A LEVEL
SOCIOLOGY

Stephen Moore
Head of Division of Social Policy
Anglia Polytechnic University, Cambridge Campus

Letts

EDUCATIONAL

First published 1994
Reprinted 1995 (twice), 1996
Second edition 1997
Reprinted 1998

Letts Educational
Aldine House
Aldine Place
London W12 8AW
Tel: 0181 740 2266
Fax: 0181 743 8451
e-mail: mail@lettsed.co.uk

Typeset by Jordan Publishing Design

British Library Cataloguing in Publication Data
A CIP record for this book is available from the British Library.

ISBN 1 85758 3930

Note for readers: Some of the information in this book is liable to change, particularly that which is directly influenced by Government policy. Such information is correct at the time of going to press but the reader should keep in touch with current affairs to ensure an up-to-date knowledge of the subject.

Printed and bound in Great Britain by
Progressive Printing (UK) Ltd, Leigh-on-Sea, Essex

Letts Educational is the trading name of BPP (Letts Educational) Ltd

Acknowledgements
The author and publishers gratefully acknowledge the following for permission to use questions in this book:
Illustrative questions (Chapters 1–3 and 7–15); question bank questions 1 (Chapters 1, 10, 13 and 15), 2 (Chapters 1, 2, 11, 12, 14 and 15), 3 (Chapters 10 and 12) and 4 (Chapter 13): Reproduced by kind permission of the Associated Examining Board. Any answers or hints on answers are the sole responsibility of the author and have not been provided or approved by the Board. Question bank questions 1 and 2 (Chapters 6 and 7): Reproduced by kind permission of London Examinations, a division of Edexcel Foundation. Edexcel Foundation, London Examinations accepts no responsibility whatsoever for the accuracy or method of working in the answers given. Question bank questions 1 (Chapters 3 and 4), 2 (Chapters 3 and 4), 3 (Chapters 1, 14 and 15) and 4 (Chapters 1 and 2): Reproduced by kind permission of Northern Examinations and Assessment Board. The author accepts responsibility for the answers provided, which may not necessarily constitute the only possible solutions. Illustrative question (Chapter 4): Reproduced by permission of the University of Cambridge Local Examinations Syndicate. The University of Cambridge Local Examinations Syndicate bears no responsibility for the example answers to questions taken from its past question papers which are contained in this publication. Question bank questions 1 (Chapters 2, 8, 9, 11, 12 and 14), 2 (Chapters 8, 9, 10 and 13) and 3 (Chapters 2, 8 and 13): UODLE material is reproduced by permission of the University of Cambridge Local Examinations Syndicate. The University of Cambridge Local Examinations Syndicate bears no responsibility for the example answers to questions taken from past UODLE question papers which are contained in this publication.

The author and publishers would also like to thank all those who have given permission to use copyright material as indicated in the text.

CONTENTS

STARTING POINTS

In this section:

HOW TO USE THIS BOOK

THE STRUCTURE OF THIS BOOK

This book, by its very nature, is a condensed version of the more detailed sociology textbooks which are available. What I have attempted to do here is to guide you through the material, pointing out the major issues, studies and debates, and, in so doing, enable you to gain more from your studies and from your wider reading.

The key aim of this book is to guide you in the way you tackle A-level and AS-level Sociology. It should serve as your study guide, work book and revision aid throughout your course, whichever syllabus you are following.

Your study guide is divided into three sections. **Section One, Starting Points** deals with study and revision skills and guides you through your syllabus requirements. **Section Two, Sociology Topics**, the main part of the book, covers the sociology topics you will need to tackle in your course. Finally, in **Section Three, Test Run**, you will find a mock exam to help prepare you for your examination.

Please note that there is a detailed Bibiliography on pp 341–3, which gives full details on all the resource material mentioned throughout the book.

In the main body of the book, the **Chapter Objectives** provide a comprehensive synopsis for each topic. They indicate what you should be looking out for in your reading and the considerations which examiners, at the end of your course, will require you to bear in mind. The objectives will help you to approach your reading analytically.

Before embarking upon your reading for a given topic, you should read through the relevant objectives very carefully to assess the full scope of the topic. When you have completed your reading and note-taking, check through the objectives and ask yourself if you have enough knowledge and acquired sufficient understanding of what you have read to give an account of each of them. When you have mastered all these points, you should be confident that you will be able to answer questions on that topic in the examination.

At the end of each chapter you will find two types of question. The first is entitled **Test Yourself**. They will help you to check what you have learned in that chapter. The second type of question is contained in the **Illustrative question and answer** and **Question bank** sections. These give you a chance to practise real questions taken from past papers. Answers and guidance are provided for both types of question.

USING YOUR SYLLABUS CHECKLIST

Whether you are using this book to work step-by-step through the syllabus or to structure your revision campaign, you will find it useful to use the checklist to record what you have covered – and how far you still have to go.

The checklist for each examination is in two parts. First there is a list of topics covered by this book which are part of your syllabus. Although the checklists are detailed, it is not possible to print entire syllabuses. **You are strongly recommended to obtain an official copy of the syllabus for your examination and to consult it when the need arises.** The examination boards' addresses are given after the syllabus checklists.

When you have revised a topic, make a note of the date in the column provided and, if there are questions elsewhere in the book, try to answer them, putting the date or dates in the final column.

The second part of the checklist gives you information about the examination, providing useful details about the time allocated for each paper and the weighting of the questions. The different types of questions which may be set are explained in detail later in this section under the heading The Examination.

SYLLABUS CHECKLISTS AND SCHEMES OF ASSESSMENT

ASSOCIATED EXAMINING BOARD
A-level Linear without coursework (0638W)
A-level Linear with coursework (0638C)
A-level Modular without coursework (0638J)
A-level Modular with coursework (0638)

Syllabus topic	Covered in Unit No	✓
Theory	1.1–1.10	
Methods	2.1–2.13	
Family	8.1–8.6	
Education	9.1–9.5	
Work, Organisations and Leisure	7.1–7.8	
Stratification and Differentiation	3.1–3.7, 4.1–4.3, 5.1–5.4	
Culture and Identity	1.10, 5.1, 5.2, 4.1, 6.2	
Crime and Deviance	15.1–15.5	
Health	12.1–12.4	
World Sociology	4.3, 14.1, 14.2, 14.4, 14.6	
Wealth, Poverty and Welfare	13.1–13.7	
Mass Media	11.1–11.4	
Sociology of Locality	14.4, 14.5	
Power and Politics	10.1–10.3, 13.4	
Coursework (Theory and Methods in Context)*	page 11, 2.1–2.8	

* A-level with coursework only

Scheme of assessment

Syllabus 0638W (Linear without coursework)

Compulsory syllabus topics: Theory and Methods; Family; Education; Work, Organisations and Leisure; Stratification and Differentiation; Culture and Identity.
Optional syllabus topics (four to be studied): Crime and Deviance; Health; World Sociology; Wealth; Poverty and Welfare; Mass Media; Sociology of Locality; Power and Politics; Religion.

Paper 1 *3 hours* 50% of the total mark.
Divided into two sections:
Section A One compulsory structured data-response question on Theory and Methods.
Section B Five structured data-response questions on the compulsory topics of the syllabus. Candidates must answer two questions.

Paper 2 *3 hours* 50% of total marks.
Divided into nine sections, with two questions in each. The sections cover the optional topics of the syllabus plus Theory and Methods. Candidates must answer four questions in total. Each question must be on a different topic.

Syllabus 0638C (Linear with coursework)

Compulsory syllabus topics: Theory and Methods; Family; Education; Work, Organisations and Leisure; Stratification and Differentiation; Culture and Identity; coursework (Theory and Methods in context).

Optional syllabus topics (two to be studied): Crime and Deviance; Health; World Sociology; Wealth, Poverty and Welfare; Mass Media; Sociology of Locality; Power and Politics; Religion.

Paper 1	*3 hours*	50% of the total marks. Divided into two sections: Section A One compulsory structured data-response question on Theory and Methods. Section B Five structured data-response questions on the compulsory syllabus topics. Candidates must answer two questions.
Paper 3	*1¾ hours*	30% of total marks. Divided into nine sections: the first eight sections consist of two questions each. The eight sections cover the optional topics of the syllabus. Candidates must answer two questions in total. Each question must be from a different section. There is only one question in the ninth section which will be on Theory and Methods. The question is compulsory.
Paper 4	*Project*	20% of the total marks.

Syllabus 0638J (Modular without coursework)

Compulsory syllabus topics: Theory and Methods.

Optional syllabus topics (combination of six to be studied): **any two from** Family; Education; Work, Organisations and Leisure; Stratification and Differentiation; Culture and Identity; **plus any two from** Crime and Deviance; Health; World Sociology; Wealth, Poverty and Welfare; **plus any two from** Mass Media; Sociology of Locality; Power and Policitics; Religion.

Paper 1	*3 hours*	50% of the total marks. Divided into two sections: Section A One compulsory structured data-response question on Theory and Methods. Section B Five structured data-response questions on the compulsory syllabus topics. Candidates must answer two questions.
Paper 5	*1½ hours*	25% of total marks. Five sections each consisting of two open-ended questions. Syllabus topics covered: Crime and Deviance; Health; World Sociology; Wealth, Poverty and Welfare; Theory and Methods. Candidates to choose **two** sections and answer **one** question from each of these.
Paper 6	*1½ hours*	25% of total marks. Four sections each consisting of two open-ended questions. Syllabus topics coverd: Mass Media; Sociology of Locality; Power and Politics; Religion. Candidates to choose **two** sections and answer **one** question from each of these.

Note: When taking the Modular A-level, Paper 1 is taken during the course of study and Papers 5 and 6 must be taken together at the final examination.

Syllabus 0638 (Modular with coursework)

Compulsory syllabus topics: Theory and Methods; Family; Education; Work, Organisations and Leisure; Stratification and Differentiation; Culture and Identity; coursework (Theory and Methods in context).

Optional syllabus topics (two to be studied): Crime and Deviance; Health; World Sociology; Wealth, Poverty and Welfare; Mass Media; Sociology of Locality; Power and Politics; Religion.

Paper 1	*3 hours*	50% of the total marks. Divided in to two sections: Section A One compulsory structured data-response question on Theory and Methods. Section B Five structured data-response questions on the compulsory syllabus topics. Candidates must answer two questions.
Paper 3	*1¾ hours*	30% of total marks. Divided into nine sections: the first eight sections consist of two questions each. The eight sections cover the optional topics of the syllabus. Candidates must answer two questions in total. Each question must be from a different section. There is only one question in the ninth section, which will be on Theory and Methods. The question is compulsory.
Paper 4	*Project*	20% of the total marks.

ASSOCIATED EXAMINING BOARD
AS-level

Syllabus topic	Covered in Unit No	✓
Theory	1.1–1.10	
Methods	2.1–2.13	
Family	8.1–8.6	
Education	9.1–9.5	
Work, Organisations and Leisure	7.1–7.8	
Stratification and Differentiation	3.1–3.7, 4.1–4.3, 5.1–5.4	
Culture and Identity	1.10, 4.1, 5.1, 5.2, 6.2	

Scheme of assessment

Compulsory syllabus topics: Theory and Methods.

Optional syllabus topics (two to be studied): Family; Education; Work, Organisations and Leisure; Stratification and Deifferentiation; Culture and Identity.

Paper 1	*3 hours*	100% of the total marks. Divided into two sections: Section A One compulsory structured data-response question on Theory and Methods. Section B Five structured data-response questions on the compulsory topics of the syllabus. Candidates must answer two questions.

Note: If you wish to convert your AS-level into an A-level, you can do it in two ways:
(i) Take papers 3 and 4
or
(ii) take papers 5 and 6 **together**.

NORTHERN EXAMINATIONS AND ASSESSMENT BOARD
A-level (Modular)
A-level (End of course)

Syllabus topic	Covered in Unit No	✓
Theoretical Perspectives in Sociology	1.1–1.10	
Social Differentiation, Power and Stratification	1.4, 3.1–3.7, 4.1–4.3, 5.1–5,4, 6.1–6.3, 7.3, 10.1–10.3, 12.2	
Methods of Sociological Enquiry	2.1–2.13	
Social Change	1.1–1.3, 1.5, 1.7–1.9, 6.1–6.3, 7.8, 10.2, 14.1–14.3	
Social Control and Deviance	15.1–.15.5	
Debates and Issues in Sociology	9.1–9.5 *or* 8.1–8.6	
Personal Enquiry (Methods of Sociological Enquiry)	2.1–2.13	

Scheme of assessment

Syllabus 4376 (Modular)

Assessment of six modules is required. Candidates may choose between *either* Methods of Sociological Enquiry *or* Personal Enquiry (Methods of Sociological Enquiry).

Each module test	*1½ hours*	One compulsory stimulus response question and three essay-style questions, of which candidates must answer one.

Note: Assessment takes place in February and June.

Syllabus 4375 (End of course)

Assessment of six modules is required. Candidates may choose between *either* Methods of Sociological Enquiry *or* Personal Enquiry (Methods of Sociological Enquiry).

Each module test	*1½ hours*	One compulsory stimulus response question and three essay-style questions, of which candidates must answer one.

Note: All modules to be assessed at the same session.

NORTHERN EXAMINATIONS AND ASSESSMENT BOARD
AS-level (Modular)
AS-level (End of course)

Syllabus topic	Covered in Unit No	✓
Theoretical Perspectives in Sociology	1.1–1.10	
Social Differentiation, Power and Stratification	3.1–3.7, 4.1–4.3, 5.1–5.4, 6.1–6.3, 7.3, 10.1–10.3, 12.2	
Methods of Sociological Enquiry	2.1–2.13	

Scheme of assessment

Syllabus 3376 (Modular)

Assessment of three modules is required: Theoretical Perspectives in Sociology; Social Differentiation, Power and Stratification; Methods of Sociological Enquiry.

Each module test   *1½ hours*   One compulsory stimulus response question and three essay-style questions, of which candidates must answer one.

Note: Assessment takes place in February and June.

Syllabus 3375 (End of course)

Each module test   *1½ hours*   One compulsory stimulus response question and three essay-style questions, of which candidates must answer one.

Note: All modules to be assessed at the same session.

INTEGRATED BOARDS (CAMBRIDGE, LONDON EXAMINATIONS, NICCEA, OXFORD AND WJEC) A-level

Syllabus topic	Covered in Unit No	✓
Theory*	1.1–1.10	
Methods*	2.1–2.13	
Social Differentiation and Stratification*	3.1–3.7, 4.1–4.3, 5.1–5.4, 6.1–6.3	
Households and Family Forms**	8.1–8.6	
Mass Media and Popular Culture**	11.1–11.4	
Community and Nation**	5.1, 14.5	
Health**	12.1–12.4	
Welfare and Social Policy**	13.1–13.7	
Education and Training**	9.1–9.5	
Work and Economic Life**	7.1–7.8	
Power and Politics**	10.1–10.3	
Deviance and Control**	15.1–15.5	
Project	page 11	

* Compulsory topic
** Optional topic

Scheme of assessment

Syllabus 9848

Paper 1   *2½ hours*   40% of total marks.
Paper 2   *2½ hours*   40% of total marks.
Both Paper 1 and Paper 2 are divided into three sections
Section A Candidates must answer one compulsory data-response question on Social Differentiation and Stratification.
Section B Candidates must answer one structured question from five questions offered (one on each optional subject)

Section C Candidates must answer one question from the ten unstructured questions (two questions from each of the five options)

Candidates answer three questions in total for each paper. The questions must, however on **different** options.

Paper 3   *2 hours*   20% of total marks.

Consists of *either*:
● an examinatin paper in two sections
Section A One compulsory structured question requiring candidates to design a piece of sociological research.
Section B Candidates must answer one structured question from four unstructured essay questions. The questions will all be on the relationship between theory and method.

or

● personal study
A project consisting of an extended piece of work on a sociological topic which the candidate is able to choose. The study must demonstrate the candidate's familiarity with Theory and Methods.

INTEGRATED BOARDS
AS-level

Syllabus topic	Covered in Unit No	✓
Theory (The Sociological Approach)*	1.1–1.10	
Methods (The Sociological Approach)*	2.1–2.3	
Social Differentiation and Stratification*	3.1–3.7, 4.1–4.3, 5.1–5.4, 6.1–6.3	
Households and Family Forms**	8.1–8.6	
Mass Media and Popular Culture**	11.1–11.4	
Community and Nation**	5.1, 14.5	
Health**	12.1–12.4	
Welfare and Social Policy**	13.1–13.7	
Education and Training•	9.1–9.5	
Work and Economic Life•	7.1–7.8	
Power and Politics•	10.1–10.3	
Deviance and Control•	15.1–15.5	

* Compulsory topic
Candidates choose between two sets of optional topics, either ** or •

Scheme of assessment

Syllabus 8748

(i) Candidates take *either* Paper 1 or Paper 2.
(ii) Candidates take *either* Section A or Section B of Paper 3.
Modular assessment pattern: Students can take the assessment in two parts, gaining 50% of the marks one year and 50% the following year.

CAMBRIDGE
AS-level (Modular)

Module	Covered in Unit No	✓
Education	9.1–9.5	
Health	12.1–12.4	
Crime	15.1–15.5	

Scheme of assessment

Assessment is by means of three compulsory written papers, one for each module. Each paper carries 33⅓% of the available marks.

Each paper lasts 1½ hours, and is divided into two sections: a compulsory data response question and a structured essay (choose one from two). Each section carries half the marks for the module.

EXAMINATION BOARDS AND ADDRESSES

AEB
The Associated Examining Board
Stag Hill House, Guildford, Surrey GU2 5XJ
Tel: 01483 302302

Cambridge
University of Cambridge Local Examinations Syndicate
Syndicate Buildings, 1 Hills Road, Cambridge CB1 2EU
Tel: 01223 553311

London Examinations
Edexcel Foundation
Stewart House, 32 Russell Square, London WC1B 5DN
Tel: 0171 393 4444

NEAB
Northern Examinations and Assessment Board
Devas Street, Manchester M15 6EX
Tel: 0161 953 1180

NICCEA
Northern Ireland Council for the Curriculum, Examinations and Assessment
Clarendon Dock, 29 Clarendon Road, Belfast BT1 3BG
Tel: 01232 261200

Oxford
University of Oxford Delegacy of Local Examinations
Ewert House, Summertown, Oxford OX2 7BZ
Tel: 01865 554291

WJEC
Welsh Joint Education Committee
245 Western Avenue, Cardiff CF5 2YX
Tel: 01222 265000

STUDYING AND REVISING SOCIOLOGY

THE DIFFERENCE BETWEEN GCSE AND A/AS-LEVEL

Sociology as a subject is probably new to you, unlike some of the other A-levels you may have chosen to study. In particular, A-level Sociology relies heavily on empirical (experimental) data and draws on a variety of different academic disciplines.

A quantitative difference: generally speaking, A-levels involve more than GCSEs: more hours in the classroom, more work at home, longer essays, more, and longer, examinations.

A qualitative difference: the most important change from GCSE work is that A-levels require a thoughtful and critical approach rather than simply churning out a previously learned set of facts. The emphasis is on understanding, applying a body of knowledge, organising material into a coherent whole, evaluation and comparison.

This approach is also reflected in the kinds of question which are set. The examiner aims to prevent the use of prepared essays which only demonstrate the candidates ability to learn. There is no 'right' answer; there are legitimate answers which must be argued for. Facts are important as a means to an end, not an end in themselves, as at GCSE.

Therefore, opinions are a feature of A-level study. You must learn to form your own which are based in fact. Reading sociological material will help you form opinions; arguments and discussions with classmates and teachers will help too, as will writing essays.

An eclectic approach one which chooses the best from a variety of sources; it is a feature of advanced studies. While the syllabus may appear to be neatly divided into sub-areas, this is by no means true. It is important not to limit your thought according to artificial divisions of the body of sociology. Intelligence is shown by combining information from different areas.

AS examinations

AS exams offer an alternative to A-level. They enable students to study more subjects while maintaining the depth of study. This means that less time is spent studying the subject, the examination is shorter and the coursework less, but the syllabus remains as broad and the questions are as difficult. It is possible to take an AS in one or two years.

STUDY STRATEGIES AND TECHNIQUES

At least 80% of your time as a student will be spent on private study, so it is very important for you to acquire those skills which enable you to study effectively. Many hours can be wasted reading books from which you learn very little, or drawing elaborate charts and diagrams which are soon forgotten.

Study will involve you in collecting information, analysing it, clarifying your thinking, assimilating knowledge and expressing yourself clearly. Nobody is born with these skills, nor are they obtained accidentally. They must be acquired by conscious effort and practise. Here are some suggestions which will help you to develop these skills and make the most of your study time.

Establish targets

Research has shown that a learning period of about 45 minutes produces the best relationship between understanding and remembering. Set yourself study breaks which can be achieved in this period of time and then take a break for 15 minutes or longer before attempting another period of work. Plan reasonable targets which you can achieve in each study session.

Focus on essentials

There are large numbers of books and articles which deal with topics in the A-level or AS syllabuses. Some of this material is inappropriate or duplicates what is written better elsewhere. Try to focus on sections of books, avoid extraneous material and select what you read intelligently.

Select key words and phrases

When you read a section of a book, select words or phrases which will help you to remember what the section is about. These words can be written down for reference and used as personal notes.

Note taking

Far too many students write notes as they write essays, in linear sequences. About 90% of what is written is wasted material and will never be remembered. It is the key words, concepts and phrases which need to be remembered. With practice, you can abandon linear notes and learn more effectively by recording only the key words. This skill takes some time to acquire and can best be learned in stages by first writing down long phrases but not sentences and then, after a time, reducing the notes to just the key words and phrases. This form of note taking is suitable for notes made while reading or during a lecture. Remember to record the author and title. Sometimes a page number is also useful for future reference. A fluorescent highlighting pen is useful for identifying key words and phrases. These are not, of course, to be used on text books or journals, but on notes you have made or been given.

COURSEWORK

The most commonly used examination board, the AEB offers a project worth 20% of marks, and the Integrated Boards offer a project worth 20%.

If you decide to do a project then bear the following points in mind.

The topic to study

The majority of candidates choose to study the media or gender issues, but there is a wide variety of other areas that could be chosen too. The starting points for the project include:

- The project should be something that interests you.

- You should have some access to sources for research. I do not mean just books or magazines but to an organisation or work place where the activity you are studying takes place.

- You must ask yourself whether the study is actually feasible. Attempting to study the social disruption caused by war, for example, may be interesting but too difficult.

- Decide upon the level of knowledge demanded by the subject; the accessibility of the material; the limits on your own time and money.

- The study is morally acceptable – a participant observational study of drug use may he extremely interesting but may also be illegal.

- Finally do not put yourself into danger by studying activities which could involve violence – such as studying the behaviour of a violent gang.

Starting the research

What interests you? Nothing much is the usual answer. But often with a bit of thought there is something you have always been curious about. One student who could not think of a coursework idea was attending a football match when he saw a fight break out and decided to study football violence. Another student had been first ignored and then bullied at primary school – she decided to follow this up. Another student was a nurse, and based her study on differences in accidents and social class.

You should start by reading anything you can obtain on the topic area in books, magazines and journals – use the school/college, public and local university libraries. There are often useful and interesting television and radio programmes on topical subjects so check the television and radio guides.

Ask members of staff for help. My experience of public libraries in particular is that staff are generally courteous and helpful. When you do find a book or article that is relevant, check to see if there are any references which you can follow up.

As your knowledge of the area increases, try to narrow down your subject into a manageable 'package' that provides you with enough to do at the right depth.

There are often pressure groups which produce information on a range of subjects relevant to their areas of interest and so it is worth writing to them with a stamped addressed envelope asking for any free literature, or catalogues of material they produce for sale.

The aims or hypothesis

By now you should have a rough idea of what is possible to study and what is not, you should also have a decent understanding of the chosen area of study. The time has come to clarify the aims of the study or to actually construct a hypothesis.

A hypothesis is a statement which makes a causal relationship between two social phenomena. This will help you to clarify what you should concentrate on in your research. You may well find that your original ideas are too difficult to put into practice. Then you should simply alter your aims or hypotheses. Do not worry too much about restricting your investigations because they seem to lead away from your original hypothesis or aims, follow the logic of your research and see where it leads you.

The methods

The methodology you choose is largely determined by the topic you choose and the circumstances in which you do your research. However, if you have a choice of methods then start off by considering the aims of the research and how best you can achieve these. You may find that you need statistical information or the opinions of large numbers of people, and in this case a survey of some kind would be most appropriate. On the other hand if you wish to see what people actually do, then it is more appropriate to use some form of observation. Of course, there is no rule that says only one method must be used, and increasingly sociologists are using a variety of approaches (**triangulation**) in order to gain greater accuracy.

The most important point to remember, however, is that you should only set out to achieve what is possible, so limit your enquiries to what you believe will be practicable.

Record and time-keeping

Your research will most likely take place over a number of months and it is important that you keep an adequate written record of what has happened and when. Reliance on your memory will result in some creative fiction when it comes to writing up the research!

You should also have a clear plan of what you must do and when. Construct an action plan and then stick to it.

Writing up the coursework

What to emphasise

The majority of people reading this will be doing the AEB coursework project and they should bear in mind that the allocation of marks by the 'skill domains' of:

- knowledge and understanding
- interpretation and application
- evaluation

all apply as much to the project as to the examination answers, and therefore you should bear this in mind when writing up the project.

Before you begin on the project ask for copies of work done by previous students at your school or college, to get an idea of what is expected.

Organising the material

The AEB helps us with this by providing guidelines to follow. By using these sensibly the project can be well organised and clear.

Rationale

This is your starting point for the project and you should provide the background for your choice of material, what you hope to achieve, and what your own views and values are. You need to introduce your choice of research method and the reasons why you chose this rather than others. If you have a clear hypothesis then state this and explain your thinking.

Context

This section gives you the opportunity to show how you read relevant research and allows you to pull together material from a wide variety of sources, in such a manner that you can demonstrate understanding of the wider debates. You should also be able to criticise the research and to apply it to your chosen area. Ideally there should be considerable theoretical input here. Do not copy large chunks from one or two core textbooks, and do try to demonstrate reading from a variety of sources, and their relevance to your interests.

Remember that just showing knowledge of material is inadequate for a good mark, you need to apply and to evaluate, as the marking scheme clearly demonstrates.

Methodology

Here you should describe and discuss the methods which were used in the enquiry and provide reasons for your choice of methods. The reasons will include both theoretical and academic considerations as well as practical ones, so a participant observational study of a fast-food restaurant is practicable because you have a part-time job and is also the most relevant as you are researching the differences between official behaviour demanded by the company and the unofficial 'forms of resistance' used by the staff. It would be impractical and inappropriate to do a survey or an experiment.

Do not forget your marking criteria of **knowledge**, **application** and **evaluation**. Show the examiner that you do know the appropriate method of research, that you can apply it usefully to the chosen area, and that you are aware of the strengths and weaknesses which this method has when used by you in the particular circumstances of the study. It is no use simply listing the advantages and disadvantages of the method by copying it out of a textbook or a course companion such as this.

Content

Never assume that the facts speak for themselves. You need to organise your material, present it clearly, and to interpret what you have obtained in such a manner that the relevance and sociological content is demonstrated to the reader.

If you simply include pages of graphs or quotes from people you have interviewed then this could not possibly cover the skill domains. You must interpret and apply your material to relevant concepts of sociology.

Incidentally, it is best not to mention people by name but to use pseudonyms.

Evaluation

This is extremely important, and often distinguishes the better projects from the run-of-the-mill ones. But remember that evaluation should take place throughout the project not just in this section. What you should do in this section is draw many of the points together into a coherent and honest discussion of the strengths and weaknesses of the study you have undertaken. You should not be afraid of dwelling on the failings, as these will have been spotted by the examiner already and she/he may well be looking for you to acknowledge these weaknesses. To gain even higher marks you should suggest ways by which you could have overcome the problems or have foreseen them.

You should evaluate your original hypothesis, your motivation for research, your ability to undertake it, your research methodology and sampling, your background context reading, your substantive findings and your conclusions.

Bibliography

This refers to all the material you have read and used. You should include a bibliography which is detailed, honest and accurate. Making up studies and books does not fool anyone.

Appendices

At the end of the study you may wish to include examples of relevant pieces of work such as your questionnaire, or a copy of the video or sound recording you made, or perhaps additional photographs etc.

Presentation

You do not have to word-process your project, and there are no extra marks for doing so. But whether you word-process or handwrite the project, the work should be neat and tidy. The tables and charts should be clear and accurate with some evidence of concern for the quality of presentation.

There should be a separate title page, which has the candidate number, the title of the project, and the centre number. The next page should be a contents page which should be of use in guiding the examiner through your work. Each section of the main body of your work should be on a separate page and the pages should be numbered. The bibliography comes on a separate sheet of paper at the back, as do the appendices.

You cannot lose marks for spelling errors, but clearly you should do all you can to demonstrate to the examiner that this is a piece of work which has been taken seriously by you, and there is no excuse for failing to use a dictionary, or if you are fortunate to have a spell-check on your computer, using that.

Assistance from others

Many students are confused over the amount of help they are allowed to ask from their lecturer or teacher. Consequently, many good students fail to make use of this most important resource. You can ask staff for:

- advice on the collection of data.
- help on presentation, structuring, analysis and evaluation.
- how to overcome problems you have encountered.

A second area of confusion is whether groups of friends can work together. The answer is that working together is perfectly acceptable, but the final writing up must be entirely your own work.

REVISION TECHNIQUES

Probably the worst part of taking an A-level course is the examination at the end, and the worst part of the examination process is not actually answering the questions but the revision that you have to do to be able to write anything down. The bad news is that there is no short-cut to revision, all you can try to do is to get organised and try to make the task as clear-cut and useful as possible. Here are some guidelines to help you.

Timetable

At Christmas time, the summer and the examination seem a long way off. However, if you look at the amount of work you need to do, then there is relatively little time. I would suggest that you start serious revision in April, and that you should spend a few days in March working out a programme of revision. The first thing you should take into account is how many A-levels you are doing. Clearly, if you are only doing Sociology then the amount of material you have to study is far less than if you are taking two or three examinations.

Go through your calendar – cross off any holiday trips or activities you know will take up much time. Then mark in the exact days of your examinations. After this, work out a balanced programme of revision allowing adequate time for each topic you are going to answer questions on.

Remember you cannot study every evening, so give yourself lots of time off, and allow plenty of time for 'getting stuck' on difficult topics. Remember, it is not the amount of time that is important but the amount of **productive** time that you can put in.

What to do

When revising, you should first read through the notes you have from college or school, and when you think you have got a grasp of them, you should tackle some of the questions which are included in this book. These are devised to test knowledge, interpretative skills and evaluative ability. Do not worry if you do not get the same answers as there are in this book. After all these are my answers, and they are bound to be different from yours. However, the answers here will help give pointers and guidelines to what the examiners are looking for. If your answers are significantly different from what is here, or you simply cannot think of how to answer the questions, then go back again and work through the material.

Before the examination

As the day of the examination arrives, do not go mad, trying to cram as much information into your head as possible. It is in the last few days, that you really should benefit from the slow organised revision. I would strongly suggest that you slow down and try to relax at this crucial period. You should try to get as much sleep as you nerves will allow you, so that you enter the examination as fresh and relaxed as possible.

THE EXAMINATION

QUESTION STYLES

There are two main types of examination question used by the different boards:

1 structured response or stimulus questions

2 essay questions.

Structured response or stimulus questions

These use a series of short extracts from a number of different sources and then ask up to four questions which can be answered partially by reference to the sources and partially from wider knowledge and understanding of sociology, which needs to be applied in a relevant way to the answers. e.g:

Item A

Simply choosing an explanation out of personal preference would not get us very far by itself. It is true that there are many occasions when human beings say they 'know' something to be true when what they really mean is that they 'think' it to be true. This would be the case if I were to say that I 'know' the Labour Party will win the next election, for example. Science however aims at much greater certainty in its explanations than this. Having arrived at an hypothesis – a plausible or appealing story about how something or other is caused – scientists do not then spend their time trying to persuade us of its truth by the logic of their argument, as philosophers do. Nor do they ask us to simply have faith in their belief, as theologians do. They try to *prove* its truth to us. This they do by *showing* it to be true.

(Adapted from Jones, P., *Theory and Methods in Sociology*, Bell and Hyman)

Item B

So how common is cheating in science? Surveys show that both in Britain and America, only about one in four scientists is prepared to provide original data when requested. Unless there is something to hide, there is no reason for such refusal. One can only conclude that scientific fraud is extremely widespread. Moreover, it is not limited to minor figures: the verdict of history is that Ptolemy, Galileo, Newton, Dalton and Mendel all tampered with some of their data.

Why then do scientists cheat? Not everyone, and perhaps not anyone, pursues science merely out of a quest for truth. At the best, people are heavily biased towards proving their own theories right, but they also want promotion, research grants and glory. Since all depend on publishing, the pressure to publish is enormous. It is obviously quicker to fake data than to run experiments and you can be sure of getting the desired result.

Another extremely common way of cheating is to run an experiment over and over again until the desired result is obtained and then publish it, quietly forgetting the negative instances. Other scientists get things wrong, not by cheating but by unconsciously seeing what they are looking for (even when it is not there) or failing to see what is there.

There is little risk of being caught. Except for the most important findings, little attempt is made to replicate; there is no prestige in redoing someone else's experiments.

(Adapted from *The Observer*, August 1989)

Item C

Most of us rather hastily and thoughtlessly regard 'science' as a sort of collection of linear accelerators and space vehicles and organic chemistry models. In fact, it is not any of these things; it is only a systematic method of gathering and testing knowledge, involving certain formal procedures: gathering information, forming an hypothesis to explain the information, predicting certain consequences of the hypothesis and performing an experiment to test the prediction. If you investigate any area of knowledge by this method, you are doing science. If you use any other method, you are doing something else.

(Adapted from Pohl, F., *The Game-Playing Literature in 'In the Problem Pit'*, Corgi)

(a) Briefly explain how scientists try to prove an hypothesis 'by showing it to be true' (Item A). (2)

(b) Item B puts forward a number of reasons why science cannot be seen as objective. What are the implications of this for the belief that sociology is a science? (4)

(c) Apart from the points raised in Item B, how far do you agree with the argument in Item C that science is a 'systematic method'? (6)

(d) Item A suggests that human beings 'know' things to be true in ways other than the scientific method. On what grounds do people claim that their beliefs or ideas are true? (4)

(e) Using information from the Items and from elsewhere, assess whether it is possible for sociology to be a science. (9)

Here are some simple hints of the best way to approach the stimulus questions:

❶ Read all the extracts and make sure you understand what is being said.

❷ Read the questions carefully, and try to work out the different skills that may be required from you.

③ Do not treat the extracts as distinctive elements which are related only to one particular question. Try to use supporting evidence and gather clues for each answer from all the extracts.

④ Remember that there is no hurry to answer the questions, and that no extra marks are gained from finishing early, so you should take some time to plan your answers and to think through all the relevant material that you should include.

⑤ Different parts of the question carry different marks, so ensure that you write enough relevant information to reply adequately to the questions. As a rule of thumb, the more marks there are the more you need to write and discuss.

Essay questions

These are used by all the Examination Boards. They require you to write a significant length essay in which the question set is fully and rigorously examined. The AEB is particularly clear on the three elements it is seeking to award marks for – these are:

Knowledge and understanding

Which is basically your ability to remember and reproduce an adequate amount of relevant information from your studies.

Interpretation and application

These refer, for example, to the abilities to interpret the relevant elements of a sociologist's writings or research, to draw from other relevant examples which are not immediately apparent, and possibly from one's own relevant experiences.

Evaluation

This refers to the ability to be critical and to appreciate the strengths and weaknesses of a position.

Writing essays

Plan

You should *always* plan your essays, so that when you are writing them, you concentrate on clarity of style and quality of answer. If you simply start writing and hope to arrive at the answer then nine times out of ten you will write a muddled essay. A plan need not be a complex and elegant affair, but simply a list of key words or concepts, or if you prefer a spider diagram.

Paragraphs

Each piece of information, relevant example of research or point you are trying to make should be put into a separate paragraph. One of the most off-putting things for a marker is to see a 'wall' of writing without breaks. Paragraphs also help you to see quite clearly how your essay is progressing, and whether you may have missed any points from your plan.

Links

Do not leave paragraphs to 'float' without connections between them. Too often, students write essays by putting together a host of unconnected points, and then expect the marker to make sense of them. This is not acceptable. Each paragraph should be related to the ones preceding and following it, and this should be made clear by the use of linking words or phrases. For example, you could say 'An opposing view to this', or 'As a result of Hobb's study' and so on.

Signposts

The most common cause of low marks comes from not answering the question. Often people start off answering the question, but then drift away. This should be prevented by sensible use of plans. However, another way of ensuring relevance, and to help the marker understand unambiguously what you are trying to do, is to use 'signpost' paragraphs. Signpost paragraphs should be used a couple of times in each essay to briefly review what has been said, and to say where the essay is going to next. This clarifies the issues for the marker, and ensures that the writer is aware of where she/he is going.

Understanding the terminology of the questions

Outline/describe

Outline simply means to describe, and is rarely asked for except in the simplest of stimulus questions. A-level almost always requires some form of analysis. If it is asked, probably in a stimulus question, then there is no need to do more than describe, as there will usually only be a few marks awarded for that question.

Analyse

This term is usually used where a fairly complex issue is the subject of the question, but there is relatively little controversy. A detailed and accurate break down of the issues involved is required.

Examine

This is very similar to analyse, but often is linked to a statement which may be controversial or only one of a number of possible explanations for a social issue. The implication for you is to be aware of alternative explanations and criticisms.

Account for

This goes one stage further than describe, as it also requires an explanation. It is generally used when there is some historical element.

Explore

This term is generally used when the student must use their own ideas and insights in answering a question, and the student is being invited to use their initiative.

Discuss

This means to look in detail at a number of different explanations for a phenomenon, and to ensure that strengths and weaknesses are pointed out. Often the examiners say 'critically discuss', to add weight to the point that you should not simply present textbook arguments.

Compare and contrast

Compare means to point out similarities and contrast means to point out the differences. They are used to get students to look at two differing explanations for a social phenomenon and then to make a structured discussion based on the similarities and differences.

Assess and evaluate

These are usually used when the examiner wants to look afresh at a well-worn topic or area of questioning. There is an assumption that a description is not needed, nor necessarily is an analysis. However, the examiner is asking for a detailed critical discussion of the strengths and weaknesses, and how the approach being examined relates to other approaches, or has influenced them.

EXAMINATION TECHNIQUES

1. Do not tire yourself out the night before the examination with intensive revision. If you do not know it by now, you will not learn much extra. Instead, try to relax so that you feel fresh for the examination.

2. Arrive in plenty of time.

3. When you are given the examination papers, take your time and read carefully through all the instructions, make sure that you understand them.

4 Read each question carefully and choose all those you feel that you might be able to do. Re-read these carefully and narrow your choice down. Do not panic if everyone else is writing. Careful choice of questions is crucial. If you think you can only answer one or two questions and you are supposed to answer four, stay calm. Very often you find that once in the swing of the examination you become less nervous and can see possibilities of answering questions which at first seem impossible.

5 Work out how much time you have to answer each question. Follow these time limits. One question answered in great depth earns fewer marks than two questions answered competently.

6 Answer the question asked – not what you would like it to be. **The main cause of low marks is failing to answer the question.** Writing all you know on a subject is of little use and gains few marks. Also, try to avoid your stating own opinions on the subject, it is an examination in sociology, not on your views.

7 Always plan your answer before beginning to write.

FINAL PREPARATION

- Check the time, date and place for the examination.
- Check you have the necessary things you need.
- Take some physical exercise before the exam to relieve tension and clear the mind.
- Arrive in good time.
- Practice relaxation techniques while waiting for the exam to start. Look forward to the conclusion of your studies.

SOCIOLOGY TOPICS

In this section:

Each chapter features:

- *Units in this chapter:* a list of the main topic heads to follow.

- *Chapter objectives:* a synopsis of the topics which will be covered in the chapter.

- *The main text:* divided into numbered topic units for ease of reference.

- *Test yourself questions and answers:* short questions and answers to test your understanding of the topics covered in the chapter.

- *Illustrative question and answer:* a typical examination question with an indication of the knowledge required and a suggested answer plan.

- *Question bank:* further examination questions for you to attempt with points to include in framing your own answers.

CHAPTER 1

THEORY

Units in this chapter

Chapter objectives

In this chapter we first of all gain an overview of the nature of theories in sociology and what their relationship is to each other. Fig. 1.1 illustrates how sociology evolved as a discipline. We then take each of the seven major theoretical perspectives and work our way through them in some degree of detail to provide ourselves with the tools of analysis to understand fully the substantive topics which follow in the rest of the book.

The first theory examined is functionalism, which stresses the positive benefits to society of the major institutions that exist. This is followed by a discussion of Marxism and the theories that have developed from Marxism. Functionalism and Marxism both stress the importance of large-scale theories to explain all of social activity. On the other hand, interactionism and ethnomethodology concentrate on looking at the activities of individuals and groups of people engaged in constructing the social world about them. A summary of the explanations of social change is provided.

The next approach studied is feminism, which criticises sociology for being concerned only with the interests of males and of ignoring women and their experiences.

We then move on to look at the more recent contributions to sociological theories provided by the post-structuralist and structuration approaches. Post-modernism is then considered.

The final unit of the chapter offers an overview of the issues of identity and culture. These are explained in more depth elsewhere in the book.

1.1 THEORIES AND CATEGORIES OF THEORY

CATEGORIES OF THEORY

We can distinguish between two different categories of theory:

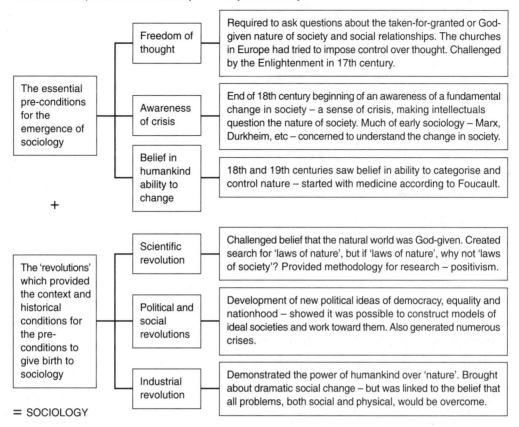

Period of development: late 17th century ⟶ early 20th century

Fig. 1.1 The origins of sociology as a discipline

1 **Macro-sociological or structural theories** attempt to construct theories which explain the whole of human action and social institutions throughout history. They place the emphasis on the wider **constraints** on individual action.

These approaches assume that man is a product of society and therefore that any explanation of human behaviour must start by analysing the structure of society and through that arrive at an understanding of individual action. Structural sociology asks such questions as: How does society hold itself together? How does change come about? Why do particular institutions and rules exist?

2 **Micro-sociological or phenomenological, or action approaches** try to uncover the assumptions underlying the routine, taken-for-granted actions of everyday life. They stress the study of individual **choice** and decision-making. Phenomenological sociology starts from the individual, and makes no claim to explain the whole of human action; rather it sets out to produce explanations of small-scale interaction, building up a catalogue of the rules that govern face-to-face interaction. Phenomenological sociologists ask such questions as: On what basis do we place people into categories (insane, criminal, normal)? What are the consequences of this categorisation of people?

Most theories fall within these two approaches, although some attempt has been made to combine the two, in particular the work of Giddens in his structuration theory.

THEORIES

Functionalism

A structural theory that stresses the **cohesive** and **consensual** nature of society. It holds that institutions and rules exist in order to help society continue to the mutual benefit of its members.

Marxism

A structural theory that tries to uncover the way in which certain groups gain power in society and then hold that power for their own benefit. It stresses above all else the **extent of conflict** as the basis of society. Neo–Marxism refers to writers within the Marxist tradition who have provided variations on the original concepts.

Symbolic interactionism

This studies the way that individuals build up rules and expectations of each other in such a way that a society can exist. It stresses the **constant negotiation** that individuals must engage in to maintain harmonious social interaction.

Ethnomethodology

This theory rejects the idea of the existence of a society based on shared beliefs and interpretations. It studies the processes by which individuals work at making sense and order of the chaos of human interactions.

Feminism

These approaches stress the nature of the **male domination** of society and explore how this power developed, its effect upon women (and men) and the mechanisms by which male power continues. It is generally influenced by structural theory.

Structuralism and post-structuralism

These develop the more traditional structural approaches and lay much greater stress on the **nature of language** as a **determinant of action**.

Structuration

This sets out to explore the unclear relationship between the constraints placed on individuals by the structure of society and the choices and decisions individuals make. This is an attempt to link **structure** and **action theories**.

1.2 FUNCTIONALISM

SOCIETY AS AN ORGANISM: DURKHEIM

The originator of this approach, Durkheim, started from the assumption that our desires are limited only by the regulation of society and that, left to ourselves, people would satisfy their own desires with complete disregard for others. Durkheim points out that laws are far less important in regulating people than is an internalised set of values. The set of basic values which everyone shares is called the **collective conscience**. If society is unable to maintain and enforce this common set of values then the members of society fall into a situation where each is for him/herself, or **anomie**.

In his *Division of Labour*, Durkheim sets out to explain how the basis of social solidarity changed as societies developed from primitive to modern complex ones. In traditional societies, there is a **mechanical** form of social solidarity which lays great stress on the importance of the group. Here, individuality is disapproved of and conformity is stressed; shared values and shared actions underlie the sense of solidarity.

In advanced industrial societies, however, this form of solidarity no longer prevails and is replaced by **organic** solidarity. Complex societies are here characterised by individuality and social diversity; but each individual needs the others (whether they realise it or not), making individuals mutually dependent. Thus solidarity is maintained in a changing society.

For Durkheim, societies were social facts rather like an organism in which the various parts (heart, lungs, etc) function to maintain its existence. His analyses therefore would seek to show the functions performed for the society by its component institutions: his study of religion stressed its role in maintaining and re-affirming the collective conscience through dramatic ceremonies (such as a mass); even crime had the function of marking the permissible bounds of action in society. It was this emphasis on functions that led the Durkheim tradition to be known as functionalism.

TALCOTT PARSONS: STRUCTURAL FUNCTIONALISM

In *The Structure of Social Action* Talcott Parsons attempted to explain both the structure of society and individual action within it. More precisely, at the structural level he wanted to explain:

● the origins of social institutions,

● the reasons for continuing existence and

● the relationships of institutions to each other.

At the individual level he sought to examine:

● how individual actions and beliefs are related through the culture to the 'needs' of society.

This was, in effect, an attempt to fuse the sociology of Weber (individual motivation) with that of Durkheim (structure and function).

Prerequisites

According to Parsons, every society must solve four problems in order to exist:

● adapting to the environment,

● providing a decision-making process,

● integrating the various institutions of society and

● coping with the psychological demands of the society's members.

These are known as **functional prerequisites**.

❶ **Adaptation** Society has to derive the necessities of life from the environment. A society that cannot feed or clothe its members is bound to collapse. The economic institutions cope with this problem.

❷ **Goal attainment** Each society must have a means of deciding how it will be organised and run. This decision-making process is the political institution.

❸ **Integration** Various subsystems have arisen in response to specific needs of the society and have developed their own sets of values. There is no guarantee that values of the various institutions will be in harmony. Specialist institutions, such as religion, therefore develop to integrate possible competing demands from the economic and family subsystems, for example.

❹ **Latency** This centres on psychological problems and has two elements: pattern maintenance and tension management.

  ● **Pattern maintenance** refers to the problem faced by a person where they have to reconcile contradictory demands from different institutions: for example, where a woman is both a mother and an executive.

  ● **Tension management** refers to society's need to motivate the individual to continue his/her active membership of society and not to 'drop out' (through deviancy, suicide, etc).

Parsons then goes on to link these prerequisites with individual action and emphasises the role that culture plays in this.

Culture and the role of pattern variables

As we have seen, for a society to exist it has to fulfil the functional prerequisites. Yet society in itself does not exist and cannot do anything: it is after all no more than a collection of individuals. Therefore, it is necessary to persuade the members to act in certain ways which will enable society to fulfil its needs and ensure its continuation. Culture performs this task by emphasising certain values which guide members to act in particular ways and thus ensure that the functional prerequisites are carried out.

These cultural values fall into five groups (or **pattern variables**) and the culture, reflecting how society solves the prerequisites, prompts people to act according to one group or another. There are no other possible choices. The five pattern variables are:

1. **Affectivity or neutrality** This is whether the society is characterised by individuals who typically have emotional involvement with each other or whether personal transactions are mainly emotional-free; for example, compare village life with town life in this context.

2. **Specificity or diffuseness** The grounds on which we relate to others can be single or numerous. For example, in a town the person who lives next door is merely our neighbour, whereas in the country we may know that person as a parish councillor or shopkeeper as well as our neighbour.

3. **Universalism or particularism** This asks the question whether rules should be applied to everyone equally or differently to different people (for example on grounds of race or birth).

4. **Quality or performance** This asks whether people should be treated on the basis that they are equal at birth.

5. **Self-orientation or collectivity orientation** Does the society stress the importance of individuality or the greater importance of the group?

These five pattern variables can be seen as a more sophisticated version of Durkheim's difference between modern (organic) and traditional (mechanical) societies.

Role

The final concept in Talcott Parson's work is that of role. A role is a pattern of action that is typically followed by a person when they hold a socially categorised position. Most individuals can be placed into social roles, for example doctor, nurse or patient. These roles allow other people to predict their action, and order is maintained in this way.

Fig. 1.2 illustrates the theory of functionalism.

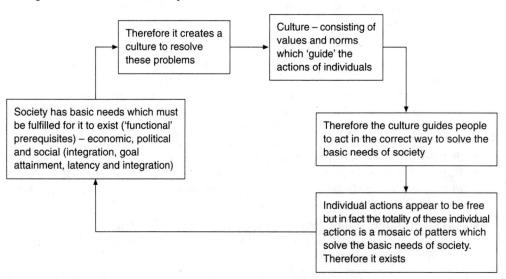

Fig. 1.2 Theory of functionalism

ROBERT MERTON: FUNCTIONS AND DYSFUNCTIONS

In *Social Theory and Social Action*, Merton responds to Parsons' work and both criticises it and builds upon it. Parsons assumes that if an institution is functional for one part of society then it is functional for all parts. Merton says that this is not true, that something can be both functional and **dysfunctional** (ie it promotes disharmony) – for example religion. An important point here, however, is that Merton is aware of power differences and that some groups can therefore manipulate social institutions to their benefit.

Merton also points out that just because an institution exists to perform a function, this does not mean that there is no other way (even a better one) of performing that function. Parsons, on the other hand, assumes that the institution that exists is, by its very existence, the best possible solution.

Merton distinguished between the intended, manifest consequences of an act to the individual involved and the unintended or latent consequences for society. In this way, an individual may perform and act for one reason, but the outcome for society may be entirely different from that intended.

CRITICISMS OF FUNCTIONALISM

There are four main criticisms of functionalism:

1 It over-emphasises the consensus that exists in society.

2 It draws an analogy between an organism and society, yet there are profound differences between these two, the obvious one being that organisms are biological with a natural life process and that societies are not. Organisms may have needs but can societies? It could be argued that the needs mentioned by Parsons are not the needs of society itself, but the needs of the powerful members within society.

3 Functionalists have problems explaining social change. If institutions exist to fulfil needs, once the needs are fulfilled there should be no need to change.

4 The version of humanity given by functionalists makes us seem like puppets not people. The possibility of choice and free-will seems excluded by the stress functionalism places on the power of the pattern variables and the functionalist concept of predictable social roles.

1.3 MARXISM AND NEO-MARXISM

Marxism and neo-Marxism derive from Karl Marx. The term **neo-Marxism** is used to describe the continuing tradition of writing according to the philosophy of Marx. Marx's thought started from the point that human society began when people co-operated to produce or obtain the articles necessary for existence. The methods people chose to obtain their economic necessities strongly influenced their forms of social life. The importance of this economic base continues throughout the history of society and is the determining force of the social structure of all societies. Hence his theoretical approach is often described as **economic determinist**. The owners of the economic structure, or **means of production** as he called it, control the society and construct values and social relationships in their own interests – the **relations of production**.

SOCIAL CHANGE

Societies evolve, becoming increasingly technologically and socially complex. As they do so, the means of production change and with them the relations of production.

Marx distinguished five *epochs*, or periods of history, each characterised by a change in the means of production:

❶ **Primitive communism**, in which people work together and ownership is communal.

❷ **The ancient epoch**, for example a society such as Rome that was based on slavery. Marx also gave an alternative: the Asiatic epoch.

❸ **The feudal epoch**, which was characterised by land ownership by the nobility and by the fact that the peasantry were tied to the land and subservient to the rich.

❹ **Capitalism** is characterised by large-scale factory production (the means of production) owned by one social class, with a much larger, lowly paid class employed in the factories. Emphasis is placed on the private ownership of property (relations of production).

❺ The final epoch, according to Marx, after the transitory one of the dictatorship of the proletariat, is **communism**, in which the means of production will be owned equally by all people.

The next step in Marx's analysis concerned the way societies evolved through these epochs. Marx, influenced by the German philosopher Hegel, suggested three stages:

● a **thesis** (an initial state);

● an **antithesis** (an opposing state);

● and a **synthesis** (the result of the clash).

Although Marx insisted that economic forces were the primary factors in understanding society, he certainly did not ignore the importance of ideas and values in shaping history. Values derive from the economic base, but in turn they have a powerful influence in the development of the economy.

THE MODEL

A model of society from a Marxist perspective can be drawn up. In this, each of the five epochs Marx distinguished is characterised by a particular means of production, owned by one group (or class), who, as a result, controls the society. This ruling class constructs a particular set of relationships of production which benefits them and they ensure that they receive a large proportion of the wealth and are given high status. Furthermore, their beliefs dominate society (the term now generally used for this is **hegemony**). The means of production are always changing, yet ideas and values change more slowly. In each epoch, the relations of production constructed by the owners of the means of production initially assist the advance of the economic structure of society. Gradually, however, they hinder the advance, as the ruling class has created a society to their own benefit and there seems little point in changing it. At a certain point the onward advance of technology can no longer be held back by the relations of production and it bursts through into a new epoch. At this point, a new group arises and introduces a different set of relations of production which both assists the onward advance of technology and reflects the interests of this new ruling group.

APPLICATION TO CAPITALISM

When the Marxist perspective is applied to capitalism, the following scenario emerges. The ruling class or the **bourgeoisie** employ workers; the **proletariat** who have no capital of their own sell their labour to the bourgeoisie. The bourgeoisie construct relations of production to their own benefit, such as the concepts of private property, free movement of labour and capital, and wage labour. The thesis is that the values that are beneficial to the interests of the capitalists are defined as good for all society.

Capitalists are in competition with each other (at least in the early stages of capitalism) and attempt to produce goods at the lowest price possible. Bankruptcies and unemployment are common as some producers are unable to remain in business. For various economic reasons, crises of overproduction occur and these will gradually become worse.

The numbers of capitalists will decline, and their wealth relative to that of the general population will increase. Intermediate groups, such as small shopkeepers, will gradually be forced out of business and join the ranks of the working class. Over time, increasing polarisation will occur between rich and poor. A crisis point is finally reached when the **dialectic** (something that controls the change of history but cannot be seen) is at the final stage of the antithesis. The productive system could advance but is being held back by the organisation of capitalist society with only a few owners controlling output. The synthesis is that the proletariat, reaching a point of desperation at their exploitation, will take over the means of production and introduce common ownership.

FALSE CONSCIOUSNESS AND CLASS CONSCIOUSNESS

The level of class conflict is both the indication and the result of the dialectic. It may appear that the bourgeoisie's exploitation of the proletariat is so obvious that the working class should rebel rather than wait to the point of desperation. The ruling class are, however, able to maintain a sense of **false consciousness** in the working class by inculcating in them values which disguise the reality of their exploitation. For example, Marxist writers such as Bowles and Gintis point out that the educational system ensures that working-class children fail, and it also persuades them that it is their fault.

Class consciousness is the situation in which workers become aware of their exploited position. Factors affecting this include the work of political activists and the existence of large-scale working-class communities, which help insulate the working class from the dominant values of society.

ALIENATION

In a society where people work for money rather than for the satisfaction and relevance that work brings to their own lives, a situation of **alienation** occurs. Many of society's problems derive from this sense of alienation. Work, in a capitalist society, destroys both an individual's sense of his or her own worth and the sense of social cohesiveness of members of society.

CRITICISMS OF MARX BY NON-MARXISTS

Criticisms of Marx include the following:

1. It is felt that Marx's concept of economic determinism places too great a stress on the economy as determining all social life.

2. The polarisation of people into proletariat and capitalists has not occurred.

3. Indeed, the middle classes have actually increased and the other two groups (proletariat and capitalists) have decreased in size.

4. The nature of capitalism has changed with democracy and the Welfare State.

5. The concentration of ownership has not occurred; indeed, there has been some limited diffusion of wealth.

6. If Eastern European countries are considered to have been Marxist, the fact that they have collapsed indicates the inaccuracy of Marxist models of society. Yet capitalist societies continue.

7. Marx ignores women and fails to analyse their particular position in society.

DEVELOPMENTS OF MARXISM: THE NEO-MARXISTS

Marx's work has become the basis for a huge amount of debate from those who are basically in sympathy with his thinking. There are too many neo-Marxists to discuss here but many examples appear throughout the book. However, the range of criticisms can be seen by examining the work of the Frankfurt School on the one hand and Althusser on the other.

The Frankfurt School: the role of values

The Frankfurt School is associated with Marcuse, Adorno and Horkheimer. It has since been developed by Habermas. These sociologists were opposed to the economic determinism of Marx and felt that the role of values in dominating people had been underplayed. They pointed to three elements of the culture of capitalism:

① **Instrumental reason** Capitalist society stresses that all thought, reason, science etc are means to an end. The Frankfurt School argues that people are discouraged from thinking about why we wish to achieve these ends or about the nature of society. Thus, for example, the never-ending search by capitalism for efficiency is not questioned.

② **Mass culture** Marcuse, Adorno, Horkheimer and Habermas stress the role of mass culture in teaching people to be supine and to accept what is offered to them. According to them, entertainment and music trivialise issues and stupefy people.

③ **Personality** All societies need to repress individuals' selfish desires because they are a threat to order and cohesion. In early stages of capitalism, there was a great degree of repression as the economic system was built up. Values of conscientiousness, work ethic and individuality were introduced. In later, or mature, capitalism these individual desires, such as sex, have been built upon and used to the benefit of capitalist society rather than being suppressed. Therefore sex is routinely used to sell things and ownership of certain types of clothes, car or perfume are equated with sexuality. In this way potentially threatening desires are incorporated into the workings of society.

Althusser: relative autonomy

An alternative version of neo-Marxist writings is provided by Althusser. He suggests three elements of capitalist society:

① **economic**: the production of material goods;

② **political**: all forms of organisation;

③ **ideological**: ideas and beliefs.

He argues that the economic structure has ultimate control, but that the economic and political elements of life have quite significant degrees of autonomy. So values and organisations develop and act as if they were completely autonomous – and largely they are – but in the ultimate analysis all these things are controlled by the economic base. Althusser does recognise that there is an element of interplay and that to a limited extent the economic base is affected by the other two elements.

Althusser has used the term **relative autonomy** to explain the relationship between economy and the other elements.

Power and the State

Much of Marx's work focuses on the nature of the State, and Althusser has developed this. He points out that the power of capitalism is maintained through the State (see Chapter 10: Power and Politics) in two ways:

① the obviously repressive elements such as the army and police – the **repressive State apparatuses**;

② and the more **subtle ideological State apparatuses** – education, the media and religious organisations.

HARVEY: POST-MODERNISM

In *The Conditions of Post-Modernity*, Harvey develops Marxism within a post-modernist framework (we discuss post-modernism on pp 38–40). Post-modernism is a movement which argues that there has been a fragmentation of society towards greater diversity, linked to the development of increasingly superficial cultures. Harvey argues that since the mid 1970s capitalism has changed. Economically, there has been a massive decrease in the power of trade unions and an increase in job insecurity, while the types of jobs have shifted from physical labour to ones based on mental or service labour. Capitalists have been successful in developing rapid shifts in fashion and style. At the same time, there has been a change in the nature of culture from nation and class-based ones to a kaleidoscope of mixed and ever-changing cultural forms caused by mass communication and travel. The development of world trade and banking has rendered national governments powerless so that real politics have been taken over by image politics. With the decline in organised labour has also come the growth of a wide range of different sources of opposition to capitalism.

1.4 SYMBOLIC INTERACTIONISM

Structural theories, such as functionalism and Marxism, concentrate on the whole of human society and behaviour. In contrast, phenomenological or action theories, such as interactionism, have a more limited design, and those who subscribe to these approaches are doubtful whether it is truly possible to study such a wide canvas in the way that structural theories set out to do. Phenomenological theories explore the day-to-day routine actions that we all perform. These approaches see individuals as creating society through their routine actions. The purpose of sociology is to study how people act and to understand why they act in this way – without looking for some overarching structure to explain it all.

Symbolic interactionism derives from the work of Mead and, later, of Blumer, and is associated with the University of Chicago. One version of it is known as **labelling theory**. Symbolic interactionism rejects the view that men and women act like puppets controlled by their socialisation or relations of production. It claims that people actively respond to the world, choosing their actions, telling lies, worrying over the best plan of action and so on.

There are three core elements to symbolic interactionism:

- the symbol,
- the self,
- the interaction.

THE SYMBOL

In order to understand the world, we need to classify millions of unique objects and people into groups and to give each group a symbol (or a name); therefore, 'car' encompasses an enormous variety of unique objects. But it is not simply inanimate objects that are classified; so too are people – woman, man, criminal etc. Classification makes the world appear simple, ordered and predictable.

Symbols applied to the classifications, however, usually imply some meaning and require some form of response: a heroine is to be admired, a villain to be despised. The world is therefore composed of symbols which are human-created and which imply *possible* courses of action. However, the line of action is not compulsory – so I could admire the villain and despise the heroine.

THE SELF

People respond to the symbolic world about them, but a *considered* response is only possible if an individual has an awareness of her/himself. I cannot decide what I ought to do in certain circumstances without knowing who I am and where my place is in the scheme of things. We develop this ability to look at ourselves from the outside by playing games in childhood. It is through these games that we are able to engage in the third and crucial element of social life: interaction.

THE INTERACTION

Society consists of individuals acting in certain regular patterns, yet no interaction is possible unless individuals are aware of others' intentions. Each individual must have the ability to take the role of others, that is to base his/her actions on their understanding of what they would do in the place of the other. Individuals assume that they share common understandings of the symbols (speech etc), then put themselves in the place of the other, and respond accordingly. Interaction is not trouble-free and people are constantly modifying their behaviour according to their changing perceptions.

CRITICISMS OF INTERACTIONISM

Interactionism has been criticised on a number of grounds. These include that:

1 It fails to look at wider *structural* factors that create the context in which the interaction takes place: why does one person have power over another person?

2 It fails to explain the *origins* of the meaning that people place upon actions: when people engage in an interaction on the basis of presumed shared meanings, where do those shared meanings originate?

1.5 EXPLANATIONS OF SOCIAL CHANGE

Table 1.1 *Explanations of social change*

	Social conflict approaches	Functionalist	Weberian-based approaches
Basis of society	Different social classes, with the ruling class exploiting the proletariat	A society based on shared values with divisions based on differences in skill	A society based on different status groups competing for prestige
Agent(s) of social change	Class conflict based on the underlying changes in economic factors. Change is *inherent* in Marxist analysis	Exterior factors which force the society to change, such as external economic factors, war, climatic change etc	Changing values
Process of social change	A ruling class is challenged by a subordinate class and a long process of social conflict occurs	The concensus shifts in response to the problem faced	Values held by certain groups come to predominate in society, e.g. Protestant values of thrift and hard work etc
Outcome	A new economic 'epoch' (or period of history) emerges with a different ruling group	A new consensus is developed which 'solves' the external	A shift in the nature of society occurs as a result of the economic and political changes which have emerged from the ability of one group to achieve dominance for its values
Criticisms include	Places too great a stress on economic factors. Historical analysis seems inaccurate	Assumption of a concensus in society is dubious. Accepts that whatever social arrangements exist are the *best* – ignores differences in power	Fails to explain the origins of values

1.6 ETHNOMETHODOLOGY

This theory derives very much from the work of Schutz but is usually linked with Garfinkel. It focuses on the processes through which people create the illusion that an ordered social world exists. Ethnomethodologists do not accept that there is a social order at all, and think instead that society seems ordered only because its members themselves construct a sense of order.

In its most extreme form, ethnomethodology actually suggests that the process of studying society is pointless as sociology uses the very same assumptions about the world as the people it is studying. How can it therefore give any insights? But most ethnomethodologists simply stick to the task of uncovering the details of the sense-making process in which people are constantly engaged. Ethnomethodology has been used mainly in studies of education and deviation. There are three core features:

1. membership,
2. indexicality,
3. reflexivity.

MEMBERSHIP

People assume that they all share a common reality and on this basis they perform social acts. Yet much of what we experience challenges this sense of common reality. Therefore, people constantly strive to clarify the actions of others and to fit them into some pattern that makes sense.

INDEXICALITY

This refers to the fact that we make sense of others' actions because we place them within a context or, as Garfinkel calls it, an **index**. In this way, what is ridiculous in one situation makes sense in another.

A second element of indexicality is that when an individual explains an action or series of actions, rather than giving a complex and detailed description and analysis of everything that happens, he or she glosses over these details. So when asked what happened at college today, the answer may be 'nothing'. Yet we know that it cannot literally be nothing – *something* happened, even if it was a waste of time. Thus both the student and the listener 'fill in' the missing details and mentally file them in the 'trivial' category.

REFLEXIVITY

This is the belief that an ordered, sensible world must exist because if it did not, life would be pointless. Garfinkel argues that people use the documentary method of pulling out of situations certain features (and ignoring others) to create the illusion of an underlying pattern. We document the reality by using examples. For example... well that is the point: if I illustrate this with an example, then I am using the documentary method.

1.7 FEMINISM

Feminist theories overlap with other types of theory, for example they often draw upon Marxist perspectives, but are primarily concerned to examine the position of women in society. In doing so, of course, they also throw light upon the position of males.

Feminist theories have been categorised into:

- liberal feminism,
- Marxist feminism,
- radical feminism,
- dual-system feminist theory,
- a subcategory which could be called black feminism.

LIBERAL FEMINISM

This is primarily concerned to examine the processes of socialisation and **sex-role conditioning** in order to show that the gender roles of male and female are not biologically based. Most early sociological studies followed this route by uncovering socialisation patterns in the family, at school, in work and in the mass media. The aim of the studies was to expose these activities and to agitate for different ways of socialising children, to offer higher schooling expectations for girls, and to change the images of women in the media.

Criticisms of liberal feminism

Critics from within feminism argue that:

1 this approach does not uncover the wider structural factors leading to female oppression;

2 it does not see that **patriarchy** (the dominance of men) is prevalent in all situations, not just in certain areas, such as the family and the media.

MARXIST FEMINISM

This approach locates women's oppression within the nature of capitalist society. Capitalism exploits and oppresses both males and females, and by exposing and then replacing capitalist society, both females and males will be liberated. Marxist feminism has examined in some detail the position of domestic labour within capitalism (see pp 28–9). Women are seen as important reproductive agents in capitalism, who physically produce and care for the next generation of labourers, and who socialise the next generation into submissive attitudes.

Criticisms of Marxist feminism

Critics from within feminism argue that:

1 there is an overemphasis on the exploitation of capitalism. Women experience as much patriarchy in non-capitalist (and pre-capitalist) societies (for example the killing of female infants in China) as they do in capitalist ones;

2 the target for women and for analysis should be patriarchy in whatever context.

RADICAL FEMINISM

This category starts from the assumption that the real cause of the oppression of women is men. Patriarchy, the power of men, exists because men deliberately or unknowingly benefit from this and wish it to continue. Women are categorised as an inferior class to men and are exploited. Some radical feminists argue that women fall into the category of the underclass because on political, social and economic grounds their experiences are significantly worse than men's.

Radical feminists have examined a wide range of issues in male–female relations that are beyond the traditional concerns of feminist researchers, in particular violence against women and sexual politics – the use of women by men in sexual relations. Radical feminism has a number of differing strands, including ones which stress lesbian rights, separatism from men, and celibacy (where the woman is heterosexual).

Criticisms of radical feminism

Critics within feminism argue that:

1 Radical feminism overemphasises the extent to which women share common experiences of exploitation;

2 following from this, it downgrades class and race relations;

3 it cannot account for the changes in the position of women over time, and could only do this within a wider structural framework;

4 it fails to take account in its analysis of other factors besides patriarchy.

DUAL-SYSTEM THEORY

This approach is recognised by many commentators outside feminism as the one which offers the most comprehensive critique of the position of women. It combines elements of radical feminism and Marxist feminism and argues that two intertwined systems of exploitation and oppression exist: the first of these is capitalism which ensures the exploitation of all workers, but in particular women; the second is that at the same time women are oppressed by men within this capitalist structure. The interconnected roles of women in the labour force and in the home combine to form a system of oppression that maintains women in their oppressed position, while benefitting men and capitalism.

Women are forced to engage in part-time, and generally insecure, employment because of the demands made on them as mothers and houseworkers. Their family and domestic commitments prevent them from taking senior positions in the labour force or in the political system, and so they remain in an inferior position.

Criticisms of dual-system theory

Critics of dual-system theory argue that:

1 the system underplays the active role of men in women's oppression – by seeing men's actions as their response to capitalism;

2 capitalism is seen to pre-date and underpin patriarchy, but radical feminists would argue that it is the other way round.

BLACK FEMINISM

This is only a partial approach to the position of women, in that it is primarily concerned with the position of black and Asian women. It claims that feminism is ethnocentric, reflecting the concerns of white and often middle-class women. It suggests that there are very different problems facing black women, and that their experiences are very different too – as is the route to liberation. Therefore they argue that issues of capitalism, patriarchy and anti-racism ought to be given equal weighting in the analysis.

1.8 STRUCTURALISM AND POST-STRUCTURALISM

The starting point for structuralism and post-structuralism is language. Levi-Strauss points out that **language structures our thoughts and actions**. The way people perceive the world is through the spectacles that language gives us. Therefore all social life and social actions are determined by language, and it is to this that we should turn our attention.

STRUCTURALISM

According to Levi-Strauss, society is an independent entity that structures social life, and the structure is provided by language, which all humans encounter. Levi-Strauss also believes that all languages have similar underlying structures: language, and therefore culture, originates in the subconscious human mind and, as all human minds work the same way, all languages are the same in structure. Cultures of different societies actually reflect the subconscious thought processes that underlie language. Levi-Strauss rejects the idea that people are able to construct their own conscious innovations, as they are constrained by the structure of language. The term 'structural' refers to the fact that Levi-Strauss sees there being a structure of action constructed by language which does not allow free will in any true sense of the word.

Those sociologists following the ideas of Levi-Strauss analyse the way in which myths and symbols can be related to social 'laws'.

POST-STRUCTURALISM

Foucault both developed and provided an alternative to Levi-Strauss. He centres his analysis on language, but rejects the argument that there are some universal common features underpinning all languages.

Foucault examines the interplay between power and the way that language is developed in respect to particular areas of social life, such as sexuality or madness. For Foucault, **the way language is structured and the meanings it has reflect power**: it directs us to understand and think about things in certain ways and excludes us from thinking about them in other, possibly challenging ways. (This has some similarity to Marxist ideas of hegemony and false consciousness, see p 29.) Foucault calls the forms of language used in particular areas **discourses**. Our knowledge and perceptions of the world are therefore determined (or 'constituted') by discourses. Foucault then studies the complex ways in which discourses come into being. In *Madness and Civilisation* he describes this process as being like the archaeologist's activity of digging through layer after layer to find the origins of a particular site.

The difference between Foucault and Levi-Strauss (apart from the terminology) is that Foucault sees discourse, or forms of language, as being constructed because of the power of certain groups of people at certain times. He is not, however, saying that the construction of discourse is conscious. Foucault argues that power creates the discourse, but then that the discourse itself creates power by limiting the meaning of language.

Foucault's analysis of madness is an example of how innovatory he was: he manages to link the closing of leprosy asylums with the creation of mental asylums and the development of the profession of psychiatry.

1.9   STRUCTURATION

As we noted at the beginning, sociological theories tend to fall into two types – those emphasising **structures** of society, such as Marxism and functionalism, which stress that social structures above and beyond people tend to determine individuals' lives, and those emphasising **action**, which tend to stress the idea that people make choices which in turn affect the structure, for example interactionsim and ethnomethodology.

Giddens (*Social Theory and Modern Sociology*) has recently put forward a theory called **structuration** which attempts to pull these two approaches together. He argues that there is a close relationship between structure and individual action, with both affecting the other. Instead of sociologists arguing that the best way to understand society is either by taking a structural perspective *or* an action perspective, he says that we should take elements of both.

The key elements of structuration are:

- structure
- agency.

STRUCTURE

This has two elements:

1 Rules are procedures generally prescribed for us by society which we follow in our everyday life. These may be written down, such as legislation or office procedures, or may be more informal. According to Giddens, rules may be changed over time.

2 Resources take two possible forms.

- *Allocative resources* refer to such things as economic goods, raw material, technology, land ownership and all the things that we require to produce or consume.
- *Authoritative resources* refer to power differences between people.

Resources and rules therefore form the structure.

AGENCY

Structures can only exist in so much as people continue to act in certain ways, and therefore there is an intimate relationship between structure and the actions of 'agents'. (Giddens calls people 'agents'). In fact, people need structure in order to engage in their actions – because it profiles the framework from which they draw upon a shared stock of knowledge and perceived appropriate behaviour, yet at the same time structure can only continue to exist if people act in certain ways. This intimate relationship of existence is called 'duality of structure' by Giddens.

Ontological security

According to Giddens, humans have a need for a sense of security, which is provided by rules and resources. People wish to believe that the 'natural and social worlds are as they appear to be'.

The desire for security and the existence of mutual knowledge help to move people towards regular patterns of social life. Regularity in turn leads to society largely reproducing itself and remaining stable.

However, change always remains a possibility. In particular, a process known as **reflexive monitoring** takes place in which agents are evaluating amongst other things, their place in society and whether their personal and family objectives are being met. If this is not the case, then people may choose to act in different ways. A simple example of this is the collapse of communism in Eastern Europe in the 1980s and early 1990s. Although an economic and political system was in existence that dominated rules and resources, eventually the failure of the system led agents to perceive that the system was flawed and to turn to different political and economic systems with different rules and allocation of resources.

Unintended consequences

Giddens makes the point that no agents can ever be certain of the outcome of their actions and that all social action has unintended consequences. When the president of the former Soviet Union, Gorbachev decided to bring in minor political and economic changes to communism, it is unlikely that he foresaw the complete collapse of the entire political and economic system. Any sociological theory must, therefore, take into account unintended consequences.

Transformative capacity

In structural theories, people are seen almost as puppets doing what the society dictates. In action-based theories, people make choices apparently with little reference to wider social restraints. This difference is often described as the difference between voluntarism and determinism. For Giddens people almost always have the power to change things, that is, in all but the most extreme situations there is choice. Therefore people can make changes in society through decisions (though, of course, they cannot be sure of the unintended consequences). This is known as *transformative capacity*.

As a way of illustrating his theory, Giddens points to Willis' *Learning to Labour* as an example of structuration, where the choices of the boys (agency) and the structure of society interact to provide an outcome that gives both free will and predictability. Willis studied a group of 12 working-class boys for 18 months at the end of their schooldays, and then briefly into their first employment. The 'lads' showed no interest in studying at school, regarding it as pointless. They passed their time by 'having a laff' in lessons and making fun of teachers and the harder-working pupils ('ear 'oles'). The lads looked forward to their time at work. Their indifference to school ensured their school failure, making it certain that they would get unskilled manual work. They treated the dead-end jobs they entered like they had their schooling and coped in much the same way. Therefore 'having a laff' at school ensured their failure but also gave them the ability to cope with the dull, repetitive nature of their jobs.

CRITICISMS

Much of Giddens' work, it could be argued, goes little further than the work of some of the founders of sociology. In fact, many would argue that Giddens is merely updating Weber. Yet strong echoes of Giddens' ideas of transformative capacity can be found in Marx – 'people make their own history, but not in circumstances of their own choosing', or even in Parsons who was fully aware that society consisted of individuals making 'patterned choices'. If they did not do so, there was no society.

Archer ('Morphogenesis versus structure and action') argues that resources are much more important than Giddens would have us believe. Economic and material resources impact strongly upon people's lives, for example terrible poverty or famine *must* limit or determine the actions of people. Secondly, Giddens' approach does not give any specific predictions of action. All Giddens says, she argues, is that in certain situations people may act in a variety of ways depending upon their choices which include reproducing previous patterns or engaging in transformative capacity. But Giddens' approach cannot predict which of these may occur.

1.10 POST-MODERNISM

Post-modernist approaches to sociology provide a powerful challenge to traditional theories which have sought to explain in one all-encompassing theory the nature of society (see Table 1.2). Post-modernism as a movement attacks the very idea of grand theories such as Marxism or functionalism or 'meta-narratives' as the movement refers to them. Post-modernism is a movement rather than any one specific theory, which seeks to locate traditional theorising within a particular historical and academic tradition. In the 18th century, a historical movement which became known as the Enlightenment was taking place. In essence the Englightenment was the application of rational thought to solving scientific, economic, political and social questions. It was believed that the natural and social worlds were governed by forces or laws that could be uncovered through scientific endeavour. The more the laws of economics and science could be uncovered, the greater would be the progress in ridding the world of hunger, disease, war and all other problems. The Enlightenment ushered in the 'modern' world in which sociology was born. All of the founders of sociology were very strongly influenced by the idea that societies were progressing from traditional or pre-modern societies through to modern ones based on science, technology and the industrial process. The belief in progress and the benefits of science and rationality, as well as unity in society, as opposed to irrationality and diversity, was taken for granted until the 1970s when the post-modernist movement began to emerge.

In sociology the search had always been for the one unified theory which would explain everything. Marxism and Functionalism both claimed to do this, but by the 1970s great disillusionment had set in amongst the majority of sociologists with these theories as clearly they were failing to explain all they claimed to explain. The first signs of postmodernism, as a reaction to modernism, occurred in architecture with the realisation that the rational, functional tower blocks were actually not good places to live and work in. An architectural movement emerged that still used scientific methods to design buildings but experimented with diversity and 'quirkiness'.

Within the social sciences, people began to reject the meta-narratives and to start to ask new questions which only emerged if one did not accept the traditional theories. In *criminology*, for example, sociologists began to ask questions about the meaning of 'crimes', and to look at other non-criminal issues such as *environmental questions*, how criminologists were *ignoring women* because the definition of crime came from male perspectives.

In the **sociology of work**, a debate emerged about the nature of **post-Fordism**, that is the move away from large-scale production-line methods of manufacture, involving thousands of (usually male) workers coming to the factory, towards more women working for smaller component companies feeding the material to an assembly factory.

In political sociology, interest shifted away from the main political parties to the fragmented, usually unorganised movements which became known as the **New Social Movements**, concerned with such issues as diverse as sexuality or the environment. A sociology of culture emerged to explore the diversity and range of expression and meaning which people had developed for themselves, as opposed to the mass culture which appeared to dominate according to Marxist writers.

BAUDRILLARD

One of the most famous post-modernists (though he does not use the term for himself) is Baudrillard. For Baudrillard, society has shifted away from the production and exchange of goods, to the production and exchange of image. Baudrillard argues that this is just one of the stages in a four-stage process:

1 Signs are a reflection of basic reality – when societies first developed words to express concrete reality

2 Signs mask or distort basic reality, but there is still a connection. This stage includes the development of concepts, such as 'honour'.

3 Signs mask the absence of basic realities. According to Baudrillard, where religions, icons and ceremonies may hide the fact that there is no God (religion).

4 The sign bears no resemblance to any reality, the sign reflects a **simulcrum**. A simulcrum is a shadowy thing that has never existed in reality. According to Baudrillard, the perfect example of a simulcrum is the Mickey Mouse character in Disneyland. This bears no resemblance to a mouse and is meant to refer the person back to another cartoon image called Mickey Mouse. There is no reality here, but nevertheless the image is the basis of a multi-billion dollar company. This idea of a shadowy world of signs expands to politics, where image replaces real power or even real meaning.

CRITICISMS

Post-modernism has been a very incisive criticism of meta-narratives. However, it has failed to provide substantial alternatives. Baudrillard, for example, uses a range of generalisations and assertions in much the same way as any other meta-theorists, possibly with less proof to support his arguments. Furthermore, the idea that there are no underlying 'structural' factors which provide a link between different phenomena is not supported by the evidence, which demonstrates clear inequalities of power and enormous structured differences in wealth and standards of living across and within countries.

Table 1.2 *Modernism and post-modernism compared*

	Modernism	Post-modernism
Aim	To uncover the natural, scientific and social rules underlying the physical and social worlds	To demonstrate that there are no 'universal rules' or scientific truths. To undermine the grand theories or 'meta-narratives' of sociology
Content	All the rational, scientific theories in the physical and social sciences. Marxism, functionalism, feminism etc	A relativist approach to understanding reality. Post-modernists pick and choose from within different approaches. Sociological theories are merely comforting mythologies pretending to explain
Approach method	Positivistic, rational methodology	Relativistic – no approach inherently has more truth than another
Best known writers/theorists	Marx, Durkheim, Weber, Parsons	Lyotard, Baudrillard, Bauman
Categorisation of social groups	Social class, nation, gender, 'race', family	Rejects traditional forms and categories arguing instead for the dynamism and fluidity of society. Consumption is more important than class. There is a fragmentation of traditional groups, e.g. families
The nature of culture	It is real and 'exists'. Derives from consensus (functionalism); economic power (Marxist); values (Weberian); Patriarchy (feminism)	Culture is that which is defined by the media. Content has become unimportant as has meaning. Style and superficiality are all important
The nature of identity	Individuals are 'located' in a culture which provides them with their sense of identity. Although adjusts it fundamentally remains throughout their lives	Identities are constantly changing. They are fluid. Our belief in one essential 'identity' is merely a myth providing us with a sense of reality and stability. As class, family and religion have declined, the media have emerged as those which provide a sense of identity
The future	Modernism foresees the onward advance of science as it categorises, understands and 'conquers' the natural, scientific and social rules	Two approaches: **Pessimistic** – Loss of identity and culture. All is what it appears to be. The possibility of manipulation by the all dominant media **Optimism** – the collapse of the certainties lead to new opportunities and new identities in terms of gender and family in particular
The modernist response to the post-modernist critique	Criticised for its relativism – if everything is of equal meaning and value, how do we measure or understand anything? Giddens points out that if there is no movement in history, how can we have moved from modernism to post-modernism?	Harvey argues that although there is a large degree of fragmentation, continuity continues in many areas of social life

1.11 IDENTITY AND CULTURE

THE RELATIONSHIP BETWEEN SOCIETY AND THE INDIVIDUAL

There are two main ways in which sociologists have sought to explain the relationship between society and individuals:

- Society as more important than individual.
- Individual as creator of society.

Society as the creator of the individual

This approach suggests that people act the way they do because of the over-riding importance of society. It is associated with structural theories such as functionalism and Marxism (see pp 24–31) In essence these approaches suggest that the 'free-will' which people believe they have is ultimately illusory. They can make their own choices, but not in the circumstances of their choosing. This sort of approach has been called 'deterministic'.

Individuals as agents with free choice

This approach suggests that individuals really do make 'real' choices, and that they actually construct society through these choices. The approach is generally associated with 'interactionist' (sometimes known as labelling or social constructionist) theories, and ethnomethodology. These approaches are examined on pp 31–35.

FACTORS IMPACTING ON IDENTITY

Most writers agree on what the factors are which help to create identity at the micro-level. However theoretically there are significant differences as shown in Fig. 1.3.

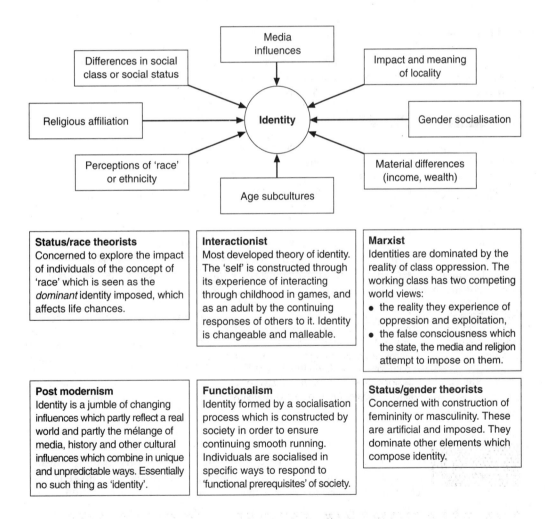

Status/race theorists
Concerned to explore the impact of individuals of the concept of 'race' which is seen as the *dominant* identity imposed, which affects life chances.

Interactionist
Most developed theory of identity. The 'self' is constructed through its experience of interacting through childhood in games, and as an adult by the continuing responses of others to it. Identity is changeable and malleable.

Marxist
Identities are dominated by the reality of class oppression. The working class has two competing world views:
- the reality they experience of oppression and exploitation,
- the false consciousness which the state, the media and religion attempt to impose on them.

Post modernism
Identity is a jumble of changing influences which partly reflect a real world and partly the mélange of media, history and other cultural influences which combine in unique and unpredictable ways. Essentially no such thing as 'identity'.

Functionalism
Identity formed by a socialisation process which is constructed by society in order to ensure continuing smooth running. Individuals are socialised in specific ways to respond to 'functional prerequisites' of society.

Status/gender theorists
Concerned with construction of femininity or masculinity. These are artificial and imposed. They dominate other elements which compose identity.

Fig. 1.3 Factors impacting on identity and their theoretical explanations

NORMS, VALUES AND CULTURES

Norms

These are expected patterns of behaviour which are closely linked to culture, but are much more specific than the general guidelines provided by culture.

Roles

These are expected patterns of behaviour associated with particular social statuses or social positions. (Social positions can be such things as jobs, for example teacher, relationships such as lover, or positions of social honour, for example hero.)

Role conflict

Most people play different roles. These will conflict on occasions, for example mother/child versus teacher/student. The situation is known as role conflict. Functionalist theory is the only one which explicitly includes this, by suggesting that all societies must develop a 'functional prerequisite called latency'.

Status

This refers to the fact that certain positions or individuals are awarded social honour. Status is closely linked to power (see p 76, and Weber's discussion of status).

CULTURE

In its most general form, culture refers to the set of values which societies need to share to a certain minimal extent in order to exist. However, within this simple and broad definition, there are other meanings which sociologists have studied.

The basis of culture

There are deep divisions within sociology concerning the exact basis of society. These have been explored elsewhere in the chapter.

Structuralism explores the relationship between language and culture – see pp 35–6. Marxists argue that the basis of the culture of society is located in the economic base of society, or as they call it, the 'means of production'. Cultural ideas are imposed upon the majority of people by the ruling class.

Functionalists argue that culture is created by society in order to solve the shared problems of society. For them, culture celebrates the shared values of society.

Post-modernists see a fragmentation of culture as modern society moves away from a shared culture whether imposed (Marxism) or reflecting consensus (functionalism).

Divisions within culture

High culture

This is probably the common sense meaning of culture. It suggests that there is a specific set of beliefs and attitudes of the higher status groups (or elite) in society, which incorporates art, music and literature, which is superior to the values and entertainment pursuits of the majority of the population.

Mass society

Those who support the idea of a superior culture of the elite, compare this with the culture of mass society. This is the belief that there is a meaningless and superficial culture of the mass of society which is closely linked to the growth of mass media. The argument of writers such as writers such as Nietzsche and Leavis is how to avoid contaminating the elite culture by the inferior mass culture and the best way to preserve it. The argument is not totally irrelevant for very significant amounts of lottery funding and government grants still go to subsidise opera, which is a minority interest, with the argument that this is a superior form of music that ought to be supported from public funds.

Radical approaches to mass society

Weberian

Weber viewed high culture as a technique of 'closure' by which he meant that social groups who wished to maintain their exclusiveness used the different forms of values and artistic appreciation as a barrier to those who wished to enter their group.

Marxist

We saw earlier that Marxists hold the view that culture derives from the ruling class's control of the means of production. It lies within the ruling class's power to impose a culture on society. This applies to the two meanings of culture – first, that the values of society reflect their interests and secondly, that elite culture is also a form of barrier to distinguish the upper classes from the rest of society. The knowledge of ballet, opera art and so on reflects the superiority of the upper class. It also gives them 'cultural capital' in that knowledge of this culture is regarded as a sign of intelligence and civilised behaviour. This argument resembles Weber's.

Marxism, modernism and culture

The Marxist based Frankfurt School, of which Marcuse is the most famous proponent, argued that mass media had produced a mass culture which had been a key method by which the spread of revolution had been prevented. Mass culture was essentially passive and meaningless. It reflected modernism in being standardised, and predictable, but most importantly, entirely trivial and devoid of any meaning. Consciousness and awareness of the world, reflecting the experiences of the majority of the population were overwhelmed by the output of television, the cinema and the published media which provided an alternative meaningless culture.

In essence, Marcuse is providing an explanation for the Marxist of 'false consciousness' whereby the working class loses the desire for revolution and accepts the status quo.

Subcultures

Subcultures refer to cultures which exist within the main dominating cultures but are quite distinctive. (They may also be in direct opposition to the mainstream cultures and are sometimes known as contra-cultures.) Subcultural theory is explored in the chapters on age (pp 127–31) and on deviance (pp 313–15).

Functionalists only rarely use the concept of subculture as it does not conform to their idea of a single consensual society. However, they do agree that there is such a thing as a youth subculture which enables young people to transfer from childhood to adulthood (p 127).

Marxist writers have used the concept in a much more radical way, and have suggested that subculture actually reflect the attempts by young, working-class people to provide a way of solving the problems they face. The content and symbolic use of dress codes, language and music can be 'decoded' to provide a way of understanding these problems (p 129). The one unifying theme of all the disparate youth cultures is that they represent opposition to capitalism.

Post-modernism and subculture

If modernism claimed that there was enormous conformity and pointed to the way that culture ensured this, post-modernism has sought to show that there is an enormous variety of styles of life. Secondly, it has attacked the idea that the culture or the subcultures actually reflect anything real. For writers like Baudrillard, there is absolutely no truth or underlying meaning in contemporary culture. Youth cultures, which Marxists believe can be decoded, in the view of post-modernists exist on the basis of a 'melange' of different values, ideas, accidental happenings, pastiches of previous fashion styles and musical approaches. There is nothing to decode, no meaning to bring out and certainly no opposition to capitalism.

SOCIALISATION

This is the process whereby people learn the values, norms and ways of behaving.

Functionalism

For functionalists, the process is relatively uncomplicated and consists of learning the correct attitudes and behaviours through the family and educational system (p 191).

Marxists

Once again, the process is relatively simple. Culture is learned through the same agencies. The difference is that these agencies are operating on behalf of capitalism to socialise people to behave in the way that the ruling class wishes. However, there are always opposing forms of socialisation going on, which oppose the values of the ruling class. These values emerge from working-class organisations such as the trade unions.

Symbolic interactionists

These have developed a detailed and elaborate explanation of the process of socialisation. Building on the work of Mead and Cooley in the early part of the 20th century, they argue that children learn norms and values through play. First they imitate their parents and later they learn to put themselves in the place of others through playing team games. Interactionism is explored on pp 31–32.

Feminist approaches

These stress the way that girls and boys are socialised differently and the concept of gender behaviour is constantly stressed (pp 33–35).

CULTURAL DIVERSITY

The issue of identity and culture are often best raised through the discussion of race and racism (p 110). The term cultural diversity refers to the fact that there is not one single culture in most contemporary western societies, but also a variety of distinctive cultures which provide a complete (as opposed to the subculturally incomplete) alternative to the values of the dominant group. In Britain there are cultures which are linked to 'ethnic groups', such as Bangladeshis and religious groups such as Jews or Muslims.

Test yourself questions and answers

Questions

1 What major division is traditionally made between types of theory?

2 Very briefly outline the underlying idea of structuration theory, relating to the division referred to above.

3 What criticisms have been made of functionalism?

4 Explain the term 'alienation'?

5 What was the Frankfurt School?

6 What are the three key elements of interactionism?

7 What are the three core features of ethnomethodology?

Suggested answers

1 Theories are traditionally divided between structural and phenomenological, or action approaches.

2 It sets out to explore the unclear relationship between the constraints placed on individuals by the structure of society, and the choices and decisions individuals make. This is an attempt to link structure and action theories.

3 Criticisms of functionalism include:
- It overemphasises the consensus that exists in society;
- the biological analogy is flawed, in particular over the issue of power;
- functionalists have problems explaining social change because of the emphasis on harmony;
- the idea of choice and interaction is excluded by functionalists.

4 In a society where people work for money rather than for the satisfaction and relevance to their own lives that their job could bring, a situation of alienation occurs. Work, in a capitalist society, destroys the sense of individual worth of people and the sense of social cohesiveness of members of society.

5 It was associated with Marcuse, Adorno and Horkheimer and has since been developed by Habermas. They were opposed to the economic determinism of Marx and felt that the role of *values* in dominating people had been underplayed. They pointed to three elements of the culture of capitalism:
- instrumental reason,
- mass culture,
- personality.

6 The symbol, the self, the interaction.

7 Membership, indexicality and reflexivity.

Illustrative question and answer

Question

1 Compare and contrast the contributions of structural theories and interactionist theories to an understanding of social life.

AEB

Suggested answer

Remember this question asks you both to compare and contrast, so do not simply give a description of each approach. There are always two ways to answer compare and contrast questions: *either* compare and contrast as you go through the two approaches *or* give an analysis of both and then draw together the similarities and differences. In theory (no pun intended!), I think the first approach is better, and I encourage students to do so in essays, but in an exam situation I would suggest that you could probably get your ideas sorted out more clearly by analysing them both separately and then look at the similarities and differences at the end of the essay.

Start by explaining the meaning of the term structuralist, pointing out that it includes both Marxist and functionalist theories. Run through these theories but do try to emphasise what they share as well as the differences. Do not forget to demonstrate that you are aware of more 'contemporary' approaches to Marxism rather than just Marx, and, similarly, for functionalism do not just mention Parsons (for example, talk about Merton, Davis and Moore).

The majority of marks will come, however, from your ability to compare and contrast. *Differences* include:

- Starting point for analysis – individual or society.

- Focus of analysis – about interaction compared to social change.

- Ability to explain different things – so interactionism struggles or ignores macro-level issues such as social change, stratification, etc, while structural theories struggle to explain the complexities of individual actions and choices. You need to explore this in some detail, and really draw out the differences.

- Value issues are closely related to structural theories in that Marxism is left-wing and functionalism is conservative. Interactionism tends to be apolitical, although here you might want to discuss Becker's famous call for sociology to be on the side of the underdog, and the criticism of him by Gouldner, a structuralist.

- Power is an interesting point of comparison – although Marxists and functionalists have very different views on it, they tend to locate power 'above' the level of individuals. More importantly, they both have a coherent view on the nature of power. It is arguable that interactionists do not have a coherent view on power.

- The nature of society: structuralists tend to accept that there is an existing 'thing' called society. Interactionists see it as simply a something existing in the minds of the people and having no existence beyond this.

- Methodology – structuralism is sympathetic to positivist methods, while interactionism is distinctly non-positivistic.

  Similarities are harder to find. All the approaches have traditionally ignored issues of race and gender. All approaches accept that sociology is possible and worthwhile, and that they can provide us with a useful understanding of the world. Ethnomethodology and post-modernism have more negative views on this. All approaches reject biological determinism, i.e. what we are is a result of genetic programming.

  Links? Giddens' structuration theory has attempted to link the approaches in a coherent way. Although he has not done any empirical studies to demonstrate his theoretical approach, he quotes the work of Paul Willis (*Learning to Labour* – see p 193) as a good example of his ideas.

Question bank

1 Assess the claim made by interactionists that the social world has to be explained in terms of the meanings that the actors give to their actions.

AEB

Points

This requires a full discussion of interactionist theory. But in the introduction you should briefly state the differences between interactionism and more structural theories. How the social world is, according to them, socially constructed through 'symbols' and how people are taught how to respond and negotiate with these symbols. Give examples from different areas of sociology. Probably the best examples are in the area of deviance (see pp 316–19). Explore implications of labelling and how action based on symbols does have 'real consequences'. Do not forget to criticise. You should stress the lack of discussion of power and of wider 'structural' issues.

2 Compare and contrast Marxist and functionalist theories of social change.

AEB

Points

Remember, 'compare and contrast' means bring out all the differences and similarities between the two. Start with functionalist theory. Explain that it is primarily a theory based on 'stasis' or harmony and has some problems with social change. Go through Parson's version of functionalism, but also use Durkheim. After this, work your way though Marxism. Explain that this is primarily a theory of social change. Look at the way that functionalism sees change coming from outside while Marxism sees an internal dynamic. Emphasise the difference between the consensual approach of the functionalists and the conflict approach of the Marxists. I would use examples from development theory – modernisation theories are functionalist ones.

3 Read the passage and answer the questions which follow.

Social order for some sociologists is based essentially on the ownership, control and domination of the means of production by a ruling class. Social values and beliefs merely serve to reinforce the continued dominance of the ruling group and act as a means of ideological control.

(a) Explain what is meant by:
  (i) the means of production
  (ii) ideological control
  (iii) the class struggle (2)

(b) Why does class struggle threaten the continued dominance of the ruling class? (4)

(c) Choosing any one institution you have studied (e.g. family, education, work, the media, religion), demonstrate how that institution contributes to the continuing dominance of society by a ruling class. (7)

(d) How might sociologists who use a different theoretical perspective criticise the view of social order outlined in the passage? (8)

NEAB

Points

(a) (i) The dominant form of technology which exists at any one time, for example, industry or agriculture.
  (ii) The way that the dominant forms of thought are imposed on the people in a society by the ruling class.
  (iii) The conflict between the different social classes in society as the ruling class attempts to impose itself on the proletariat and their response to this attempt.

(b) Threatens because it reflects growing consciousness of the working class of their position. On a deeper note, the increase in class conflict reflects the movement of the dialectic between the means and relations of production.

(c) One of the following: *family* – reproduces the workforce physically and ideologically, maintains the (male) worker; *education* – reproduces the workforce in terms of ideology and skills; *media* – key role to play in ideological reproduction and false consciousness.

(d Best to take the functionalist position of shared values leading to social order through consensus. Use the Parsonian theory approach and illustrate with Davis and Moore. You might also illustrate by giving examples from functionalist approach to education and to the family.

4 'An understanding of social life can only be achieved by combining theories of social structure and theories of social action.' To what extent do you agree with this viewpoint?

NEAB

Points

You need to clarify the meaning of social structure which is essentially Marxist and functionalist. You then need to define the theories of social action. These are interactionist approaches and Weberian-based approaches. Very briefly, outline the strengths and weaknesses and then say that the current attempt to bring the two together is the work of Giddens with his idea of 'structuration'. Briefly explain and, if necessary, illustrate with Willis' *Learning to Labour* (p 193).

RESEARCH

Units in this chapter

Chapter objectives

The study of methodology – how sociologists go about gathering information and constructing theoretical explanations for action – is possibly the most important area of study for the student of sociology. If the methods of data collection and theory building are flawed, then so are the resulting explanations of human action. Much criticism has been made by outsiders of sociological methods: in particular, they argue that the methods used are naive, value-laden and insufficiently rigorous. Sociologists have responded in a variety of ways, and these are explored in this chapter.

We begin by discussing the nature of science itself and the relevance of this to more traditional approaches to sociology. We then analyse whether sociology is, or should be, a science and why the debate occurs. Sociologists' answers to these questions tend to be variable, and we therefore continue to examine these issues by looking first at those who believe sociology is a science and then listing the criticisms from those both inside and outside sociology.

The next issue concerns the place of values in sociology. Once again sociologists are divided on whether personal and political values are central to an understanding of the social world, or whether they interfere with a neutral, scientific dissection of social phenomena.

The following sections of the chapter explore the actual process of research and how to do it well. We start by looking at how to undertake a social survey, and the best methods to utilise in order to obtain an accurate picture of the population you may wish to study. We then explore the relative merits of questionnaires and interviews, and give a comprehensive guide to their strengths and weaknesses. After this we look at a variety of other ways, besides surveys, to study the social world. Possibly the most important, and useful approach is that of observation. At first sight this seems an obvious form of research, with very few problems; however, we see that to do an observational study well there are numerous problems and pitfalls to be overcome.

The final section of the chapter is an example of how we can take the same social phenomenon – in this case suicide – and come to profoundly different conclusions about it by making different assumptions at the start, and then following these through.

2.1 WHAT IS SCIENCE?

DEFINITION

Science can be defined in terms of:

- a set of key **components** which can be related to
- a methodological **process**.

THE COMPONENTS

Science has four components:

1. It is **empirical**: it deals with measurable phenomena.

2. It is **theoretical**: it seeks to uncover causal relationships between phenomena – it does not simply describe events.

3. It is **cumulative**: it builds up knowledge, moving towards greater understanding of the world.

4. It is **objective**: values, bias and personal attitudes have no place in science. It concerns itself with the 'objective' discovery of the truth.

THE PROCESS

Science involves using a particular method, which is based on the following process:

- phenomena are observed;
- a hypothesis is formed to explain tentatively the phenomena;
- an appropriate form of experiment is devised in order to isolate key variables;
- the process of data collection is carried out, usually in the form of an experiment;
- the data are analysed;
- the hypothesis is confirmed, modified or rejected;
- conclusions are drawn and, in most circumstances, a theory is formed. This may be tested in further experiments.

2.2 SOCIOLOGY AS A SUBJECT AND ITS STATUS AS A SCIENCE

Sociologists have disputed the scientific nature of the sociological enterprise for over 120 years. For non-sociologists, the question is why should they be so concerned? There are two reasons:

1. **Prestige** Since the 19th century, the subjects regarded as scientific have been accorded the highest prestige in the educational world, and among the public. Therefore 'scientific' medicine has greater prestige than 'unscientific' homeopathy.

2. **Finance** Partly as a result of this, the amount of funding for research, teaching posts and 'space' in the curricula of schools, colleges and universities depends upon the level of academic prestige.

Currently 'positivistic' sociology lays claim to make objective, policy-oriented research which is of use to governments and official organisations.

ARGUMENTS FOR SOCIOLOGY AS A SCIENCE

Sociology is a science because it fulfils the key components and processes of a science. That is, it is:

- theoretical,
- empirical,
- cumulative and
- it follows the relevant process of observation/experimentation/theory formation.

Theoretical

Theory involves making causal connections between phenomena and predicting behaviour as a result. The more accurate the theory, the greater the accuracy of the prediction. Individuals may be relatively unpredictable, but the behaviour of groups of individuals is quite predictable. For example, insurance companies can work out the risks involved for various types of driver and car. They can do this on the basis of accident records for age groups and car types. They do not claim to predict the behaviour of individual drivers.

Empirical

Sociology deals with facts, in just the same way that any other science does. So it collects and analyses statistics and observes human behaviour. The original proponent of this argument was Durkheim, writing at the beginning of the 20th century, who points out that there are clear patterns of behaviour which exist in society and which can be observed in similar ways to other non-social facts. For example, statistics on marriages, crimes, suicides and health are all objective facts that can be observed and counted.

Cumulative

Sociology seeks to accumulate a body of knowledge using new research to build on the advances in knowledge gained by previous research.

The process model

Sociologists have developed methodological approaches such as interviews, questionnaires and sample surveys, which allow them to follow the scientific processes.

CRITICS OF SOCIOLOGY AS A SCIENCE

Critics of sociology as a science can be divided into two very broad groups:

- physical scientists, who criticise from outside the discipline, and
- subjectivist sociologists from within sociology itself.

Physical scientists

Physical scientists have criticised some sociologists who claim that the subject is a science. Their criticisms are on empirical and theoretical grounds.

1 **Theoretical** The essence of theory is to predict. But people, unlike objects, are unpredictable because they have free will. Therefore, true prediction and useful theory is impossible.

2 **Empirical** Sociologists have not developed adequately sophisticated and valid ways of measuring phenomena as the physical sciences have done.

Subjectivist sociologists

A significant proportion of sociologists argue that sociology is not, and should not claim to be, a science, on theoretical, empirical and cumulative grounds.

1 **Theoretical** Although it is accepted that sociology is theoretical in intent, there are great problems with the nature of sociological theories. In particular, people are concerned that the theories of sociology are based upon assumptions concerning the nature of reality, which are themselves really based on theories or ideologies. For example, most theories in sociology until the 1980s were **malestream**, in that they were based upon assumptions concerning the roles of women in society. Once these assumptions were exposed many of the basic theories looked threadbare.

2 **Empirical** It is not possible to accumulate facts in the same way as physical scientists do, since social facts such as statistics are really social constructs and do not reflect an objective reality. Sociology needs always to take into account the meanings that people ascribe to actions. So an objective reality does not exist in sociology; sociologists deal more with subjective perceptions of reality. See Fig. 2.1.

Critics of the scientific status of sociology point to the way governments manipulate unemployment figures in order to make them as low as possible: by allowing only certain groups to be officially considered as unemployed, the extent of unemployment is altered in official figures. A similar process occurs with hospital treatment waiting lists. A detailed discussion of this process with regard to the massaging of criminal statistics can be found on pp 311–12. The question must be whether there are really any objective statistics upon which sociologists can base their objective measurements.

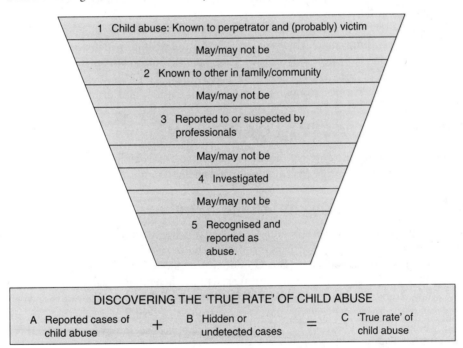

(*Source:* S. Taylor, 'Measuring child abuse' in *Sociology Review*, February 1992)

Fig. 2.1 An example of how statistics may not reflect 'reality': from abuse to reported abuse

3 **Cumulative** Kuhn (*The Logic of Scientific Method*) points out that no science is cumulative, but progresses through **paradigm shifts**. By this he means that a theory is believed to be correct, and so all research and newer theories are based upon this foundation, on the principle that this represents the truth. Alternative theories or explanations of reality are dismissed. However, at a certain point, another totally different competing explanation for reality shows itself to be so overwhelmingly true that the old paradigm is abandoned, and with it all the research associated with it. Reality is shown to be false. It could be argued, for example, that this is what is happening with Marxist theory, as the States that have claimed to be based on this have collapsed.

2.3 OBJECTIVITY AND VALUE FREEDOM

A major concern for sociologists has been whether or not sociology is so riven with value judgements as to make absurd any claim it has to be a neutral, objective science. On the one hand, the more 'positivistic' sociologists claim that it is possible to put aside one's own values. On the other hand, the more vocal sociologists claim either that it is impossible to keep one's values from influencing research or, indeed, that we should actively seek to put our values into our research.

In this section we look first at the argument for objectivity and then at the opposing arguments for sociology as value-laden.

THE CASE FOR OBJECTIVITY

The nature of sociological research is no different from the nature of research in the natural sciences. There are, it is claimed, objective social facts such as divorce statistics, crime statistics, opinion polls, which are like any form of phenomenon, and the biases of the researcher are irrelevant, as long as they do not deliberately distort or alter the findings. If the researchers are biased, however, and they publish the methods used in their research, plus the raw data if necessary, then other sociologists can check their research process to make a judgement about their objectivity.

It is accepted that individuals have free will, but conformity and predictability are normal and indeed the very things upon which society is based and without which no social life would be possible. Unpredictable people are regarded as mad or disturbed in our society. Therefore free will is less important than has been suggested by critics.

Finally, sociology studies groups of people not individuals and groups *are* predictable.

SOCIOLOGY AS VALUE-LADEN

Many critics within sociology reject the idea that a value-free sociology is *possible*. Secondly, a number of sociologists argue that a value-free sociology is not *desirable*.

The historical background to the debate

The late 19th- and early 20th-century sociologist Max Weber has traditionally been associated with the argument that personal values could/should be kept separate from the research and teaching of sociology. But Gouldner points out (*Anti-Minotaur: The Myth of a Value-Free Sociology*) that Weber was writing at a time when intellectual freedom was under strong attack from the government of Prussia/Germany. Gouldner claims that Weber's writings were a ploy to prevent the government from interfering and possibly preventing sociology being taught. This ploy has passed into the canons of sociology as an **eternal truth**, but should be seen in its historical context.

A VALUE-FREE SOCIOLOGY IS NOT POSSIBLE

Certain branches of sociology, as well as individual sociologists, hold that a value-free sociology could not exist.

Feminists

Feminists point to the way that sociology has focused on male concerns and its disinterest in women's concerns. Thus the role of houseworker and the economic contribution of this work was ignored until feminist researchers took it up. Similarly, the issues of women in the workplace and women and crime were other areas where male sociologists introduced their biases by choosing areas of study and by basing their work on certain (sexist) assumptions.

Neo-Marxists

Neo-Marxists point to the way that sociology has accepted the values and social structures of capitalism and has sought answers within the framework of capitalism.

Finance

Those who pay for research often control the direction of that research. As most research funding comes from government and institutions funded by large corporations, research may operate within the framework set by them. In Britain, the Department of Health retains copyright on all research that it funds and can prevent publication of critical research.

A famous example of government funding of research was Operation Camelot in the 1960s which was research funded by the US military to find ways of undermining the social stability of 'unfriendly' countries. It is suggested that some of the information gained was used by the US military to help destabilise Argentina and overthrow the Socialist government.

Personal values and interests

Sociologists, like anyone else, have a desire to improve their careers and to make a name for themselves. They also have personal values, interests and prejudices. They may come from certain racial or social class backgrounds. All these factors influence the choice, methods, direction and interpretation of research.

Phenomenology and reality

Sociologists who subscribe to phenomenological approaches to sociology argue that the process of scientific method, the concept of science and the very basic underlying concepts of sociology are themselves products of society and reflect only the social activities of people attempting to construct a reality. In essence, sociology is a product of the very thing that it is trying to study. The belief of the more extreme approaches – in particular ethnomethodology – is that sociology as a subject can achieve no more than to uncover what people mean through their taken-for-granted assumptions. But no value-free sociology in the conventional sense can be undertaken.

Foucault

A similar argument is put forward by Foucault in his study of the development of knowledge. Foucault argues that what is considered knowledge reflects no more than the process of certain powerful groups attempting to construct a reality. Yet this reality is not substantial, composed as it is of a mixture of contradictory and essentially meaningless beliefs and values. Foucault rejects any sense of order or meaning in society. Value freedom is impossible.

SHOULD SOCIOLOGY BE VALUE-FREE?

In the 1970s a famous debate took place between Becker (*Whose Side are We On?*) and Gouldner. Becker claims that values are always present in sociology and that it is wrong to pretend that sociologists can be neutral scientists. Sociologists should therefore make up their minds who they represent. Becker suggests that sociologists' research ought to put forward the viewpoint of the underdog, the criminal, the deviant and the pupil. This is because power and the sympathy of society are on the side of the top dogs – the police, the teachers etc. By focusing research on the underdogs a different perception of reality could be built up.

Gouldner criticises Becker for this view by arguing that Becker is actually dissociating himself from the main issues of the debate. The type of research advocated by Becker (labelling theory, see p 31) documents the lives and views of the powerless. This type of research seems like it could be helpful, but in reality it documents the *results* of the oppression by the rich and powerful, rather than concentrating on those who create the oppression and who benefit by it. Indeed, Gouldner claims that the spotlight of research should be on the powerful and on the mechanisms they use to oppress the majority of the population.

THE OUTCOME OF THE DEBATE FOR SOCIOLOGY

This debate on oppression and the call to be value-committed has been taken up by a number of sociologists, so that most feminist and anti-racist researchers have consciously made the decision to express professional support and sympathy for women and ethnic minorities in their research.

2.4   POSITIVISM

Positivism is the name given to the form of sociology that takes as its model the scientific approach of attempting to gain hard facts.

POSITIVISTIC METHOD

Positivistic approaches to sociological research are based on the belief that as far as possible sociology ought to utilise similar methods to those used in the natural sciences. Therefore, the model of procedure of the natural sciences is used, which moves from observation and hypothesis, through data collection and analysis, to theory formation and modification. Most researchers set out to disprove the initial hypothesis, on the basis that it is impossible actually to prove anything, the best course of action then being to show that despite the researcher's best attempts to disprove the initial hypothesis, the explanation still appears to hold true. Contrarily, if the researcher is testing a hypothesis (perhaps made by someone else) which he/she disagrees with, then the best attempts are made to prove the hypothesis.

A good example of this is the classic affluent worker studies of the late 1960s, by Goldthorpe, Lockwood et al (*The Affluent Worker in the Class Structure*), where the researchers did not agree with the argument that large sections of the better paid working class were being absorbed into the middle class. Nevertheless, Goldthorpe and Lockwood tried their best to prove the hypothesis correct. It was only when they felt they had done the best they could to prove it and not succeeded, that they felt confident that the theory was inaccurate.

VARIABLES

The aim of the research process is usually to find out the relationship between two or more **variables**: that is two phenomena having a relationship of some kind, so that changes in one **(the independent variable)** bring about or cause changes in the other **(the dependent variable)**. The usual outcome of successful research is to:

- isolate the independent variable,
- measure the relationship and
- explain the nature of the relationship.

REPRESENTATIVENESS

To judge this, the sociological researcher asks whether the group under study is typical or representative of those about whom he/she wishes to generalise. If not, the research is of limited value. This emphasises the importance of **sampling** (see pp 56–7).

THE EXPERIMENTAL METHOD

Experiments are used in order to ensure complete control over all known variables, so that the researcher can isolate the key variables and be certain that he/she knows exactly what each variable does or responds to. Sociologists rarely use experiments because:

- it is impossible to recreate normal life in the artificial environment of an experiment;
- there can be ethical problems relating to performing experiments – even sociological ones – on people;
- there is the possibility of the **experimenter effect**, by which we mean that people respond to what they perceive the experimenter wants from them. The most famous example is the Hawthorne studies.

Occasionally sociologists use **field experiments**, where a form of experiment is undertaken in the community. Rosenhan sent 'normal' people to psychiatric institutions in the USA in the 1960s to see how they were treated by the staff. (The staff treated ordinary behaviour as evidence of insanity.)

THE COMPARATIVE (OR STATISTICAL COMPARATIVE) METHOD

Because of the problems associated with the experimental method, sociologists have frequently used the **statistical comparative method**. When a sociologist is interested in a particular phenomenon, he/she collects information from different groups or societies in the search for clear statistical patterns. If these are found, and they differ from one society to another, the sociologist searches for the relevant social differences which may cause the variations. The most famous example of this is Durkheim's *Suicide* (see pp 63–8).

METHODOLOGICAL ARTEFACTS

There are a number of important concepts that are of concern in considering methodological artefacts. **Reliability** and **validity** are two of the most important concepts that affect both questionnaires and interviews.

Reliability

This refers to the difficulty of comparing like with like in interviews and questionnaires. Is each interview and, to a lesser extent, questionnaire the same thing? If two people are interviewed by the same interviewer is *exactly* the same social event happening? Issues of personal dislike or mutual attraction, differences caused by race, age, class or gender could intervene to a greater or lesser extent in each interview. The context of the interview may be particular – for example two interviews taking place, one in a hurry and the other at a more leisurely pace. All these factors influence the outcome of the interview so that when all the survey results are put together the individual interviews or questionnaires may not be the same.

Validity and indicators

Sociologists are concerned to study and measure concepts which have been created theoretically to explain aspects of social life. The problem of research is to find a true (or valid) way of measuring abstract concepts through real behaviour or expressed attitudes. The problem is exactly *what* behaviour and *which* attitudes can be take as true measures of the concept.

Indicators

Related to validity is the issue of **indicators**. Research often has to find concrete and clear ways of measuring the beliefs, values and activities that people hold or do. Often there are no conventional methods of measuring these beliefs or activities, so the researcher must invent them. The question is how accurate these forms of measurement or indicators are?

In her study of husband and wife relationships, Pahl (*Money and Marriage*) decided that two factors were important:

- who controls the finances?
- did the couple have a happy marriage?

Having decided that these were important concepts, she then had to devise indicators to measure these two factors. For financial control she devised a four-category scale:

1 husband-controlled;

2 husband-controlled pooling;

3 wife-controlled pooling;

4 wife-controlled.

For happiness, she asked couples to place themselves into one of the two categories:

1 happy/very happy;

2 average/unhappy.

The point is that if these indicators do not reflect 'reality', then they invalidate the study.

2.5 SURVEYS AND SAMPLING

Surveys are used (among other methods of research) by positivism in its attempt to gain hard facts. In order to attain the best possible survey, various sampling methods are used.

SURVEY AND PILOT SURVEY

A survey is a study made of a large group of people in order to find out specific information about them. A survey usually involves composing questionnaires and then either directly asking individuals in a form of interview or delivering the questionnaires to the selected individuals.

A pilot survey is a small-scale study which is intended to:

- evaluate the usefulness of the larger survey;
- test the quality and accuracy of the questions;
- test the accuracy of the sample; and
- check whether any technical difficulties that emerge can be learned from and avoided in the main study.

SAMPLING

Sociologists may wish to find out the beliefs and habits of a section of the population. In most cases they are unable to ask everybody: for example to find the political preferences of voters, it would be difficult to question over 20 million people. However, through careful sampling an accurate statistical picture can be drawn up.

There are two main types of sampling:

- random sampling and
- quota sampling.

Random sampling

This is based on the idea that by choosing randomly, each person has an equal chance of being selected. Those chosen are therefore likely to be a cross-section of the population. Random sampling operates on the same principle as a prize draw.

A major advantage of random sampling is that, using statistical tests (of confidence), it is possible to check just how random, and therefore typical of the population, any random sample is likely to be.

There are a number of different ways of conducting random sampling. These include:

- simple random sampling,
- strata sampling,
- cluster sampling,
- multi-phase sampling.

Simple random sampling

Individuals' names are chosen at random from a list or some other form of **sampling frame**. This is the easiest and clearest method of sampling, and in non-professional research the most commonly used.

A sampling frame is some form of a list from which the sample is drawn. If the sampling frame is inaccurate, this can lead to great errors in the final findings. Therefore it needs to be a true reflection of the sort of people whom the researcher wishes to study. Typical sampling frames are electoral registers or GP's patient records.

Strata sampling

The population under study is divided according to known criteria, for example 51.9% women and 48.1% males are chosen to reflect the sex composition of the UK. Within this broad strata people are then chosen at random. The strata can become quite detailed, for example including age, social class, geographical location. This method does have similarities with the quota sampling method (see below).

Cluster sampling

The population under study may sometimes be spread over too great a geographical area for the researcher to visit and study. So the researcher attempts to 'cluster' the samples together, though still choosing at random. If a researcher wished to examine voting patterns in the UK, he/she might first choose a number of constituencies at random, then within these a number of wards, and within these a number of polling districts. Finally, he/she may then choose a number of households within these randomly clustered polling districts.

Multi-phase sampling

This form of random sampling usually occurs when a researcher, after an initial study has been done, wishes to return to the area to ask a small number of sampled people detailed questions. The researcher chooses at random a small subsection of the original sample.

Quota sampling

This form of sampling is used by market research companies and by large-scale university studies. It almost always involves street interviews conducted by trained staff. Assistant researchers are sent out to find a specific quota of people with certain characteristics which reflect the exact make-up of the population under study. There is no element of randomness involved.

The idea is that as sociologists now know almost exactly the main social characteristics of the UK population (age, income, occupation, location, ethnicity etc), so researchers are given a particular portfolio of individuals whom they must find and question. When the results are pieced together, rather like a jigsaw, the replies should be an accurate reflection of the population as a whole. This form of sampling can only be done where the major characteristics of the population are accurately known before the quotas are constructed.

The major advantage of quota sampling over random sampling is the very small number of people needed to build up an accurate picture of the whole. For example, the typical surveys made of voting preferences in journals and newspapers use a quota sample of approximately 1,260 to represent the entire British electorate.

2.6　QUESTIONNAIRES

Questionnaires are a series of printed questions that are handed or mailed to respondents who complete them on their own, giving their own judgements. Questions may be open or closed:

- Open questions: any reply that the respondent wishes to give is acceptable.
- Closed questions: The respondent is presented with a short list of possible answers from which he/she must choose. Typically a box is given and the respondent is asked to tick his/her choice.

THEIR USEFULNESS

Questionnaires are a useful method of research when the researcher wishes to question a large number of individuals (especially if they are geographically spread) and where the researcher wishes to find relatively simple facts. They are likely to be more reliable than interviews (see p 50) because of the lack of interviewer intervention and bias. They can also be used successfully to study embarrassing areas, such as sexual conduct, because the questionnaire is completed anonymously.

THE DESIGN

Questionnaires are best if they:

- are short;
- ask precise, unambiguous questions;
- use clear language; and
- are designed so that the answers given allow the researcher to measure accurately the issue being studied (the problem of validity, see pp 55–6).

THE DRAWBACKS

There are several difficulties associated with using questionnaires as a form of research. They cannot explore issues in depth. The researcher can never be sure that the person given the questionnaire will actually complete it him/herself. The researcher has no way of confirming the truth of the replies, except by including 'check' questions (some questions which are essentially the same are asked in different ways to ensure that the respondent gives similar answers). If he/she does not there is the risk that they are lying. Questionnaires have very low **response rates** (the ratio of questionnaires given out to those returned). Response rates are important because the fewer the number of people who reply, the less the researchers can rely on the results; this is because they do not know what the non-respondents would have said, whether there would have been a range of opinion or whether they all might have had the same opinion.

2.7　INTERVIEWS

Any form of oral questioning made to obtain information is an interview. As with questionnaires, questions may be open or closed. The style of questioning may vary from structured (or formal) to unstructured (informal). This means that at the most formal, it is merely an oral questionnaire with the interviewer being instructed to read out the words in a particular way, and not able to elaborate if the interviewee asks questions. The most informal interviews can take the form of a structured conversation.

THEIR USEFULNESS

Interviews are a useful method of finding detailed information from people in face-to-face situations, allowing interviewers to explore issues in depth, where necessary. Interviewers are also able to compare replies given with their own observations in order to make a judgement about the truthfulness of the reply.

THE DESIGN

Depending upon the level of structure in the interview, the design can be simple and unambiguous or simply guidelines to enable a trained interviewer to follow through certain themes. Having said this, interviews do allow opportunity for detailed, individualised comments to be made.

THE DRAWBACKS

Interviews can be time-consuming and therefore expensive if the interviewer is being paid. There is also a much greater possibility of bias (and therefore reliability problems) than with questionnaires as the interviewer and interviewee must interact in some way. Factors such as social class, age, gender and ethnicity may affect the outcome of interviews.

2.8 SECONDARY DATA

Secondary data is all data which are not obtained first-hand by researchers. They can be compared with **primary data**, which are obtained through the sociologists' own direct research.

THEIR USEFULNESS

Secondary data are used when researchers are unable to obtain primary data; where published data are more useful/accurate/appropriate; and to back up and support first-hand investigation.

It may not be possible to obtain primary data in the following circumstances:

- when historical data are needed and the participants in the events are dead;
- when the researcher is unable to visit places to collect data from other cultures;
- if the subject of the research is illegal activities and it is unsafe for the researcher to go to collect data;
- if data need to be collected from closed groups, such as religious orders, where the researcher is forbidden to enter.

Published data are more useful, accurate or appropriate because:

- official statistics often provide far greater scale and detail than a sociologist could gather;
- the published statistics are cheap;
- the information is much easier to obtain;
- the information covers a long time span;
- the published data may be the focus of the researcher's investigations.

TYPES OF SECONDARY DATA AND PROBLEMS ENCOUNTERED IN USING THEM

The most common types of secondary data used by sociologists include:

- official statistics,

- official reports,
- the mass media,
- diaries,
- oral history (usually recorded),
- letters,
- novels and works of fiction, and
- other researchers' works.

Official statistics

These are collected for administrative reasons and the classifications used may be different or inappropriate for sociologists (eg the definitions of social classes used by government departments). Official statistics may be affected by political considerations, such as when they are used to assist the image of the government of the day. They may also reflect a complex process of interaction and negotiation, such as crime statistics, and may indeed be worthy of investigation themselves for this reason.

Official reports

These are constrained by their remit, which states the limits of their investigations. The government or other powerful lobbies are therefore able to exclude discussion of issues which they do not want to be brought into the public domain; the Scarman Report on the inner-city riots was limited in this way.

The mass media

The major problems of using the mass media as secondary data lie with the selection of material – on exactly what grounds are items included and excluded? – and with the sociologists' interpretation of the chosen material. The temptation in both cases is to include (deliberately or subconsciously) only material that supports the case of the researcher. This particular criticism was made of the Glasgow Media Group's publications such as *Bad News* and *More Bad News*, which were critical appraisals of television news. It was claimed that they were selective in their choice of material and that they applied their own interpretations to the selections.

Diaries, oral memories and letters

These are particularly useful sources of secondary data when the individual assessed or lived through a period that is of interest to the sociologist. Problems can occur, however, if individuals have distorted views of what happened or if they justify or glorify themselves in their accounts of what happened, which is often the case. Almost any politician's memoirs prove this. Other difficulties are that letters will often have been written with a particular purpose in mind and that diaries of important people are often intended for publication and so are written with the reader in mind.

Novels

Novels can give an insight into the attitudes and behaviour of particular groups, especially if the author is drawn from one of those groups. However, they are fiction and will exaggerate actions and values for the sake of narrative. Writing books is typically a middle- or upper-class activity, which limits the insight that can be gained about the particular group featured.

Other researchers' works

Most sociologists rely on the work of previously published research to form part of their own research. However, it should be taken into account that there are possible errors in methodology in the published research, that there is a possible bias in the research and in the choice of topic area, and that there may have been defects in the previous research, upon which the sociologist based his/her research. A famous piece of anthropological research which was used for 40 years before it was found to be centrally flawed was Mead's *Coming of Age in Samoa*.

2.9 OBSERVATIONAL STUDIES

THE RELATIONSHIP BETWEEN INTERACTIONIST PERSPECTIVES AND OBSERVATIONAL STUDIES

Interactionists are interested in how people define and respond to the social world. In order to explain this it is important to get as deeply as possible into the mind of those being observed. Joining them and becoming one of them allows the researcher the greatest possibility of understanding their perceptions of reality.

Positivists are more interested in statistical evidence which proves or disproves a particular hypothesis. For them, the attempt to enter the minds of groups under study is not scientific or rigorous as there is such a great possibility of bias. Reliability, representativeness and validity are all major concerns.

THE DIFFERENT ROLES OF THE OBSERVER

There are four main roles the observer can play in the groups under study; they may also overlap. These are:

- covert *versus* overt observation,
- participant *versus* non-participant observation.

Covert observation

This is the approach of pretending to be one of the group under study. It is linked to the participant observational approach (see below). An example of this is Patrick's *A Glasgow Gang Observed*.

Advantages

The researcher is able to enter forbidden areas and can immerse him/herself totally in the group to be studied.

Disadvantages

The researcher could be in danger if the false role is uncovered or if the role forces the researcher into immoral or illegal activities. There are also methodological problems associated with recording events.

Overt observation

This method involves making clear that you are an observer, and can be linked to both participant and non-participant observational roles. An example of this method is Judith Oakley's study of Gypsies.

Advantages

As a trusted outsider with no problems of rivalry, the researcher may receive the confidences of the group members. The researcher is able to play an honest and clear role.

Disadvantages

There will be many activities occurring in the group that only the trusted insider may join; the researcher gains no experience of these and is therefore not able to use these in his/her research.

Participant observation

The researcher effectively joins the group under study and participates in their activities. However, the researcher can choose to be covert or overt in his/her role.

Advantages

A full and complete understanding of the feelings and beliefs of the group can be gained by the researcher, possibly as well as an experience of their way of life.

Disadvantages

There is a greater chance of bias with this method than with others as the observer is drawn closely into the world of the group and may begin to be clouded by their perspective.

Non-participant

As far as practicable, the observer merely watches and records the actions of the group, without attempting to join in or become one of the group. This type of observation is almost always overt.

Advantages

There is a greater chance of eliminating bias compared to the method of participant observation.

Disadvantages

The researcher is less able to empathise with the beliefs and actions of the group being studied.

2.10 FEMINIST RESEARCH

Feminist research has derived from the belief of feminist sociologists that there is a need to:
- expose the oppression of women;
- uncover and explore specifically female views of their experiences;
- help explain these experiences; and
- show how women resist oppression.

The nature of feminist research is explicit in its value biases. Feminist researchers such as Roberts and MacKinnon argue that **malestream sociology** is just as biased but that the male sociologists are less aware of their bias.

Feminist researchers use a wide variety of methods, in much the same way as other sociologists; however, they also use biographical and autobiographical accounts of life to explore the meanings to women of their experiences.

Skeggs ('Confessions of a feminist researcher') suggests that there are significant differences between female and male sociologists doing research.

❶ Those who try to tackle subjects from a feminist perspective which questions taken-for-granted assumptions about such things as sexuality are often prevented from gaining access to subjects for their research. She cites the example of being prevented from researching sexuality with students in an FE College.

② Women are excluded from a significant number of public areas; for example they may find it more difficult to stay out alone in the streets at night without fear of harassment.

③ She argues that male and female researchers are able to obtain very different types of information from people they interview because of the different expectations of and responses to the sex of the interviewer. Therefore, feminist and male research may arrive at very different points of view. In particular, she points out how female researchers are able to gain access to areas both geographical (toilets at clubs) and emotional (rape) which are simply closed to males.

④ Linked to this is the fact that during research, the female researcher may be given intimate information which presents her with the dilemma of colluding (with such things as domestic violence or incest) by keeping silent, or challenging this form of behaviour.

⑤ Skeggs also points out that female researchers may themselves be the subject of sexual harassment.

2.11 CASE STUDIES

This is where one small-scale group or event is studied in great detail. The case study need not be representative of wider society, though often it gives detailed information on certain social processes which allow more general application or at least the generation of hypotheses. An example is Hugh Beynon's *Working for Ford*.

2.12 PANEL STUDIES

This is where a carefully selected representative sample of the population is surveyed regularly over a length of time to note the changes that take place in their behaviour or attitudes. This method was first used in voting studies in the USA to track changes in voter preferences. The most well-known example is the *British Election Survey* based at the University of Essex.

2.13 EXAMPLE: SUICIDE

An examination of Durkheim's classic study of the causes of suicide gives us a good example of the differences between the positivist and phenomenological approaches. Durkheim takes the positivist approach, which stresses the reality of the social world on a par with the reality of the physical world. The phenomenological (or subjective) approach, by contrast, stresses the creation of the world through interaction. These two approaches have led to very different sets of conclusions about suicide. In sociology in general there is a major split between these two approaches.

THE WIDER RELEVANCE OF THE DEBATE ON SUICIDE

Durkheim's study often seems to be rated as too important by newcomers to the subject. However, it is not really suicide itself that is the real centre of the debate but the methodological issues that surround it.

The debate on suicide has passed through a number of stages:

1 Durkheim chooses suicide as the key issue to prove the usefulness of sociology as a means of understanding social phenomena.

2 He uses sophisticated methodological techniques that become a model for other sociologists to follow.

3 Durkheim's work is elaborated and built upon by other researchers, using his original framework.

4 His entire framework is attacked by Atkinson ('Societal reactions to suicide') and Douglas (*The Social Meanings of Suicide*), who argue that his methodology is fundamentally flawed.

5 Durkheim's research is used as an illustration of the two major methodological approaches used in sociology:

- positivism, as shown in the work of Durkheim;
- phenomenological perspectives, as shown in the work of Atkinson and Douglas.

DURKHEIM'S ORIGINAL RESEARCH ON SUICIDE

Durkheim undertook the research on suicide to prove the unique contribution that sociology could make to understanding social actions. He wished to show that other forms of explanation including psychology were inadequate by themselves.

Durkheim chose suicide because it is one of the most individual acts possible: if he could explain as individual an act as this (which most people explain through a psychological perspective), then he could explain any act.

The methodological background

Durkheim started from the premise that society is more than just a collection of individuals. For him society could best be described as an 'entity' which makes demands upon people and determines the way they act. It is only a slight exaggeration of Durkheim's position to compare us to puppets with society as the puppeteer.

As society determines our actions, it is of little interest to study the individual's perception of the world and his/her actions, as they are determined by society.

Research, according to Durkheim, ought to be directed at the necessary level of society in order to understand the actions of the individual. Accordingly, the researcher ought to:

- clearly define what it is he/she is studying – the social phenomenon;
- collect as much information at the social level as possible, in the form of statistics, for example;
- understand that this (statistical) information reflects 'social facts' or the 'reality' of the situation far more than any individual's perception of it (for example divorce statistics give you the 'facts' on broken marriages etc);
- if possible, pull out from the collected information the key factors which influence the phenomenon studied; and
- study the same phenomenon across different societies in order to see the variations that exist, if this could be useful.

This approach to the study of society has since become known as positivism.

What is suicide?

Durkheim defines suicide as 'every case of death resulting directly or indirectly from a positive or negative act performed by the victim himself which he knows will produce this result'. A positive act would be actively to kill oneself (eg with poison), while a negative act would be to allow oneself to die in certain circumstances (eg 'going down with the ship').

Rates of suicide

The first thing that Durkheim did was to collect suicide statistics for different societies and groupings within societies. He found quite conclusively that suicide is not a random phenomenon:

- levels of suicide varied from society to society, for example Italy had (and still has) lower suicide levels than Britain;
- the differences in levels of suicide remained constant over a number of years;
- within each society, the suicide rate varied (again on a regular basis) from one group to another, for example married people are less likely to commit suicide than single people.

Durkheim argues that if suicide were entirely an individual act, how could these regular patterns exist – surely they would fluctuate at random? The only answer, according to Durkheim, was that there has to be some aspect of the society or social structure that influences (regularly) the level of suicide. The answer lay in the levels of social and moral integration.

Social integration

Durkheim argues that all societies consist of an integrated group of individuals who share a common set of values, beliefs and attitudes. Society can only exist if all the members of society are closely bound together through various forms of organisation or group, such as the family, which direct our behaviour and give us a feeling of belonging. Membership of groups is therefore necessary for social integration, and social integration, in turn, is a necessity for the existence of society.

Moral integration

According to Durkheim, men and women have infinite desires that have to be controlled if they are not to get out of hand and cause social chaos (**anomie**). Society sets limits on what is achievable (**social goals**) and the limits of that achievement. Individual satisfaction can therefore be achieved through attainment of a set of limited goals set by society.

THE LINK BETWEEN INTEGRATION AND TYPES OF SUICIDE

Social and moral integration are needed to hold society together; but 'incorrect' levels of integration (too much or too little) can have consequences that can be related to suicide. 'Suicide varies with the degree of integration of the social group of which the individual forms a part', according to Durkheim. He suggests that there are three relationships between suicide and integration:

- egoistic,
- altruistic and
- anomic.

Egoistic suicide

This is the most common form of suicide. It is based upon a person committing suicide because of **excessive individualism**, where a person is more concerned about his/her worries than anything else.

Relationship to society

It occurs in societies that lay heavy stress on the individual and his/her importance. In Durkheim's time this was typical of Protestant societies.

Relationship to integration

Durkheim found that:

- people who were not members of groups – the single, widowed, divorced, for example – were likely to commit this form of suicide;

- Protestants were more likely to commit suicide than Catholics. He argued that this was because Catholicism offers a much closer sense of belonging and community, as does the Jewish faith, for example;
- in times of war, suicide declines, as people are drawn together.

Altruistic suicide

This suicide type is the very opposite of egoistic suicide. It occurs when an individual sees his/her own life as of little importance compared to that of everybody in the rest of society.

Relationship to society

This occurs in societies that lay little stress on the individual but great stress on the importance or the needs of the society. A good example that is contemporary to ourselves but not to Durkheim, is traditional communist society.

Relationship to integration

This type of suicide is found among highly integrated members of groups, such as the army which has its own code of honour, where not living up to the ideals of the group leads the person to have a sense of personal failure and hence to commit suicide.

Anomic suicide

This occurs when the normal rules and guidelines of society are weakened and so the constraints which guide people and give them satisfaction are lost.

Relationship to society

People need restraints to be placed upon them by society, without which they would never be satisfied. In certain periods of crisis, these constraints collapse.

Relationship to integration

This suicide type occurs in any society in which the 'moral integration' has broken down. Examples could be in periods of rapid prosperity or dramatic financial collapse. An example (not used by Durkheim) would be when a couple win the pools and simply cannot cope with their new-found wealth.

CRITICISMS ACCEPTING DURKHEIM'S FRAMEWORK

Urban and rural divisions

In 1930, Halbwachs suggested in *The Causes of Suicide* that Durkheim's work could be re-interpreted to prove that the major social factor relating to social integration and suicide was, in fact, the difference between urban and rural life. Suicide levels were higher in the cities because of lower levels of social cohesion there.

How do you measure social integration?

Gibbs and Martin have argued (*Status Integration and Suicide*) that Durkheim left no valid measurement of social integration, and they suggest instead that suicide occurs where people have little **status integration**. They mean by this that if a person has a status in one area (employment) which is very different from his/her status in another (education or level of income), then there is an incompatibility of status which can lead to discontent and therefore suicide.

THE PHENOMENOLOGICAL APPROACH

This approach to sociology suggests that the only way to understand why people act the way they do is to understand the meaning and motivations they bring to their actions. Douglas and, separately, Atkinson have concentrated their attention on the phenomenon of suicide from the phenomenological perspective. Two areas of interest emerge:

● the judicial process of categorising an act as suicide, and

● the meaning of the act of suicide to the person committing suicide.

The judicial process

Both Atkinson and Douglas point out that the key to Durkheim's study is the collection of statistics on the number of suicides in any particular region. They therefore turned their attention to understanding how these statistics were constructed.

In Britain (and there is a similar system in the USA), a coroner (a form of magistrate) investigates the circumstances leading to death. A coroner makes a decision on the nature of death according to the evidence available to him/her. He/she does this by reconstructing a possible course of events. In essence this consists of the coroner thinking:

● 'If I were this person, in these circumstances, would I have considered suicide?' This question involves the coroner searching for reasonable motives – financial or emotional worries etc.

● 'Secondly, are the circumstances of death reasonably consistent with suicide?' Here the coroner is saying that people choose certain forms of death such as poison or hanging, but would be unlikely to beat themselves or stab themselves to death.

According to his/her conclusions the death is classified as suicide, accidental death, or natural causes etc. The point that Atkinson and Douglas are making is that we never know whether a person has committed suicide or not (because they are dead and cannot tell us), so we rely for our statistics on the taken-for-granted assumptions of the coroner as to what leads a person to commit suicide. The statistics are therefore a reflection of the assumptions of the coroner, not the objective reality of the number of suicides.

The consequences for Durkheim's analysis

The point of the research on suicide is that the official statistics of suicide rates are a reflection of the social process of the coroner's enquiry. In this, they reflect his/her thought processes. This seriously undermines Durkheim's claims of statistical relationships.

The meaning of suicide to individuals

Suicide is usually defined as an act where someone kills him/herself. Yet this ignores the fact that people kill themselves for a variety of reasons. The act may be the same, yet the meaning differs. Douglas points out that if the *meanings* are different, surely we are talking about completely different social phenomena? Some of the different meanings that underlie suicide include:

● **a move to a better place** – the person is unhappy and hopes that death will take them to heaven (or possibly oblivion);

● **revenge** – the person wants to make someone else sorry for having hurt them, for example in the case of the jilted lover;

● **atonement** – someone is sorry for what they have done.

The consequences for Durkheim's analysis

Each suicide has such different motivations that it cannot be classified simply. Suicides are different *social* phenomena with different causes, even if the outcome is the same.

UNEMPLOYMENT AND SUICIDE: SUPPORTING DURKHEIM'S ARGUMENT?

Research on suicide by Krietman and Platt over a period of 14 years found that there is a close relationship between levels of unemployment and suicide (as well as attempted suicide).

Table 2.1

Duration of unemployment	Risk of attempted suicide of unemployed to employed
Less than 6 months	6:1
6–12 months	10:1
Over 12 months	19:1

The figures in Table 2.1 do suggest that social factors and suicide rates can be linked and that the criticisms of Douglas and Atkinson should not completely destroy attempts to explore the relationship between suicide and social factors.

Test yourself questions and answers

Questions

1 What are the four components of science?

2 What are the stages of positivistic method?

3 Identify the criticisms of sociology as a science.

4 Is a value-free sociology possible?

5 Explain reliability and validity.

6 What types of sampling are there?

7 What are the limitations of questionnaires?

8 What do we mean by secondary data? Give examples.

9 What possible disadvantages are there with diaries and letters?

10 What is meant by feminist research? Why should it be necessary?

Suggested answers

1 It is empirical, theoretical, cumulative and objective.

2 Phenomena are observed and a hypothesis is formed. An appropriate form of experiment is devised to isolate key variables. Data collection is carried out, usually as an experiment. The data are analysed. There is confirmation/modification/rejection of the hypothesis. Conclusions are drawn.

3 A significant proportion of sociologists argue that sociology is not, and should not claim to be, a science. They argue that it is not possible to accumulate facts in the

same way as physical scientists, because social facts such as statistics are really social constructs and do not reflect an objective reality. Sociology needs always to take into account the meanings that people ascribe to actions. So an objective reality does not exist; it is more a subjective perception of reality. Secondly, although it is accepted that sociology is theoretical in intent, there are great problems with the nature of sociological theories. In particular, people are concerned that the theories of sociology are based upon assumptions concerning the nature of reality, which are themselves really only theories or ideologies. Thirdly, Kuhn points out that no science is cumulative, but progresses through 'paradigm shifts'.

4 Many critics within sociology reject the idea that a value-free sociology is possible.
   ● Gouldner claims that Weber's writings in which he proposed a value-free sociology were a ploy to stop the government from preventing sociology being taught.
   ● Feminist writers point to the way that sociology has focused on male concerns, excluding women's concerns.
   ● Neo-Marxists argue that sociology has accepted the values and social structures of capitalism and has sought answers within that framework.
   ● Those who fund research often control the direction of that research.
   ● Personal values and interests of sociologists must influence their activities.
   ● Sociologists who subscribe to phenomenological approaches to sociology argue that the process of scientific method, the concept of science and the very basic underlying concepts of sociology are themselves products of society, and reflect only the social activities of people attempting to construct a reality.

5 Reliability refers to the problem of comparing like with like. Is each interview and, to a lesser extent, questionnaire the same thing? Validity refers to the problem of finding a true way of measuring abstract concepts through real behaviour or expressed attitudes. The problem is exactly *what* behaviour and *which* attitudes can be take as true measures of the concept.

6 Strata sampling, simple random sampling, cluster sampling, multi-phase sampling and quota sampling.

7 Limitations of questionnaires are:
   ● They cannot explore issues in depth.
   ● The respondent who completed the questionnaire is not always the person actually wanted.
   ● Are the replies true?
   ● Low response rates.

8 Secondary data refers to information sources that are not the result of the sociologist's own original research. The most common types of secondary data used by sociologists include official statistics, official reports, the mass media, diaries, letters, oral history (usually recorded), novels and works of fiction, other researchers' works.

9 Problems can occur when:
   ● individuals have distorted views of what happened;
   ● individuals often justify or glorify themselves;
   ● letters will often have been written with a particular purpose in mind;
   ● diaries of important people are often intended for publication and may be biased by this.

10 Feminist research is sociological research conducted by women on subjects that are of importance to women, and which they argue have been ignored by 'malestream' sociology. It aims to uncover the oppression of women, to explore specifically female views of their experiences, to help explain them and to show how women resist oppression.

Illustrative question and answer

Question

Item A

Simply choosing an explanation out of personal preference would not get us very far by itself. It is true that there are many occasions when human beings say they 'know' something to be true when what they really mean is that they 'think' it to be true. This would be the case if I were to say that I 'know' the Labour Party will win the next election, for example. Science however aims at much greater certainty in its explanations than this. Having arrived at an hypothesis – a plausible or appealing story about how something or other is caused – scientists do not then spend their time trying to persuade us of its truth by the logic of their argument, as philosophers do. Nor do they ask us to simply have faith in their belief, as theologians do. They try to *prove* its truth to us. This they do by *showing* it to be true.

(Adapted from Jones, P., *Theory and Methods in Sociology*, Bell and Hyman)

Item B

So how common is cheating in science? Surveys show that both in Britain and America, only about one in four scientists is prepared to provide original data when requested. Unless there is something to hide, there is no reason for such refusal. One can only conclude that scientific fraud is extremely widespread. Moreover, it is not limited to minor figures: the verdict of history is that Ptolemy, Galileo, Newton, Dalton and Mendel all tampered with some of their data.

Why then do scientists cheat? Not everyone, and perhaps not anyone, pursues science merely out of a quest for truth. At the best, people are heavily biased towards proving their own theories right, but they also want promotion, research grants and glory. Since all depend on publishing, the pressure to publish is enormous. It is obviously quicker to fake data than to run experiments and you can be sure of getting the desired result.

Another extremely common way of cheating is to run an experiment over and over again until the desired result is obtained and then publish it, quietly forgetting the negative instances. Other scientists get things wrong, not by cheating but by unconsciously seeing what they are looking for (even when it is not there) or failing to see what is there.

There is little risk of being caught. Except for the most important findings, little attempt is made to replicate; there is no prestige in redoing someone else's experiments.

(Adapted from *The Observer*, August 1989)

Item C

Most of us rather hastily and thoughtlessly regard 'science' as a sort of collection of linear accelerators and space vehicles and organic chemistry models. In fact, it is not any of these things; it is only a systematic method of gathering and testing knowledge, involving certain formal procedures: gathering information, forming an hypothesis to explain the information, predicting certain consequences of the hypothesis and performing an experiment to test the prediction. If you investigate any area of knowledge by this method, you are doing science. If you use any other method, you are doing something else.

(Adapted from Pohl, F., *The Game-Playing Literature in 'In the Problem Pit'*, Corgi)

(a) Briefly explain how scientists try to prove an hypothesis 'by showing it to be true' (Item A). (2)

(b) Item B puts forward a number of reasons why science cannot be seen as objective. What are the implications of this for the belief that sociology is a science? (4)

(c) Apart from the points raised in Item B, how far do you agree with the argument in Item C that science is a 'systematic method'? (6)

(d) Item A suggests that human beings 'know' things to be true in ways other than the scientific method. On what grounds do people claim that their beliefs or ideas are true? (4)

(e) Using information from the Items and from elsewhere, assess whether it is possible for sociology to be a science. (9)

AEB

Suggested answer

(a) Most commonly scientists may set out through experimentation to show that their explanation or hypothesis is the most accurate in predicting the outcome of events. However, it cannot be proved to be true – it can only be shown to be the best available explanation.

(b) The findings have no specific implications for sociology as a science in that it merely shows that scientists do not attain the aim of objectivity and scrupulous scientific research procedure. If science is seen as a process or series of procedures which give us the best possibility of making accurate explanations, then sociology must still strive for this. The item just shows that problems exist for physical sciences in much the same way as for sociology.

Of course you could subscribe to the belief that sociology is a not a science nor should seek to be, and in this case the item is support for this position.

(c) The answer you give will depend upon your belief and understanding of the nature of sociological enquiry. My view would be that all science is really a series of steps and guidelines to help us arrive at the best possible explanation whatever we wish to study. If it becomes a series of rigid methods or procedures, then it will prevent rather than help the search for explanations. However, we have learned from experience that there are some procedures and methods which are better than others, and that researchers ought to at least attempt to follow these where possible.

(d) This refers to the fact that science searches for some sort of objective, testable truth. However, in normal life people do not place their beliefs under such scrutiny. Knowledge of the world derives from socialisation processes and from the reinforcement of these ideas through contact with other people, the media and schooling. People also subscribe to ideologies which provide ready-made structures of thought providing clear answers to issues. These can range from political ideologies, such as Marxism, to religious ideologies.

(e) This is a commonly asked question and you should be well prepared for it.

You need to cover the question, What is the nature of science? Here you should refer to the various processes and procedures plus the need for objectivity, theory and empiricism. You should then look at the particular problems faced by sociology in terms of the nature of evidence/statistics and objectivity. You should then look at the way in which the natural sciences themselves fail to achieve 'science', and a conclusion to the effect that it is not necessary for sociology to be a science as long as it is rigorous.

As a final comment you may wish to discuss why people are so concerned about it being a science and raise the issues of funding, careers and prestige.

Question bank

1 'Whether researchers adopt participant and/or non-participant roles when observing they cannot avoid having some influence on those they study.'

Compare and contrast the role of the researcher in both participant and non-participant observation. Illustrate your answer with examples of sociological studies using these techniques.

Integrated Boards

Points

Start by explaining what participant and non-participant observational research is, and then run through the points about the degree to which the influence of the participant distorts their perception and prevents them from having a detached overview versus the ability to understand fully what is happening. You should also point to the difficulties of recording information accurately when participating, and to the other problems of entry, personal relationships and exit.

However, it is important that you point out that these differences tend to exist more in textbooks than in reality. When researchers have been merely observers initially, they are almost always drawn into the social network of the people they observe. Patrick's *Glasgow Gang Observed* is a classic of participant observation, and you can compare this with Parker's *View from the Boys* which is supposed to be observational only, but inevitably he is drawn into the research. Other examples where the line between being an observer and just a participant is blurred are Hobb's *Doing the Business*, a study of life in the informal economy of East London life, and Collinson's study of drug squad detectives, *Police, Drugs and Community*.

Point out that it is not inevitable that the observer will influence the group being studied however. The degree of influence depends upon such factors as how important to the group the researcher becomes, whether he or she gives advice or is asked for it, and the cohesion of the group. Thus Parker probably had more influence than Patrick, even though his was a non-participant role – however, the 'boys' looked to him for advice in their dealings with the police.

2 Assess the influence of feminist perspectives on sociological research.

AEB

Points

Start by explaining what 'feminist research' is. Compare it to the male-biased research which has dominated sociology. Point out the reasons for the ignoring of women by male researchers and writers.

Move on to look at the specific contributions of feminist researchers. These include:

- the obvious one that half the population had previously been ignored;
- feminist research helped to point out the male values and biases underpinning research;
- the categories of research such as social class were not appropriate for women and were therefore inaccurate;
- different forms of research were necessary to obtain information from women;
- new areas of research were uncovered (caring for the sick and disabled, family violence, etc.).

3 'Secondary data provide sociologists with a variety of sources of information ranging from government statistics and newspapers, to diaries and autobiographies.'

Outline and discuss the strengths and weaknesses of using a range of secondary sources in sociological research. Illustrate your answer with examples of how secondary sources are used by sociologists.

Integrated Boards

Points

You are being asked to discuss the benefits of secondary documents in research.

Secondary data includes all information which the researcher has not actually found from his or her own first-hand research and includes all documents. The following questions always have to be asked:

- Why was the material written in the first place? Diaries because people wish to be important, government statistics to bolster the position of the government, newspapers to reflect the stories which will sell to the public.
- What are the values underlying the documents, for example, what political beliefs, social class and gender was the diary writer?
- How accurate are the data contained? Very often the content of diaries are written in a very biased manner as are newspaper articles, etc.

But you need also to put in a word of caution about primary data. Primary data can be inaccurate, full of errors and value biased. The advantage is that the sociologist at least has the chance to tackle these and is very often aware of the problems.

4 Assess the view that the subject matter of sociology is inappropriate for scientific investigation.

NEAB

Points

This question is asking whether sociology is a science, and whether the methods of the 'natural' sciences are appropriate.

You need to discuss what a science is, and the best way to define this is by saying that it is a commitment to the use of certain methods and procedures. You should briefly outline these and say why they are useful.

You need to demonstrate your knowledge of the debate within sociology between the 'positivists' and 'non-positivists'. Go through the arguments that sociology should and can use scientific methods and then criticise them. You should then examine the argument that sociology is not dealing with non-thinking objects or creatures and consequently must use different approaches. You should argue however that as long as the search is for accuracy and honesty, then the debate is in some senses spurious and rests upon dubious. 19th-century beliefs about the assumed superiority of 'science'.

CHAPTER 3

STRATIFICATION: SOCIAL CLASS AND MOBILITY

Units in this chapter

Chapter objectives

This chapter explores the way in which divisions are made between people, and the consequences that this has for society. For the sake of clarity, it concentrates mainly on social class but, in order to emphasise the links between social class, race and gender – all of which are examples of stratification, we have included some discussion of race and gender.

The chapter begins with a discussion of the theories of social class, and contrasts Weberian, Marxist and functionalist approaches to the subject. This is a long debate which allows us to put into practice many of the ideas that are suggested in Chapter 1: Theory.

The second section of the chapter is a discussion of the changing nature of social class in the UK. No conclusions are drawn as to whether class has been superseded by other forms of stratification, such as race and gender, but it is clear that very substantial changes have taken place in the structure of social class in the UK. There are separate parts on the changes in the working and middle classes, and on the possible emergence of an underclass of deprived and marginalised people.

We then look at the very topical debates on the relationship between social class and race. The debate centres on the question of which is the more socially significant division – social class or race; social class or gender.

The following sections deal with the ruling class and the related issue of the concentration of wealth and income in the hands of relatively few people.

There follows a detailed discussion of the problems of **operationalising** social class. How does a researcher actually use the very helpful concept of social class to give a true picture? In this section we also include discussions of the places of race and gender and their relationships to social class.

The final part of the chapter discusses social mobility, which is the movement up and down the stratification system. What factors allow, or even promote, some people to rise from the bottom, and others (though many fewer) to sink down?

3.1 THEORIES OF SOCIAL CLASS

The main theoretical approaches are:

- Marxist and Neo-Marxist,
- Weberian,
- functionalist.

MARXIST APPROACHES

For background information see the examination of Marxist theory on pp 27–31.

All capitalist societies are divided along class lines. Class has two elements, an objective one and a subjective one.

The objective element

Marx defined this part in terms of its relationship to the **means of production**. The class that owns the means of production is the ruling class and they will exploit the rest of society. Marx was aware that there will always be a variety of groups in society and that these are not necessarily social classes. Within capitalism, the two social classes are:

- the **bourgeoisie**, who own the industry and commercial institutions;
- the **proletariat**, who sell their labour to the bourgeoise and receive wages. They do not have any significant ownership of industry or commerce.

The subjective element

A class only truly became a class when it first became aware of its **class identity**, with an awareness of its own interests. Marx argued that the dynamics of capitalism meant that there was constant conflict between the two social classes. However, the ruling class seeks to prevent the proletariat ever becoming aware of its own sense of shared exploitation. The ruling class, therefore, constantly seeks to divide the working class amongst itself and therefore destroy its class identity or **class consciousness**.

Marx did recognise the existence of two other groups, apart from the two main social classes:

- the **petty bourgeoisie**, who were small businessmen and women;
- the **lumpen proletariat**, who were the fringe group of undesirables, comprising criminals, for example.

Marx saw both groups being gradually absorbed into the working class. Over time, the working class would grow and its conditions worsen as the people were increasingly exploited by the bourgeoisie.

Criticism of the Marxist approaches

Critics of Marx claim that:

- there are more than two social classes;
- social class is not based solely upon production but increasingly upon consumption;
- the class conflict Marx claimed always existed is only one of a number of divisions including age, disability, race, gender; these divisions were seen as secondary to social class, yet feminists and anti-racists argue these are more important;
- the increasing polarisation and crystallisation of the social classes has not occurred, as predicted by Marx.

Neo-Marxist developments

Marxist writings on social class have continued unabated throughout this century. Given the importance of social class in Marxist analysis, this is not surprising.

Dahrendorf: divisions of authority

Dahrendorf argues in *Class and Class Conflict in an Industrial Society* that the growth of companies from small-scale, personally owned ones to multi-nationals owned by thousands of shareholders means that ownership is too dispersed for there to be clearly demarcated ownership/non-ownership-based social classes.

Wright: contradictory class locations

One of the major problems has been to clarify the rather vague division made by Marx between the owners of the means of production and the proletariat. Wright suggests that there are three main classes in society:

1. **capitalist** – owners of significant capital;

2. **proletariat** – who sell their labour; and

3. the **petty bourgeoisie** – smaller, independent business people.

He believes, however, that these do not cover all the types of employment that now exist. Therefore he also delineates groups such as managers, supervisors, the self-employed and those who employ only a very small number of people. These groups which fall outside the main classes he argues are in **contradictory class locations**, by which he means that the members of these classes do not subjectively believe they are in the proletariat, do not act in the appropriate way, and associate themselves with the ruling class. However, objectively, they are in the same position as the proletariat.

THE WEBERIAN APPROACH

Weber suggests that social class is based upon three elements:

1. **Class**: the income and wealth that a group of people are able to obtain for their labour.

2. **Status**: the prestige that groups of people are given by others.

3. **Power**: the ability to persuade or coerce others into doing what that group wants.

Weber points out that the three elements are generally linked together, but need not be. Indeed, they can be independent. So a person could be high in status and yet low in class, for example a member of the clergy.

Weber substitutes the concept of **status group** for social class, and suggests that this is a more accurate and flexible description of society. Status groups share similar life-chances and standards of living. The advantage of the Weberian model compared to the Marxist one is that it gives a much more dynamic and flexible model of social class.

Criticism of the Weberian approach

There are some problems with Weber's model of class/status. Weber fails to provide the basis of status – why are certain positions given more prestige than others? He suggests that this may be to do with tradition, but this really begs the question of how it became tradition in the first place. Nor does he explain adequately why some groups are able to obtain higher income and wealth than others. He claims that this is because there is a greater demand for their skills in the 'market place'. Yet, why are some skills rewarded more highly than others? This has similarities with the functionalist debate and criticism of Davis and Moore in the following section.

Post-Weberian approaches

W. G. Runciman

Runciman has developed the Weberian ideas of class, status and power but has altered them slightly, calling them:

- **ownership** – of property,
- **control** – of power,
- **marketability** – of skills.

At the top of the hierarchy is the tiny upper class with access to all three elements, and at the bottom is the underclass with virtually none of the three elements. The majority of people fit into two very broad social classes (middle and working) which are themselves highly fragmented according to differences in ownership, control and marketability. So Britain has a class structure which is then further subdivided into status groups.

F. Parkin

Parkin developed Weberian ideas, but laid greatest emphasis on occupational status. According to him, ownership of property is not that important in contemporary society, as it was in Marx's time. Instead, we are generally accorded prestige and rewards dependent upon the status of the job we do.

Parkin suggests that the class structure is therefore headed by higher professionals and the lowest group is composed of unskilled manual workers.

The most innovative idea of Parkins is that of 'social closure', by which he means that groups seek to enhance their status by denying other groups access to status. Class boundaries are made by this process of exclusion rather than by some objective relationship to the ownership of the means of production.

Giddens

Giddens is the most recent writer in the post-Weberian tradition and once again suggests that there are three elements, which he calls 'market capacity', that determine a person's class position. However, he links one of these with each social class. Giddens suggests that:

- the **upper class** is based upon the market capacity of **ownership of capital**,
- the **middle class** is based upon the market capacity of **educational qualifications**,
- the **working class** is based upon the market capacity of **labour power**.

THE FUNCTIONALIST APPROACH

This approach is based on the idea that divisions in society reflect the real needs that society has to survive and prosper.

Talcott Parsons: the need for positions of authority

According to Talcott Parsons, the division of labour leads to the development of different skills demanding different levels of ability. The complexity of the division of labour is such that it inherently requires someone to co-ordinate the jobs – that is to take positions of authority. Talcott Parsons holds the view that status may be inherited.

Davis and Moore: the functional importance of jobs

In a famous argument, ('Some principles of stratification'), Davis and Moore claim that some jobs are more important to society than others and that these jobs require the most able people to fill them. In order to attract people to compete for these and to undergo the long periods of training, the key positions should have greater rewards and prestige attached to them.

Criticism of the functionalist approach

Critics of the functionalists' arguments point out:

- Who decides which are the key positions?
- In reality there appears to be little rational link between wealth/income and useful jobs.
- There is no discussion of the role of power.

3.2 THE CHANGING CLASS STRUCTURE

THE WORKING CLASS

Overview of the debates on the working class

The traditional view which existed until the 1950s of the working class being comprised of male manual workers who have a sense of class solidarity has been shown to be inaccurate. All commentators agree that a breaking down of the working class has taken place, but the direction of the **decomposition of the working class** is a matter of dispute. In essence the debates since the 1960s have been polarised between two positions:

- those who see the working class becoming absorbed into the middle class, or into some classless society – the debate on the new working class;
- those who see a proletarianisation of the labour force in Western societies, with a process of deskilling taking place and skilled work available only to a few.

The debate on the 'new' working class

Many factors have suggested that a division has taken place between the more affluent 'new' working class, and the more traditional working class: the success of the Conservative Party in remaining in power in the 1980s and much of the 1990s, the changing structure and nature of employment (see pp 139–41), in which wide divisions have opened up between those in secure employment and those in insecure occupations or even unemployed; the growth in housing developments; the increasing emphasis on materialism; the decline of the traditional working-class culture and solidarity.

The new working class are said to be characterised by:

- home ownership,
- well paid employment,
- a materialistic life style,
- declining allegiance to the Labour Party.

Origins of the sociological debate

The debate about the restructuring of the working class has taken place over a 40-year period. In the late 1950s the claim was being made that a division was taking place. In the 1960s the classic **affluent worker** studies of male manual workers in Luton car and chemical industries (no women were included in the study) suggested that a new type of affluent worker had emerged who were different from the traditional male manual workers. They were also distinct from the male office workers included in the study. The differences centred on:

- income,
- status,
- friendship patterns (see Table 3.1).

Table 3.1

	Traditional male working class	Affluent male workers	White-collar male workers
Income	• Low. • Rented houses.	• Higher through overtime. • Owned houses.	• Similar to the affluent workers, but not through overtime. • Owned houses.
Status	• Traditional working-class images of society – working-class, middle class, rich.	• Saw themselves as classless, or at least that class related to income only.	• Saw themselves as middle class.
Friendship patterns	• Working-class male patterns of solidarity.	• Great emphasis on home life, and few outside social links.	• More traditional middle class with people invited for meals etc.

Feminisation of the intermediate class

As routine white-collar work has expanded, it has been women who have filled these roles, so that 75% of routine white-collar posts are now taken by women. The lower position of clerical workers can be seen as simply reflecting the lower position of women in our society generally. Furthermore, this tells us that we need to study class as only one element of stratification.

Does the new working class really exist?

Arguments for

1 **Changes in employment patterns** There has been a major shift away from unskilled manual work, related to the heavy industries of the North and Midlands. Today, there are approximately 8 million manual workers, compared to almost 15 million in 1951; they comprise less than half the workforce. The nature of manual work has changed, with the majority of workers engaged in some form of skilled work. The decline has taken place in the employment of unskilled (male) workers.

2 **Affluence** There are now higher real wages for the more skilled workers. Consumer credit controls abandoned in the 1980s allowed the explosion of purchase through credit. There has been a growth in the number of two-earner households. All these factors contribute to the increase in real affluence.

3 **Home ownership** Over 70% of homes are now owned or being purchased through mortgages. Rented properties are in steep decline. There has been a move out of inner-city areas to suburbs.

4 **Family life** There has been a move towards a more integrated and shared family life – particularly with the growth in women working. Women still retain the prime responsibility for household chores, however.

5 **Leisure** There has been an increase in home-based pursuits, and purchase into traditional middle-class activities, such as squash and golf.

6 **Politics** A process of de-alignment from class-political party loyalties has taken place. Working-class voters look for immediate benefits to themselves and their families.

Arguments against

In a study of over 2,000 people in the UK and drawing from comparative studies elsewhere, Marshall et al in *Social Class in Modern Britain* argue that social class is still very important in people's lives and remains the clearest guide to attitudes, behaviour and life chances. Furthermore, the apparent divisions within the working class are not new and have been commented on as far back as the 19th century. The mistake was ever to see the working class as homogeneous.

THE UNDERCLASS

There are two ways of defining this class – the structural and the cultural.

- Structural – associated with Field and Giddens. This defines the class in terms of income levels, so underclass is a group below the working class whose members are the very poorest. Usually, the underclass subsists on state benefit. According to Field, the underclass is primarily composed of the sick, the elderly, single parents and the long-term unemployed. The state benefit system is seen as the main culprit in maintaining the underclass – because it pays such low benefits, it is impossible to have a decent standard of living.

- Cultural. This is a much more negative view of the poor and derives primarily from an American commentator Charles Murray. According to Murray, there exists a group of poor who have little or no interest in contributing to society. They have a distinctive set of values which justify crime, living off state benefits and are uninterested in finding employment.

Is the underclass a 'class'?

Whether or not the underclass is actually a social class in sociological terms, or just an ill-defined group, is a matter of argument.

Dahrendorf, in particular, argues that although there are people who are marginal to the working class as a result of changes in the demand for labour and changes in family structures, this does not mean they form a distinct social class. To be a class, they would need to form a very distinct group with its own identity and lifestyle. However there seems to be very little evidence for this.

Heath used material from British Attitude Surveys, and found that there were few differences in values between what would be defined as them embers of the underclass and the 'traditional' working class.

THE MIDDLE CLASS

Development of the middle class

The 18th and 19th centuries saw the emergence of the professions such as law and medicine and the development of a salaried civil service. In the 20th century there has been a large extension of the middle class, particularly after 1945, largely because clerical work, which had grown rapidly, began to change and to demand professional status.

The professions have more than tripled in number since the 1950s. This is because of:

- a growth in the size of the State, particularly in health, welfare and education;
- a demand for more technical work;
- the adoption of professionalisation as an occupational strategy;
- the decline in manual work;
- the more than doubling of the number of managers since 1950.

Divisions in the middle class

According to Goldthorpe (*Social Mobility and Class Structure in Modern Britain*), the middle class can broadly be divided into two:

- the **service class**, composed of professionals and managers, and
- the **intermediate class**, composed of routine white-collar workers.

The service class

Goldthorpe used this term to indicate that this group runs industrial societies but does not actually own them. Using a Weberian analysis, he suggests that their situation can best be described through three areas:

- market situation,
- work situation and
- status situation.

1 Market situation The service class are generally able to sell their skills for relatively high rates of pay.

2 Work situation They are generally in charge of their work situation, particularly those in the higher professions (as opposed to the marginal professions such as teaching or social work). Their work is rarely unionised, but the strategy of professionalisation was chosen. Key factors distinguishing them from other workers are the availability of a career path, and the power over others' lives.

3 Status situation Managers and professionals have successfully manipulated the definitions of what constitutes high-status work.

You should turn to pp 154–6 for greater discussion of professionalisation.

The intermediate class

According to Goldthorpe, this is composed primarily of routine white-collar workers employed as clerks, shop workers, service industries workers etc. A key point in understanding this group is the **feminisation** of this sector of employment as males have moved away from this type of work into management (or unemployment). White-collar jobs are therefore divided by **gender**, with the higher paid and higher status jobs taken by men.

Table 3.2

	Market situation	Status situation	Work situation
For proletarianisation	• Clerical skills not needed, technology pushing them aside. • Decreasing levels of pay – overtaken by much manual work.	• No longer high-status work. • No longer viewed as part of management. • Style of life indistinguishable from clerical and manual workers. • Unionisation has taken place amongst white-collar workers.	• Style of offices (open plan) is similar to the shop floor – demonstrates parallel with manual work. • The introduction of computers has deskilled workers.
Against proletarianisation	• There has always been an overlap between clerical and manual pay. • Differences remain in the work situation and the provision of a range of benefits such as job security, pensions, holidays etc.	• Union growth is an attempt to maintain differences between white collar and manual not to join the working class. • The similarity in lifestyles comes from the more affluent members of the working class altering their lifestyles.	• Promotion prospects still exist. Stewart et al studied the career prospects of male clerical workers and found a majority were promoted out of it, while 30% left for manual work. • Clerical work is therefore transient. • The *work* of clerical workers has been proletarianised, but *not* clerical workers. • Information technology is not so much deskilling as providing new skills.

Proletarianisation

One argument centering on the intermediate 'class' is that of **proletarianisation**. The debate is organised on the lines of:

- market situation,
- status situation and
- work situation (see Table 3.2).

3.3 RACE AND SOCIAL CLASS

The relationship of ethnicity or race to social class is a complex one, and one that is a matter of dispute for sociologists. There are a number of competing models, including:

- race as caste;
- race as a subsidiary element of analysis;
- the divided working class thesis;
- racialised class fractions;
- the underclass.

RACE AS CASTE

This issue is associated with Lloyd Warner (*Social Class in America*) and applied to the USA. Warner claims two types of stratification exist: class and caste. No matter how high the position of the black person is in the class structure a barrier of caste exists between ethnic groups.

RACE AS A SUBSIDIARY ELEMENT OF ANALYSIS

Westergaard and Resler (*Class in Capitalist Society*) argue that using race as a tool of analysis for social divisions simply draws attention away from the fundamental and more important class divisions based on ownership of capital.

THE DIVIDED WORKING CLASS THESIS

Castles and Kosack studied immigration patterns in Europe (*Immigrant Workers and Class Structure in Western Europe*) and argue that, initially as a result of the lack of people willing to do the less pleasant jobs in the wealthier societies, immigrants are encouraged to enter to do these. A division develops between the indigenous working class who take the better jobs and develop affluent lifestyles and the immigrants and later their children who tend to do the worst jobs.

RACIALISED CLASS FRACTIONS

Miles suggests that social classes are divided into a number of **factions** based upon such things as locality, gender, types of employment and ethnicity. Therefore race should be seen as just one of a number of divisions.

THE UNDERCLASS

This is discussed on p 80. Its application to race was originally made in the UK by Rex and Tomlinson (*Colonial Immigrants in a British City*). They suggest that the ethnic minorities in the UK are separated from the mainstream society by economic, political and status barriers.

Economic

There is clear evidence that, in the entire range of economic variables used to indicate quality of living standards, race is an important factor. Members of the ethnic minorities tend to have lower wages, work longer hours, in less pleasant conditions and have fewer chances of promotion. The concept of the **dual labour market** has been put forward to explain this partially. There are jobs in the **primary employment market** which are well paid and secure, with long-term benefits. On the other hand there is a **secondary labour market** with less secure, generally lower paid jobs with fewer insurance/pension benefits. This is the labour market in which a higher proportion of the members of the ethnic minorities are employed.

Political

Few black or Asian political agencies exist which have any serious influence or even press coverage; possibly the only one which receives coverage is the Islamic Parliament.

Status

Racial discrimination and racism (reaching the extremes of racial violence) are apparent in a wide range of experiences of ethnic minorities in the UK.

3.4   THE UPPER CLASS

A RULING CLASS

The main thrust of Marxist analysis is that Britain is controlled by a ruling class, who own the main industries and commercial institutions and use the power deriving from economic control to gain and continue to enjoy political power. Sociologists are particularly interested in the distribution of wealth for, if it is truly in the hands of a few as suggested by Marxists, then there is support for their theories; if, on the other hand, wealth is spread across the society (even if fairly unevenly) then one main prop of the theory falls.

Westergaard and Resler (*Class in a Capitalist Society*) argue that there is a clear, **monolithic ruling class** comprising 5–10% of the population, who are the very rich and either directly or indirectly very powerful. They claim that they are linked through a network of intermarriage and mutual benefit. The system of capitalism with its political, social and economic structure exists to benefit them and to prevent the development of other forms of society.

The ruling class is able to reproduce itself from one generation to the next through:

- direct transfer of capital,
- social and cultural capital (public schools and then Oxbridge),
- mutual appointments in senior positions in business, arts and finance etc.

SCOTT: A COALITION OF INTERESTS

A more critical evaluation of this thesis has been given by John Scott in a series of books (including *The Upper Classes: Property and Privilege in Britain*). According to Scott, in the 19th century there were three overlapping strata of the upper class:

- landowners,
- financiers,
- manufacturers.

The most united were the financiers who consolidated their links through intermarriage.

In the 19th century, the firms became larger and larger and gradually moved away from direct family control. By the end of World War II, the top three strata had become almost indistinguishable through intermarriage and financial overlap. In the last part of the 20th century, the proportion of shares owned by individuals has declined as pension funds and unit trusts have begun to hold the majority share. At first sight this would appear to support the managerial revolution approach, but Scott rejects this.

The business class

He claims that a **business class** has emerged which comprises the directors, top executives and main shareholders of the 1,000 largest British companies, which Scott estimates as about 0.2% of the population. A further peripheral group consists of those senior people in the armed forces, the Church and the universities.

The business class can further be subdivided into:

① **Entrepreneurial capitalists**, who have large shareholdings in their own firms. These are the remains of the traditional family firms. Those still existing include Tesco, Sainsbury's, Rothschilds (bankers), and Baring Brothers (bankers).

② **Internal capitalists**, who are senior executives working for companies and who are in employment, though often with some shareholdings.

③ **Finance capitalists**, who are involved in the financing and ownership of more than one company. These are particularly important in linking ownership and control of different firms through a network of overlapping directorships. This ensures a continuity and a coherence of response to perceived trends and problems.

Very often the finance capitalists own, or part own, merchant banks.

3.5 CHANGES IN THE DISTRIBUTION OF WEALTH

DEFINITIONS OF INCOME AND WEALTH

Income is earnings from employment, investments or State benefits. Wealth is the ownership of property, shares or other assets. However, the issue of exactly how to define wealth in discussing its distribution across the population has caused some controversy. Wealth can be defined as including one's own home – which is correct, except that for most people this is a necessity, not something that is disposable. Wealth can also be defined to include only that which is sellable, and which excludes the home. Finally, wealth can also be said to include occupational and pension rights – this tends to even out the extent of wealth inequalities.

WEALTH DISTRIBUTION

As Table 3.3 shows, ownership of wealth has remained very unequal, although there had been a decline in the extent of inequality among the various groups throughout the 20th century until the late 1970s, when the decline stopped. This was the result of government policies to maintain inequalities in wealth distribution.

The main trends are that the wealth has shifted from the richest 1% to the richest 25%; this reflects the ability of the very rich to distribute their wealth within their family and thus avoid duties payable on death. There has been no significant spread of wealth across the population as a whole. Today, the wealthiest 10% of the adult population owns 50% of all marketable wealth.

Table 3.3 *Distribution of wealth[1] in the UK, 1976–93*

	1976	1981	Percentages 1986	1991	1993
Marketable wealth					
Percentage of wealth owned by:					
Most wealthy 1%	21	18	18	17	17
Most wealthy 5%	38	36	36	35	36
Most wealthy 10%	50	50	50	47	48
Most wealthy 25%	71	73	73	71	72
Most wealthy 50%	92	92	90	92	92
Total marketable wealth (£ billion)	280	565	955	1,711	1,809
Marketable wealth plus occupational and state pension rights (latest valuation)					
Percentage of wealth owned by:					
Most wealthy 1%	13	11	10	10	10
Most wealthy 5%	26	24	24	23	23
Most wealthy 10%	36	34	35	33	33
Most wealthy 25%	57	56	58	57	56
Most wealthy 50%	80	79	82	83	82
Total marketable wealth (£ billion)	472	1,036	1,784	3,014	3,383

[1] Applies to adult population aged 18 and over. Estimates for 1976, 1981, 1986 and 1991 are based on the estates of persons dying in those years. Estimates for 1993 are based on estates notified for probate in 1993–94. Estimates are not strictly comparable between 1993 and earlier years.

(*Source: Social Trends 26*, Table 5.21 (Inland Revenue), p111)

Share ownership

Share ownership increased significantly in the 1980s and early 1990s as a result of government privatisation schemes. In 1981 approximately 7% of the population held shares and this had increased to 22% by 1992. However, there are rarely significant levels of individual shareholdings, and the bulk of shareholdings remain in the hands of the top 5% of personal shareholders. The proportion of all shares held by individuals has fallen over the last 30 years from 50% in the 1960s to less than 20% today. There has been a large increase in shares held by such organisations as pension companies, banks and insurance companies. This supports the writing of Scott, who pointed out the increasing importance of the finance capitalists as powerful members of the ruling class.

INCOME DISTRIBUTION

This is much less unequal in its distribution than wealth, as shown in Table 3.4.

Nevertheless, significant inequalities exist so, for instance, whereas the bottom 20% of the population receive only 10% of the income, the top 20% earn approximately 35%. The gap between the two extremes has been growing since 1979 (as shown in Table 3.4.).

THE DECLINE OF SOCIAL CLASS

By the 1980s sociologists such as Pahl, Saunders and Parkin were questioning whether social class had much use as a concept for sociology. According to them the changes which had taken place in society were so great that social class had been superseded by other, more significant types of groupings. These arguments can be gathered together under the headings:

Table 3.4 *Distribution of disposable household income in the UK*

						Percentages
	Quintile groups of individuals					
	Bottom fifth	Next fifth	Middle fifth	Next fifth	Top fifth	Total
Net income before housing costs						
1979	10	14	18	23	35	100
1981	10	14	18	23	36	100
1987	9	13	17	23	39	100
1988–89	8	12	17	23	40	100
1990–91	7	12	17	23	41	100
Net income after housing costs						
1979	10	14	18	23	35	100
1981	9	14	18	23	36	100
1987	8	12	17	23	40	100
1988–89	7	12	17	23	41	100
1990–91	6	12	17	23	43	100

(*Source: Social Trends 24*, Table 5.20, p77)

- consumption,
- the feminisation and organisation of employment,
- social class fragmentation,
- New Social Movements.

Consumption

Historically, one's position in the class structure was determined by occupation, which was also linked to social prestige and levels of income. However, from the 1960s wage levels were not linked to the traditional divisions of white-collar and manual employment – traditionally prestigious white-collar employment might well pay less than manual employment. At the same time, there began to emerge a culture based on consumption – the purchase of goods and leisure. Once again traditional divisions became blurred. Foreign holidays, leisure activities such as playing golf or eating in restaurants, fashionable clothes were increasingly consumed by the working class as much as the middle class (it was claimed). The result today is that people are measured on their possessions and their leisure pursuits rather than in the origins of their money – their occupations.

Feminisation and organisation of employment

We have touched upon these points in the section above. Traditional class divisions were primarily based upon male occupational differences. The growth in employment of women to the point where they form the majority of the workforce, once part-time employment is taken into consideration, means that the male-based occupational divisions are largely obsolete. Separate to this is the decline in male-based manual labour. New jobs are increasingly being created in office and service industries. The manual/white-collar division is irrelevant when almost 70% of the workforce is now in white-collar work.

Finally, the development of post-Fordist work practices means that the production line and the traditional solidaristic male work environment has been fragmented.

Social class fragmentation

A number of factors have helped to break up the traditional social classes.

1 The upper class has been entered by highly paid managers who are not necessarily owners of the companies. Their loyalty is not automatically given to the traditional class of people with inherited wealth.

2 As the middle class has enlarged, so it has been entered by large numbers of males and females from working-class backgrounds, on the basis of educational success, rather than inherited class position. Within the middle class significant fragmentation has taken place depending upon the type of employment – the newer marginal professions such as teaching or social work, which are relatively poorly paid and have relatively low status, and the traditional well-paid professions such as barristers. A third group of managers and the self-employed has grown too who have little in common with the professions. Finally, there has been the growth of minimally skilled white-collar work which 'enjoys' very much poorer conditions of work compared to the professions and managers.

3 The working class has been affected by the decline of traditional industries and the emergence of post-Fordist working practices. Traditional male-based beliefs of social solidarity have declined in line with these.

4 A new lower working class or 'underclass' has developed of the long-term unemployed and those who live off state benefits.

New Social Movements

The 1990s has seen a decline in clear-cut ideological differences between the major political parties. In their place Social Movements (or New Social Movements) have emerged which have encapsulated sets of values that do not easily fit into traditional party divisions. Issues such as the environment, concern about cruelty to animals, the building of new roads, the position of women and ethnic minorities in society have partially replaced traditional class conflict as the central concerns of a significant proportion of the population. These cut across class and so weaken class solidarity. Linked to this has been the emergence of race, religion and gender as 'organising structures' which significant groups of the population have used as part of their social identities.

The continuing significance of social class

Not all sociologists agree that social class is dead.

Scott argues that social class is still the dominant form of stratification in Britain, which largely determines life chances, though he recognises that it does so in a close relationship with other factors such as age, race, religion and gender. In an international study in the 1980s, Marshall (*Social Class in Modern Britain*) also concludes that social class remained crucial, not just in Britain but across Europe. He points out the continuing divisions based on income, ownership of property, cultural values and lifestyles, as well as political divisions.

3.6 MEASURING SOCIAL CLASS

OCCUPATION AS AN INDICATOR FOR SOCIAL CLASS

Social class forms an important theoretical concept in sociology, and most commentators accept its existence and importance. The main problem, however, is **operationalising** social class, or using the concept in actual research. A number of solutions have been proposed for operationalising social class, all of which are based upon a person's occupation.

Occupation is important because:

● it determines income, which allows a certain lifestyle;
● it also reflects educational and cultural attributes and differences between people.

SOCIAL CLASS CLASSIFICATIONS

Classifications based on occupations include:

● the Registrar-General's classification,
● the manual/non-manual classification,
● Goldthorpe's model,
● feminist models.

The Registrar-General's classification

This model is used in most government surveys and publications. It has six divisions (or more accurately five, with the third division divided into two); see Fig. 3.1.

I	Professional occupations
II	Intermediate occupations
IIInm	Skilled occupations (non-manual)
IIIm	Skilled occupations (manual)
IV	Partly skilled occupations (manual)
V	Unskilled occupations (manual)

Fig. 3.1 The Registrar-General's Classification

Criticisms of the Registrar-General's classification are that:

● it ignores the very rich as it starts with the professions;
● its categories are too broad – so small and large farmers, for example, are classified together; and
● it places routine non-manuals above skilled manuals, even though they earn less.

Goldthorpe's model

This is used in the Oxford Mobility Study, discussed on pp 92–3.

The Service Class

I	Higher professionals and managers of large establishments, large proprietors.
II	Lower professionals and administrators. Managers of smaller establishments. Supervisors of non-manual workers. High-grade technicians.

The Intermediate Class

III	Routine white collar workers in administration and commerce. Sales personnel. Other rank and file employees in services.
IV	Small proprietors, including farmers and small-holders. Self-employed artisans. Other own account workers.
V	Lower grade technicians, supervisors of manual workers.

The Working Class

VI	Skilled manual workers.
VII	Semi and unskilled manual workers in industry and agricultural workers.

Fig. 3.2 Goldthorpe's Model

The **advantages** of using Goldthorpe's model are that it:

- distinguishes between different levels within occupational groups, eg higher and lower professions;
- clearly distinguishes the self-employed;
- clearly distinguishes routine clerical workers from supervisors and from skilled manual workers;
- ranks by occupational group, grouped by coherent social class.

The **problems** associated with it as a method of classification are that it:

- places routine white-collar workers above skilled manual workers;
- ignores the very rich (the upper class);
- takes no account of the unemployed;
- is inappropriate for female employment patterns.

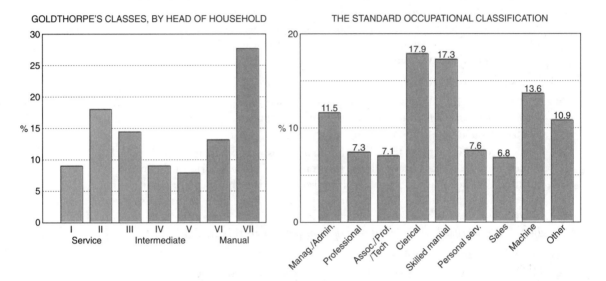

Fig. 3.3 An example of how using different social categories can produce very different results in measuring people's social class

Fig. 3.3 shows the different 'shape' of the social class structure, using different classifications. In the standard occupational classification, often used by government surveys, there are larger numbers in the 'middle' categories and fewer in the 'lower', or working class.

Feminist models

Many contemporary sociologists have characterised these traditional approaches as **malestream**. By this they mean that these classifications are inappropriate for classifying women:

❶ Orthodox approaches are designed to distinguish between male occupations.

❷ The important male distinction between manual/non-manual is far less important for women given the dominance of non-manual work for women.

❸ Within occupational groups, women are typically employed at lower levels.

❹ The same job can be very different in terms of its implications, eg clerical work for a man could be a route into management, for a woman a job in itself.

❺ Where are housewives in traditional occupational-based classifications?

❻ In most of the classifications, women who work are still based upon their husband's social class, as he is considered the head of the household.

❼ 14% of households are now headed by women in single-parent families.

Feminist alternative bases for social class classifications

1 Individualistic model

- It is used by Marshall et al (*Social Class in Modern Britain*).

- It gives every individual a class position based on their present or past occupations. When applied to 'housewives', it gives their last occupation; yet if this was 20 years ago, is it accurate?

- Also, as based solely on an individual's position in the labour market, it excludes a variety of domestic circumstances of women. But couples may mutually support each other, or the wife may give up her possibilities of employment to support the husband. The model ideally should take into account the domestic circumstances, particularly whether the individual is married.

2 The patriarchal model

- It is used by Walby (*Theorising Patriarchy*).

- This model rejects the whole idea of attempting to locate males and females together within a class model. Completely separate categories are needed, as class implies some form of common position of men and women. Feminist theorists adhering to this view suggest instead that the significant and meaningful division is that between the two genders.

3 The cross-class model

- Britten and Heath ('Women, men and social class') in E. Gamarnikow et al, *Women, Men and Class* found a very significant number of women in non-manual occupations married to men in manual occupations.

- This approach recognises that there are many cross-class partnerships in which women in middle-class occupations, for example, may be married to men in working-class occupations. The resulting series of **life chances** are significantly better than couples where both partners are drawn from the working class; they are also significantly worse than where both partners are drawn from the middle class. So, the nature of the *relationship* is important in this model.

4 The class-accentuation model

- This is put forward by Bonney (*Gender, Household and Social Class*).

- This approach takes a similar line to that used by the cross-class model but argues instead that most marriages represent a *strengthening* of class, because couples tend to marry those from similar backgrounds. As two-earner households become the normal domestic arrangement, this will strengthen the divisions.

Examples of alternative feminist classifications

A number of feminist writers have suggested alternative classifications which they claim reflect more accurately the position of women:

1 Women-only classification

Dex suggests the following classification, which could be useful for classifying women but not men:

I	Professional occupations
II	Teachers
III	Nursing, medical and social occupations
IV	Other intermediate and non-manual occupations
V	Clerical occupations
VI	Shop assistants and related sales staff
VII	Skilled occupations
VIII	Childcare occupations
IX	Semi-skilled factory work
X	Semi-skilled domestic work
XI	Other semi-skilled occupations
XII	Unskilled occupations

❷ A feminist classification for both men and women
Arber, Dale and Gilchrist suggest the following scale which could accommodate both males and females:

I   Higher professionals
II   Employers and managers
III   Lower professionals
IV   Secretarial and clerical staff
V   Foremen, self-employed manual workers
VI   Sales and personal services
VII   Skilled manual occupations
VIII   Semi-skilled manual occupations
IX   Unskilled occupations

❸ A radical feminist position
Delphy, a radical feminist, has rejected all such attempts at classification based on occupations, arguing that they reflect patriarchal relationships which exclude the **domestic sphere of consumption**.

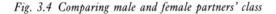

		FEMALE PARTNER'S CLASS			
		Service	Intermediate	Working	TOTAL
MALE PARTNER'S CLASS	Service	95 (48)	82 (42)	20 (10)	197 (100)
	Intermediate	32 (18)	96 (54)	51 (28)	179 (100)
	Working	21 (10)	89 (42)	103 (48)	213 (100)
Row percentages in brackets.				TOTAL	589

Fig. 3.4 Comparing male and female partners' class

Goldthorpe's reply to his feminist critics
Goldthorpe has replied to criticisms that his is a malestream approach by arguing that what is most important is the social class of the *household*. Therefore the person whose class is most significant for the household should give the class to those in the household. Goldthorpe suggests that dominance (level of job) and worktime (number of hours worked) play a key role here in determining whose class is most significant; usually it is the male but it could also be the female.

3.7   SOCIAL MOBILITY

DEFINITIONS

Social mobility may be defined in five contexts:

❶ Inter-generational The social class position of a child compared to a parent – usually this is the son compared to the father.

2 Intra-generational The present social class position of a person compared to a previous point in time – usually their first 'proper' employment.

3 Self-recruitment The extent to which children of members of a social class remain in that class.

4 Meritocracy The extent to which people achieve their position in the social class structure through their ability alone.

5 Open/closed systems Social systems that allow/do not allow movement between social classes.

WHY STUDY SOCIAL MOBILITY?

The extent of social mobility tells us the degree to which a society can be said to be **meritocratic**. High degrees of both upward and downward social mobility suggest an open society which rewards the more able. This would undermine the Marxist position on social class, for example.

High levels of upward social mobility with little downward mobility suggest a change in the occupational structure with an increase in jobs traditionally rated as high status. This would not necessarily indicate a meritocratic society. There would have to be some significant degree of downward mobility to support the meritocratic thesis, in this situation. High levels of downward mobility, without corresponding upward mobility, would indicate a contraction of the occupational structure.

THE RESEARCH

A major recent post-war study has been the Oxford Mobility Study, which concentrated on men aged between 20 and 64. This used the Goldthorpe Model explained on pp 88–9. See also Fig. 3.5, comparing relative mobility chances of two generations.

Upward mobility

Far more men move up the social scale than move down. Over 50% of those from social class I come from other social classes. But entry to social class I decreases the 'lower' the social class starting point of the male; eg 29% of class I come from class II, only 6% from class VII.

Downward mobility

Relatively few people move down the class structure; eg only 6% of men with fathers in class I moved down to class VII.

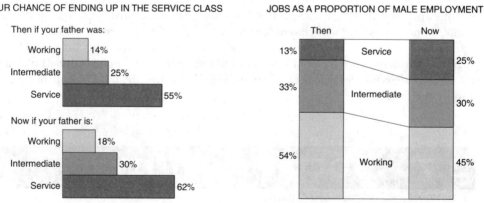

(*Source:* adapted from *The Sunday Times*, 13 January 1980)

Fig. 3.5   Comparing relative mobility chances of those born in 1908–17 with those born in 1938–4

Self-recruitment

Three social classes had noticeable levels of self-recruitment:

- social class I = 45%;
- social class VI = 30%;
- social class VII = 35%.

Most of the other social classes could best be described as transitional – particularly III, which is routine white collar. This is occupied by men moving up into management.

Overall summary

There has been a significant increase in the amount of movement into the top two social classes. Relatively few men move downward.

CONTENTIOUS ISSUES

There are some problems, however, and these centre on:
- methodology,
- female social mobility.

Methodological issues

Social mobility studies use the methodology of social class classifications and therefore have all the problems inherent in them (see pp 88–91). They also exclude the very rich and concentrate only on the bulk of the employed workforce.

The meaning and status of jobs change over time – so that being a clerk in the 1950s had far more status than it does today. Is it therefore possible meaningfully to compare movement over time by jobs? Geographical variations in employment mean that in certain parts of the country the possibility of advancement in employment is greater than in others, because the level of jobs (number of white collar and number of unskilled manual) varies.

Female social mobility

Most studies of social mobility have been male-oriented and have simply ignored female mobility.

Heath (*Social Mobility*) used evidence from the General Household Survey, and found that women were concentrated in class III (routine white-collar work). Compared to their fathers' social class, there appears to be greater downward than upward mobility with women. Single women, however, are more likely than single men to be upwardly mobile. This suggests that employment 'success' and marriage do not coincide. Female upward mobility was most notable in the areas of welfare, education and health.

CAUSES OF CHANGING PATTERNS OF MOBILITY

The changing occupational structure

This is the single most important reason for upward mobility. There has been a massive decline in the percentage of manual jobs available and a significant increase in professional, managerial and white-collar jobs. Over one-third of the workforce now classifies itself as 'professional', for example. The result is that a majority of the workforce can claim to be in higher-level occupations, and this therefore gives the illusion of upward mobility.

Patterns of reproduction

The higher social classes have consistently failed to reproduce themselves and therefore have left open spaces for those from lower social classes.

Education

The Oxford Mobility Study indicates that, for a man, there is a link between educational qualifications and membership of higher social classes. Those who are educationally highly qualified move up the class structure no matter what their class origins are. However, we know that those from social classes I and II are more likely to be educationally successful. Therefore education both provides a route and simultaneously ensures reproduction of the class structure.

Test yourself questions and answers

Questions

1 What is the meaning of the term 'contradictory class locations'?

2 What three elements to stratification are there according to Weber?

3 What criticisms of the functionalist theory of stratification have been made?

4 What is the meaning of the term 'the new working class'?

5 What relationship has been suggested between stratification and 'race'?

6 Why is occupation used as an indicator of social class?

7 Explain why feminists criticise 'malestream' classifications.

8 What are the main causes of upward social mobility?

Suggested answers

1 Erik Ohlin Wright has suggested that groups which fall outside the main Marxist division into two social classes are in 'contradictory class locations', in that the members of these classes do not believe they are in the proletariat and associate themselves with the ruling class. However, objectively they are in the same position as the proletariat.

2 Class, status and power.

3 Critics of the functionalists' arguments question who decides which are the key positions and point out that in reality there appears to be little rational link between wealth/income and useful jobs. There is also no discussion of the role of power.

4 A group of affluent working-class people whose living standards, patterns of home ownership and leisure activities are noticeably different from the traditional working class.

5 A variety of links have been proposed including:
- race as caste;
- race as a subsidiary element of analysis;
- the divided working class thesis;
- racialised class fractions;
- the underclass.

6 Occupation is important because it determines income, which allows a certain lifestyle. It also reflects educational and cultural attributes and differences between people. Finally, it is simple to operationalise in research.

7 Criticisms include:
- Orthodox approaches are designed to distinguish between male occupations.
- The important male distinction between manual/non manual is far less important for women given the dominance of non-manual work for women.
- Within occupational groups, women are typically employed at lower levels, and in a narrower range of jobs.
- The same job can be very different in terms of its implications: eg clerical work for a man could be a route into management, for a woman a job in itself.
- Housewives are not placed in traditional occupational-based occupations.
- In most of the classifications, women who work are still based upon their husband's social class, as head of household.
- 14% of households are now headed by women in single-parent families.

8 Causes of upward mobility include:
- the changing occupational structure, with an increase in middle-class occupations;
- the failure of the middle and upper class to produce enough children to fill these positions;
- higher standards of educational attainment of the working class and lower middle class.

Illustrative question and answer

Question

Item A

The measurement of class

Although sociologists constantly refer to social class as a major dimension of people's lives, it is not always easy to determine which class a person is in. There are two major types of definition of class: objective and subjective. The main objective indicator of class is occupation and the most used classifications of occupations are the Hall-Jones' and the Registrar-General's. However, there are serious drawbacks to using these two scales, not least of which is that they ignore the subjective dimension of class. Which class people think they are in is important, because it is likely to affect the way they act.

(Adapted from Lawson, T., *Concise Sociology*)

Item B

Changes in occupational structure of Britain

Higher-grade professions; predominantly male. There has been an overall increase in the number of males in this category, especially between 1951 and 1971. The number of females has remained fairly static, showing a slight increase in the decade 1961–71.

Employers and proprietors; predominantly male. There has been a decline in the number of males in the category and a slightly smaller decline in the number of women within it.

Administrators and managers; mainly male. There has been an increase in the number of males in the group, but the number of females declined between 1921 and 1931 and subsequently increased in recent years.

Lower-grade professionals; more men than women. There has been a steady increase in the number of males in this category, especially after 1951. There has been a similar increase in the number of males and females in this category.

Clerical; predominantly female. There has been a very small increase in the number of males but it is an occupational group which has seen the greatest increase in the number of women employed.

Supervisors, foremen; both men and women in roughly equal proportions. There has been a steady increase in the number of males and females in this category.

Sales personnel and shop assistants; predominantly female. The employment of males has fluctuated and numbers have declined since 1931. For women, there has been a steady increase until 1961 when a small decline became apparent.

(Adapted from Selfe, P., *Advanced Sociology*)

Item C

| | Personal wealth: distribution among adults of marketable wealth | | | |
	1966	1979	1984	1985
Percentage of wealth owned by:				
Most wealthy 1% of adults	33	22	21	20
Most wealthy 5% of adults	56	40	39	40
Most wealthy 10% of adults	69	54	52	54
Most wealthy 25% of adults	87	77	75	76
Most wealthy 50% of adults	97	95	93	93

(*Source:* Inland Revenue statistics)

Item D

Fragmentation has occurred within the middle class; three major groupings can be identified. The first is the traditional middle class. These are the owners and top managers of businesses and the traditional professions like doctors and lawyers, who have high status and income. The second group are the 'new' professionals or intellectual middle class like teachers, social workers, University lecturers etc. These are mainly found in the public sector rather than the private. The third group are the routine white-collar or non-manual middle class who have been growing in size since the Second World War. These workers are sometimes put with the lower professionals like the nurses and technicians.

(a) With reference to Item A, name two social characteristics other than occupation which might be used as objective indicators of class.   (2)

(b) What criticisms other than those raised in Item A, could be made of the Hall-Jones' and Registrar-General's classifications of occupations?   (6)

(c) What explanations have sociologists offered for the differences between male and female patterns of non-manual employment, as shown in Item B.   (6)

(d) What pattern can be identified in Item C about the changing distribution of marketable wealth among adults?   (1)

(e) The author of Item D suggests that the middle class in Britain is fragmented. Assess the argument that Britain's class structure as a whole is increasingly fragmented.   (10)
AEB

Suggested answer

(a) education, lifestyle, income level, house ownership or house type etc.

(b) The main criticisms have centred around the following:
  ● they are both outdated and refer to groupings which are not necessarily the most appropriate today;
  ● they have broad and vague categories which link inappropriate groups together;

- both forms of classification are based on male occupations and ignore women;
- both forms of classification have significant problems classifying households rather than individuals, as it could be argued that household is a more significant measure given the development of two-earner households.

(c) You need to refer to the range of factors which limit women's ability to enter higher-level managerial and administrative posts. Arguments put forward usually centre around the way in which the roles of women outside work have placed a great limitation on their ability to have a successful career.

You should point out that the roles of mother/wife and carer still predominate in the UK, and show how childhood socialisation at home and at school plus social control later in life all constrain women to place their domestic roles above their career roles. Women are therefore more likely to work part-time, to take service work which is low paid and has less opportunities for promotion etc.

(d) Overall, a remaining concentration of wealth in the hands of relatively few people. However, there has been some dispersal of wealth down among the 50% most wealthy.

(e) This question is worth 10 marks and therefore deserves a considerable amount of work and thought. You should begin by pointing to the traditional perceptions and (limited) evidence for a homogeneous working class. You could also relate this to the Marxist perspective which stressed the divisions between the proletariat and the bourgeoisie. You should then move to look at the changes in class structure which became clear in the 1960s with the studies of the so-called affluent workers. You should point to evidence from the voting studies of Crewe among others and from the evidence of the increase in overall affluence and home ownership. Then move on to discuss the increasing awareness of issues of race, gender and disability, as well as of the ways that divisions between public and private employees have grown – the work of Wright is important here. You might then conclude by bringing in the work of Marshall et al, who argue that class is still an extremely important element in determining peoples' lives.

Question bank

1 For Weberian sociologists social class, based on market relations of supply and demand, is only one form of social stratification. Other forms of stratification are social status based on social honour and political relationships based on unequal access to decision making positions.

Weberians stress that all three concepts may well be needed to explain fully the life chances of individuals and groups.

(a) Explain what is meant by:
    (i) social stratification;   (2)
    (ii) social honour.   (2)

(b) What evidence has been used to support the view of social stratification outlined in the above extract?   (5)

(c) What evidence had been used to question the view of social stratification outlined in the above extract?   (5)

(d) With reference to any one area of social life (e.g. educational opportunity, health, career opportunities), explain the effect that social stratification has on the life-chances of individuals and groups.   (5)

(e) Explain and illustrate what Weberian sociologists understand by the 'terms,' 'class', 'status' and 'power'.   (6)

NEAB

Points

(a) (i) Social stratification can be defined as the allocation of people to groups based on social factors which then determine their access to the distribution of material goods and status.

    (ii) Social honour is the element of stratification based on prestige.

(b) Studies of a variety of groups have indicated that social prestige is not solely distributed along lines of ownership and wealth. Groups such as nurses, doctors and teachers receive higher prestige than those in the City. Social class divisions in the UK are not clear cut, but merge with other divisions such as race and gender.

(c) Marxists have pointed to the continuing importance of class in determining life chances and the continuing concentration of wealth in the hands of a few.

(d) Education – access to exam results and higher education still linked to class. You will need to produce some statistics to show this.

    Employment – same as above.

(e) Class – position in the market place.

    Status – linked to traditional values according to Weber. Rather weak.

    Power – different status groups have different levels of power, which they use to maintain or enhance their positions.

2 'Social stratification is to everyone's benefit, rich or poor, powerful or powerless, because it allows society to achieve efficient role-allocation and performance.' Critically assess this statement.

NEAB

Points

This is a discussion and critique of the functionalist approach. You should run through the arguments of Davies and Moore, and Parsons, which are actually summed up for you in the question. The best and most-gifted get the top jobs and the highest rewards. Criticisms are legion, but you could use Weberian (status group closure) and Marxist critiques. You should explore the issue of power to define what is most important.

GENDER AND SEXUALITY

Units in this chapter

Chapter objectives

This chapter provides only a small proportion of the information on women in this book. I have generally sought to place the discussion of gender issues in the relevant chapters of the book rather than to collect them in a separate chapter. If you do not find the information in this chapter, it will be in the related subject chapter elsewhere in the book – for example for information about gender and poverty read Chapter 13: Poverty and Welfare.

The chapter starts with a discussion of how being male or female is as much a matter of socialisation as of biology. This section examines the main process of becoming a woman, in the sense of being expected to behave in certain ways. This is known as the **female gender role**.

However, once constructed, the role has to be maintained, and there is a discussion about the way that this process of social control continues. For example, many feminists have argued that the public space is really men's space, while the only place regarded as appropriate for women is the domestic sphere. There are many **sites of oppression** for women, and these are discussed throughout the book; perhaps the most obvious one is that of work. The chapter then moves on to explore the ways in which women encounter a patriarchal society in their work, with their lower wages and lower chances of career success. But for most women work also includes unpaid housework, and the nature of this is also discussed.

The next section looks at the roles of women in a broader perspective, in particular looking at women outside the advanced industrial societies, since, after all, these form the overwhelming majority of women in the world. It considers the traditional roles of women and the effects of modernisation on their lives.

The final unit looks at the traditional role of the male and at New Man.

4.1   FEMALE GENDER ROLES

GENDER ROLES

Gender roles – the behaviour expected from members of a particular sex – are socially constructed, that is they are not biologically based, according to sociologists. Evidence for this comes from cross-cultural studies where women and men behave in very different ways than in Western societies. Two key elements of female gender roles are:

- socialisation,
- social control.

Socialisation

The media

The media present different images of males and females. Males are presented as dominant, active characters. Females have their own specialist literature ('women's magazines') which guide them into appropriate behaviour.

Lobban studied the main characters of children's adventure stories and concluded that generally the main action character or 'hero' was male. Females play a subordinate role. Weitzmann et al carried out a survey of the most widely used pre-school children's books and also found a clear difference in the roles attributed to the sexes. Males outnumbered females by 11 to 1. Girls were also much more likely to be passive and engage in indoor activities. Ferguson (*Forever Feminine*) studied women's magazines over 20 years. She found a **cult of femininity** in which the dominant values regarding women were enshrined. Today the message of the magazines is that the ideal woman combines a successful career with motherhood. (It should be noted that most educational publishers have clear policies regarding the balance of roles in newly published books, and what we are seeing is the gradual phasing out of such traditional roles in books.)

The school

Through the **hidden curriculum** (that is the assumptions which teachers make regarding the appropriate behaviour and aptitudes of the two sexes), teachers act differently towards male and female pupils. Research by Walker and Barton (*Gender, Class and Education*) suggested that girls are rewarded for silence, neatness and conformity, but the more rebellious attitudes of boys were tolerated by both male and female teachers.

1 **Race, gender and school** Bryan et al (*Learning to Resist: Black Women and Education*) found in their research of black female pupils that they tended to be initially enthusiastic about school but gradually became disillusioned as teachers labelled them troublemakers. However, this was not the view of Fuller's study ('Black girls in a London comprehensive School') of black female pupils, where the importance of future career was emphasized by the girls. Indeed, the female pupils of Afro-Caribbean origin were likely to be more successful than the white girls in Fuller's study.

2 **Reputation and social control** Lees' study (*Losing Out*) suggested that female pupils were very concerned about 'reputation' especially concerning sexual behaviour (or perceived sexual activity) and that this had a strong effect upon self-perception and behaviour. Girls were concerned to avoid being labelled into the extreme categories of promiscuous or not sexually active.

3 **Subject choice and gender** More noticeable than different levels of attainment between the two sexes are the different subjects which males and females study and achieve success in. Once pupils have the choice of subjects at GCSE/GNVQ and beyond, males choose maths, science, technology and computing, whereas females are more likely to take humanities, caring subjects, human biology and clerical/business studies.

The significance of subject choice is that it strongly influences the choice of higher education and the choice and possibilities of employment.

The home

Parents have different expectations of boys and girls – they treat them differently in terms of language used towards them, clothes they dress them in and toys they either buy them or permit them to buy. However, even when parents set out to combat gender stereotyping, they experience difficulties. Statham (*Daughters and Sons: Experiences of Non-Sexist Childraising*) studied 30 middle-class adults heading 18 families. The families were committed to raising their children in a manner which broke down gender roles. However, they found it very difficult to combat the influence of the wider society and even the expectations of their relatives.

Social control

The family

Parents exercise stricter control over daughters than they do over sons, regulating where they go and at what time they should return. Husbands similarly have expectations of wives concerning their behaviour; in the extreme this leads to marital violence (see pp 322–3). Dobash and Dobash argue that marital violence is commonplace and rather than being an aberration performed by a disturbed individual it is a *normal extension* of the husband role.

The peer group

Girls' behaviour is constrained by the fear of gaining a reputation, eg for being sexually available. The power of the peer group (both male and female) to label females is much stronger for girls than it is for boys. Lees studied 16-year-old girls in three London comprehensives and found that they were concerned not to be labelled as 'slags'. This influenced their behaviour, form of dress and speech. Willis' study of Midland schoolboys (*Learning to Labour*) found that boys sought out girls defined as 'easy lays' but did not want a long-term relationship with a girl like that.

The public sphere

Women are controlled in public through fear of male harassment or even violence if they go out in the streets at night or into pubs, for example, alone. Hammer and Saunders found that women were inhibited by fear of sexual assault and violence. The only way to overcome their fear was to request the company of a male, thereby creating a situation of dependency on men who are the cause of the trouble in the first place.

Employment

Women are usually employed in least responsible positions and have male managers. They are also paid less than men. This means that they are directly controlled and supervised by men in employment. See the section below.

SEXUALITY

The social construction of sexuality

There is a common belief that sexuality is constructed solely by biology – and that therefore heterosexuality is normal and natural. Sociologists have not necessarily disagreed, but have added that sexuality is also socially constructed. Influences identified by Weeks and Foucault include religion, law, medical beliefs and differences in power between various groups.

According to Metcalf and Humphries (*The Sexuality of Men*), sexuality like most aspects of what is defined as masculinity requires men to dominate and control women sexually. Women, however, have their sexuality more tightly controlled than men. Women, may approach sexual activity differently than men, placing sex within a framework of emotion, rather than an activity in itself.

Writers, such as Seidler (*Rediscovering Masculinity*), argue that women have been exploited in sexual relationships with sex being defined as primarily for the pleasure of males and centring on sexual intercourse rather than other acts of pleasure which women may prefer.

An example of how discourses in sexuality are socially constructed can be found in the perceptions of homosexuality.

Homosexuality

Traditional accounts of homosexuality treat it as deviant and abnormal, despite studies such as Wellings in 1994 which suggested that 6% of males and almost 4% of females had had homosexual/lesbian experiences.

Historically, homosexuality was common, with homosexual love (between males) regarded as a 'higher' form of love by the Ancient Greeks than heterosexual love. Today, homosexuality is illegal in many countries and in the UK, the law still distinguishes between heterosexual and homosexual activity on the age of consent.

However, sociologists have suggested that sexual identities are not as clear cut as generally believed, and that there is a case for arguing the normality of bisexuality. Weeks (*Sexuality*) argues that the early stages of Christianity involved attacking the commonly accepted belief at the time of sex as activity purely for pleasure. Yet it took a period of almost a thousand years for the gradual emergence, in the 12th and 13th centuries of the only true form of acceptable sexual activity being that between husband and wife for reproductive purposes. And it was not until the 19th century that the only accepted form of 'normal' sexuality was heterosexual sex, with other forms of sex coming to be regarded as deviant. Indeed, the term 'homosexuality' was only devised in 1860, both reflecting and helping to construct the emergence of a clear-cut sexual identity.

Foucault (*The History of Sexuality*) points out that the first time that governments became interested in population and birth control was in the 18th and early 19th centuries. As a result of this interest 'discourses' or ways of thinking and discussing sexuality developed. The discourses that developed as a result of government interest in population control divided sexuality into four types:

● women's sexuality,

● children's sexuality,

● married sex,

● homosexuality.

Women were not supposed to have the same sexual drive and needs as men. Children were removed from sexuality altogether. Married sex was normal (though not necessarily pleasurable). Finally, homosexuality was clearly a form of perversion engaged in by 'perverts'.

Foucault suggests like Weeks that a category of person – the homosexual – is 'invented' at this time. Foucault argues that the ability to construct a discourse reflects differences in power, so that the discourses on sexuality reflect the power of heterosexual males. The very construction of the discourse is part of a process of controlling homosexuals (and women).

Categories of homosexuality

Plummer argues that the idea that there are 'homosexual' people or gays and lesbians and heterosexual or 'straight people' is too simplistic and that at least four categories of males who have engaged in homosexual activities can be distinguished:

● **Casual homosexuality** refers to a brief encounter or passing homosexual act, often happening in periods of sexual experimentation during youth.

● **Situated activity** describes the situation where people whose preference in normal circumstances would be heterosexual turn to homosexual actions because of various constraints. This occurs in prisons, for example.

● **Personalised homosexuality** is where homosexuality is the preference of the person, but he or she is unable to express it openly. Homosexual activity therefore becomes furtive and occurs in hidden encounters.

● **Homosexuality as a way of life** occurs when people have 'come out', and have integrated into alternative 'gay' or lesbian cultures which provide a network of links and social relationships.

The social construction of homosexuality

The work of sociologists suggests that homosexuality can be viewed less as a deviant form of personality caused by psychological or biological 'abnormalities', and more of a *social status* imposed upon certain categories of acts.

Furthermore, sexual acts between those of the same sex are more common than the stigmatised category of 'homosexual' would suggest, according to social surveys. Therefore many heterosexuals have engaged in homosexual acts, as we saw earlier. Plummer's categories suggest that people can switch from one form of sexuality to another depending upon how it is defined by others. For example, in both female and male prisons, homosexuality is normal, even though the majority of people in there would define themselves and others as heterosexual. On release the majority of people resume their heterosexual activities. Another of his categories, casual homosexuality, refers to a stage that many young people go though, which involves experimenting with peers of their own sex. This is a passing phase, and if not defined by the individuals involved or others as homosexuality, then the individual does not retain that label.

Plummer, Foucault and Weeks all suggest that sexuality is one of many power struggles which occur in society, and whether or not a group becomes stigmatised is less to do with the sexual acts themselves than the amount of power resources that group holds. So, since the 1980s gay and lesbian pressure groups have been extremely effective in challenging the discourses on sexuality, demanding equal rights and challenging the traditional negative view of homosexuality.

4.2   WOMEN AND WORK

WHO BENEFITS FROM WOMEN'S LABOUR?

Housework

Delphy (*Close to Home*) argues that it is men who benefit and that they therefore block women's attempts to escape. Marxist-feminists argue that capitalism benefits in producing a well looked-after worker.

Paid employment

Dual labour market theorists Barron and Norris ('Sexual Divisions and the Dual Labour Market') argue that there are two types of job:

1. secure, with the possibility of promotion;

2. secure, with no definite future and no benefits, such as pension paid holidays etc.

Women are more likely than men to be trapped in the second marginal labour market.

Breugal (*Women as a Reserve Army of Labour*) puts forward a Marxist argument that claims that women are a cheap, available pool, or **reserve army**, of workers that employers use and dispense with, as they feel necessary.

Fig. 4.1 shows the pay differences between men and women in the same occupations.

HOUSEWORK

Housework is almost exclusively performed by women. Its key elements are that it:

- is not regarded as 'work',
- is unpaid,
- has low status.

Rather than diminishing with the introduction of labour-saving devices, such as dish washers, washing machines, hoovers etc, these have merely raised the standards expected. Oakley (*The Sociology of Housework*), starting from the premise that housework is work, studied 40

London housewives and concluded that housework has the following elements:
- long hours,
- monotony,
- excessive pace of work,
- fragmentation,
- no pay, based instead on personal relationship to family.

PAID EMPLOYMENT

The pattern of women's employment

Women's employment 'work-cycles' are influenced by child-bearing. There is a peak of women in employment before they have their first child and after their last child starts school. However, the length of the child-bearing period has reduced, as has women's willingness to remain at home as full-time mothers and houseworkers. This means that the time out of employment for child-rearing is becoming increasingly shorter.

The type of employment

Over 70% of full-time female workers are employed in clerical or service work and in the 'lower' professions. Women are therefore effectively segregated in the lowest wage areas. This is known as **horizontal segregation** by sex. This happens because the power of gender roles leads us to define certain work – usually the lowest paid – as appropriate for women. Men therefore control entry to the better jobs. Figures for part-time employment show that 44% of women in employment are part-time and 90% of part-timers are women. This happens because there is an expectation of women to perform domestic duties.

The level of employment

Women are more likely to be found in the lower levels of any occupation; eg 24% of males are managers or professionals while only 9% of females are (and these are likely to be the 'lower' professions such as teaching/social work). Yet 61% of women are in routine non-manual occupations compared with only 17% of males. This is known as **vertical segregation** by sex. The reasons which have been suggested for this have been:
- male prejudice;
- the fact that women often interrupt careers to have children;
- low expectations by women themselves as a result of gender role socialisation.

Women's pay is significantly lower than men's: women earn approximately 75% of male net earnings.
   There are several reasons for women's low pay:
- Women are concentrated in jobs that pay less (see above).
- Women are less able to work overtime because of the nature of their jobs (clerical work offers little overtime) and because of their domestic responsibilities.

4.3   WOMEN IN NON-INDUSTRIAL SOCIETIES

WORK

Generalisations are so great in talking about non-industrialised nations that it is arguably a worthless exercise. However, it is generally accepted that women work longer hours in non-industrial societies than men. Generally, they do as much work as men for the general 'income' (it may be non-monetary) of the household, but they also engage in the range of services we associate with women in the West: cooking, washing etc for the males of the family.

For example, Oakley in *Subject Women* shows that 60–80% of the food of two Phillippine societies (the Tanulong and the Fedilizan) is produced by women. Boserup, in a study of the contribution of women to farmwork in Asian societies found that on top of all domestic work, women also perform 40–75% of farmwork. It would seem that the double role of domestic tasks and productive labour is performed in non-industrialised societies in much the same way as it is in industrialised ones.

QUALITY OF LIFE

Various studies have been carried out to measure the quality of life of women in non-industrialised societies. This sort of study is fraught with problems, according to what indicators are used to measure quality of life. Blumberg has created a list of seven criteria based on sexual freedom, educational opportunities, power within the household etc. Giele has suggested six areas of measurement:

- political expression,
- work,
- family formation, duration and size,
- education,
- health and sexual control,
- cultural expression (images of women).

THE EFFECTS OF MODERNISATION ON THE ROLES OF WOMEN

Traditional theories

Most theoretical approaches to development have seen industrialisation as a means for women to liberate themselves. Conservative modernisation theory, for example, stresses the development of Western-style family units in which the women are liberated to become 'good' mothers, providing a high standard of mothering to their children. Marxist writers have stressed the liberating aspects of their theories as industrialisation will inevitably lead to a Marxist revolution which would gain women their freedom.

Feminist approaches

Only feminist writers have suggested that the underlying power of men, or **patriarchy**, will mean that men will control the changing technology and so retain their power. There is considerable evidence for this approach. Oakley argues that economic production can be divided into three types:

1. activities which create goods (and agricultural produce);

2. the exchange of goods and services;

3. the cyclical reproduction of labour power involving caring for children, husbands, animals and performing domestic work.

Women are engaged primarily in the first and third of these. As the economy changes from small-scale domestic agriculture to work outside the home, women tend to be excluded from the new form of wage labour and therefore made dependent upon men. At the same time, the third form of labour (**cyclical reproduction**) is not regarded as a high status area as it is not measurable directly in terms of income (women are not paid for being mothers). They therefore suffer a decline in status compared to the wage-earning male.

INDUSTRIALISATION AND WOMEN IN THE THIRD WORLD

The development of industrialisation in the Third World has mainly been through the activities of large international organisations in their search for cheap labour. The cheapest labour available is often that of young women. So manufacturing industries recruit these on a large scale to undertake work that needs considerable manual dexterity. The outcome, according to Elson and Pearson ('The subordination of women and the internationalisation of factory production'), is to affect the position of women in one of three possible ways:

- intensification,
- decomposition,
- recomposition.

Intensification

Here the existing pattern of gender roles is intensified by the activities of the multi-national corporation. They give the example of the multi-national company operating in Malaysia, which tries to strengthen the traditional subservient role of the female in order to use this to create discipline within the factory.

Decomposition

In this situation, the process of industrialisation weakens the traditional gender roles. Elson and Pearson give the example of how Western-style views of women are developed among employees (through fashion contests, disco dancing etc). The result is to provide women with alternative models of femininity which they point out may undermine such traditions as arranged marriages. Elson and Pearson do not claim that this is necessarily a good thing, as they may be exchanging one form of subordination for another.

Recomposition

This follows on from decomposition and is where traditional forms of subordination are substituted by newer forms. Elson and Pearson suggest that the authority of the male family member over women may often be replaced by the authority of the male factory bosses. The subordination to men continues, therefore, but in a different form.

4.4 MASCULINITY

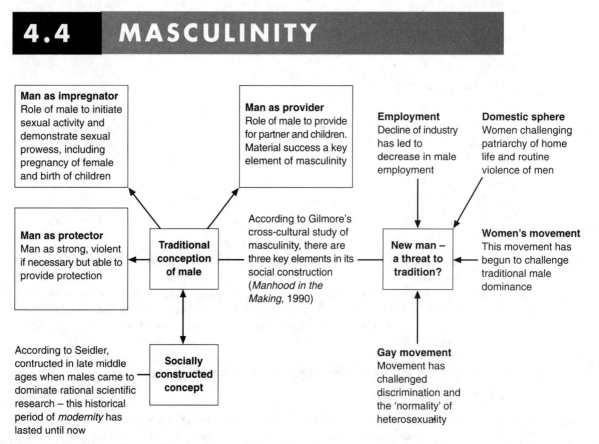

Fig. 4.1 Masculinity: from tradition to threatened New Man

Test yourself questions and answers

Questions

1 What are the two key elements in the construction and maintenance of gender roles?

2 What is the role of the media in helping to construct gender roles?

3 Explain what the term 'dual labour market' means.

4 Outline the key elements of housework.

5 Are the majority of women in employment in full-time or part-time work? Explain the reasons for this pattern.

6 How can the quality of life of women be measured?

7 What are the effects of industrialisation on women?

Suggested answers

1 Socialisation and social control.

2 The media present different images of males and females. Males are presented as dominant, active characters. Females have their own specialist literature ('women's magazines') which guide them into appropriate behaviour. Ferguson, in her study of women's magazines over 20+ years, found a 'cult of femininity' in which the dominant values regarding women were enshrined. Today the message of the magazines is that the ideal woman combines a successful career with motherhood. Lobban studied the main characters of children's adventure stories and concluded that generally the main action character or 'hero' was male. Weitzmann et al studied preschool children's books and also found a clear difference in the roles attributed to the sexes.

3 This derives from the writings of Barron and Norris who argue that there are two types of jobs:
   ● secure, with the possibility of promotion;
   ● insecure, with no definite future and no benefits such as pension, paid holidays etc.

   Women are more likely than men to be trapped in the second, 'marginal', labour market. This system is known as the dual labour market.

4 Its key elements are that it:
   ● is not regarded as 'work',
   ● is unpaid,
   ● has low status.

   Oakley adds that it is characterised by:
   ● long hours,
   ● monotony,
   ● excessive pace of work,
   ● fragmentation,
   ● no pay, based on personal relationship to family.

5 Part-time; the expectation is that women perform their domestic duties first and their paid employment is expected to fit around this.

6 Blumberg has created a list of seven criteria based on sexual freedom, educational opportunities, power within the household etc. Giele has suggested six areas of measurement:

- political expression,
- work,
- family formation, duration and size,
- education,
- health and sexual control,
- cultural expression (images of women).

7 There are three possible outcomes, it has been suggested:

- Intensification: the existing pattern of gender roles is intensified by the activities of the multi-national corporation.
- Decomposition: the process of industrialisation weakens the traditional gender roles.
- Recomposition: following on from decomposition, where traditional forms of subordination are substituted for newer forms.

Illustrative question and answer

Question

Outline and discuss the social processes that produce and reinforce definitions of femininity and masculinity.

Cambridge

Suggested answer

You should first clarify the issue of the debate about gender as a social construction and the biological nature of the sexes of male and female. You need then to discuss the main processes responsible for gender construction of socialisation and social control.

These take place in the home, school, and in the place of employment as well as in public places. They are performed by family members, peer groups, the media and through the general culture of UK society.

Childhood socialisation needs discussion to show how girls learn to be different from boys and to learn to express themselves and define themselves in different ways as a result of the female gender roles. You could refer to studies by Oakley such as *Subject Women* to prove your point.

Interaction in schools could be brought in with some discussion of the importance of teachers' expectations and attitudes – you could look at Stanworth here. There is also considerable research from feminist writers on the content of school books, (Campbell, Lobban) and the way that girls are marginalised in science lessons by boys and even by some teachers (Kelly). Lees' work has stressed the control of girls by other girls. However, a rather different note has been struck in research by Driver, for example, who actually found that girls of Afro-Caribbean origin were very clear on their determination to succeed.

To complete your essay you should go on to discuss the social processes in the workplace and the stereotypes reproduced by the media.

Question bank

1 Consider the reasons why, despite legislation, divisions and inequalities still exist between males and females.

NEAB

Points

Point out you are aware that there is an Equal Opportunities Commission and that legislation regarding equal pay was introduced in the early 1970s. Point out also that recently the European Court (the one which clarifies European Union law) has passed a number of judgements which have continued to strengthen the rights of women, despite the opposition of the UK government.

You should then turn to an examination of feminist theories which share the belief that the continuing inequalities between men and women are largely determined by patriarchy or the power of men to impose their view of reality on the world. You should illustrate this by looking at:

● the continued differences in work patterns between males and females
● the family responsibilities which have limited the chances of women
● the caring role which women continue to have, etc. You should also consider images of women in the media.

2 'Despite increasing evidence to suggest equality in educational performance, women still remain occupationally disadvantaged in earnings, job-security and promotional opportunities. Their primary roles are still seen as domestic.' What explanations have sociologists offered for the continuing subordination of women in society?

NEAB

Points

You should prove that you know some of the statistics on educational performance, employment, etc. You should then go on to demonstrate the changes over time. Explain what is meant by the 'domestic roles' reference in the quote. Then move on to look at feminist theories and their explanations for this position. Make sure you distinguish between the various approaches.

CHAPTER 5

RACE, ETHNICITY AND NATIONALISM

Units in this chapter

Chapter objectives

Where appropriate, I have integrated discussions of race into the relevant chapters. This chapter therefore only contains part of the information on race and if you are searching for an issue such as race and poverty, you should turn to Chapter 13 Poverty and Welfare.

The major discussions in this chapter centre first on understanding the notions of race, ethnicity and, to a lesser extent, nationalism. These are still important concepts in understanding the divisions within and across contemporary societies.

The second section looks at the background to immigration in the UK and the reasons for the different settlement patterns of those people of Afro-Caribbean and Asian origins, though it is important to realise that large numbers of other migrant groups have settled in the UK over the last one hundred years, including the Irish, Jews and numerous central and East European groups.

The third section of the chapter looks at the various and opposing explanations for racial prejudice and discrimination. The final section examines the reality that this discrimination and prejudice has helped to create for those British people of Asian and Afro-Caribbean origins.

5.1 THE NOTIONS OF RACE, ETHNICITY AND NATIONALISM

RACE

The term race has been used to indicate a group that is assumed to share some common biological and social traits. There appears to be little evidence, however, to support the idea that there are such things as biologically distinct races.

ETHNICITY

The concept of ethnicity has been suggested to replace the term race. An ethnic group refers to a group which distinguishes itself, or is distinguished by others on the grounds of cultural or religious differences, real or perceived. These differences allow boundaries to be set up between groups. The boundaries are strengthened by real differences in economic position, status and power.

However, the idea of ethnicity has been criticised by those who argue that it tends to promote the idea that ethnic groups are entirely homogenous with few differences within the groups. References are made to 'Asians' or 'Muslims', without distinguishing between Asian groups or variations within Islam.

Contemporary writers on ethnicity such as Hall argue that what is more important to study is not the structural differences between the groups (in terms of employment, housing, education, etc) that we look at in this chapter, but with the very concept of race and 'difference' which persists over time and across societies – even though there is little support for biologically based differences between groups. According to Hall, the concept of ethnicity is one which applies to all groups in British society and rather than using it solely for understanding the position of those of Afro-Caribbean or Asian origins for example, it can be used to understand the position of any group in society.

NATIONALISM

Nationalism has been defined by Giddens as a 'set of symbols and beliefs providing the sense of being part of a single political community'. The key elements of nationalism are shown in Fig. 5.1. In many ways nationalism is a parallel concept to race, in that the world is seen as being divided into groups or nations with distinctive characteristics. Usually, nationalists believe that their 'nation' is superior to others.

KEY ELEMENTS

Perceived differences
(people believe they are distinctive and linked)
But *exactly* what is different may be unclear

Ambiguity
Lack of clarity as to exactly what this basis is. Usually linked to perceptions of ethnicity, race or possible religion. But *exact* membership unclear

Locality
Nationalism is linked to a place which is symbolic as the 'home' of the group. Myths and beliefs about places and historical events reinforce. But *exact* boundaries are unclear

Sovereignty
The concept of nation is connected to the desire for self-rule, ie a form of government led and controlled by members of the national group

THEORETICAL EXPLANATIONS

Wallerstein: Nationalism linked to international nature of capitalism:
- Race as a construct emerged from need to justify exploitation, also capitalism created mobility which mixed these 'races'.
- Nations emerged from 'empires', eg colonial division of Africa created artificial nations.
- Nations emerged with growth of competitions amongst core Western nations. National beliefs allowed rulers to maintain control and cohesion within state boundaries.

Hall: Sees a 'dialectic' between capitalism and nation-states.
Capitalism created nationalism and nation-states initially. But globalisation of economies and knowledge have led to break-up of empires (USSR) and the wakening of nation-states, as regions and ethnic groups have taken the opportunity to re-assert their claimed distinctiveness. This has been possible because of the construction of supra-national agencies, such as the European Union.

Fig. 5.1 Key elements of nationalism

People have probably always felt an affinity to some form of group – a family, tribe or religious community, but nationalism or the belief in the distinctiveness of a nation-state only developed as we know it in the 19th century. The development of nation-states in the 18th and 19th centuries created the belief that each people should have a territory of its own which ensures that they can develop their own culture as they wish. This belief has probably been the cause of more wars than any other single belief in the last two hundred years.

In traditional societies, the borders between them were unclear. The power of the central government was also limited by communication factors amongst other things. Traditionally, too, the state was based upon the monarch or the sovereign rather than on any sense of shared cultural identity. In the 18th and 19th centuries nation-states developed which sought to eradicate minorities and to subordinate the various groups into one nation. In the latter part of the 20th century, however, various subordinate groups within nation-states have made claims to distinct historical identities which they claim to make them nations in their own right. In Europe the most obvious examples are the Scottish, the Irish (in Northern Ireland), the Basques in Spain and the Serbs, Croats and Slovenians of the former Yugoslavia. These groups are now demanding, or have obtained nation-stte status based on their claims to be nation-states. Concepts of race and nationalism are not completely separate and may overlap. The idea of multi-culturalism as expounded by Hall earlier is seen by nationalists as threatening the very idea of a nation, as they claim that a multi-ethnic society is one with no clear roots and no history.

5.2 THE PATTERN OF ETHNICITY IN BRITAIN

PEOPLE OF AFRO-CARIBBEAN ORIGINS

Most came to Britain during the 1950s and early 1960s, recruited by British companies with offices there, such as London Transport and the NHS, to fill the vacancies caused by the post-war boom. Over half of Afro-Caribbeans came from Jamaica, then others from the islands of Trinidad and Tobago, Barbados, and from Guyana on the South American mainland. It is important to realise that the 'West Indians' come from a wide range of different island cultures and are not homogeneous. Their home language is English (and local Creole dialects) and they were educated in English, in schools based on the British educational system. The religion of the Caribbean islands and Guyana is Christianity and Rastafarianism.

Original settlers who came here believed that they were coming to the 'motherland' and were shocked at the hostile racist reaction they received. The original generation was strictly conformist to British values and symbols, seeking to integrate themselves. However, successive sociological surveys have shown that racist attitudes continue and that West Indians are one of the groups in Britain with the fewest **life chances** in education, employment, housing and law enforcement.

Pryce (*Endless Pressure*) distinguishes a number of adaptations of Blacks to British society. The extremes of these are:

- the Saints – respectable people who belong to Pentecostal Churches;
- the 'in-betweeners' – young blacks who are politically aware, and eager to confront a racist society;
- the Rastas – who have developed an alternative cultural lifestyle which involves a rejection of white society for a version of the Rastafarian religion, allied with a strategy of 'getting by' on the streets. Lea and Young's writings on black inner-city youth have stressed their **marginalisation** from mainstream society, caused by high rates of unemployment (or at best having the worst jobs) and repressive policing.

PEOPLE OF ASIAN ORIGINS

East African Asians

A fifth of Asians are of East African origin. Most had originally gone to East Africa, with British encouragement, from North India and Pakistan. There they formed the commercial and administrative middle class, usually highly educated and fluent in English. They are generally Muslims and Hindus. They left East Africa in the 1960–70s under pressure from countries like Kenya, Uganda and Malawi which adopted a policy of Africanisation – handing over businesses and senior jobs to Africans.

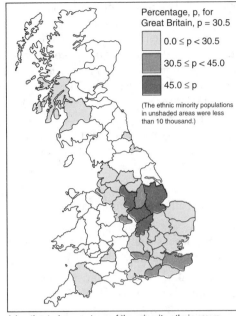

(a) estimated percentage of the minority ethnic group population of Indian origin, by county or region, 1986–8

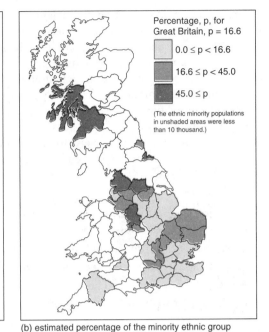

(b) estimated percentage of the minority ethnic group population of Pakistani origin, by county or region, 1986–8

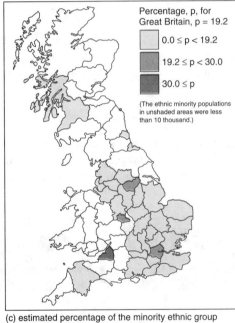

(c) estimated percentage of the minority ethnic group population of West Indian origin, by county or region, 1986–8

(d) estimated percentage of the minority ethnic group population of mixed ethnic origin, by county or region, 1986–8

(Source: Population Trends 63, HMSO)

Fig. 5.2 Settlement patterns of ethnic minorities in the UK

Because of high levels of education allied to a great stress on career success, this group comprises some of the most successful immigrants on a par with the Jews.

Pakistanis

These people came from Kashmir and Punjab, both groups speaking Punjabi, and also from the North-west Frontier Province, speaking Pashto. Educated Pakistanis can speak and write Urdu. There is a major division between urban Pakistanis, who are generally well educated, and rural Pakistanis, who may have more traditional customs and not be as literate. The families of the original immigrants are still arriving. Most of these people live in Yorkshire, Manchester, Lancashire, West Midlands, Glasgow and Cardiff.

Anwar studied Pakistanis in Rochdale (*The Myth of Return*). The original settlers here encouraged family friends to migrate and also provided support. The result over time is a form of 'chain' from Pakistan to England, leading to a closely knit community which protects Pakistanis from a hostile white society. Their society is based on the **extended family** who generally form one household, sharing a house. This extended family can include distant relatives from the same village of origin. An alternative is the **joint family**, consisting of nuclear families living in separate households but taking all major decisions on a joint basis. All families are **patriarchal** and close links are maintained with Pakistan. The connecting mechanism holding Pakistanis together is the concept of *Biraderi* – this is the term covering mutual obligations that all Pakistanis from an area or extended family owe each other.

Pakistanis here are effectively isolated (or **encapsulated**) by religious differences, racism and the fact that they are concentrated in low-paid jobs, living in inner-city areas.

Indians

These people came to Britain in the 1950–60s originally, although families are still arriving. Immigrants came mainly from two States:

- Sikhs from the Punjab (often recognisable by the turbans they wear). They speak Punjabi. (At Independence Punjab was split between Pakistan and India.)
- People from Gujarat. These are mainly Hindus, speaking Gujarati and writing Dunagri. Educated people can use the official Indian language of Hindi.

Sikhs settled in Leeds, West London, the West Midlands and Glasgow. Gujaratis live mainly in north and south London, Leicester, Coventry and Manchester.

Bangladeshis

Bangladesh is the poorest of the Indian subcontinent nations. Males came in the 1950–60s to take up low-skilled, low-paid jobs. Most came from the rural Sylhet district, speaking Sylheti but writing Bengali. The main single area of settlement is east London. These are some of the poorest people in Britain.

Other migrant groups

Other large ethnic minorities in Britain include the Chinese from Hong Kong; Poles who came after World War II; Jews who have settled here over a period of 100 years; Italians who came in the 1950s to Bedfordshire. The single biggest 'immigrant' group in Britain is the Irish.

5.3 EXPLANATIONS FOR RACIAL DISHARMONY

There is no doubt that racist attitudes and behaviour exist to a considerable extent in contemporary Britain. This is not a new phenomenon: there are accounts of anti-Irish riots in the latter part of the 19th century, as well as organised racist attacks on black seamen in Liverpool in the 1930s.

Sociologists have attempted to explain why racism exists, and what factors aggravate it. The following approaches exist:

1 Immigrant–host model;
2 Weberian models, including
- cultural differences,
- power differences,
- struggle over scarce resources;
3 Marxist models, including
- culture,
- scapegoating,
- threat.

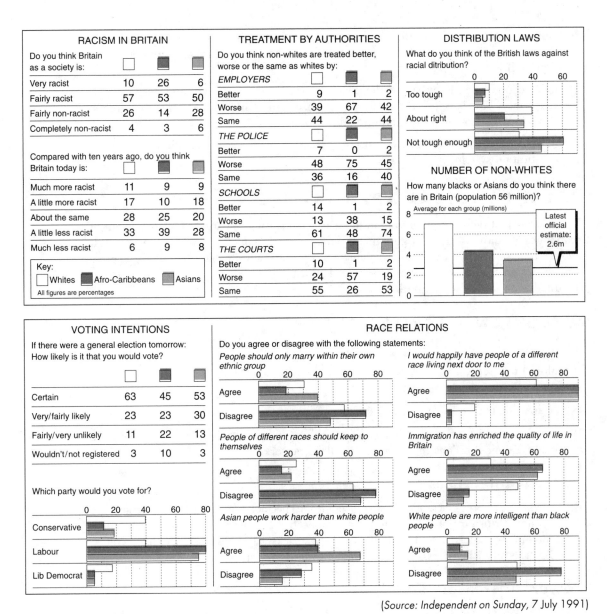

(Source: Independent on Sunday, 7 July 1991)

Fig. 5.3 Are the British racist? The results of a survey in 1991

Fig. 5.3 shows the results of a survey conducted in the *Independent on Sunday* in 1991. It gives the attitudes of whites, Afro-Caribbeans and Asians towards racism in Britain.

THE IMMIGRANT–HOST RELATIONSHIP

This approach is associated with the functionalist perspective, based on a model of immigrants arriving in a culturally integrated and homogeneous society. It is argued that there are a number of possible outcomes upon the arrival of the immigrants, with consequently different levels of racism. These outcomes include:

● **complete rejection**, where two groups attempt to oust each other, eg Jews and Palestinians;

● **assimilation**, where there is total acceptance of immigrants by the hosts;

● **integration**, where the immigrants adapt themselves and are accepted in certain **universal spheres of association**, but still retain their own identity, eg Jews;

● **self-segregation**, where the immigrant group voluntarily segregates itself, eg colonial Britons.

According to Patterson, three factors determine which of the above outcomes occur.

① **Demographic**: the *size* of the immigrant group, *rate* of entry, *duration* of time over which they arrive, *density* of settlement patterns (whether they are clustered or dispersed).

② **Socio-economic** and **cultural**: the degree to which the immigrant and host are compatible. This is influenced by education, occupation and whether the immigrants are from a rural or urban background.

③ **Structural**: the amount and type of employment available and the rigidity of the stratification system.

PSYCHOLOGICAL APPROACHES

These stress that racism derives from individual personality problems and is not a result of economics or culture. Adorno argues that a rigid upbringing in childhood can lead to adult *authoritarian personalities*, who are extremely conventional and unable to accept or express tenderness, so that they have no outlet for their emotions. They, therefore, use certain identifiable groups as **scapegoats** (see over).

WEBERIAN APPROACHES

These approaches stress:

● cultural differences,

● power differences and

● the struggle over scarce resources, eg housing.

Weber saw that society was composed of various groups vying for social honour and economic advantage. Ethnic divisions fit into this overall framework.

Cultural differences

British whites perceive blacks and Asians through the spectacles of centuries of colonial rule during which British people learned to regard themselves as superior. This has implications for contemporary social interaction; for example blacks have lower status than whites. Compare this with the Marxist view on the culture of racism, below.

Power differences

One of the key elements of Weber's analysis of society is the concept of power. Power is something that enables people to gain authority and to have their wishes recognised as being more important or justifiable than the wishes of others. Society is composed of groups who believe that they have certain characteristics in common; it is fragmented when differences arise among groups and one group tries to exert power over another. One kind of fragmentation in society is based on perceptions of race. Racial disharmony can therefore be located within the wider struggle over power that is engaged between different groups.

The struggle over scarce resources

A good example of the constant competition between groups in society is given by Rex and Moore in *Race, Community and Conflict*, their study of the Sparkbrook area of inner Birmingham. They found that immigrants were forced to live in overcrowded inner-city areas as no-one wanted them to live elsewhere. As renting was difficult, the immigrants bought houses, paying for them by subletting; the resulting overcrowding confirmed stereotypes already held. Similar conflicts can develop in other areas over scarce resources: education, politics, health services etc.

MARXIST APPROACHES

Marxist-based explanations such as the work of Castles and Kosack, stress the more *deliberate* aspects of racism, locating its origins in the racist culture that was inherited from colonialism.

They also stress the need to split the proletariat so that they blame each other rather than the ruling class for their problems. There are three elements to the Marxist approach:

● culture,
● scapegoating,
● a threat.

Culture

In order to colonise foreign countries, the ruling class erected racist beliefs which allowed the British working class (who also formed the military) to see the colonised people as subhuman. Today whites inherited this culture. The difference between this approach and the Weberian is the deliberate erection of racist culture in the Marxist approaches in comparison with the Weberian culture of British superiority.

Scapegoating

The ethnic minorities are blamed for the problems created by capitalism eg inner-city crime, unemployment. The scapegoating is carried out primarily by the media but institutions such as schools contribute. The ethnic minorities lack the power to reject the cultural image in which they are portrayed.

A threat

Ethnic minorities were encouraged to come to Britain and Europe during the post-war boom. As the boom declined, the blacks and Asians formed a **reserve army of labour** which appeared as a threat to the working class, hence antagonism was strengthened.

5.4 THE REALITY OF RACISM

The reality of racism, then, is that British people of ethnic origin draw the short straw in terms of housing, relations with the police, employment, education and health.

HOUSING

People of Afro-Caribbean and Asian origins are more likely to live in houses built before 1945 than are the majority white population, and are twice as likely to live in terraced properties. 35% of Asians live in 'overcrowded' conditions, compared to 3% of the white population. In 1990 those of Afro-Caribbean origins were four times more likely to be renting from local authorities than those of Asian origins, and twice as likely as whites.

A wide range of studies funded by the Commission for Racial Equality based on Tower Hamlets, Edinburgh and Southwark has found that there is clear existence of discrimination by housing authorities against non-whites. This often includes being put in the 'worst' estates and being given the least desirable accommodation (such as high rise flats, for example).

POLICING

According to the Prison Reform Trust, the black imprisonment rate for England and Wales is 775 per 100,000 of the black population, compared to 98.2 per 100,000 of the population as a whole. The National Association for the Care and Resettlement of Offenders (NACRO) claims that black people are more likely than white people to be stopped and searched by the police, to be prosecuted and to receive a prison sentence.

In 1990 fewer than 1% of police officers in the UK were drawn from minority ethnic groups, and the highest ranking black police officer in Britain was a superintendent. This is the result not simply of a failure to recruit from the Afro-Caribbean and Asian communities, but of racist practices within police forces. For example, in 1989, 26 out of 35 black or Asian recruits to the Metropolitan Police left the force.

A study of the Metropolitan Police in the mid-1980s by the Policy Studies Institute, and another by Lord Gifford of the Merseyside Police in 1989, found that there was widespread racism at all levels within the police.

EMPLOYMENT

The PSI survey of 1984 shows that ethnic minorities are less likely than whites to get the better types of employment. This affects Afro-Caribbeans in particular. An exception is East African Asians.

Wage levels are significantly lower on average for ethnic minorities than for whites. However, it is also true that Asians of East African origin are particularly successful.

Table 5.1 shows the percentage of employees in managerial and professional occupations, differentiating between ethnic groups and gender.

Table 5.1 *Employees in managerial and professional occupations by ethnic origin and sex, 1987–9*

	Men	Women
White	35%	27%
All ethnic groups	34%	29%
West Indian/Guyanese	17%	31%
Pakistani/Bangladeshi	27%	23%
Indian	41%	Not available
All other origins	43%	30%

(*Source: Department of Employment, 1991*)

Unemployment rates are higher on average for all the ethnic minorities than for whites, see Table 5.2.

Table 5.2 *Economic status of people of working age: by gender and ethnic group, Spring 1995*

	White	Black[1]	Indian	Pakistani/ Bangladeshi	Other[2]	All ethnic groups[3]
Males						
Working full time	72	49	65	41	51	71
Working part time	5	8	7	8	8	5
Unemployed	8	21	10	18	12	9
Inactive	15	22	18	33	29	15
All (= 100%)(thousands)	16,993	273	306	216	224	18,017
Females						
Working full time	38	37	36	12	30	38
Working part time	29	15	19	6	16	28
Unemployed	5	14	7	7	8	5
Inactive	28	34	38	75	46	29
All (=100%)(thousands)	15,420	296	279	191	238	16,428

[1] Includes Caribbean, African and other Black people of non-mixed origin.
[2] Includes Chinese, other ethnic minority groups of non-mixed origin and people of mixed origin.
[3] Includes ethnic group not stated.

(*Source: Social Trends 26*, Table 4.3 (Labour Force Survey, ONS), p83)

EDUCATION

There are significant differences in educational attainment between ethnic minorities and whites, on average (see Fig. 5.4). However, it is also true that Asians of East African origin are particularly successful.

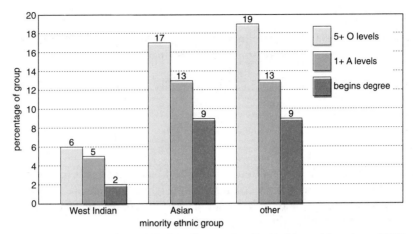

(*Source:* Statham et al, *The Education Factfile,* Hodder and Stoughton, 1989)

Fig. 5.4 Education attainment of different ethnic groups in Great Britain, 1981–2

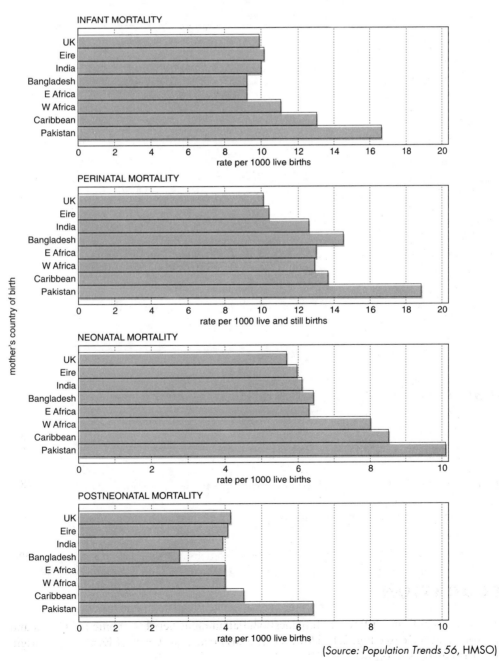

(*Source: Population Trends 56,* HMSO)

Fig. 5.5 Infant, perinatal, neonatal and postnatal mortality rates by mother's country of birth, 1982–5, England and Wales

HEALTH

Significantly higher levels of mental illness among people of Afro–Caribbean origins have been observed, and the suggested reason is that it is linked to awareness and experience of racism in daily life.

There are also much higher levels of infant mortality from mothers of ethnic minorities not born in the UK (see Fig. 5.5).

FAMILY

Table 5.3 shows the reasons for children of white and black families being taken into care. There appear to be quite clear differences, for example white children are a third more likely to be taken into care for parental neglect than black children. Yet black children are more likely to be taken into care for financial circumstances and for family relationships.

Table 5.3 *Reasons for children being taken into care, by 'race', in percentages*

Reason	Black	White	All
Family relationships	24	21	22
Financial/material circumstances	15	12	13
Parental neglect/inadequacy	21	33	27
Failure to thrive/medical health	1	6	3
Mother's mental health	11	5	8
Mother's ill-health	5	6	5
Homelessness/housing	11	11	11
Suspected child abuse	15	18	16
Child's behaviour	15	26	20
TOTAL	(294)	(270)	(564)

The total refers to overall numbers in care. Actual percentages do not add up to 100 because of the multiplicity of reasons that could be recorded.

It shows significant differences in the reasons given and that, overall, there are more black children in care than white ones.

Test yourself questions and answers

Questions

1 What Weberian-based models have been suggested to explain racial disharmony?

2 Outline the Marxist approaches to explain the causes of friction between different groups in society.

3 When we use the terms Black and Asian in what ways can we risk stereotyping?

4 When we discuss ethnic minorities it is usually taken to mean people of Indian, Pakistani or Afro-Caribbean origin. Which other significant groups live in the UK?

5 Explain the meaning of the term 'scapegoats'.

6 What significant differences emerge in the housing status of those of Afro-Caribbean origin compared to the white population?

7 According to table 5.1, which group have the highest percentage of managerial and professional jobs and which group the lowest? (Excluding category "all other origins").

Suggested answers

1 Weberian-based models of cultural differences, power differences and the struggle over scarce resources (eg housing) explain racial disharmony.

   Weber saw society composed of various groups, among them groups based on racial or religious differences, vying for social honour and economic advantage. Cultural differences occur because historically British (white) people had been brought up to perceive themselves as superior. An example of the competition between groups in society over scarce resources is Rex and Moore's study of housing conditions in inner Birmingham.

2 Marxist approaches locate conflict in the racist culture inherited from colonialism as well as the need to split the proletariat so that they blame each other rather than the ruling class for their problems.

3 There are a wide variety of groups within those 'categories', who have vastly different beliefs and backgrounds. For example 'Asians' can include Pakistanis, Bangladeshis, Indians (who come from widely differing parts of India, and those who came from Africa). There are also those who are born and raised in the UK. They also represent a range of religion.

4 Should include Jews, Irish, Poles, Ukrainians, Cypriots, Italians etc.

5 This is a group of people who are blamed for the social problems of a country. Usually they are the least powerful and very often they are in an ethnic minority. The most infamous example is the scapegoating and murder of millions of Jews by the Nazis.

6 More likely to live in council or 'social housing' and least likely to own their own homes. The quality of the homes they receive from local authorities appears to be worse than the average.

7 Lowest = West Indian/Guyanese males
   Highest = Indian

Illustrative question and answer

Question and suggested answer

Please note that the following question combines two elements of stratification – race and gender. Furthermore, the answers are combined with their separate question elements.

Item A

Women to take half of all jobs 'by 2000'

Women are expected to make up more than half Britain's work-force by the turn of the century, according to a survey by the influential Henley Centre. At present, women account for more than one in three jobs, but their changing role in society, together with the restructuring of the family, means that there will be more female employees than male by the year 2000. Three-quarters of all jobs created during the 1990s are expected to be filled by women. The proportion of women in full-time professional occupations or senior management will increase from its present 5 per cent.

The forecasting centre attributes the rise in female employment to the importance women now place on careers as well as the much larger numbers who delay having children or who return to work before their off-spring reach school age. Leading corporations, such as the High Street banks, are trying to make it easier for women to return to work after having children, and to encourage older women to work. "Pressure is on single-parent women to work to provide for their family. Furthermore, divorce and illegitimate births are also set to rise significantly, adding still further to the disruption of the traditional family base," the report says.

Source: Adapted from *The Guardian* August 1989

Item B

The extent to which an ethnic minority culture is absorbed into the majority culture can be presented in the form of a model as follows:

Extent of ethnic minority absorption into the majority culture:

Total absorption			No absorption
←			→
Assimilation	Integration	Pluralism	Separatism

Ethnic assimilation occurs when an ethnic group becomes fully absorbed into the majority culture. An example of assimilation is the case of the French Huguenots whose ancestors today appear to have little or no ethnic identity other than perhaps some memories of their forebears.

Ethnic integration occurs when an ethnic group retains its own identity and practices but also fully participates in the 'mainstream' life of a society. The Jews are a good example of a group which has adapted this way. Many continue to practise their characteristic religious and cultural rituals and behaviours whilst also working and socialising with non-Jews.

Ethnic pluralism occurs when an ethnic group retains a high degree of separate identity and lifestyle from the majority culture. Certain groups of Asian origin tend to fit this pattern. Thus, a large number of British-Bangladeshis – notably in the Tower Hamlets area of London – do not speak much English and participate relatively little in life outside their own families and ethnic community.

Total **ethnic separation** within a majority culture is virtually impossible (though it is sometimes put forward as a goal). In Britain, some Rastafarians argue that a return to Africa is the only way blacks will ever achieve social justice.

Source: Adapted from *Culture and Identity in Multi-ethnic Britain* in *Social Studies Review* Volume 5 No. 3 January 1990

Item C

A definition of underclass

Underclass: A term sometimes used for the poor who are also denied full participation in their societies. It may refer to employed workers who do the least desirable jobs and are also denied the basic legal, political and social rights of the rest of the labour force. Illegal migrant labourers are the most cited example, but the term is sometimes extended to cover all or most of those in the 'secondary sector' of a 'dual' labour market. Alternatively, it may refer to particular groups whose poverty derives from their non-employment: the long-term unemployed, single-parent families, the elderly. Membership of these is often ascriptive: black or brown skin, females, the elderly.

Source: Student Encyclopedia of Sociology, M. Mann (Macmillan)
AEB

(a) Give a reason why a 'total ethnic separation within a majority culture is virtually impossible' Item B   (1)

This would involve breaking away to form a separate state, as there is always some form of interaction in a society between groups, even if only for commercial or employment reasons.

(b) Using the information in Item B and elsewhere, assess sociological evidence concerning the extent to which ethnic minorities in Britain are absorbed into the majority culture. (8)

Note that this question is worth a full 8 marks and therefore it deserves an adequate discussion.

The extract in Item B actually gives a number of examples, and some reference should be made to this approach. However, you should go on to look at the extent to which Blacks and Asians suffer from discrimination in a wide range of commercial and cultural areas such as housing, employment, education, racial violence, politics etc. This information would challenge the models presented in the extract and would suggest that it is not a matter of the willingness of the immigrant ethnic groups to assimilate, but the willingness of the majority group to allow them integration or ethnic pluralism.

(c) Suggest *two* ways in which leading corporations might make it easier for women to return to work' (line 13) Item A. (2)

You should rely on your discussions in sociology classes and your general reading here. Examples could include: crèches or financial support for child rearing, changing the working hours/working year to fit with school attendance, regular retraining and updating sessions for female employees who leave work to have children.

(d) What implications does the information contained in Item A have for sociological views of the class structure? (6)

The issue here centres around the way that traditional perceptions of social class have been male based. There are two implications of this you should discuss

1   The reality of life for individuals where there is likely to be more women employed than men, and the income of women becomes a major factor in the standard of living of the household.

    The division might not be between middle and working classes, but between families with two or one income earner.

2   The awareness of social class by people. The majority of new jobs are white-collar and if women are employed in these there will be large numbers of cross-class marriages. The sense of class and clarity of divisions will change.

A separate set of issues surrounds the increase in male unemployment and the possible changing perceptions of gender which arise.

(e) Evaluate the usefulness of the concept of an 'underclass' (Item C) as a description of the position of *women* in the class structure. (8)

The item gives a clear framework for analysing the concept of the underclass and its application or otherwise to women.

You should point out that women are excluded from areas of social life which are regarded as normal for members of society, in particular they have worse

- economic status,
- social status
- political status.

You should provide evidence for all of these, by referring to the lower wages, and job opportunities for women; by noting that they receive lesser status than men, and that their role in society is dominated by 'caring concerns'; finally you should point out the lack of political representation women have, for example in Parliament, and the possibility that the economic and social status of women are lower because of this lack of power.

Do not forget to be critical of the concept by arguing that there are divisions between women on the grounds of race and class which may well prevent them sharing a common position.

Question bank

With reference to relevant research, demonstrate how ethnicity affects the life chances of individuals.

NEAB

Points

You cannot waffle on this one, I'm afraid. It requires you to provide evidence for the differing life chances of individuals. You should know statistics or research studies on education, housing, health, criminal justice, employment and unemployment. These can be found throughout this book.

You should then offer explanations based on Weberian concepts of status groups and closure, on Marxism, on dual labour market theory and on straight racism.

STRATIFICATION: AGE

Units in this chapter

Chapter objectives

In this chapter we examine childhood, youth, old age and death. We note that the first three categories are social constructions more than they are biological realities.

In the section on childhood we explore the demography of childhood, the variations across time and cultures in the nature of childhood, and the different theories explaining the social construction of childhood.

In the second section on culture the emergence of youth as a specific period of life is examined and the competing explanations from Marxists and functionalists are compared and evaluated. The functions for society or capitalism are then discussed. We take an example of one particular subcultural study of youth to show how these debates can help us to understand the nature and style of particular youth cultures. We examine gender and youth as a very distinct experience for females and males. Finally, we look briefly at the relationship between age and race.

Old age is traditionally viewed as a negative period in people's lives and we try to unravel the differences between the biological and the social effects of ageing. We start by looking at the demography of ageing and move on to look at the quality of the lives of older people. We then examine the stigma faced by elderly people and try to understand why there is a lack of integration of older people in our society.

The final section considers why death is no longer viewed as a part of everyday life. It also examines the processes of dying and looks at the role of professionals in helping people to negotiate death.

6.1   CHILDHOOD

DEMOGRAPHY OF CHILDHOOD

There have been very significant changes over the last 30 years in the numbers of children and the style of family life. The changes in fertility, cohabitation and divorce have all changed the nature of childhood in Britain.

The fertility rate has been stable since 1977, although there may be some increase in the number of births in the late 1990s as a result of the 'baby-boom' which occurred in the 1960s.

The decline in marriage and the increase in cohabitation has been associated with a rapid increase in births outside marriage. In 1991, 44% of all conceptions occurred outside marriage, and more than 30% of these ended in abortion. More than half of the conceptions outside marriage appear to be to cohabiting couples. Over 2.2 million children now live in single-parent families, with 90% of them headed by a woman.

However, for the majority of children, being in a lone-parent family is just a temporary situation as over half of divorced women and three-quarters of divorced men remarry within five years. The result of this is that by 2000, 2.5 million children and young people will be growing up in some form of step-family.

VARIATIONS IN CHILDHOOD

According to Prout and James (*Constructing and Reconstructing Childhood*), childhood is best viewed as a social phenomenon which has been constructed by social forces. It is not simply a period of biological immaturity.

The way that childhood is experienced is varied for different social groups. The childhood of a white working-class boy, for example, may be not at all the same as that of an Asian-origin, middle-class girl. Differences in lifestyles as a result of social class and race are discussed in Chapter 3: Stratification: Social Class and Mobility, and Chapter 5: Race, Ethnicity and Nationalism.

One simple example of the variations in the experience of childhood today is the difference in family incomes, differences which cross boundaries of race, class and gender. In 1990, 22% of all children were living in poverty – if that is measured as being in families on or below income support level. If the poverty line is shifted to represent 140% of income support, then the total rises to 30% of all children, numbering approximately 3,750,000.

Childhood varies across cultures and history, and our expectations of what is natural in childhood and parenthood have been challenged by numerous studies. Malinowski, in his study of the Trobriand Islands in the early part of the 20th century, shows how distinctly different the lives of Trobriand Island young people were from those in the West. They were much freer, were openly engaged in sexual activity and were not regarded as being subservient to their parents. Turnbull (*The Mountain People*) shows how groups of children, abandoned by their parents, and aged only three to five, were able to survive. In contemporary Brazil and Peru, gangs of street children survive by street trading, theft and other marginal activities. As a result of their perceived threat to adults in the larger cities, groups of vigilantes, reputed to be off-duty police officers, have murdered significant numbers of them.

THE EMERGENCE OF CHILDHOOD

Moral entrepreneurs

Aries (*Centuries of Childhood*) argues that in medieval society the concept of childhood did not exist, and that as soon as the child was no longer an infant (in terms of being totally reliant upon maturer people) then he/she was regarded as equivalent to our concept of an adult. Aries argues that children were included in all types of social activity including sex, fighting and work. He claims that from the 15th century onwards the integration of children into adult life came under criticism from religious theorists and educators, who claimed that there was something 'special' about young people and that they should be treated differently from adults. Children, it was claimed, were 'fragile creatures of God' who needed to be both safeguarded and (re)formed from their natural state of 'original sin'. As the concept of childhood developed so did new ideas of what constituted the 'family' and what were appropriate family relationships. Aries claims that such things as the privacy and the separation of family members began to develop at this time.

The motivation behind the move towards the **construction of childhood** comes from the activities of what is described as **moral entrepreneurs**, that is groups of powerful people who were able to create a situation of change.

Functionalist views

Musgrove (*Youth and the Social Order*) stresses that the nature of childhood alters with the economic usefulness of children. In areas where they are of great economic use, the idea of children as naive and gentle creatures is underplayed. Thus in peasant societies where they are of use working on the land, and in societies in the early periods of industrialisation, the concept of childhood, as we know it, was not present. On the other hand, when children are of little economic use, such as in the UK at the time when compulsory schooling was introduced and laws were passed forbidding child labour, then the nature of childhood changed. As children were no longer economically important the numbers being born declined and, at the same time, they began to be seen as weak and dependent.

Related to this is the fact that modern industrial societies are extremely complex and require members to undergo a long period of socialisation and skilling. The period of childhood was therefore extended to allow for this. This period of prolonged education allows young people to be graded by skill and allocated an appropriate position in the occupational structure.

There are very close parallels to be drawn on the emergence of childhood with the changes in the status of women in the 1830–1950s. This led Firestone (*The Dialectic of Sex*) to argue that women and children shared oppression.

Marxist views

In many ways, the Marxist views reflect those of the functionalists in stressing the importance of the economic structure in altering the position of the child in society.

Here the argument is that as children were no longer needed in the workforce, and as the nature of tasks grew more complex, it was in the interests of capitalism to draw the children away from being exploited in factories so that they could acquire the necessary attitudes and skills which would allow them to become the workforce of the next generation.

Marxists have pointed out that the modern patriarchal family which emerged in the 19th century was a particularly useful way of helping younger people survive and be socialised. The family provided shelter, food, clothing and basic care entirely at the expense of the other family members. The single male wage was used to do this, and the ideology of the **responsibility of parents** ensured that they could make sacrifices to ensure that the children survived. As education was funded by the State which obtained the money by taxes paid by the working class, the result was a system of training and rearing the next generation of workers that cost little to the employers.

6.2   YOUTH CULTURE

FUNCTIONALIST VIEWS

The origins of youth culture

Youth culture developed after World War II. It was directly related to:

- the growing affluence of the young, who had cash to spend on 'consumables';
- the development of the mass media, including radio, hi-fi, records and specialist magazines;
- the extension of education so that large numbers of 'youth' were placed together and 'isolated' from adults;
- the manipulation of youth by commercial interests, who wished to make a profit from the youth market (clothes, records etc).

The functions of youth culture

All societies need to ensure order and continuity through sharing central values. Without agreed values and ways of behaving, societies would collapse.

In 'simple', pre-industrial societies, there is usually only one set of values which is easily learned in childhood from adults. When the child has learned the skills and values needed to become a fully contributing member of society, he/she undergoes a ceremony which unambiguously marks their entry into adulthood. This ceremony is known as a **rite of passage**.

In complex, advanced, industrial societies, there is a variety of different values and the process of socialisation is much more complex than that in simple societies. According to Parsons and Eisenstadt, for example, the values of the family which stress affection, equality etc clash with the adult world where the work ethos of individualism and competition dominate. In these societies, the shift into adulthood is much more complex, with a considerable number of stages. There is no clear, unambiguous rite of passage.

Youth culture developed, according to Eisenstadt, to perform the task of aiding the transition from childhood (and its associated values) to adulthood (and its values). It does this by helping youth to break away from the family by providing an alternative set of standards, both in clothes and values. Furthermore, the youth culture provides emotional security in a difficult period of transition, as youths feel they belong to a particular culture. They know they belong because they have the appropriate clothes and like the currently popular music: entry to the youth culture is simple. The result is that youth can move out of the family, prepare for the adult role and be provided with a sense of security and belonging.

The content of youth culture

For functionalists, the content of youth culture – that is the concept of a youth style – is unimportant, as style has no particular meaning. As long as youth culture is expressed by clothes and music that are different from the parents' culture, then youth culture is performing its function.

Criticism of the functionalist approach

The main problem is that it ignores the variety of styles of youth culture – why, after all, do so many different types of youth subculture exist side by side?

MARXIST-BASED EXPLANATIONS

The nature of capitalism

In capitalist society, the small ruling class, comprising the owners of the major industrial and commercial institutions, oppress and exploit the majority of the population. Control of the population is maintained in a number of ways, but the main method is through control of the values and beliefs of society – persuading people that the way society and the economic system are organised is 'natural' and the best way possible. In sociological language this control of values is known as **hegemony**.

Youth culture and the nature of capitalism

Most people accept the dominant values of capitalism and are further tied to it by economic and social pressures, such as their job, mortgage and family commitments. However, young people have few, if any, of these commitments; they are therefore more able to express their resentment and opposition to capitalism. The form that their opposition takes is not necessarily political, but is instead through youth (sub)cultures, which express, in a complex, often hidden way, their rejection of the system which provides most working-class youth with a bleak future (dead-end jobs, low-pay routine).

The nature of youth culture

Youth cultures provide working-class youths with solutions to their bleak future and a means of opposing the system that oppresses them. However, the solution they have adopted (youth culture) does not really solve their problems: it merely gives them the illusion of doing so. In this sense, according to Brake (*The Sociology of Youth Culture and Youth Subcultures*), youth culture is 'magical'.

The essence of the Marxist approach is that, although working-class youth is rebelling against capitalist society, they may not be fully aware that this is the real cause of their problems. Their rebellion is *inarticulate*, in the sense that they are aware of oppression and they seek to express this, but having no *political* awareness, they show their resistance through the styles of clothes they wear, the music they listen to etc. It is the task of the sociologist to unravel the content (or 'style') of the youth culture and to explain the hidden meanings. The study of signs is known as **semiology**.

An example of the Marxist subcultural approach

One of the earliest studies using this form of analysis was that of Phil Cohen, who analysed youth in east London in the early 1970s. Cohen suggested that the only way to understand the meaning of youth cultures was to examine them in:

- their immediate context and
- the wider context.

1. **The immediate context** Cohen argued that during the 1960s the fabric of east London society had been ripped apart as a result of redevelopment, the loss of jobs in the dockyards and the decline of the extended family. Large numbers of people had been moved out into new towns, or if they remained they were likely to live in high-rise apartments. Partly as a result of this, the close-knit street life was lost. The price of property in the East End rose as developers began to realise the potential of an area so close to the centre of London. Small workshops and businesses were driven out as rents and rates rose.

   The economy of the traditional East End had been based on the docks and the closeness of housing to employment had helped to create the feeling of belonging and community. After the decline of the docks in the 1960s both the economic structure and one of the props of the community were destroyed.

   Partly as a result of the other two factors, the working class extended family also declined. This had consisted of a network of family members who provided each other with mutual support. Youth in the 1960s, therefore had grown up without the traditional East End community to support them.

2. **The wider context** The 1960s came as the benefits of greater affluence had percolated through to large sections of the population. Ownership of houses and consumer goods had risen sharply over the previous decade and a whole new ideology of affluence had begun to develop. This ran alongside the continuing existence of poverty and deprivation in inner-city areas.

Youth cultures developed, according to Cohen, to cope with the loss of community; they also reflected the divisions in the wider society. Cohen suggests that two different responses occurred among youth:

1. One element adjusted its sights and aspired to the new ideology of affluence – the mods. Their style was to show that they had money and knew how to spend it, on such things as mohair suits and Lambretta scooters.

2. The other looked back to the more traditional working-class community and through their clothes and actions adopted the short hair, the DMs, braces and tunic shirts of traditional working-class men. These were the skinheads. By dressing this way, they were 'magically' saving the community of east London.

Fig. 6.1 illustrates how the twin 'pulls' of the new affluence and the traditional community values produced a variety of youth subcultural styles.

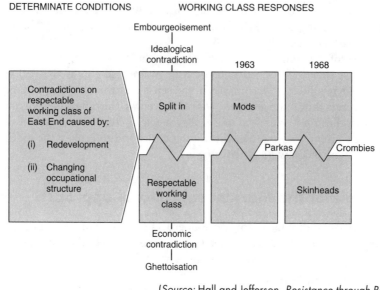

DETERMINATE CONDITIONS   WORKING CLASS RESPONSES

Embourgeoisement

Idealogical
contradiction   1963   1968

Contradictions on
respectable
working class of   Split in   Mods
East End caused by:

(i) Redevelopment   Parkas   Crombies

(ii) Changing
     occupational   Respectable   Skinheads
     structure   working
                                  class

Economic
contradiction

Ghettoisation

(*Source*: Hall and Jefferson, *Resistance through Rituals*, 1977;
reprinted in Moore, *Investigating Crime and Deviance*, 1996)

Fig. 6.1 The production of a variety of youth subcultural styles

Criticisms of Marxist approaches

Marxist approaches have been criticised because they emphasise social class to the exclusion of other relevant factors, such as race and gender.

The semiological approach has been criticised for the fact that the way Marxists make sense of the signs is biased in that it arrives at a definition which supports their contention that subcultures are forms of resistance. Cohen has pointed out that other interpretations can be made that would not support a **'resistance' approach**. How, therefore, can one interpretation be proved as more accurate than another?

GENDER AND YOUTH CULTURE

Youth culture studies have traditionally focused almost exclusively on males. Lees' (*Losing Out*) writes that females have largely been considered **marginal**. According to Lees, the fact that sociologists have ignored females is simply a typical example of the way that females are **invisible** in society generally. Male sociologists simply overlooked them and took for granted their subordinate position on the edges of youth cultures. According to Heidensohn (*Women and Crime*), male sociologists argue that girls were not available for research on the streets as boys were. Heidensohn claims that the real reason girls were ignored was that sociology as a subject area has been dominated by males who have focused on *male* concerns.

The male model is inappropriate for females because they are socialised differently into a subordinate role. They experience the world in a different way because of this and have developed very different means from boys of solving their problems through a different form of youth culture.

Research on female youth culture

Griffin (*Typical Girls?*) studied a group of white working-class girls at school and then at work, over a three-year period. This was backed up with 180 interviews with a wide variety of schoolgirls. She set out to see if Willis' model of male youth behaviour was appropriate for females (see p 197). It is *not* she concludes. She gives four reasons for this:

❶ She found no evidence of gangs of girls hanging around together – friendships were usually between two girls, for example.

2 Deviance for the lads was based on toughness, for girls it was defined through sexual activity.

3 For Willis there was a clear division between the working and middle classes in their attitude to the job market; for the girls in Griffin's study, there was no such clear division.

4 No clear division emerged between pro- and anti-school groups, such as the 'lads' and the 'ear 'oles' distinguished by Willis.

Lees studied three schools over a two-year period, interviewing 15–16-year-old girls in friendship groups at school, using open, non-directed discussion. Lees sees that girls' experience of youth is totally dominated by the concept of sexuality. Behaviour at school was strongly influenced by the concept of the 'slag' – a girl who has slept with a number of boys. Girls did not want to be known as this, but nor did they want the label of 'tight bitch' (a virgin, not interested in sex). The result was a control of their own behaviour to conform to the expected role of a girl. Lees also saw that girls viewed their lives in terms of the inevitability of marriage and child-raising – but did not look forward to the prospect with joy. They thought that an important aim of their lives was to delay marriage for a number of years.

McRobbie and Garber (*Girls and Subcultures*) studied girls in one school who lived on a single council estate. They argue that parental control and gender attitudes that effectively prohibit females from hanging around street corners, create a 'bedroom culture'. Girls go round to each others' houses to stay in listening to music, dancing and chatting. But the culture exists in private – at home, which is regarded as the appropriate place for females in our society.

RACE AND YOUTH CULTURE

There has been relatively little work on ethnic minority youth cultures, and the work done on Asian and Afro-Caribbean male youths has used the Marxist conflict perspective.

Black youths, for example, express their resistance by adopting and adapting Rastafarian beliefs and styles. The original Rastafarians believed that the human body is of little importance compared to spiritual development and therefore they left their hair to grow – thus developing locks. This symbol of Rastafarianism provided a distinctive look for young blacks anxious to have a style which could be said to be their own. The colours of green and gold which are worn by Rastas are the national colours of Ethiopia, the promised land of the original Rastafarians.

This approach has been criticised, however, for focusing on the few deviant subcultures of black and Asian youth. Pryce (*Endless Pressure*) shows in his study of Afro-Caribbeans in Bristol that there is a wide variety of responses to being black in a white, racist society. They range from the illegal to the most highly conformist.

6.3   OLD AGE

DEMOGRAPHY OF OLD AGE

The most noticeable trend of demography is the ageing of the population (see Table 6.1). In 1850, less than 5% of the population was aged over 65, by the year 2000 the proportion will be 15%, and 20 years later it will have jumped to nearly 20%. The main long-term factor leading to the rise in the numbers of the elderly has been the increasing expectation of life. This has resulted from higher living standards, better nutrition and warm homes. Women have longer expectations of life than men and by the age of 85 they outnumber men by 400%.

Table 6.1 *The growth in the number of over 65s in the UK population*

	Numbers (millions)		% of total population	
	Aged 65–79	Aged 80+	Over 65	Over 80
1901	1.3 (65–74)	0.5 (75+)	4.7	1.3 (75+)
1921	1.9 (65–74)	0.7 (75+)	5.9	1.5 (75+)
1951	4.8	0.7	10.9	1.4
1971	6.1	1.3	13.4	2.3
1981	6.9	1.6	15.0	2.8
1989	6.9	2.0	15.6	3.5
Males	3.0	0.6	6.3	1.1
Females	3.9	1.4	9.3	2.4
Projected 2001	6.7	2.5	16.0	3.8

HOUSEHOLD STRUCTURE

Today, 77% of older people live with their partner, their family or very near their family. This contradicts the image of older people as being largely lonely and lacking care or attention. There are gender differences, however, as only 20% of women aged 75 are still married, compared with 66% of males. About 5% of older people live in institutions such as EPHs (elderly persons' homes), but the older the people the greater is the likelihood that they will be in care.

STANDARDS OF LIVING

Older people form the second largest group in poverty in the UK, and almost 60% of older people have an income below the poverty line. Poverty in old age is a direct reflection of poor pension levels.

GENDER, RACE, CLASS AND THE QUALITY OF LIFE

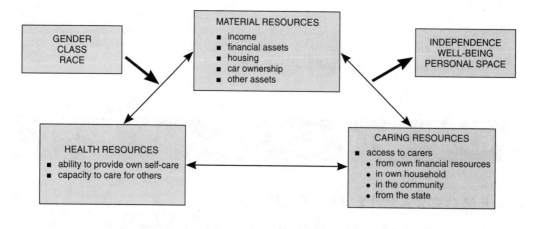

Fig. 6.2 Three key resources influencing independence and dependence

Fig. 6.2 shows that the quality of life when a person is old varies according to a number of factors, and that old age is not one (primarily biological) condition, but a number of states.

SOCIAL LIFE AND OLDER PEOPLE

Two explanations have been offered as to why older people have limited social lives:

- disengagement,
- exclusion.

Disengagement

This approach stresses the voluntary withdrawal, or **disengagement**, of people from social life, as they make active choices to stay at home and not to entertain. This is seen as part of the lifecycle. Writers, such as Erickson (*Childhood and Society*), suggest that there are stages through which people typically move. Each stage is associated with particular work patterns, family relationships and attitudes. Erickson suggests that the attitudes most favourably associated with 'the ageing years' are 'a sense of fulfilment and satisfaction with one's life' and 'a willingness to face death'.

Exclusion

This approach stresses the fact that older people are excluded from a whole range of activities, such as employment, entertainment and sport and, just as importantly, that they are excluded by social attitudes and arrangements.

As people age, factors such as poverty, ill-health or frailty and the attitudes of younger people all conspire to lead to their loss of significant roles (and therefore identity), and their difficulty in maintaining independence and control. Entry to old age is a rite of passage which is not valued and leads to a significant loss of prestige because it is a move from the role of an employed citizen to that of 'pensioner'.

LABELLING, STIGMA AND OLD AGE

Old age is a stigmatised identity for most people, and is regarded as having very few positive characteristics. According to Lehr (*Stereotyping of Age, and Age Norms*), the aged are perceived as ill, 'retarded', tired, slow and inefficient in their thinking, and are regarded as having no sexual interest, unless they are odd or perverted.

The majority of older people reject labelling themselves as old and commonly understand that while other people see them as looking old they themselves know that 'inside' they are still young.

However, the combined loss of role and identity can lead some people to accept the label of being old because they lose their self-confidence and begin to take on the characteristics (such as indecision) that others ascribe to them. Harris (*Sociology of Ageing*) calls this a **negative feedback loop** see Fig. 6.3.

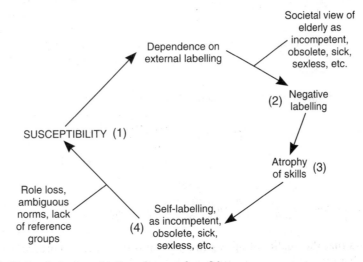

Fig. 6.3 Labelling and the loss of independence and confidence

6.4 DEATH AND DYING

Throughout history death was regarded as a fact of everyday life – the idea of old age was unthinkable for the vast majority of people. A person born into a working class or agricultural family up to the mid-19th century was more likely to die before the age of 16 than to survive, for example. But once childhood had been survived, accidents, disease and malnutrition all combined to wipe out significant proportions of the population of all ages. Death was not always natural, as *infanticide* was a common practice if too many children were born, or they were of the 'wrong' sex. Older people too were abandoned, neglected and even killed when they were not able to be productive economically. This practice is known as *geronticide*.

Towards the end of the 19th century, higher standards of living, better housing and, to a much lesser extent, medical advances began to increase the chances of survival into old age. This process, fuelled by the same three factors has continued right until the present day, creating the demographic structure we saw earlier. Whereas death was seen as a normal part of life for all people 150 years ago, death today is associated with the old.

THE REMOVAL OF DEATH FROM SOCIETY

Cultural removal

Historically, religious beliefs linked life and death together. Most societies promoted the belief that death was merely the move from one form of life to another. The decline in religion and the association between old age, infirmity and death have culturally isolated death from the rest of life.

Physical removal

The majority of people reading this book will never have seen a death. For someone 100 years ago, this would be unimaginable. Death was everywhere, and people tended to die at home. Contemporary society has transformed death into a medical issue. Death occurs when medicine fails. This 'failure' takes place in hospitals or nursing homes where paid carers or medical staff attend the dying person. Thus death has become isolated physically from everyday life.

THE PROCESS OF DYING

Kubler-Ross (*On Death and Dying*) suggests that death for those who are not the very elderly in western cultures involves five stages:

1. **Denial** – the person simply does not wish to accept that it is going to happen to him or her and usually he or she avoids contact with anything that suggests the certainty of his or her death.

2. **Anger** – the person begins to accept death but asks the question 'Why me?'. The person feels that it is unjust and unfair when others continue to live.

3. **Negotiation** – here the person thinks that maybe death is not inevitable and a 'deal' can be struck with God to allow life to continue.

4. **Resignation** – a period of depression after realisation that it is going to happen.

5. **Acceptance** – this is the final stage where the dying person accepts the situation, but sets out to use the remaining time constructively – perhaps organising his or her farewell with the family, for example. A similar process is said to occur with bereavement. Those who are left behind may at first deny and only after a significant period can they actually come to accept the death of a loved one.

However, Lund (*Older Bereaved Spouses*) and others have criticised this linear view of death, suggesting that there are a wide variety of responses to death, including those who initially seem to accept death and only later have feelings of anger and even denial.

NEGOTIATING DEATH: THE ROLE OF PROFESSIONALS

When people die in hospitals or hospices, they are almost always cared for by professionals. These individuals experience death so often that they develop routines which allow them to cope with the stress of such occasions. They do this by developing routines. Glaser and Strauss have suggested that there is a 'dying trajectory'. This is the prediction made informally by staff of the length of time that the person has to live, and on the basis of this how best to act. This guides staff on how to act towards the person and the relatives. It also dictates the amount of and quality care to be given.

For those who are labelled as certain deaths about which nothing can be done, social death actually precedes physical death. In Sudnow's study of two US hospitals, the dying patient may no longer be given medical treatment, personal belongings may be taken away and relatives may be prepared. Indeed, on one occasion, a nurse was seen closing the eyes of the patient before she was dead, as it is more difficult to do this after death. This trajectory is not automatic however, and there are factors influencing how the professionals behave. For example, younger people are more likely to be treated as 'alive' longer than older patients.

Test yourself questions and answers

Questions

1 Why do sociologists argue that age is a social rather than solely a biological concept?

2 What explanations are there for the emergence of childhood?

3 What do we mean by youth culture?

4 Outline the factors which led to the development of youth culture.

5 Briefly outline the differing explanations for the content or 'style' of youth cultures.

6 In what ways can we see old age as a stigmatised period?

Suggested answers

1 Age is related to expected patterns of behaviour and to different levels of social status. The differences are not the same across societies and history, although the biological process of ageing is similar across them.

2 There are a number of competing explanations including that provided by
   - Aries,
   - Marxists and
   - functionalists.

   Aries has argued that the concept of childhood emerged as a result of a change of attitude in the 17th century onward to a belief that children could be moulded into moral adults. Certain forms of behaviour (including sexual activity) became seen as inappropriate for children. Children were distanced from adult life and concerns and also became powerless. Various cultural influences have affected their treatment since then.

Marxists see childhood emerging with changes in the economy so that it is a period in which young people are trained in the skills and values necessary to become the next generation of workers.

Functionalists also see childhood emerging as a period of socialisation and skill training. Unlike Marxists, however they also see it as being beneficial to both the children and society.

3 Youth culture is a distinctive set of attitudes and behaviour patterns associated with an age group between childhood and adulthood, generally accepted to be 15–20. However, it is important to remember that there are a number of different youth cultures existing at any one time reflecting differences in the wider culture, social class, gender and race, among other influences.

4 Youth culture emerged in the 20th century in response to the lengthening of the non-productive early period of a person's life and the extension of schooling. It is also linked to the development of the mass media which targetted the emerging youth market.

5 There are a number of different explanations for the style of youth cultures:
   ● Functionalist writers have little problem explaining it as, for them, the style has no specific meaning – it is merely a way to distinguish the youth from the adults.
   ● However, Barthes suggests that youth attach meaning to the symbols they adopt from the wider society, and then subvert these symbols into a meaningful reality.
   ● Brake also claims that working-class youth cultures are an attempt to work out the problems facing youth, even though the attempts are doomed to failure.
   ● Writers, such as McRobbie, have suggested that female youth undergo a very different experience from males, and this reflects the greater range and standards of controls on females in society.
   ● The work of Pryce on black youth in Bristol emphasises the range of ways in which they respond to the particular circumstances of being young and black. He argues that there will be a number of 'responses' not just one.

6 Old age is a stigmatised period because older people tend to have much lower status in UK society, lower incomes and less power, and tend to be regarded as of limited usefulness to society. However, the low level of income and power is not the same for all groups of older people, and the divisions created by social class remain into old age.

Illustrative question and answer

Question

'Youth subcultures are noted more for their differences than for any underlying unity between them'. Discuss.

AEB

Suggested answer

You should begin by delineating the various approaches to youth culture in particular distinguishing between Marxist and functionalist approaches, and of course the divisions within them.

The functionalist approaches stress the problem solving function of youth culture and see it emerging in response to rapid social change. The Marxist approaches also see it as problem-solving, but solving the problems of capitalism. The main point you ought to make and explain is that the meanings of the content of youth cultures are viewed diametrically by functionalists and Marxists.

Finish your essay by discussing the omission of gender and race. Point out too the stress upon working class youth cultures. You should make it very clear that you think there are a number of youth cultures at any one time.

Question bank

1 'The notion of a unified youth culture is a sociological misconception.' Explain and discuss.

London Examinations

Points

You should point out that the claim for a unified youth culture comes primarily from the functionalists. You should then criticise this on the grounds of social class, gender and race. You should also demonstrate the differences between the contents and symbols adopted by the differing youth cultures as a response to their situations.

2 Why do youth sub-cultures develop?

London Examinations

Points

This requires you to discuss first of all the nature of youth subcultures, and then to look at the origins which are suggested by the explanations.

The functionalists point to the importance of rites of passage in traditional societies and how these have disappeared in modern societies. They argue that the origins of youth sub-cultures came about through the need to move from childhood to adulthood and to have a period of adjustment. They tend to stress the intervention of the mass media in the 1950s.

More radical approaches see working class youth cultures as developing specifically to help solve the problems of the working class in a 'magical' fashion which presents an apparent solution but ultimately not a true one. The origins can be traced back to capitalist society.

CHAPTER 7

WORK, UNEMPLOYMENT AND LEISURE

Units in this chapter

Chapter objectives

This chapter explores the way in which people experience their employment, their state of unemployment and their leisure. In order to do this, it looks at the changing nature of the economy and the influence that this has on social life.

The chapter begins with a description and explanation of the changes that have occurred in the occupational structure, showing how the sorts of job available have changed over time.

This is followed by an analysis of the contemporary debate over the move towards what has been called **post-Fordism**. By this we mean the shift from the style of work which requires (usually male) workers to labour on production lines for a working life, to a style that means far less security of labour, greater employment of women (in relatively poor conditions) and often in small-scale work groups. This dramatic change in the patterns of work and employment may be having equally dramatic effects on gender relations and social class structures.

The second section considers de-industrialism and post-industrialism, Japanisation and McDonaldisation and their implications. The next section discusses ownership and control of the economy, and the changes that have taken place over this century. For, although employment patterns may be changing and so too may work practices, the ownership of industry appears to be concentrated in few hands.

The fifth section deals with the experiences of people in work and the levels of satisfaction they gain from their jobs. We also examine theoretical explanations for the variations in job satisfaction and the different kinds of industrial action that are possible.

The next part of the chapter looks at the place of the professions in commerce and industry, and examines the reasons for the growth of the professions and the impact they may have on work.

However, increasingly large numbers of people are experiencing unemployment rather than employment as the major factor affecting the quality of their lives. We therefore look at the extent of unemployment, who is more likely to become unemployed and the impact that unemployment has on people's lives.

The final section examines issues surrounding the changing nature of leisure.

7.1 THE CHANGING OCCUPATIONAL STRUCTURE

THE THREE SECTORS OF THE ECONOMY

Employment in Britain occurs within three distinct areas or sectors. All employment takes place within these:

1. **Primary (extractive)** Employment is in extracting natural products from the land or sea, eg agriculture, mining and fishing.

2. **Secondary (manufacturing)** This includes the entire range of industries which manufacture some article.

3. **Tertiary (service industries)** This includes all non-manufacturing activities, such as insurance, banking, retailing etc.

THE CHANGING NATURE OF THE OCCUPATIONAL STRUCTURE

Historically, industrialisation brought a move away from agriculture towards manufacturing. However, some extractive industries, such as coal mining, boomed. The 150 years from the beginning of the 19th century to the middle of the 20th saw the vast majority of the population employed in the secondary sector as Britain was one of the countries dominating world manufacturing.

Since 1950, and at an increasingly fast pace, there has been a move towards the tertiary sector (see Fig. 7.1). Indeed, more people are now employed in this than in manufacturing. Agriculture has shrunk to a tiny proportion of the workforce, accounting for only 2% of employment. This has led some commentators, such as Daniel Bell, to refer to Britain (and the USA) as being in a **post-industrial society**. Certainly, there is no doubt that Britain is de-industrialising, if we mean by that a decline in manufacturing industry. In 1966 there were approximately 8 million people employed in manufacturing and today the figure is less than 5 million. A simple example of the change in the status of manufacturing in Britain is that today Britain imports more manufactured goods than it sells.

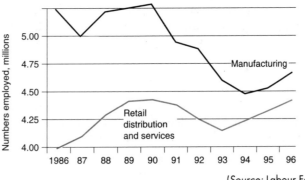

(*Source:* Labour Force Survey, ONS)

Fig. 7.1 The changing nature of the occupational structure

Changes in occupations

Since the beginning of the 1970s, the major changes in the nature of employment are that:

1. Manual work has declined, in line with the decline in manufacturing. Overall, manual workers now form less than half those in employment, although there are differences between the sexes. Today, approximately 56% of men and 36% of women are employed in manual work.

2 Non-manual work has, in comparison, expanded rapidly. Since 1950, the number of clerical workers has increased fourfold.

3 There has been a similar expansion in the numbers of people defined as managers and administrators.

4 The most rapidly expanding occupational group since 1950 has been that defined as 'professional', seeing a fivefold increase.

5 The self-employed account for approximately 8% of the working population.

Full-time and part-time employment

The changes in the sectors of the economy have been closely related to the changes in the hours and conditions of employment. Full-time employment has decreased since the 1960s, and this process has speeded up since 1980. Since 1960, more than 4 million full-time jobs have disappeared in Britain. The full-time jobs that have been lost are those traditionally regarded as 'male', and generally concentrated in the older, heavy manufacturing industries. Part-time employment has increased dramatically. Today there are more than 5 million people in part-time employment, of whom 90% are female. Most of this increase in part-time employment has been in the service sector. Today, 23% of all employment is part-time.

Unemployment

Long-term unemployment developed in Britain in the 1970s and intensified greatly in the 1980s. This was the result partly of government policy and partly of the changes in economic sectors. Unemployment does not hit all groups equally: unskilled manual workers, particularly in the traditional heavy industries have the highest rates of unemployment. Also, the ethnic minorities have significantly higher levels of unemployment than do whites. Official statistics show that male unemployment rates are higher than those for females – but this is possibly the result of obstacles to married women registering as officially unemployed, for example.

Class structure and class consciousness

One of the consequences of the changes in the nature and types of people's jobs has been the effect on social class and people's perception of their class. The enormous growth in the non-manual occupations, and in particular the growth in the 'professions', has meant that the middle class has now grown at the expense of the working class. The reality of employment in routine clerical work may be one of boring, low paid labour, but the perception of it is of middle-class work.

Politics

One of the reasons for the Conservative Party's dominance of politics in the 1980s has been its ability to capture the vote of the new 'middle class' whilst appealing to the affluent sections of the working class. The weakness of the Labour Party has been that its traditional base of male, manual workers in heavy industry has largely disappeared at least as an electoral force.

CAUSES OF CHANGE IN THE SECTORS OF THE ECONOMY

Restructuring of the economy

There has been a major restructuring of the British economy since 1950. This has been due to:

1. **The growth of a world economy**, in which Britain has had to compete increasingly against newer industrialised nations. In itself, this may not have caused great change in manufacturing; however it can be linked with the growth of multi-nationals.

2. **Multi-national companies** now dominating the world economy. These companies (such as Ford, Mitsubishi etc) search out the cheapest places where production can take place, and therefore have a tremendous advantage over companies that are located in higher wage economies. In the past this has often led to the multi-nationals producing in Third World countries (even though the profits flow back to the owners in the First World). However, as Britain is now a low-wage economy and presents a cheap production site for companies (such as Nissan cars) who wish to produce in the EU, this flow out of Britain of manufacturing jobs may be slowed down.

3. **The development of new technology** was initially perceived by writers on the deindustrialisation thesis as a way to eliminate the boring jobs and free workers for the more interesting and rewarding ones. This does not generally appear to be the case. The introduction of computer-aided machines and robotics has generally replaced workers rather than enhanced their jobs. So the numbers in manufacturing jobs have declined.

State intervention

Although, throughout the 1980s the Conservative government was dedicated to cutting back the State and spending on the public sector, the role of the State in the economy and in employment has remained very influential. Approximately 25% of all employment is State-related, as there has been massive growth in health and social welfare provision. Indeed, the growth of the professions in the post-war years has been primarily as a result of the expansion of the State.

FORDISM AND POST-FORDISM

In contrast to Braverman's thesis in *Labor and Monopoly Capitalism* that there is an ever-increasing tendency to move towards specialisation and deskilling, for which the term **Fordism** has increasingly been used, there is a group of writers who claim that in manufacturing industry there has been a gradual emergence of flexible production methods, which has been described as **post-Fordism**. There are four elements to this:

1. **Technology**: the use of computerised control of manufacture and computer-aided design robots to undertake particularly repetitive or tedious work.

2. **Products**: the ability to use robotics and high technology to produce small numbers of different designs as opposed to the mass manufacture of identical items.

3. **Jobs**: the need for versatile and possibly more highly skilled workers rather than the unskilled production line worker. All workers can do all jobs.

4. **Contracts**: in many processes there is no requirement for all employees to be working to their maximum. New forms of employment mean that workers can be moved around the factory at any one time, or that more part-time workers are employed to be brought in at times of peak output and sent home when not needed. Finally, work may be contracted out to other companies.

The wider implications of post-Fordism

Post-Fordism has greater importance than just describing a change of production practices: it also helps to understand the changes that have taken place in the wider society. The changes that post-Fordism may have brought about are summarised in Table 7.1.

Table 7.1

Relevant social area	Fordist description	Post-Fordist description
Industrial production	• Low technology, mass production, centralised planning. • Acceptance of poor-quality products.	• Innovation in production, smaller numbers of identical products produced and greater variety. • High quality.
Work relations	• Hierarchy, bureaucracy, trades unions. • Generalised wage bargaining.	• Organic structures with limited hierarchy. • Individualised wage structures.
Social class	• Solidaristic social class.	• Class fragmentation and decomposition.
Politics	• National parties along class lines.	• Development of new social movements – feminism, ecology, anti-racism.
Welfare Regime	• Centralised, prescriptive Welfare State.	• Decline of class. • Challenges to centralised 'prescriptive' welfare.
Consumerism	• Mass consumption of identical products.	• Likelihood of more individualised products.

Criticisms of post-Fordism

① Wood (*The Transformation of Work?: Skill, Flexibility and the Labour Process*) has criticised post-Fordism as exaggerating relatively minor changes to a radical change in society. Wood suggests that a more accurate term is **neo-Fordism** – meaning that the changes stay within the tradition of Fordism and merely extend it in different ways.

② Jones (*Work and Flexible Automation in Britain*) and Lane (*Industrial Change in Europe*) found limited empirical support for post-Fordism in Britain compared to Japan or western Germany.

③ The extent of flexible and part-time working seems to have been exaggerated in manufacturing industry, as the bulk of the extension has been in the service industries and government employment.

④ It could be argued that the changes which have taken place in the broader society reflect more a change of balance between employers and unions, with the employers more able to inflict their desire for cheaper, more flexible labour on a weaker and less unionised workforce.

⑤ Marxist analyses would also adequately explain much of the changes in industry and possibly society, too.

It is likely that post-Fordism does not fully describe the current situation of industry in the UK. However, it does point to a growing tendency in work patterns and their influence on social life.

The core–periphery division

An interesting development of the Fordism–post-Fordism debate is Atkinson's work on core and periphery workers ('The changing corporation', in Clutterbuck, *New Patterns of Work*). Atkinson argues that the changing production system has created a **core–periphery division** between types of employment or work situation. At the core are workers who are employed full-time in large core industries; core workers are characterised as white and male. On the periphery are industries that subcontract work out to smaller industries and even self-employed individuals who receive payments for work they undertake; but there is no guarantee of employment. A second set of workers exists in the periphery who are often on fixed-term contracts, work part-time, job-share or are involved in some government training initiative. The peripheral workers are disproportionately female and black or Asian.

7.2 NEW FORMS OF INDUSTRIALISM AND POST-INDUSTRIALISM

DE-INDUSTRIALSM AND POST-INDUSTRIALISM

Industrialism brought with it particular types of social relations, most of which continue today. Over the past 20 years a process of de-industrialisation has taken place which has brought about many of the changes we saw earlier in terms of employment, unemployment, class structure and politics as well as a change in gender relations.

It has been argued by writers such as Bell (*The Coming of Post-Industrial Society*) and Toffler (*The Third Wave*) that a period of post-industrialism has arrived, based upon the use of information technology (IT) and the growth of the service sectors. Bell argues that the future of employment will involve less manufacture of products andmore in the manipulation, storing and processing of data. Advances in global communications will also impact on the work environment. According to Bell, the decline of fabrication would also lead to the decline in social class, and divisions in society would be based upon knowledge of, and access to the new global communication networks. Bell is extremely optimistic in his analysis arguing that IT will provide more interesting work and greater time for leisure. Finally, the additional wealth it is capable of generating through efficiency can increase standards of living overall.

Kumar (*From Post-Industrial to Post-Modern Society*) takes a more critical view, arguing that:

- there has always been a very significant service industry – even at the height of industrialism,
- the social class divisions have not disappeared as the result of IT and service industries,
- the crucial division of wage-labour and ownership of wealth remains,
- there are still large numbers of poorly paid and insecure jobs as in industrialism – only the types of jobs have changed.

JAPANISATION

This refers to the increasing use of Japanese-style production methods and the adoption of their social relations at work in contemporary UK industrial companies. The model is based upon:

- **Flexibility** – workers do a range of different jobs and there is very little specialisation. So, if there is work to be done, people are moved across to do it. This is in contrast to the traditional concept of demarcation.
- **Quality** – the highest possible standards are achieved with every product. This may seem obvious, but the model previously used in the UK and imported from the USA was that a number of defective items were inevitable in the production process and this should be accepted. The process of ensuring that components and products are perfect is known as 'total quality management'.
- **Teamwork** – small groups of workers take responsiblity for their work, *as a group*, so each worker in the team is responsible to the other members of the team. This

gives group solidarity, but also ensures peer-group pressure to maintain quality and speed. Linked to this and to total quality management is the concept of quality circles where workers meet on a regular basis to discuss what improvements can be made to the process of production.

● **Just-in-time production** – traditionally in UK companies large stocks of components were held by the factory so that they would never be short of components. Sometimes these could lie in yards or warehouses for months. Just-in-time involves having components delivered at exactly the right time, and by implication of the highest standards so that there are no defective parts.

Implications for employment

Although the actual numbers of employees of Japanese or Far Eastern companies is relatively small in the UK (approximately 22,000), these methods have been influential in a wide range of other companies. Japanisation has the following social implications:

● Traditional social divisions between workers and management are eroded.

● Workers owe loyalty to their team not to any broader group of skill category as happened previously.

● Trade unions may not be recognised or only one union recognised.

● No-strike agreements are often signed.

● Just-in-time production is based upon a large number of small suppliers competing, rather than on one or two large companies being given the contract. This can fragment the supplying workforce.

● Emphasis on quality involves workers in the production process.

McDONALDISATION

Ritzer (*The McDonaldisation of Society*) also takes a negative view of the changes in post-industrial society. Ritzer points to the forms of work associated with the fast-food outlets, and in particular McDonald's.

Ritzer points to the rationalisation of work with every job timed and controlled to precision. Workers are on hourly rates of pay, with no job security and few receive paid holidays or sick leave. The overwhelming majority of workers are casual and part-time, which means that McDonald's has little responsibility for longer-term commitments such as pensions, maternity allowances, etc. Finally, in the workplace the workers have to behave in a particular way (politeness, smiling and cheeriness).

7.3 THE NATURE OF WORK

TYPES OF WORK

Sociologists following the work of Pahl (*Divisions of Labour*) and Gershuny (*Social Innovation and the Division of Labour*) on the one hand and feminist writers, such as Stacey ('The division of labour', in Abrams et al, *Practice and Progress*), on the other point out that there has traditionally been too great an emphasis on the **formal economy** of the employed and self-employed who are in official employment, paying tax and national insurance etc, and covered by what legal protection is offered to employees. This, however, is only part of the picture: there are other forms of work which are equally important, particularly the **informal economy** and the work performed without pay at home. The following types of work can therefore be delineated:

● the formal economy;

● the informal economy.

The formal economy

This consists of formal, publicly paid employment which is typically covered by legal boundaries and constraints. Within it are the three sectors of the economy described on p 139. Definitions of social class and calculations of wage levels are based upon these forms of occupation.

The informal economy

This consists of work that either is not paid (paid in 'kind') or is paid outside the tax system. There are three types of work within the informal economy:

1. **Household economy**: production of goods and services by members of a household for other members of the same household, substitutes for which may have to be paid for (eg the work of a 'housewife').

2. **The hidden economy**: work that is remunerated but which is not declared for tax purposes (eg work for 'cash in hand' payment).

3. **Communal economy**: production of goods or services for which the group would normally have to pay, but which is not for the consumption of the producers themselves (eg voluntary work).

The significance

The significance of these divisions is that traditionally all discussions of work have centred on the formal economy. Statistics on economic activity, on levels of pay and on attitudes to employment have all been based on formal occupations.

In reality, work performed outside the formal sector is central to understanding all the 'facts' mentioned above. An understanding of the roles men and women play in the home and the amount of work done there helps us to understand the different situation of men and women in the **formal workplace** of the factory and the office. The stress on the formal economy has helped in the process of making women 'invisible' that has underpinned sociology. Until relatively recently, the major part of the workforce was male (today they still dominate in full-time employment), and so the sociology of work was the sociology of men in full-time occupations. Work was seen as a 'male' activity. The inclusion of the informal economy helps us to understand what work women do, and how much it contributes to the economy.

Similarly, in discussions of the best way to help the elderly and disabled, and the 'costs' of this, the fact that the overwhelming majority of the elderly and disabled are cared for (usually by women) at home, without pay (**communal economy**) helps us to see the 'real' costs.

Pahl's study of work outside the formal economy, and the research of Ditton (*Part-Time Crime*) on soft types of crime, such as 'fiddling', show that the real wages that certain groups get are actually higher than the official statistics show. In particular, Pahl shows that those who are doing well out of the formal economy are also more likely to be successful in the informal one: for example skilled electricians who receive relatively high wages and are able to supplement their income with private work.

Divisions by sex

The workforce is changing significantly in its composition (see Tables 7.2 and 7.3). In 1961, for example there were 16.5 million men working and only 8.5 million women. By the late 1980s, there were 15 million men and 11 million women. Women now represent over 40% of the labour force and by the end of the 1990s the number of women at work should be almost equal to, or possibly greater than, the number of men. However, it is important to note that women tend to be concentrated in lower paid work and in a narrow range of occupations, particularly in the clerical and service industries, with fewer responsibilities.

Table 7.2 *Percentage of employees working part time, Spring 1996*

United Kingdom	Percentages		
	Males	Females	All
16–19			
In FTE[1]	97	99	98
Not in FTE[1]	12	26	19
All aged 16–19	51	65	58
20–24	11	23	17
25–44	3	42	21
45–54	3	47	25
55–59	7	54	30
60–64	16	71	38
65 and over	73	84	78
All aged 16 and over	8	45	25

[1] Full-time education.

(*Source: Social Trends 27*, Table 4.7 (Labour Force Survey, ONS), p76)

Table 7.3 *Employees, by gender and occupation 1991 and 1996[1]*

United Kingdom	Percentages			
	Males		Females	
	1991	1996	1991	1996
Professional	10	12	8	10
Managers and administrators	16	19	8	10
Associate professional and technical	8	8	10	10
Clerical and secretarial	8	8	29	26
Personal and protective services	7	8	14	16
Sales	6	6	12	12
Craft and related	21	17	4	3
Plant and machine operatives	15	15	5	4
Other occupations	8	8	11	9
All employees	100	100	100	100

[1] At Spring each year. Excludes those who did not state their occupation.

(*Source: Social Trends 27*, Table 4.8 (Labour Force Survey, ONS), p76)

The causes of the increase in women working are:

① The desire of women to return to work as soon as possible after having children, usually after the birth of the last child. In addition, women are having fewer children, compressed into fewer years.

② They are less well paid than men and are therefore attractive to employers.

③ They are willing (because of their domestic role) to work part-time and are therefore flexible and unable to claim a number of employment rights (such as not being laid off at the employer's will, entitlement to redundancy money, etc).

Studies of women working have tended to ignore the issue of, or at least not make the links between, women as workers in the formal economy and women as workers in the informal economy, where they are particularly active in the domestic and communal spheres. Here their work is financially unrewarded and has low status.

Divisions by ethnic group

Just as there are divisions in the labour market along the lines of sex, there are also divisions by ethnic group. Overall, the ethnic minorities are more likely to:

- have lower status occupations,
- receive lower wages,
- have significantly higher levels of unemployment,
- be discriminated against in obtaining a job in the first place, and then in gaining promotion.

However, the overall category of 'ethnic minorities' hides clear differences that exist between the various groups. Those of Afro-Caribbean origin, for example, are most likely to be in semi- and skilled employment. Those of African-Asian backgrounds are likely to be overrepresented in the professions and management. Those from Bangladeshi backgrounds are concentrated in the unskilled jobs.

7.4 OWNERSHIP AND CONTROL

Sociologists are interested in the patterns of ownership and control of industry in Britain. Apart from the obvious importance of understanding the nature of ownership and the distribution of wealth, much sociological theory derives from the belief that a small ruling class controls British industry and as a result these people have a crucial influence on the political and social life of Britain.

THE CONCENTRATION OF INDUSTRY

The 20th century has seen growth in the **concentration of industry**. In areas of production like cigarettes, petrol products, cars, alcohol and food, five companies in each sector account for over 70% of all sales. In banking, the four biggest banks took approximately 90% of all deposits in the middle 1980s. Another way of examining the concentration of industry in Britain is in terms of assets: the largest 200 manufacturing firms in Britain account for approximately 90% of all assets.

In the service and leisure industries, the levels of concentration are rapidly overtaking those in the manufacturing industries, with companies like Grand Metropolitan and Rank dominating the sector.

Multi-nationals

The development of a world economy has seriously affected Britain in the field of manufacturing, as companies search for the cheapest labour costs and then import to Britain. Large companies do set up branches in Britain, but in times of difficulty these are most likely to be lost.

However, Britain is still a major investor abroad, and investment out of Britain (by British companies) is much higher than investment into the country by foreign multi-nationals. The effect of outward investment is to lose jobs in Britain, although the profits return to the companies' shareholders.

THE MANAGERIAL APPROACH

In the 1930s Berle and Means (*The Modern Corporation and Private Property*) and later Burnham (*The Managerial Revolution*) argued that a crucial division had occurred between the owners of capital and those who managed it on their behalf. Until the end of the 19th century those who owned factories and commercial institutions actually ran them themselves. However, in the 1870s, with the growth of the joint stock company, in which shares in the company were sold, it became possible for ownership to be spread among a number of individuals or groups. As the size of companies and the number of shares available grew, the possibility of any one individual owning enough shares to dominate the company seemed remote.

Berle and Means divide control into three types:

1. **Majority control**: a small group of investors own a majority of the shares to ensure that their views predominate.

2. **Minority control**: a group of shareholders hold enough shares to ensure that their views dominate if they pool their shares. They do not have a majority of the shares but other shareholding is too dispersed to challenge them.

3. **Management control**: no group or coalition dominates as the share ownership is so widespread. This results in a vacuum, and so the managers can make the decisions. This is the situation which Berle and Means and Burnham argue is occurring in 20th-century capitalist societies. In the 1920s Berle and Means estimated that 44% of non-financial institutions were **management controlled**, while in the 1960s according to Larner, the figure had risen to 83%.

The point is that the dominance of capitalism by the owners had been weakened, and replaced by the control of **technocrats** – the managers. The interests of managers and owners were not regarded as necessarily being the same. Berle and Means argues that managers were likely to be more concerned with the public good, while Nichols and Beynon (*Living with Capitalism*) argue that they would be more likely to follow their own interests. In 1981, Herman showed that management control existed in advanced capitalism but that the managers were heavily constrained by the key financial institutions, such as banks and insurance companies. Herman describes this as **constrained management control**.

Criticisms of managerialism

Critics have pointed out that the ownership of shares is not as widespread as the managerial approach would have us believe. Indeed, banks, insurance companies and other financial institutions are increasingly dominating the ownership of shares in companies. Writers, such as Zeitlin, have argued that it is the banks and insurance companies which control the activities of companies; Zeitlin has used the term **bank minority control** to define this and Kotz claims that over a third of US business is controlled by financial institutions.

THE NEO-MARXIST POSITION: MANAGERS AS OWNERS

The managerialist argument suggests that managers are different from owners, yet the evidence suggests that there is considerable overlap.

Top managers are different from the ordinary managers in that the majority of them really are substantial shareholders. Their shareholding may be small in relation to the entire bloc of shares, but it is still worth a considerable amount. Indeed, according to Scott (*Corporations, Classes and Control*), top corporate management and personal shareholders are usually one and the same. The shareholdings give them a direct incentive in the company and in the interests of shareholdings.

Furthermore, there is still a considerable number of the old-fashioned owner-managers in British business. Indeed, in over half of Britain's biggest 250 companies there are dominant shareholders with minority or majority control (Sainsbury's, McAlpine, Marks and Spencer).

Writers, such as Westergaard and Resler (*Class in Capitalist Society*), claim that the directors are linked together through a chain of **interlocking directorships** (see Fig. 7.2), which ensures that control is spread across a wide spectrum by a few people (usually male). Fig. 7.2 shows how in recent years various companies have come to own shares in each other and so the directors/owners are able to control a far wider range of industries than at first appears. In this figure, 11 people have a total of 57 directorships in the top 250 companies. Of the 11 people, 9 form the chain illustrated which actually links 39 companies. This overlap is a reflection of the fact that wealth is concentrated in the hands of a few – with 23% of the wealth held in the hands of only 1% of the population. This evidence leads Marxists to argue that ownership is as concentrated as ever, and so is power.

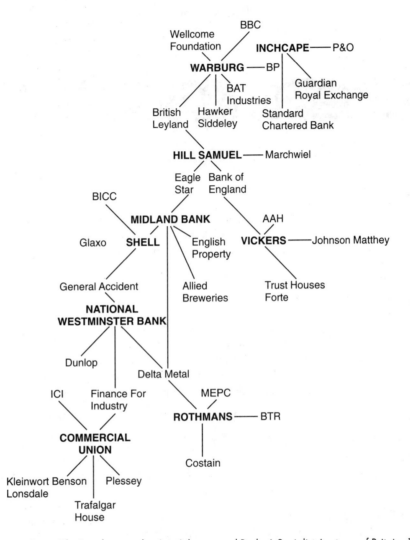

(*Source:* Scott, 'The British upperclass', in Johnston and Bush, *A Socialist Anatomy of Britain*, 1985; reprinted in Abercrombie and Warde, *Comtemporary British Society*, 1988)

Fig. 7.2 Interlocking directorships

SCOTT: CONTROL THROUGH A CONSTELLATION OF INTERESTS

Scott (*The Upper Classes: Property and Privilege in Britain*) argues that, although there is some truth in the neo-Marxist and managerialist positions, these oversimplify the complex reality. In most companies, major shareholders can join together to form a minority bloc (which is enough to have their way), but these majority shareholders have too diverse interests to follow common policy. The agreements that the major shareholders come to are likely to be unstable and short-lived, but at that time the management has to follow the line laid down. In general, the major shareholders, which are generally financial institutions (banks etc) rather than individuals, are able to agree on the composition of the board of directors, but then may disagree on most other issues. Scott calls this **control through a constellation of interests**, and clearly stresses the dynamic element of it.

In his research, he found that there was an increasing growth in the power/ownership of financial institutions so that, whereas in 1963 institutions held 30% of company shares, by 1981 this had risen to 58%. Furthermore, of the top 250 companies, Scott shows that:

- 36% are controlled by a few shareholders with a majority control,
- 20% are controlled by a few shareholders with a minority control,
- 40% are controlled by constellations of interest (mainly financial institutions, a situation which is increasing).

7.5 WORK SATISFACTION

ALIENATION

Marx

The concept of alienation derives from Marx and reflects his view that as long as people are not the owners and controllers of their work they will never fully experience satisfaction from it. According to Marx, work is drudgery unless it consists of an extension of the personality of the individual.

Blauner

In the 1960s the concept of alienation re-emerged as an issue, but it had been changed somewhat from Marx's original idea that satisfaction could not be achieved without abolishing capitalism, to one in which capitalism itself was not the cause of alienation, rather that certain factors *within* the work situation were. Blauner (*Alienation and Freedom*), developing Marx's description of alienation, suggests that it has four elements:

1. **Powerlessness**: where people have no control over their work ouput.

2. **Meaninglessness**: where the tasks seem unrelated to the finished product and of little importance.

3. **Isolation**: where the work process cuts them off from social contact with their colleagues.

4. **Self-estrangement**: this is the closest to Marx's original concept and is where the work becomes a means to obtain money to gain self-fulfilment.

Blauner suggests from his studies that the type of production method determines the extent of alienation. Comparing (all-male) craft workers, machine minders, assembly line workers and process production (chemicals) workers, Blauner found that the greater the degrees of control and skill the worker had over his (sic) job the lower was the degree of alienation experienced.

Braverman

Braverman, writing within a Marxist perspective, argues that the most noticeable process occurring within capitalism has been the increasing deskilling of labour. He means by this the influence of **scientific management** first introduced by Taylor at the turn of the century and usually known as **time and motion studies**. This approach to increasing efficiency was to look at the component actions that constituted someone's job and then to see what improvements could be made. This was not to benefit the worker but to increase his/her productivity. Indeed, the worker was viewed as a machine. Braverman argued that this process of deskilling had occurred in manual labour and was also being extended to white-collar labour. According to him, the future of employment is an increasing deskilling of the workforce and with it a worker's ability to demand high rates of pay for his/her skills.

There have been several critics of Braverman's thesis:

1 Friedman argues that Braverman underestimates the extent of workers' ability to gain autonomy both formally through unions and informally (see p 152) to create some degree of control and freedom from authority.

2 Beechey argues from a feminist perspective that Braverman's views on deskilling reflect inaccurate assumptions about the degree of skill involved in typical 'women's work'. The deskilling Braverman refers to in which skills are taken away from (male) workers and given to unskilled (female) workers is sexist, by assuming that women are somehow less skilled. The situation is less one of deskilling workers than patriarchy in practice.

3 Finally, it is not at all clear that there is a process of deskilling going on. Many of the underlying arguments for post-Fordism suggest that many workers are actually being given greater skills.

THE EXTERNAL CRITIQUE

The debates about satisfaction at work centre on the belief that the degree of skill a person uses in his/her employment determines the level of work satisfaction experienced. According to both Blauner and Braverman, the crucial determinant is the technology used in a person's work.

However, this has been criticised by Goldthorpe et al (*The Affluent Worker in the Class Structure*) who found in their study of Luton car workers that the male workers had chosen their jobs with the knowledge that they would have very little satisfaction, but were prepared to swap this for high levels of pay (an instrumental orientation to work). Therefore, satisfaction at work was affected by choices made outside the place of employment rather than by the technology.

Gallie (*In Search of the New Working Class*) suggests that the culture of the society is just as important as the technology in determining workers' satisfaction. He compared the attitudes of oil refining workers in England, France and Scotland and found significant variations in the French workers' attitudes to work and different management thinking and practices. The result was greater dissatisfaction among French workers and higher levels of industrial conflict.

THE INTERACTIONIST POSITION

A different perspective on work satisfaction comes from studies that stress the ways in which workers develop **coping strategies or strategies of resistance** at work. Examples include:

1 **Daydreaming** Ditton studied work in a bakery and found that production line workers could pass their shift simply thinking about other things.

2 **'Having a laff'** Willis' study of young males from school into unskilled manual employment (*Learning to Labour*) found that they had numerous strategies to gain some form of enjoyment from their work situation, including practical jokes, rude jokes etc.

3 **Sabotage** Taylor and Walton ('Industrial sabotage: motives and meanings', in Cohen, *Images of Deviance*) found numerous examples of industrial workers deliberately causing damage to the machinery in order to enjoy a rest or to gain revenge on their employers. Beynon found similar practices among car production line workers.

INDUSTRIAL ACTION

There has been a change in the pattern of industrial dispute over the last 20 years (see Fig. 7.3).

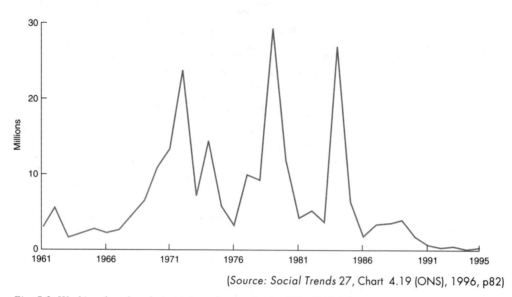

(Source: Social Trends 27, Chart 4.19 (ONS), 1996, p82)

Fig. 7.3 Working days lost during labour disputes in the UK, 1961–95

Workers attempt to gain control of their work by a wide variety of means, both informal and formal.

Informal methods of control

These include controlling output levels, controlling the information that is made available to managers, sabotaging products, stealing and taking various short-cuts to make the work process easier or quicker.

Taylor and Walton examined the activities of industrial workers and found examples of informal activities:

1 **Reducing frustration** Workers set fire to a carpet factory because they felt there was no other way to express their resentment and grievances at their treatment by employers.

2 **Easing the work process** Workers in an aircraft factory engaged a short-cut in bolting on the wings. This seriously weakened the structure of the wing, but the process allowed the workers to complete the work within the allocated time.

3 **Attempts to assert control** This occurs where the workers feel themselves powerless to confront their employers. They therefore resort to sabotage, such as Beynon's example (in *Working for Ford*) of Ford car workers using emergency stops to bring the production line to an endless series of halts after management refused discussions with union representatives over the pace of the production line.

Formal methods of control

The most common formal method of control is strike action. However, other methods are to take legal action and to boycott various disputed practices.

Strike action

The extent of strike action is related to:

1 **Government action** The Conservative governments of the 1980s and early 1990s, according to Hyman (*Strikes*), were strongly opposed to trades union action and set about a campaign to weaken the power of unions and, particularly, their ability to conduct effective strikes. In 1980 and 1984 new employment acts restricted secondary strikes, limited picketing, required unions to ballot their employees, allowed selective dismissal of strikers and lowered the social security payments to strikers' families.

❷ **The state of the economy** When there are high levels of unemployment, as in the UK in the 1980s and 1990s, people in employment are very concerned about the security of their jobs and are therefore less likely to join in industrial action. With the growth of the post-Fordist economy, in which there are peripheral workers increasingly being used on short-term contracts, self-employed people and those in part-time work, striking is not possible.

Economic factors are most commonly perceived as being the reason for strikes – and officially 90% of strikes can be attributed to demands for better pay. However, Lane and Roberts (*Strike at Pilkingtons*) suggest that pay demands are an excuse for workers striking for other reasons. They argue that striking is only regarded as culturally legitimate for pay reasons, therefore if there is dissatisfaction for other reasons, such as a change in management style, the workers express their dissatisfaction by striking for higher rates of pay.

❸ **Technology** Blauner argues that the type of technology used in the workplace is an important determinant of work satisfaction and that work satisfaction in turn determines the propensity of workers to strike. It follows, therefore, that production line work is particularly strike-prone. However, there is some dispute about this, in that Gallie found in his comparison of French, English and Scottish oil refinery workers that, with a similar technology, the French workers were more likely to strike. Gallie suggests that not simply technology but also cultural attitudes are important.

❹ **Community** Kerr and Siegel, in what is now a historical study ('The inter-industry propensity to strike'), find that workers in certain settled working-class communities based on a limited range of industries were far more likely to exhibit a form of class-consciousness, or at least class solidarity, and to engage in strike action. The demise of coal mining, ship building and the steel industry in the UK makes this of little importance today.

The decline of the unions

Fig. 7.4 shows that from 1979 there has been a consistent decline in union membership in the UK.

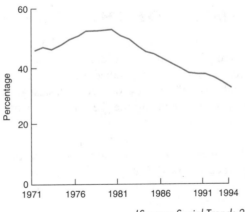

(*Source: Social Trends 27*, Chart 4.20 (ONS), p82)

Fig. 7.4 Trade union membership in the UK as a percentage of the civilian workforce in employment, 1971–94

Expression of class conflict

According to Marxists, the extent of formal industrial action, such as strikes, and informal industrial action, such as sabotage, indicate the degree of class conflict in society. Therefore, as capitalist societies are class-conscious and breed conflict, strikes are normal in capitalist society.

Are strikes the best way to measure industrial conflict?

From the information presented so far, it is clear that strikes are only one form of conflict; therefore when the government claims that strikes are at their lowest since the 1939–45 war, it may not be that industrial conflict is at its lowest.

Edwards and Scullion (*The Social Organisation of Industrial Conflict*) claim that it is necessary to see all forms of industrial conflict within a continuum, with different types of conflict occurring depending on the circumstances and balance of power. They describe three forms of management/employee relations:

1. **Turnover of labour** Women workers in garment manufacturing were strictly controlled and paid by piecework. There was little to gain by absenteeism or sabotage. Therefore workers left their employment as soon as they could for other work.

2. **Shopfloor control** Edwards and Scullion also studied a large metal production factory. Here the financial situation of the firm and their lack of ability to pay high wages led to the employers being weak in imposing their will on workers. Generally, the workers took control of the work process and the industrial relations were good. It was only when the employers attempted to impose controls on the workers that industrial conflict broke out.

3. **Subtle control** This involved sophisticated and subtle control, where workers were allowed some degree of autonomy over their work; in particular, they did not have to clock on or off, and there was a feedback mechanism for workers to express their views. This gave the workers some (possibly illusory) sense of control. The employers, however, were very strict on attendance and quality of work. Their control was subtle and they spoke individually and privately to workers whom they considered to be slacking.

The point of the research is that there is a wide variety of employer–employee relationships, and the outcome of industrial action reflects the ways in which the conflicts are managed.

7.6 THE PROFESSIONS

THE DEVELOPMENT OF THE PROFESSIONS

Today, approximately 14% of the British workforce is employed in some form of profession. Generally, the professions are divided into the **older established ones**, such as the law and medicine, and the newer ones (sometimes called the **marginal professions**), such as teaching, nursing and social work. The professions are the fastest growing area of employment in the British occupational structure, alongside the growth in white-collar workers.

The older professions developed in the last century, when a number of occupations mangaged to gain royal charters giving them monopolies over their area of work. Thus solicitors, barristers and doctors all gained the title and status of professions, and effectively pushed aside competing practitioners in their areas of employment, such as homeopaths. The professionals were overwhelmingly self-employed, or at least employed in private practices, and they charged fees for their activities.

The modern development of the professions, however, comes from the massive growth in the State in its various forms. In particular, the NHS, social work, teaching and local government all created new posts in areas of technical expertise. These posts were not necessarily managerial but required judgements and involved a level of responsibility that could not be classified as clerical. The new professionals differed from their established counterparts in that they were:

- employed primarily by the State,
- in large organisations,
- with a specific position in the hierarchy of the organisation,
- without a royal charter.

The result of this **process of professionalisation** is that the new professions occupy a slightly ambiguous or marginal position with regard to the older established professions: the marginal professions are worse paid, subject to the authority and the salary levels of the State or large organisations, and have lower status.

THREE VIEWS ON THE NATURE OF THE PROFESSIONS

Although there is general agreement on the growth of the professions in Britain since the 1950s and the fact that this has been partially caused by the changing nature of the economy, there is less agreement over the nature of the professions. Three quite distinct viewpoints emerge on the professions: these are the Marxist, the functionalist and the Weberian (derived) ones.

The Marxist approach

The Marxist approach to the professions is less a discussion of the professions as institutions and more an examination of how and where professional-type occupations fit into the **Marxist theory of social class**. Marx argues that there are only two classes in capitalist society: the owners (the **bourgeoisie**) and those who sell their labour (the **proletariat**). Marx admitted the existence of two other groups in society – the **petty bourgeoisie** (roughly speaking, small businessmen) and the **lumpen proletariat** (the 'rough' working class). Marx foresaw an inevitable polarisation of the two classes into a tiny bourgeoisie and a massive proletariat, in the process of which the petty bourgeoisie would be absorbed into the proletariat. The key distinction between the classes is the ownership or non-ownership of capital.

This analysis has posed considerable problems for neo-Marxists in recent years, with the growth of the middle-level occupations, including management and professional ones. Many professionals can be seen to share standards of living similar to those of the owners of capital. Some managers and professionals exercise authority and control which is similar to that exercised by owners. Furthermore, those in senior managerial and professional occupations perceive themselves as closer (in class terms) to the owners than to the working class.

A number of explanations of the social class position of professionals have been put forward. For writers such as Westergaard, the professionals represent a buffer group between the working class and the owners of capital, although they are ultimately not owners and are still selling their labour. They, therefore, belong to the working class. For Wright, professionals are situated in **contradictory class locations,** by which he means that they cannot simply be located in the working class or among the owners. Wright suggests that the best way to understand their position is to look at the degree of autonomy in the work situation, the extent of the authority exercised by an individual or group, and the rewards. Through this, Wright is able to show how workers in Britain are divided into clear-cut categories of the working class and those who are in **intermediate positions**, such as professionals.

Underlying these debates about the exact class position of professionals is the agreement that professionals collude in controlling the working class. For example, doctors keep the working class fit and healthy, according to Navarro (*Medicine under Capitalism*), so they will be more productive. Lawyers and barristers operate the oppressive legal system, giving the impression that it is fair to all while really controlling the working class.

The functionalist approach

This approach develops from the **general functionalist position on stratification**, that the more important positions in the occupational structure which require the highest talents and skills are more highly valued and rewarded. However, the more specific argument within the general functionalist approach is associated with Talcott Parsons (*The Social System*), who argues that the professions developed because they deal with people who are particularly vulnerable to exploitation. In the case of barristers, their clients may be at risk of prison, while doctors' clients are ill. If no control were imposed on people in these occupations, then charlatans might cheat clients. As a result of this, professional associations were formed in order to create and maintain the highest possible standards. Parsons was concerned primarily with doctors in his analysis, but his ideas are valid for the entire field of professionals. He says that 'The ideology of the profession lays great emphasis on the obligation of the physician to put the "welfare of the patient" above his personal interests and regards "commercialism" as the most serious and insidious evil with which it has to contend... The general picture is one of sharp segregation from the market and price practices of the business world.'

The functionalist approach then goes on to list a number of traits of professionals. The more of these traits an occupation has, the greater the likelihood of it being (or becoming) a profession. The following traits are identified:

1. **Systematic theory**: that underlying their actions is a body of knowledge.

2. **Professional authority**: that the client accepts unquestioningly the opinion of the expert.

3. **The sanction of the community**: that the public accept the exclusive right of the profession to deal in their area of expertise.

4. **Code of ethics**: that the profession controls its own members according to a strict code of ethics.

5. **A professional culture**: that the profession has a common way of presenting itself to those outside, and a sense of its own importance and cohesiveness.

The functionalist model is, however, very naive and takes for granted the claims of the professions concerning their lack of interest in income and their attempts to maintain the highest standards. Other approaches point to the fact that occupations forming themselves into professions is an excellent method of raising incomes and gaining work autonomy.

The Weberian Approach

This approach looks at professions in relation to the **Weberian theory of stratification**. Weber suggests that a group's position in the stratification system depends upon three factors:

1. **Class**: the result of one's position in the 'marketplace'. What you have to sell in relation to the demand for your skills. The result is your salary.

2. **Status**: the prestige in which the group is held by others.

3. **Power**: the ability to influence decisions.

Professions are an excellent way of improving all three of these factors. Sociologists within the Weberian perspective, such as Friedson (*Profession of Medicine*), and Parry and Parry (*The Rise of the Medical Profession*) all argue that professions are means of looking after the interests of their members. They identify the following elements:

1. **Restriction of entry into an occupation** The entrance examinations which are supposed to limit entrants by quality in fact limit entrants to create scarcity, thus allowing professionals to charge more.

2. **Control of the conduct of its members** This allows professions to create the impression that all its members are equally competent. By disciplining its own members, the professions prevent outsiders investigating their affairs.

3. **Monopoly of the service** Professionals can control rival groups which might threaten their dominance of a particular area. This also allows them to mystify the techniques and knowledge required.

Parry and Parry point out the difference in the situation of teachers and doctors. Doctors were organised before the government became their major employer after the introduction of the NHS. Doctors formed themselves into the BMA in 1832 and gained their monopoly in 1858. Teachers and social workers were largely a creation of the State, and the State controlled entry standards and the supply of new teachers. Teachers were therefore always in a much weaker position than doctors as they had (and have) little control over their **market position**.

7.7   UNEMPLOYMENT

THE EXTENT OF UNEMPLOYMENT

Fig. 7.5 shows the unemployment rates in different regions of the UK.

The official statistics of the numbers of people unemployed have been criticised by those who claim that they are an *overestimate* and by those who claim that they are an *underestimate*.

Scotland

11% and above

9–10%

below 9%

Northern Ireland

North

Yorkshire & Humberside

North West

East Midlands

West Midlands

East Anglia

Wales

South East

South West

(*Source: Poverty: The Facts*, C. Oppenheim, 1993, p141)

Fig. 7.5 Unemployment rates in October 1992 by region of the UK

Overestimate

The claim has been made by Conservative politicians that significant numbers of people who are classified as unemployed actually work and claim the job seekers' benefit. However, no evidence has been found by researchers to indicate that significant numbers of people are actually in this situation. The general agreement in sociology supports the work of Pahl, who found in his study of the employed and unemployed in Kent that the unemployed were those whose skills were less wanted and who were less likely to be able to find additional (part-time) work than those already in employment.

Underestimate

There has been a constant series of adjustments to the categories of people considered to be officially unemployed. Groups excluded are, among others:

● women not eligible for benefits;

● those on training schemes;

● those under 18 years of age (many of whom are officially supposed to be on training schemes);

- those over 60;
- those who consider it not worth their while to register because they believe there are no jobs, and as they cannot claim benefit there is no incentive.

The TUC believes that these groups could add up to 1–1.5 million people extra who would like to work full-time if they could.

THE GROUPS WHO COMPRISE THE UNEMPLOYED

The numbers of people who are out of work change with the overall situation of the economy. However, there have been very significant changes in the British economy over the last 15 years, which seem likely to maintain a permanently high level of unemployment.

Certain groups in the population are more likely than others to be made unemployed; these include:

The least skilled

As automated machinery has replaced them, the least skilled workers become unemployed. Indeed, unemployment levels for unskilled manual workers can be as high as six times that of professional workers.

People living away from the south/south-east of England

The south-east of England has a number of advantages for employers, including a skilled workforce, proximity to Europe, and a large, affluent population to purchase the goods or products.

People living in inner cities

There are higher rates of unemployment in inner cities throughout the UK and in the declining industrial areas.

Ethnic minorities

Partly as a result of racism, and partly because skill levels are lower overall among Afro-Caribbeans and some of the Asian communities, there are significantly higher levels of unemployment amongst the ethnic minorities. It is estimated that twice as many blacks and Asians are unemployed as whites.

Women

Official rates of unemployment for women are lower than those for men (see Fig. 7.6). However, bearing in mind the points made earlier about the official statistics, it may be that women's rates are similar to men's. The sort of work that women do is in greater demand however, with short-term, low-paid and part-time work fitting the emerging post-Fordist styles of employment.

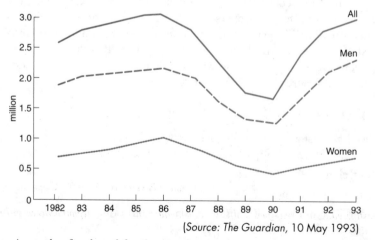

(Source: The Guardian, 10 May 1993)

Fig. 7.6 Changing paths of male and female unemployment

THE TYPES OF UNEMPLOYMENT

Economists distinguish between different types of unemployment:

- short-term (or **frictional**) unemployment,
- long-term (or **structural**) unemployment,
- cyclical unemployment.

Short-term unemployment

This occurs when workers move from one post to another within a few months. This is not regarded as particularly significant as an indicator of the economic health of a country.

Long-term unemployment

This occurs when there are no jobs available in the economy for those seeking work, or when there are jobs that require different skills from the ones that the unemployed have.

Cyclical unemployment

This occurs when the economies of industrial nations go through a period in which they all suffer from overproduction and lack of work. These slumps occur in fairly regular cycles.

Subtypes of unemployment

Regional unemployment occurs where vacancies and the unemployed are not in the same geographical area. This accounts for the significant amount of movement from the north of the UK to the south.

Sectoral unemployment occurs where the decline in some industries leaves significant numbers of workers with inappropriate skills for the newer opportunities (see Fig. 7.7).

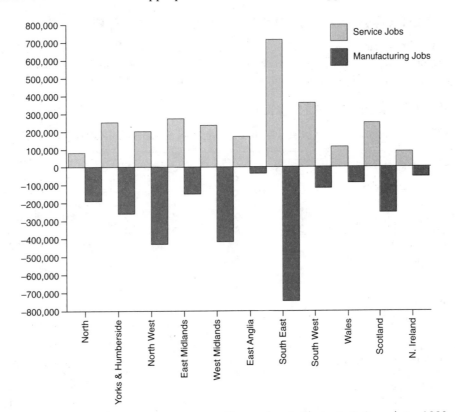

(*Source: Poverty: The Facts*, C. Oppenheim, 1993, p141)

Fig. 7.7 Charting gains in service jobs and losses in manufacturing jobs by region between 1976 and 1992

7.8   WORK AND LEISURE

Leisure is a difficult concept to define, as work and leisure can overlap – particularly if work is a pleasure for some people. Most sociologists have asked what determines the nature of leisure. Answers include the arguments that:

● work determines leisure;
● work and leisure are likely to become fused together and indistinguishable;
● age determines leisure patterns;
● leisure is determined by individual choice;
● leisure is determined by the needs of capitalist society.

WORK DETERMINES LEISURE

This derives from Parker (*The Sociology of Work and Leisure*), who claims that the nature of working life broadly determines the nature of leisure patterns. After studying a range of white-collar workers and linking this to sociological studies of occupations, he concluded that there were three key relationships:

1 **Extension (leisure as an extension of work)** Here workers enjoyed their jobs and took work home with them, so that their working and social lives were intermingled. One example is a university lecturer.

2 **Opposition (leisure as compensation for work)** Workers find their work exhausting and turn to leisure to compensate them. Examples are manual workers going fishing for the peace and quiet.

3 **Neutrality** No clear pattern emerges. This occurs in jobs which are neither particularly interesting nor particularly exhausting. Leisure is often family-centred or at least home-based.

THE FUSION OF WORK AND LEISURE

Wilensky ('Work, careers and social integration', in Smith et al, *Leisure and the Family Life Cycle*) argues that as work becomes more interesting and technology offers us the chance to work from home, the division between home and work will cease to be clear-cut.

GENDER AND LEISURE

Table 7.4 *Changes in home-based leisure activities in Britain, 1977–94*[1]

| | Percentage | | | | |
	1977	1980	1986	1990–91	1993–94
Males					
Watching TV	97	97	98	99	99
Visiting/entertaining friends or relations	89	90	92	95	95
Listening to radio	87	88	87	91	91
Listening to records/tapes	64	66	69	78	79
Reading books	52	52	52	56	59
DIY	51	53	54	58	57
Gardening	49	49	47	52	51
Dressmaking/needlework/knitting	2	2	3	3	3
Females					
Watching TV	97	98	98	99	99
Visiting/entertaining friends or relations	93	93	95	97	96
Listening to radio	87	88	85	87	88
Listening to records/tapes	60	62	65	74	75
Reading books	57	61	64	68	71
DIY	22	23	27	29	30
Gardening	35	38	39	44	45
Dressmaking/needlework/knitting	51	51	48	41	38

[1] Percentages of those aged 16 and over participating in each activity in the four weeks before interview.

(*Source: Social Trends 27*, Table 13.5 (General Household Survey, ONS), p215)

Table 7.5 *Do men help at home in their leisure time? Hours spent on household tasks by parents[1] in the UK, August 1996*

	Hours and minutes per week	
	Fathers	Mothers
Cooking/preparing meals	2:50	13:30
Cleaning	2:00	13:15
Washing and ironing clothes	0:55	9:05
Spending time just with the children	5:05	8:45
Shopping	2:50	5:50
Washing up	2:00	3:40
Driving children to school	1:45	2:55
Gardening	3:00	2:00
Sewing/mending clothes	0:10	1:20
Other household tasks	2:25	1:40
All household tasks	23:00	62:00

[1] Adults with children aged 18 and under

(*Source: Social Trends 27*, Table 13.4, p161)

AGE AND LEISURE

The Rapoports argue that leisure is increasingly determined by lifecycle and have distinguished between the following phases of life:

1. **Adolescence** The search for personal identity and pleasure. This is a period of transition to adulthood.

2. **Young adulthood** The search for a social identity. This lasts for approximately 10 years after leaving school.

3. **Establishment** This lasts from the ages of 25 to 55 and is the main period of life, during which home and family become the central concerns.

4. **The later years** This is a period of increasing reflection on past life; the amount of activity depends upon health and income.

INDIVIDUAL CHOICE (THE PLURALIST PERSPECTIVE)

This reflects the free choices that people are able to make in a relatively wealthy society. Individual interests and income largely determine leisure choice. Roberts' own research on employed males in Liverpool does not support the argument put forward by Parker that work determines leisure.

CAPITALISM AND LEISURE

Clarke and Critcher (*The Devil Makes Work: Leisure in Capitalist Britain*) argue that leisure activities are largely determined by the State and by capitalist industries. They show how there has been a process of increasing control over the working classes, and how they have been disciplined into an obedient workforce. They claim that the State and capitalist enterprises have together defined leisure pursuits:

- the State: through licensing (betting, alcohol) and support (fitness for all, leisure centres etc);
- capitalist enterprises: through provision of a leisure industry and the selling of leisure commodities (videos, magazines, holidays etc).

Clarke and Critcher argue that the provision of sanctioned forms of leisure helps to keep a compliant workforce, while the commercialisation of leisure help to make large profits for the few large industries providing leisure activities. Marcuse (*One Dimensional Man*) has suggested a similar argument in that people are manipulated through the media and leisure industries into an uncritical acceptance of capitalism.

Test yourself questions and answers

Questions

1 What social consequences have occurred as a result of changes in economic sectors?

2 What is the meaning of the formal and informal economies?

3 Explain the increase in the numbers of women working.

4 Summarise the divisions in employment by ethnic group.

5 What are the key elements of post-Fordism?

6 How did Blauner alter Marx's concept of alienation?

7 Give examples of 'resistance' at work.

8 To what factors is the level of strike action related?

9 Which social groups are most likely to be unemployed?

Suggested answers

1 A wide range including changes in social class, and in levels and meaning of unemployment (with consequences for youth and crime). The changing role of women and the possible ramifications for the nature of the family. Education has moved to training. Social cohesion with jobs for life and security has also been threatened. The development of informal economies.

2 The formal economy consists of formally, publicly paid employment which is typically covered by legal boundaries and constraints. The informal economy consists of work which is either not paid – the payment is in 'kind' – or where payment is outside the tax system.

3 The reasons for the increase in women working include the desire of women to return to work as soon as possible, usually after the birth of the last child. This is aided by the fact that women are having fewer children, compressed into a shorter length of time. Women are less well paid and therefore attractive to employers and are willing (because of domestic role of women) to work part-time, making them flexible and unable to claim a number of employment rights (such as not being laid off at the employer's will, entititlement to redundancy money).

4 Overall, the ethnic minorities are more likely to have:

   lower status occupations;

   lower wages;

   significantly higher levels of unemployment.

   People of Afro-Caribbean origin, for example, are most likely to be in semi-skilled and skilled employment. Those of African-Asian backgrounds are likely to be over-represented in the professions and management. Those from Bangladeshi backgrounds are concentrated in the unskilled jobs.

5 ● The use of computerised control of manufacture, computer aided design and robots to undertake particularly repetitive or tedious work.
   ● The use of high technology to produce small numbers of different designs, as opposed to the mass manufacture of identical items.
   ● The need for versatile workers, as opposed to the unskilled production line worker.
   ● New forms of employment mean that workers can be moved around the factory at any one time, or that more part-time workers are employed in order that they can be brought in at times of peak output and sent home when not needed.
   ● Work may be contracted out to other companies.

6 Blauner altered the concept of alienation from Marx's original idea, in which satisfaction could not be acheived without abolishing capitalism, to one in which capitalism itself was not the cause of alienation but certain factors *within* the work situation. He suggested that it had four elements:
   ● powerlessness: no control over work ouput;
   ● meaninglessness: the tasks seem unrelated to the finished product and of little importance;
   ● isolation: where the work process cuts workers off from social contact with their peers;
   ● self-estrangement: this is the closest to Marx's original concept and means where the work becomes a means to obtain money to to gain self-fulfillment.

7 Examples could include such things as:
   ● controlling output levels;
   ● controlling information available to managers;
   ● sabotaging products;
   ● theft;
   ● various short-cuts to make the work process easier or quicker;
   ● fiddling the books.

8 ● Government action: In 1980 and 1984 Employment Acts restricted secondary strikes, limited picketing, required unions to ballot their employees, allowed selective dismissal of strikers and lowered the social security payments to strikers' families.
   ● The state of the economy: Where there are high levels of unemployment those in employment are frightened and are therefore less likely to join in industrial action.
   ● The growth of the post-Fordist economy: With peripheral workers increasingly on short-term contracts, self-employed, or in part-time work, this limits the possibility of striking.

- Production-line work: This is particularly strike prone.

     However, there is some dispute about this, in that Gallie (*In Search of the New Working Class*) stresses the importance of attitudes to work.
- Community: Workers in working-class communities based on a limited range of industries were far more likely to engage in strike action. The demise of coal mining, ship building and the steel industry in the UK limits this form of class consciousness.
- Expression of class conflict: The extent of formal action such as strikes and forms of informal industrial action indicates the degree of class conflict in society. Therefore strikes are normal in capitalist society.

9 The groups more likely than others to be made unemployed include:
   - the least skilled;
   - those living away from the south/south east of England;
   - Ethnic minorities;
   - Women: official rates of unemployment for women are lower than those for men. However, given the problems with the official statistics, it may be that women's rates are similar to men's.

Illustrative question and answer

Question

Item A

New ways of producing goods

This is a description of two factories in Livingston New Town, Scotland.

     Companies like Apollo don't operate in markets defined by mass production and standardisation. They sell their highly specialised products in targeted markets with sophisticated sales teams. And instead of many layers of management and rigid separation between workers and executives, they cultivate all employees' commitment to the product. The company unifies the work-force by calling everyone staff, sponsoring higher education, offering the same holidays (25 days) to everyone, providing free cancer screening, a smart gym on site and private health insurance. It has compressed the management structure and assembly staff travel along the line with the computer they are making.

     Japanese companies operate differently. Mitsubishi has stiff discipline, guaranteed by regular quality checks and campaigns which monitor workers' timekeeping, records of faults – and housekeeping: workers clean up their own work-stations. Unlike Apollo, workers don't travel with a commodity – the product travels along a traditional assembly line. But like Apollo, Mitsubishi prides itself on the flexibility of its workforce, and the way it takes care of its employees. "It is like being members of a family and we want to let them know what is happening in the family," claims personnel officer Bill Barker. By which they mean, presumably, an old fashioned patriarchal family, in which wives, children and servants know their place.

(Adapted from Campbell, B., *Guardian Tomorrows* Wednesday, 16 August 1989)

Item B

... The new technology is having a major impact at work, for a number of reasons. The relative price of products which have had microelectronics incorporated into them has fallen. As manufactured goods have become relatively cheaper owing to increased labour productivity in manufacturing, there has been a relative increase in consumer spending on services. Hence employment has been shifting from the factory to the offices, leisure-related industries and so on. The incorporation of microelectronics in products and manufacturing processes is likely to accelerate this trend. Another impact of new technology at work is the way in which products are manufactured. Those incorporating microchips are made in a markedly different way from the more conventional products they have replaced. As one microchip usually replaces many mechanical parts, the amount of labour needed in assembly is reduced. Some of the remaining assembly tasks are more easily automated. Hence there is less routine manual work to do and the relative proportion of white-collar workers within factories rises.

(Francis, A., *New Technology at Work*, Oxford University Press)

Item C

Technology and alienation

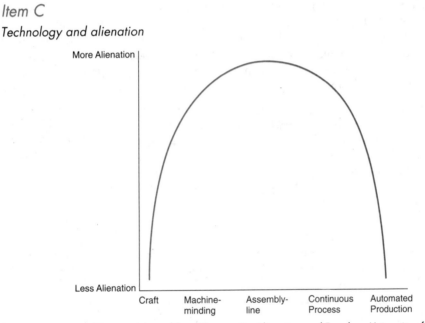

(*Source:* Adapted from Blauner, R., *Alienation and Freedom*, University of Chicago Press)

(a) What strategies have Apollo and Mitsubishi (Item A) employed to overcome the high level of alienation on assembly lines, as suggested in Item C? (2)

(b) What does Item B suggest has been the impact of microelectronics on the distribution of jobs within factories? (1)

(c) Item C suggests that alienation will decrease with the introduction of automation. To what extent do sociological studies support this view? (8)

(d) Using information from Item A and elsewhere assess the relative merits of human relations and scientific management theories. (8)

(e) Discuss the contributions which sociologists have made to an understanding of the impact of new technologies on levels of employment. (6)
AEB

Suggested answer

(a) They both look after their employees and make them feel part of a team or a family. How they do this is very different: Mitsubishi operates on strict traditional lines, whereas Apollo has emphasised the workers' association with her/his product.

(b) Less routine work and relatively higher proportion of white-collar workers.

(c) The results of studies are somewhat contradictory in that alienation can be seen as caused by technology, according to Blauner among others, or by factors outside the workplace altogether, for example Goldthorpe and Lockwood. Indeed, the very definition of what constitutes alienation is a matter of debate, with the original definition of Marx referring not to an attitude to a job but to the soul-destroying nature of capitalism.

You should refer to the debates and then argue that it is not the technology which leads to isolation, but the perceptions individuals have of the meaning of their jobs and of the effects of the wider culture. The research of Gallie is relevant here.

(d) This is a straightforward analysis and comparison of two approaches to how to control people at work. Human relations essentially sets out to control people by creating a sense of team membership and allegiance to the company. The control comes less from the employer rather from other group members. Nevertheless the control remains. The scientific management approach developed earlier in the 20th century and sees the worker as a type of machine that can be made more efficient. The writings of Braverman are particularly important here.

(e) Two approaches are needed here. The first one relates to the specific impact of new technology. Studies by Jenkins and Sherman in the late 1970s painted a gloomy picture of the role of technology and automation in replacing workers, and Gill has suggested that a cut can result in up to 50% of jobs where technology is introduced. However, Hawkins has argued that it is not necessarily technology as such which has led to a reduction in jobs, but also the shift of manufacturing employment away from the UK and the fact that the impact of technology is only one of many influences leading to a decline in employment.

A second and wider strand to this question could focus on the way in which styles and patterns of work are changing and the changing nature of the workforce. This includes such things as part-time and impermanent employment, and the growth in number of low-paid jobs taken by women. You could then go on to mention, and comment on, dual labour market theory, the reserve army of labour, and possibly the underclass.

Question bank

1 What have sociologists contributed to our understanding of industrial conflict?

London Examinations

Points

Main points that the essay should make are:
- Traditionally, and in common sense, the explanations for strikes are seen as economic. Sociology shows this is only partly true.
- Sociology has shown that strikes are only one form of a variety of types of industrial conflict. You should examine the various explanations that exist for striking, pointing out in particular the debate over technology, wider cultures etc. You should also explain the variety of types of industrial conflict (sabotage, theft etc.) and explain where strikes lie in this continuum of activities.

2 Assess the view that technological progress will eliminate alienation at work.

London Examinations

Points

This essay requires you to discuss the meanings of alienation and the differences between the Marxist one and that put forward by Blauner. The argument would be that Blauner's view is that alienation is caused by technology, while the view of Marxists is that the nature of capitalist society creates alienation. You should look at the evidence which supports and contradicts Blauner's views. In particular the work of Gallie. It is difficult to prove or disprove the Marxist view, but you can argue that only the demise of capitalism will eliminate alienation according to this approach.

THE FAMILY AND MARRIAGE

Units in this chapter

Chapter objectives

In this chapter we explore whether the family is, as claimed, an institution so basic to human societies that it is found, in some form, in all societies known to sociologists.

We then look at the different theoretical approaches to the family including:

● the functionalist,

● the phenomenological,

● the Marxist,

● the feminist,

and we note the fact that they have very different views about how beneficial the family is to the lives of its members.

The next section examines the structural changes in the family, and the importance of the economy in bringing about those changes. The next topic upon which sociologists have done research is the changing relationships between spouses in the family and, in particular, the changes in the position of women in the family.

One of the most significant debates in current sociology for social policy is the changing nature of the family and its fragmentation or possible decline. The family in the UK today reflects a range of factors, including Britain as a multi-ethnic society, differences in social class and as a society in which many women choose or are forced to head families by themselves. A significant section of the population chooses not to marry at all; are these people posing an alternative to the family? The final section explores the stresses in the family that have led to the constant increase in divorce in the last half century.

8.1 IS THE FAMILY A UNIVERSAL INSTITUTION?

It has been argued that the family in some form is present in all societies. In 1949 Murdock surveyed over 250 societies (in *Social Structure*) and concluded that some form of family existed in all of them.

Before we continue, we ought to be clear what sociologists mean when they refer to the family.

DEFINITIONS OF THE FAMILY

Nuclear family

This has traditionally been defined as the **basic family unit** of adult partners and their dependent children. When Murdock refers to the family, he means the **nuclear family**. However, feminists now suggest that the basic unit should be regarded as the mother and her dependent children. They point to the increasing numbers of such families in Europe and the USA, and how it has been institutionalised in parts of the Caribbean over decades.

Extended family

Bell and Vogel (*A Modern Introduction to the Family*) define this as 'A grouping broader than the nuclear family which is related by descent, marriage or adoption.'

EXCEPTIONS TO THE RULE OF UNIVERSAL EXISTENCE

However, a number of exceptions have been discovered to Murdock's findings, including:

1. **The Nayar in Sudan** In a historical study of this group, Gough discovered a family which was based upon the women; there were no husbands, nor were there necessarily long-term sexual relationships.

2. **The Kibbutzim in Israel** In the Kibbutzim that follow traditional values, the Kibbutz replaces the family as the centre for economic and social activities.

3. **The West Indies and Guyana** The household is headed by a woman alone and it is unusual for there to be a stable father figure. This does not meet the definition of the nuclear family as given by Murdock.

4. **The UK today** It could be argued that with the growth of single-parent families in the UK and the rest of Europe, the traditional nuclear family as defined by Murdock may be under threat.

8.2 THEORETICAL APPROACHES

The main theoretical approaches that have contributed to our understanding of the family are:

- functionalist,
- phenomenological,
- Marxist,
- feminist.

Each approach is, of course, distinctive, but one clear difference emerges in that functionalist analyses broadly see the family as a good thing for society, and for the individuals in the family. The other approaches are largely critical of the family, seeing it as an essentially harmful institution.

FUNCTIONALIST APPROACHES

Functionalist sociologists (see Chapter 1: Theory) have traditionally stressed the positive role of the family in society, regarding it as beneficial. However, they have disputed between themselves the changes in the functions performed on behalf of the family for its members and society in general.

The underlying argument behind the functionalist approach to the family is that it serves a number of very important **functions** which help to maintain the very existence of society.

The functions of the family

In traditional, pre-industrial societies, the family fulfilled central functions for the survival of society itself and for its individual members. Murdock claims that the family universally performs four functions:

1. **Sexual:** it contains a controlled outlet for sexual gratification which could otherwise lead to conflict and jealousies.

2. **Reproductive:** it allows adults to know the biological parents of children, therefore avoiding incest and delineating lines of descent.

3. **Economic:** it functions as a productive and consumption unit, thus ensuring the survival of the family members.

4. **Educational:** it passes on knowledge and skills from one generation to the next.

Other writers, such as McIver and Page (*Society*) have gone even further and suggest that there is a wider range of services the family traditionally provided, such as leisure and health.

The relationship between the family, the individual and the wider society

Bell and Vogel developed a model of the relationship between the family and society which shows a very close interchange between the wider society and the family. The economy and the family interrelate through the exchange of wages from the economy and workers from the family, the purchasing of goods, and the ploughing back of savings into the economy. The relationship between the political subsystem and the family is one in which the polity gives leadership in return for loyalty and compliance.

The loss of functions

Functionalist writers disagree on the extent to which the family in modern society continues to perform its roles, and there is a general acceptance that the family has lost a number of its functions to other institutions:

1. **The education system** This now teaches individuals the skills required, as the rapid pace of change does not allow skills to be passed on from one generation to the next.

2. **The Welfare State** As geographical mobility has prevented families from giving personal aid, the Welfare State has developed to provide help in times of crisis.

3. **The health services** Owing to the standards of medical knowledge, it is no longer possible for help to be provided by the family members, therefore specialist medical knowledge has developed.

The result is that the importance of the family in contemporary society has been greatly reduced.

A different standard of functions

Fletcher (*The Family and Marriage in Britain*) comments that it is unlikely that the family ever did perform functions in the areas of health or education to any standard worthy of categorisation. He says that the family has not lost functions for they were never performed to the standards of today. If anything, the family has *more* functions than ever before.

The irreducible functions

Parsons has suggested that the key, or **irreducible**, functions left to the family are primarily emotional in that the family provides a place of safety, affection and security for family members. The other functions mentioned by Bell and Vogel and by Murdock are of much less importance to individuals or society.

The two key functions suggested by Parsons are:

1. **Primary socialisation** It is through the family that the individual is socialised into the norms of society and given the basic individual personality. The complexity of these tasks requires intensive teaching in a secure, individualised environment.

2. **Stabilisation of adult personalities** As adults, the place where emotional security is provided is the home, with the family. It is the place which provides the emotional 'harbour' against the stresses and anonymity of industrial society.

This argument is largely supported by Berger and Berger (*The War over the Family*), who claim that there is no alternative to the family for the socialisation process, and they comment critically on the Kibbutzim which, they claim, create adults with little individuality.

Criticisms

Functionalist approaches give a view of the family which uncritically accepts it as good and beneficial. Other approaches to family life show the negative elements. Morgan points out that other institutions could just as easily perform the functions of the family and that it is not necessary to have a *family* as such.

Conclusion

The functionalist approach to the family stresses the roles it plays in the **maintenance of society**. Debates are over the extent to which the family's role may have been altered by the loss of functions rather than over the benefits to society.

PHENOMENOLOGICAL APPROACHES

Phenomenological approaches are upheld by writers such as Cooper (*The Death of the Family*) and Laing (*The Politics of the Family*). They argue that the family can be a place of great emotional pain and unhappiness for its members. Both writers point to the way in which the process of socialisation which Parsons and the Bergers see as being a very positive aspect of the family, is to them essentially harmful. They see individuals, and particularly children, trapped within the family, and having emotional demands made upon them which lead to a submissive and conformist adulthood.

Criticisms

The phenomenological approach to the study of the family has been criticised for its lack of awareness of how certain family members are inherently powerless because of the structure of the family. Feminists have pointed out that it is not necessarily the family as such that creates oppression and unhappiness, but the *patriarchal* nature of the family: the root cause of the unhappiness lies in the power of men to shape the family to their own benefit.

MARXIST APPROACHES

Marxist approaches have some things in common with functionalist approaches, in that they search for the functions performed by the family for the maintenance of capitalist societies. The great difference is that Marxists view this process as essentially harmful and exploitative, as they are critical of capitalist society.

A line of descent

The starting point is the writing of Engels (*The Origins of the family: Private Property and the State*) who argues that the family and marriage represent the males' early attempts to ensure that they would be certain to pass on their property to their own sons. By ensuring the sexual fidelity of the female through marriage, the male was able to ensure that the children were 'his'.

However, it is doubtful whether this is a historically accurate description of the origins of the family, even though the analysis may in fact be useful for drawing attention to the social construction of marriage which benefits males.

Reproduction for capitalism

Marxists argue that the family maintains and helps the continuation of capitalism in two ways:

1. **Ideological reproduction** The values of capitalism are passed on from one generation to the next. Feeley (*The Family*) claims that values such as discipline, hard work, respect for authority and 'passivity not rebellion' are passed on from one generation to the next. The mother is usually the main agent in this transmission.

2. **Physical reproduction** The family is the agency which produces and rears the next generation of workers. This is very cheap for capitalists for they do not have to bear directly the costs of the reproduction of the labour force. One wage allows the entire family to live (the family wage).

Criticisms

The Marxist approach does have a number of failings. These include:

- the omission of any discussion of the oppression of women;
- the failure to accept any positive or beneficial elements of the family to its members;
- essentially functionalist (or **teleological**) nature of the analysis. The Marxist approach starts with the assumption that if the family exists in a capitalist society, then it must be there to benefit the continuation of capitalism. As a result of this assumption, Marxists then seek out what the exact functions of the family are in a capitalist society. The resulting 'analysis' therefore starts with an assumption which, in itself, is debatable.

FEMINIST PERSPECTIVES

Feminist perspectives overlap and extend the Marxist critiques of the family. Whereas the Marxist approaches tend to view family members as experiencing similar exploitation under capitalism, feminists have pointed to the very **unequal exploitation** that takes place, and that it is usually the *women* (and often the children) who are in a worse position than the males. Tables 7.5 (p 161) and 8.1 show that women still bear the burden of domestic tasks.

The differences between feminist writers is on the extent to which women's exploited position in the family is a result of male actions (**patriarchy**), or the capitalist system (Marxist feminism), or both.

Table 8.1 *The unequal division of housework*

	Task done by (%)			
	Female (entirely or mainly)	Both	Male (entirely or mainly)	Other
(a) Female partner employed more than 30 hours per week				
Task				
Washing-up	40	40	10	10
Cleaning the house	65	27	4	4
Washing clothes	91	9	0	0
Cooking	70	21	7	2
(b) Female partner employed less than 30 hours per week				
Washing-up	62	33	2	3
Cleaning the house	87	10	2	1
Washing clothes	97	2	1	0
Cooking	82	16	2	0

A feminist Marxist approach

Benston ('The political economy of women's liberation') takes a fairly orthodox Marxist position. She points to:

- the amount of work the woman does as wife and mother and its advantages for capitalism. The wage of the male pays for two workers.
- the extent to which the family acts as a mechanism to control workers who will not cause disruption at work for fear of harming their families.

A critical view of the stress placed on capitalism rather than on patriarchy is taken by Delphy (*Close to Home*), who takes a radical feminist perspective when she argues that the family consists of men exploiting women, and that it is *inherently* exploitative, as a result of male wishes, not of capitalism.

Radical feminist approaches

Barnard (*Whose Marriage?*) argues that the family operates for the benefit of men, and to the discomfort and illness of women. She claims that the pressure and the oppression of the woman's role in the family actually makes women physically and mentally ill.

Barrett (*Women's Oppression Today*) claims that the family is the seat of women's oppression in society. This oppression derives from two sources:

1 the economic power held by men over women: generally men control household finances as the main 'breadwinner' of the family;

2 the ideology in which women are expected to be subservient to men.

Oakley's original research on the exploitation of women through housework (*The Sociology of Housework*) shows that women work long hours, doing dull, repetitive work, and receive little status and no wage. She argues that the family does not benefit the woman, but actually harms her.

Ansley argues that the wife plays an important emotional role for males in that society allows men to vent their anger on their partners, to help absorb their own feelings from work of powerlessness and oppression.

Abuse in the family

Feminist writers have also drawn attention to the way that the family, or at least the ideology of the family, masks physical abuse of women and both physical and sexual abuse of children. No one knows the extent of violence in the home, as attacks are rarely reported to the police.

But in a Scottish study by Dobash and Dobash (*Violence against Wives*), 25% of all assaults reported to police were by husbands on wives. Dobash and Dobash argue that violence against female partners is embedded in our culture:

1 **Historically** Throughout history the use of a limited degree of violence by husbands has been culturally (and legally) acceptable.

2 **Culturally** The values of family life are of a dominant male and a submissive wife who should perform her duties to a very high standard. Women who fail to do so can reasonably be coerced.

3 **Specifically** Dobash and Dobash do not dispute that specific factors such as alcohol or jealousy may not spark off violence, but this can only occur where there is a cultural context which allows this.

The family as an agency of oppression to those not in traditional families

Barrett and McIntosh (*The Anti-Social Family*) argue that the ideological support for the traditional nuclear family actually oppresses those outside this family model and, as a large proportion of those who are single (particularly the elderly) and the heads of one-parent families are female, the very ideology of the family makes those outside the traditional 'normal', nuclear family feel excluded and marginalised.

8.3 THE CHANGING STRUCTURE OF THE FAMILY

THE FAMILY AND INDUSTRIALISATION: THE FOUR STAGES OF THE FAMILY

Young and Willmott have suggested the family has passed through three stages and might possibly pass through a fourth. These stages can provide a useful structure for discussing the changes.

Stage One: the pre-industrial family

Here the family, composed of husband, wife and the unmarried children, is an economic unit producing goods for self-consumption or for sale. There is a very limited emotional tie between the partners as the economic aspects override the emotional ones.

According to Laslett (*The World we have Lost*), the family in pre-industrial Britain was nuclear and not extended as has been commonly believed. The other major characteristic was that of **primogeniture** – the term used to describe the situation where the eldest child (or more usually the son) inherited all the land or property from the parents. This had two consequences, according to Harris (*The Family*):

1 that ownership of the land remained intact and that the male who inherited was likely to be well off;

2 that the sons and daughters who did not inherit formed a mobile labour force which went in search of employment.

Harris argued that the fact of primogeniture and consequent mobile labour force resulted in the family actually creating the situation whereby industrialisation could take off in Britain; industrialisation took a different pattern in continental Europe, where primogeniture was not the norm.

This is the opposite of the functionalist approach which sees the changes in the family coming about as a result of the impact of industrialisation on it.

Stage Two: the family in the early period of industrialisation

Parsons and, separately, Goode (*World Revolution and Family Patterns*) claim that the Industrial Revolution actually weakened the (extended) family by taking away crucial economic and social functions from the family.

However, an alternative approach comes from Anderson (*Approaches to the History of the Western Family*), who has argued that the early industrial family actually helped to form extended families. Using data from the 1851 Preston census, Anderson found that 23% of households contained family members other than those in the nuclear family. This is a higher figure than in either pre-industrial England or contemporary Britain. Anderson argues that the extended family of the period was a response by the working class to the difficult circumstances (poverty, high levels of disability and illness, lack of housing) of the early period of industrialisation and was, essentially, a method of mutual assistance. There was no Welfare State and extremely limited charitable assistance, so the kin network was able to provide some level of help. Rather than industrialisation breaking up the extended family, and bringing about the nuclear family, Anderson's work suggests that the very opposite occurred.

Young and Willmott suggest that the extended family that developed at this time was constructed primarily by the women for their own and their children's benefit. The mother–daughter bond was very strong, while the husband–wife relationship was relatively weak. Families were headed by women, because of the relatively young age of death of the husbands. Young and Willmott reached these conclusions after they studied family life in the mid-1950s in Bethnal Green, East London (*Family and Kinship in East London*). This was a traditional working-class area which reflected the patterns that had developed over 100 years. Two-thirds of the locals had kin living within three miles.

Stage Three: the symmetrical family

In the 1970s Young and Willmott conducted another, this time much larger, study on the family (*The Symmetrical Family*). This consisted of a survey of almost 2,000 people in and around London. They suggest that the extended family of Stage Two had altered and been replaced by distinct nuclear families, but which still remained in contact by telephone and car. The second difference was the development of the **symmetrical family** (also discussed on pp 176–7). This was a family in which husband and wife undertook activities together and perceived themselves as equal partners. The husband was much more active in the home than in previous times.

Young and Willmott argue that family changes are linked to two not necessarily compatible factors: that extended families emerge in times of economic need, and decline in periods of affluence, and that values percolate down from the higher social classes to the lower ones. Changes are therefore more likely to appear first in the higher social classes. This concept of values beginning with the middle class and then filtering through to become widespread working-class values is known as **the principle of stratified diffusion**.

The Stage Four family

Young and Willmott suggest that a possible fourth family type may be emerging, which they first found among the better paid managing directors in their 1970s study. These men enjoyed their job and put it before family life. They were work-centred rather than home-centred. These families were more **asymmetrical** than the Stage Three ones. However, there seems little evidence to support the emergence of this fourth type in the population as a whole.

THE FAMILY NETWORK TODAY

The most contemporary evidence comes from a study by Willmott ('Kinship in urban communities, past and present'), conducted in the mid-1980s in north London to find out the extent of the continuing contact between family members at that time. His study shows that the strength of the family as a whole was based upon distinct nuclear family groups that maintained regular contact with each other, even though they may be living some distance apart. In his study he found that about 70% of respondents saw at least one relative weekly. Cars and telephones were used to maintain regular contact with those living some distance away.

Willmott suggests that three family types exist in contemporary UK:

1 **The local extended family** This comprises two or three nuclear families living separately but near each other and maintaining daily contact. This applies to about one-eighth of the UK population but is more common among the working class, in stable communities and in the other areas of the UK excluding southern England.

2 **The dispersed extended family** This is the most common type today and is composed of nuclear families living some distance apart and with consequent less frequent contact. Contact is still typically fortnightly, and aid is provided in emergencies and less often on a routine basis. This applies to about half the population.

3 **Attenuated extended families** For these, kinship is less important, but individuals and nuclear families may come together on ritual occasions and also keep in touch so that contact is not lost. For many, such as students and young couples, it may be a phase of life and re-entry to one of the other family types may occur in later life.

These descriptions of family life are supported by other research. In particular, Allen (*Family Life, Domestic Roles and Social Organisation*), in a study of a village in East Anglia, uncovered a sense of mutual obligation and contact between family members. In this particular study, however, the range of kin who are considered important is restricted and could not be accurately described as 'extended'; instead Allen uses the term the **elementary family**, which implies a restricted network rather than some form of closely interrelated family in the more traditional sense of the word.

CONCLUSION

The structure of the family seems remarkably resilient in responding to and shaping economic changes. The evidence suggests that the extended family network still exists and, although many families are physically spread over a wide geographical area, communication occurs with the aid of cars and telephones.

8.4 RELATIONSHIPS BETWEEN THE SPOUSES

CONJUGAL ROLES

In the 1950s Bott coined the terms **segregated conjugal role relationships** and **joint conjugal role relationships** to describe the different relationships between husbands and wives. In general, she argues (on the basis of a study of 20 couples) that couples either:

- led separate lives, with very different tasks within the home – the segregated conjugal role relationship. This was more typical of the working-class families;

or

- tended to do leisure activities together and perform similar household tasks – the joint conjugal role relationship. This was more typical of the middle-class families.

SYMMETRICAL FAMILY

By the 1970s, Young and Willmott's study gave some support to the idea that there had been a move toward the joint or, as they call it, the **symmetrical family**, in which there is a greater sense of partnership between couples and a mutual sharing of tasks. The basis of this conclusion was that the majority of husbands reported helping their wives at least once a week with the household tasks.

Reasons for the development of the symmetrical family

1 There was a decline in the need for mutual aid with the rise in affluence.

2 The increase in the activities of the Welfare State led to there being less need for assistance from family members.

3 Geographical mobility dispersed the family (although contact continued).

4 There was a decline in the number of children being born, and increased stress on spouse relations.

5 There was an increase in the number of women working, giving them greater power.

6 The home has become a more attractive place for people (and particularly husbands) to want to stay in.

THE PATRIARCHAL FAMILY: CRITICISMS OF THE SYMMETRICAL FAMILY

The Young and Willmott study claimed that a sign of symmetry was the husband helping his wife once a week. But can this really be seen as a sign of symmetry? In the first place, once a week seems very limited; secondly, the words, 'helping the wife', assume that this is her work and that she is responsible. This is often claimed as a good example of male thinking in sociology.

The reality of housework

Shortly after Young and Willmott's study, Oakley studied 40 married women, aged between 20 and 30, living in North London and with at least one child. She found very little evidence of their husbands sharing the housework. Only 15% had a husband who shared domestic work to a significant level, and 25% whose husband had a significant level of responsibility in childcare. In Edgell's study of middle-class families (*Middle Class Couples*), no evidence was found to support the argument that a symmetrical family existed with equal sharing of household tasks, although half the sample did share child-rearing responsibilities.

Even this limited evidence for sharing child-rearing has been challenged by Boulton (*On Being a Mother*), who claims that husbands merely help with particular tasks, or play with their children. But if the definition of child-rearing is one in which the child takes priority in the life of the carer, including their life outside the home, then in less than 20% of her sample (of 50 London families with a non-employed mother) did the husband have a major share of responsibility for childcare.

The annual *European Social Attitudes Surveys* which include a national survey of British attitudes to, and activities in the home conclude that women still have primary responsibility for housework and childcare.

POWER AND CONJUGAL ROLES

Who is the dominant partner within the marriage?

In the 1950s studies of Bethnal Green, Young and Willmott conclude that the dominant partner was the mother/wife. By the 1970s they argued that there was symmetry and a degree of equality within the home. However, most feminist commentators have disputed this and argued that the family remains a **patriarchal** institution.

One way of deciding the issue has been to look at who controls the family finances. Edgell argues that the major decisions regarding finances are taken by the husband, in particular over house moves, hire purchase agreements and car purchase. Day-to-day decisions on the budget which were defined as less important by the husband were the responsibility of the wife. Pahl (*Money and Marriage*) studied 102 couples with at least one child under 16, and found four ways in which couples organised their finances:

1 **Wife control** Major decisions are taken by the wife. Typically low-income or debt households, where the woman makes a significant contribution to the household budget.

② **Wife-controlled pooling** There is a joint account from which the wife pays the major bills. This is typical of middle-income couples where the wife has an independent income.

③ **Husband control** There is no joint bank account and the husband typically gives his wife money for household expenses. He decides the amount. This occurs in marriages where the wife does not work.

④ **Husband-controlled pooling** This is typical of high-income households, particularly where the wife is employed in a lower status job than the male. There are joint accounts but the husband pays the major bills.

Overall, Pahl found that the finances of approximately 60% of couples were controlled by the husband either entirely (group 3) or from a joint pool (group 4). One interesting fact was that there was a greater chance of a couple defining their marriage as happy where there was joint decision-making over finances than where the husband alone made the decisions.

CONCLUSION

There seems to be no evidence that women in general have achieved equality within marriage. Husbands still appear to be the dominant partners – at least in terms of patterns of housework and financial control. It would appear that where women have employment they may well have both work and household duties to combine, although their own employment does allow them to make financial decisions. As both Allan and Pahl point out in their studies, women start off with a disadvantage because of the underlying social (or ideological) assumptions concerning the nature of marriage and the role of women.

There is further discussion on the role of women and the family in Chapter 4: Gender and sexuality.

8.5 MARRIAGES, HOUSEHOLDS AND FAMILIES

We have discussed the debate concerning the move from extended to nuclear families in Britain. However, this debate may well have been overtaken by the changing nature of households and family in contemporary Britain.

The family in the UK today consists of a wide variety of types. These include variations by:

- ethnic and cultural factors,
- social class,
- remarriage and divorce.

There is also opposition to the very structure of marriage from cohabitation.

ETHNIC AND CULTURAL VARIATIONS

Britain is a multi-cultural society with a variety of ethnic groups. Two of the major groupings are people of Afro-Caribbean origin and Indian, Bangladeshi and Pakistani origin.

Afro-Caribbean origin

Barrow suggests there are three main types of family among this group ('West Indian families: an insider's perspective'). These are:

1 **The conventional nuclear family** This is the traditional UK-style nuclear family, although Driver has suggested that the woman has a far more important family role than in most other UK families.

2 **The common-law family** This exists among the less well off, and consists of unmarried partners with children of one or both partners.

3 **The mother household** This is a **matriarchal** family in which there are no permanent males. It is based on a wider female kinship and a friendship support network.

Indian, Bangladeshi and Pakistani origin

According to Ballard ('South Asian families'), these families have suffered relatively little disruption in their extended family networks. Contact is maintained both in the UK and with relatives in the country of origin (where appropriate). The second generation is able to switch from UK styles of life to more traditional South Asian ones and is thereby able to continue to support the traditional kin network without being excluded from the broader UK culture.

SOCIAL CLASS

There remain differences in social classes in terms of financial decision-making, and the extent of sharing of household tasks and child-rearing.

LONE PARENTHOOD

About 1 in 7 families is now headed by a single parent (usually the mother); this compares with only 1 in 12 only 10 years ago. Now, 1 in 6 households with children under the age of 16 are headed by a single parent. The causes of this are:

1 **The death of one spouse**: 14% of women over the age of 16 are widows, and 4% of men are widowers.

2 **Divorce and separation**: this is the single biggest cause, which affects 9% of all families. 1 in 20 women in Britain today are divorced.

3 **No marriage**: accounting for approximately 5% of all families.

See Fig. 8.1.

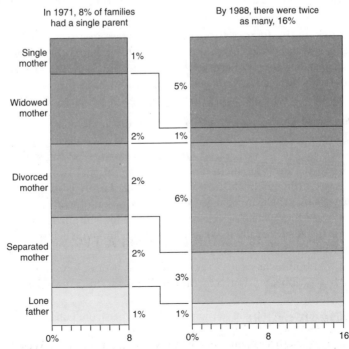

(*Source: The Independent,* 6 December 1989)

Fig. 8.1 Single parents by composition

Fig. 8.2 shows the age of the children in divorcing families; it finds that nearly 25% of divorcing families have a 16-year-old child and 10% have an 8-year-old child.

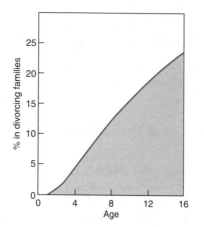

Fig. 8.2 The age of children in divorcing families in the UK

The statistics in Figs 8.1 and 8.2 have been used by such commentators as the Rapoports (*Families in Britain*) to argue that the traditional 'cereal packet' family is less common than in the past.

CRITICISM OF THE 'COLLAPSE OF THE FAMILY' ARGUMENT

Chester ('The rise of the neo-conventional family') argues that the decline of the conventional family has been exaggerated, and that family life still remains a central and vibrant element of society. He points out that there are two areas of confusion:

1. **Misuse of the statistics** Chester points out that the argument is based on the fact that the number of traditional families as a proportion of *households* is small. He says that the only accurate guide is to count the families as percentages of *people*, so instead of there being of only 32% of households composed of the traditional family of parents and dependent children, he states that 49% of people live in families so composed. So Chester argues that the breakdown of the family into diverse types is not so advanced as many people claim.

2. **The dynamics of the family lifecycle** Families are in a constant state of change as the parents age and the children grow up and leave home. Statistics of the family only show a snapshot at any one time. In fact, there are families being formed, such as young married couples (20% of people), and families in the stages of decline, such as married couples with independent children (8% of people).

Chester concludes that approximately 60% of the population live in households comprising parents and children.

Cashmore (*Having To: The World of One-parent Families*) in his study of poor single mothers found that the ideal for them remained the traditional two-parent family. So the idea that people are deliberately shifting away from the family is inaccurate.

Chester suggests that the main change in the family is that of women working, which has led to different roles for women within the family. This shift from a male head of the household who is the single breadwinner to the husband and wife being dual earners has led him to use the term the **neo-conventional family**.

COHABITATION

Another perceived threat to the conventional family is that from cohabitation. In the last 15 years the number of people cohabiting has trebled, so that today almost 13% of 18–24-year-olds are cohabiting, and approximately 7% of those over 25 are. It has been suggested that this is an alternative to marriage.

Chester points out, however, that only about 2% of women are cohabiting on a permanent basis, and that the majority of cohabitees are in a stage which precedes marriage (see Fig. 8.3) or is the result of the break-up of a marriage. Chester claims that couples usually marry when they have a child or when the female becomes pregnant.

However, the statistics do not fully bear out Chester's argument that cohabitation is merely a stage which takes place before or after marriage. Today, about 30% of births are outside marriage (see Table 8.2), and about 13% of these are registered by both parents living at the same address. This would imply a long-term commitment, which is similar to marriage in permanence. These figures fit in with what has already happened in Scandinavia, where almost 40% of couples cohabit rather than marry.

Fig. 8.3 *Proportion of women in the UK who cohabited with their future husband before marriage, by year of marriage*

Table 8.2 *The changing pattern of births within and outside marriage in the UK, 1961–90*

	1961	1971	1981	1990
Total all live births (thousands)	944	902	731	799
Total live births within marriage (thousands)	887	830	636	575
Total live births outside marriage (thousands)	57	72	95	224
Extra-marital births as a % of all live births	6	8	13	28

(*Source: Social Trends*, 1992)

DECLINE IN THE PROPORTION OF PEOPLE MARRYING

Marriage rates have declined steeply across Europe in the last 20 years. In 1961 there were 340,000 first marriages, yet in 1990 this had fallen to 241,000. Partially to compensate for this, the number of people marrying for a second time has increased from 5,000 to 47,000, and now re-marriages form 36% of all marriages in the UK compared to 14% in 1961. In 1971 only 4% of women remained unmarried by the age of 50; in the mid-1990s the figure is 17%. From these statistics, it is clear that people are marrying older and fewer of them are marrying.

Although this would appear to suggest a large-scale shift to cohabiting, Chester disputes this and argues that it represents a delay in people getting married, so that they cohabit at first and then marry with the birth of children. This has an effect on the statistics. However, the statistics do support the argument that fewer people marry. Government statistics show that 50 per 1,000 eligible women marry today compared to 80 per 1,000 30 years ago. But Britain still has the second highest marriage rate in Europe after Portugal. It also has the second highest divorce rate after Denmark.

8.6   MARITAL BREAKDOWN

THE EXTENT OF MARITAL BREAKDOWN

Table 8.3   *The rise in the divorce rate, 1961–90*

	1961	1971	1981	1989	1990
Total divorces					
(decrees absolutes granted in UK, thousands)	27	80	157	164	168
Divorce rate					
(persons divorcing per thousand married people in England and Wales)	2.1	6.0	11.9	12.7	12.9

(*Source: Social Trends,* 1992)

There are three elements to marital breakdown:

1 **divorce**: the legal dissolution of marriage;

2 **separation**: where partners live apart;

3 **empty-shell marriages**: where the partners continue married but have no shared emotional or social life.

Since 1971, the number of marriages has fallen by one-fifth and the number of divorces has doubled; on the face of it, this suggests a collapse in the institution of the family. However, it could be argued that all that has happened is that unhappy marriages are more likely to end formally in divorce and that the number of empty-shell marriages has declined.

EXPLANATIONS FOR MARITAL BREAKDOWN

Legal changes

The divorce rate, to some extent, reflects legal changes. The Divorce Reform Act came into force in 1971 and in 1984 the period that a couple had to be married before they could petition for divorce was shortened. On each occasion that the law is liberalised, there is a large increase in the numbers of people applying for divorce. This is not a cause of divorce, but a reflection of unhappy marriages. Goode has argued that this process of liberalisation is part of a wider process of secularisation in Western societies.

Changing expectations of marriage

Goode has suggested that, historically, marriage was not based upon love, but was often merely an economic relationship with limited expectations of companionship. The contemporary marriage is based upon true love, and the partners expect that all their emotional needs will be fulfilled within it. This fits with the argument put forward by another functionalist, Parsons, who claims that the family has lost its wider functions and instead provides the emotional needs that are not available in the broader society.

The decline in the extended family and the move to the nuclear family places greater emotional pressures on the fewer family members, changing people's expectations of marriage.

Shorter (*The Making of the Modern Family*) has made similar points in his historical account of the development of the modern family. He argues that capitalism brought about a degree of individual freedom from family and community pressures to conform. This enabled romantic love to develop and with it the potential emotional instability of marriage. It also meant that marriage came to be viewed as a very different institution than had previously been the case. This is explained in the section on the value of marriage, below.

The result of all this emotional loading is that the family becomes an emotional pressure cooker with great propensity to explode. If the family fails to provide all the emotional and social needs, then the marriage breaks down.

The value of marriage

Paradoxically, the increase in divorce and the numbers of people cohabiting could suggest that the value of marriage is actually higher, and that people expect very high standards from marriage (see Fig. 8.4). They may be doubtful about entering such an institution or may be keen to leave it, because they have an ideal of what marriage should be, which is sanctioned by society. This fits closely with the change in the expectations of marriage that has already been discussed.

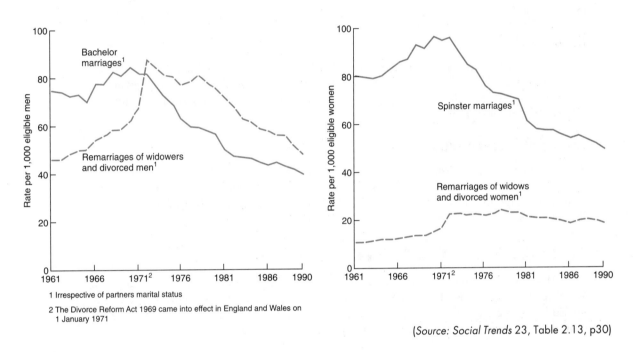

1 Irrespective of partners marital status

2 The Divorce Reform Act 1969 came into effect in England and Wales on 1 January 1971

(*Source: Social Trends* 23, Table 2.13, p30)

Fig. 8.4 Although people in the UK are more ready to divorce, they still value marriage

The changing attitudes of women

The majority (73%) of divorces are initiated by women. This could suggest that women's increasing economic independence and their greater belief in their own rights have allowed them the opportunity and desire to divorce if they perceive it as being possible to do so. Previously, the fact that men were often the sole earner in the household meant that they could prevent the wife initiating divorce proceedings. The rise in the numbers of women working, the extension of legal aid for divorce, and the increasing ease of divorce have all enabled women to initiate proceedings.

Hart (*When Marriage Ends*) argues through a Marxist analysis that, even though women now generally have paid employment, they are still expected by men to do the majority of housework and child-rearing. The tension that the different demands these roles can place on both partners can often lead to divorce.

Decline in community pressure

It is claimed that social controls and restraints, such as the social stigma attached to divorce, which kept individuals together have weakened as a result of increasing urbanisation and the related decline in community.

SOCIAL STATUS AND DIVORCE

Marital breakdown occurs with greater frequency among certain social groups than others. Three factors contribute:

- social class,
- age,
- cultural differences.

Social class

There are higher divorce rates among the lower working and lower middle classes that in other social classes. This reflects the economic and social pressures which are experienced by those on the margins of social classes and who aspire to the majority standard of living in that class.

Age

The younger the partners at marriage, the higher the chances are of divorce. This reflects possible emotional immaturity, the fact that the woman is more likely to be pregnant at marriage, and the fact that their personal development may take place at different speeds and in different directions.

Cultural differences

Those who come from very different backgrounds have increased chances of divorce. Thomas and Collard (*Who Divorces?*) argue that divorce often occurs because the couple are unable to communicate their feelings to each other. Therefore they are unable to work through their differences and problems.

THE STABILITY OF THE FAMILY

More than 95% of people still marry today. Although divorce rates are high, remarriage rates are high too, suggesting that people may reject their partners but are not rejecting the institution of marriage. Cohabitation is increasing rapidly and reflects a change in society's attitude to religions and the weakening of community pressures.

Test yourself questions and answers

Questions

1 Is the family universal?

2 What are the two 'irreducible functions' of the family, according to Parsons?

3 Briefly summarise the Marxist view of the family.

4 What are the four stages of the family, according to Young and Willmott?

5 When sociologists talk of 'family diversity', what are they referring to?

6 What criticisms have been made of the concept of the symmetrical family?

7 Did Willmott conclude in his north London study that families were nuclear and isolated?

8 Is cohabitation replacing marriage as a 'normal' form of relationship?

9 Name three possible causes of marriage breakdown.

Suggested answers

1 It depends upon what you mean by universal and what you mean by a family. The vast majority of societies have some family structure, but there have been attempts, such as by the Israeli Kibbutzim, to replace it. What is probably true to say is that the mother–child link is universal.

2 Primary socialisation and the stabilisation of adult personality.

3 Engels suggested that the family provided a line of descent, though it is doubtful whether this is a historically accurate description. Two roles which contemporary Marxists delineate are:
   ● ideological reproduction, where the values of capitalism are passed on from one generation to the next;
   ● physical reproduction, in that the family is the agency which produces the next generation of workers.

4 ● The pre-industrial family – basically an economic unit.
   ● Early industrial – an extended family.
   ● Symmetrical family – found from the 1960s onward.
   ● Type four family – where the importance of male careers means that he spends less time at home.

5 Families in the UK today consist of a wide variety of types, including variations by:
   ● Ethnic and cultural factors – for example, extended Asian and Bangladeshi families, or the female headed Afro-Caribbean households.
   ● Social class.
   ● Remarriage and divorce, and cohabitation.
   Do not forget there are also a wide range of household types.

6 Young and Willmott claimed that a sign of symmetry was the husband giving 'help' once a week to his wife. Is this 'symmetry'? Once a week seems very limited, and by saying 'helping' the wife, the assumption is that this is her work. Oakley studied 40 married women with at least one child, of whom only 15% had a husband who shared domestic work to any significant level. Similar criticisms have been made by Boulton and Edgell concerning child-care. Even this limited evidence for sharing child-rearing has been challenged by Boulton.

7 Willmott's study showed the strength of the family which was based upon distinct nuclear families that maintained regular contact with each other even though they may be living some distance apart. He found about 70% of respondents saw at least one relative weekly. Willmott suggests three family types exist in contemporary UK society:
   ● The local extended family which comprises two or three nuclear families living separately but near each other and maintaining daily contact.
   ● The dispersed extended family, composed of nuclear families living some distance apart and with consequent less frequent contact, but contacts are still likely to be typically fortnightly.
   ● Attenuated extended families, for whom kinship is less important, but individuals and nuclear families may come together on ritual occasions and also keep in touch, so that contact is not lost.

8   In the last 15 years the numbers of people cohabiting has trebled, so that today almost 13% of 18–24 year olds are cohabiting, and approximately 7% of those over 25 are. Chester argues that only about 2% of women are cohabiting on a permanent basis, and that the majority of cohabitees are in a stage which precedes marriage or as the result of the break-up of a marriage.

However, the statistics do not fully bear out Chester's argument that cohabitation is merely a stage which takes place before/after marriage. Today about 30% of births are outside marriage, and about 13% are registered by both parents living at the same address, implying a long-term commitment. These figures fit in with what has already happened in Scandinavia, where almost 40% of couples cohabit rather than marry.

9   Possible causes include:
   ● legal changes making divorce easier;
   ● higher expectations of marriage partners;
   ● increased value of the meaning of marriage;
   ● changing attitudes to cohabitation, single parenthood etc;
   ● decline in the community sanctions to keep people married.

Illustrative question and answer

Question

Item A

Some writers emphasise the cost effectiveness of the conjugal family in reproducing labour power. This argument is based on the assumption that unpaid domestic labour (that is, the labour of the housewife) lowers the minimum cost of labour to the advantage of capital. This is because workers would have to buy in domestic and child-care services if the family did not exist. This would add to their living costs and raise wage levels. Other writers have suggested that the family not only secures unpaid domestic labour for capitalism but also provides a reserve army of labour. Housewives can be drawn upon in periods of high demand for labour and, when no longer needed, can return to the family without appearing in unemployment statistics.

(Adapted from Elliott, F. R., *The Family: Change or Continuity*, Macmillan)

Item B

Feminists argue that 'welfare' legislation has incorporated the partriarchal ideology of the society that originated it. Acts such as the Factory Acts of the nineteenth century, which were supposedly designed to protect women from working long hours in unsafe conditions, in fact were designed to take them out of the workforce and keep them in the home, no longer competing with men for jobs. The 1911 National Insurance Act insured male workers but excluded married women, who were thought to be the responsibility of their husband and dependent on him. The Beveridge Report adopted the same approach: 'the attitude of the housewife to gainful employment outside the home is not and should not be the same as that of the single woman. She has other duties…'

(Trowler, P., *Investigating Health, Welfare and Poverty*, Unwin Hyman)

Item C

Functionalists regard the family as an important 'organ' in the 'body' of society. It is what the family 'does' or the functions of the family that most interest them. For example, we can look at sex and reproduction. According to functionalists, marriage and the nuclear family provide the best opportunity for the socially controlled expression of the sex drive. More importantly, they provide the necessary institutional stability for the reproduction and nurturing (bringing up) of children. The bringing up of children requires considerable time and effort: human maturation takes longer than that of any other species relative to life-span. To be brought up effectively, children usually require the help of more than one person (for practical if not emotional reasons). In most societies the two people who produce a child are expected to take responsibility for its upbringing.

(O'Donnell, M., *New Introduction to Sociology*, Nelson)

(a) Which sociological perspective is illustrated by Item A.   (1)

(b) Explain briefly what is meant by 'patriarchal ideology' (line 1) Item B.   (2)

(c) Item C states that 'in most societies, the two people who produce a child are expected to take responsibility for its upbringing'. How far is this view supported by sociological evidence?   (5)

(d) Assess the contribution of feminist perspectives to an understanding of the family.   (8)

(e) Items A and C suggest very different views about the functions of the family in modern society. Discuss these points of view and assess their relative merits.   (9)

AEB

Suggested answer

(a) Marxist.

(b) Note that as only two marks are awarded there is no need to go into depth. Your answer should refer to the power that males have to create a set of dominant values in society which benefit them at the expense of women.

(c) It is probably true to say that this is the case in the majority of societies; but they may well do so within a wider kin network. However, a more accurate statement would be to suggest that in the overwhelming majority of societies the mother has the main responsibility, with the role of father having different interpretations in different societies.

   To prove your point you could give examples of child-rearing in contemporary UK and refer to the growth in single-parent families and, within two-parent families, to the dominant role of the mother. You could also give examples of the importance of the wider kin for Asian-origin families.

(d) This question is worth eight marks and therefore deserves spending some time on. You should state the traditional view of the family put forward by Marxist and functionalist writers, and comment upon the gender blindness of interactionist theories. You should then point out how feminist perspectives helped to lay clear the dimensions of power both within the family and the wider society, and showed how women are oppressed by men. You could refer to studies and arguments by Oakley, Delphy, Benston and Barnard.

(e) The two points of view are the Marxist and the functionalist. You need to examine each viewpoint in turn and suggest what positive insights they provide and what weaknesses they have. Then you should look at the similarities and differences between the two approaches.

   The functionalists examine the positive functions of the family for both its members and for the wider society. Debates over exactly what the functions are persist within the functionalist perspective. The roles of the family members are taken for granted and are seen to reflect very much biological imperatives. The structure of the family is closely linked to the needs of society. Problems occur in the functionalist viewpoint in that it has a considerable number of historical mistakes; the family is shown to have a more negative side with violence by males towards females and children, it ignores the issues of power and women.

Marxist perspectives stress the family as a means by which capitalism can reproduce its workforce both physically and ideologically. The family benefits capitalist society, but not its members. Criticisms have been made that it has historical inaccuracies – particularly Engel's ideas; the fact that family can also be beneficial to its members; and that the Marxist position has largely ignored the position of women.

Both approaches stress the importance of the family to society, although they interpret whether it is good or bad for society in very different ways. Both approaches ignore women and tend to take a male perspective.

Question bank

1 What has been the contribution of feminist sociology to our understanding of relationships within the family?

Integrated Boards

Points

Need to show how feminist perspectives have demonstrated that contrary to earlier functionalist analyses, the family does not benefit all its members. Instead, it is argued that the family largely benefits men. Furthermore, this has led to analysis of the benefits to children and the argument is that for many children the family is harmful.

- Delphy and Leonard have pointed to the importance of domestic labour and how this has been overlooked.
- Finch has shown the extent of the caring role which women have had to undertake which has benefited others but not them.
- Boulton has pointed out the exaggeration of the extent to which the 'new man' helps in the home.
- Edgell has pointed out the continuing dominance of the male in the family.

2 (a) Briefly explain what sociologists mean by the concept of 'joint conjugal roles'. (4)

(b) Briefly describe how two aspects of modern social life might be changing the nature of relationships within the family. (4)

(c) What evidence is there for the view that relationships within the family are becoming more democratic and egalitarian? (7)

(d) Evaluate the view that the contemporary family meets the needs of its members.

(10)

Integrated Boards

Points

(a) Sharing of tasks by cohabiting partners (etc)

(b) Changing attitudes of women, changing role of children or employment patterns, such that both partners go out to work.

(c) Studies by Gershuny and by Edgell both suggest that men dominate in terms of their decisions being the final ones. Also that women still do more housework, even when taking into account employment patterns.

(d) Point out this is a functionalist argument, and then run through the argument that the family performs various functions for its members. The criticise by pointing out the reliance on women and the continuing oppression of children. You could use the work of Esterton to point out the psychological damage it is claimed the family does.

3 'Households today take so many different forms that the idea of a "normal" nuclear family no longer applies.' Critically assess this statement.

Integrated Boards

Points

This question refers to the argument that the traditional nuclear family of father/mother and dependent children all living together is only a small and declining proportion of all households. You should start with evidence supporting this, pointing out the increase in divorce and the growth of never-married mothers living alone, as well as the increase in cohabitation as a perceived alternative to marriage. You should then move on to discuss this. It is important to distinguish between the household and the family first of all, and secondly to point out that the family is dynamic, passing through a number of stages. In terms of households it is a declining proportion because of the growth in households of single people, of elderly people and of those cohabiting. In terms of families, however, the proportion remains historically high. The 'normal' family referred to is a phase in the family life-cycle. Point out that it is still true the majority of cohabitees marry and the majority of divorcees remarry.

EDUCATION

Units in this chapter

Chapter objectives

In this chapter we set out to explore the social characteristics of the educational system. In particular, the chapter provides an overview of the major issues which sociologists have identified.

The chapter begins with an overview of the major theoretical traditions which have been used to analyse education. The major competing approaches are the functionalist, which sees the education system as providing a positive educational experience which benefits the children and the society, through to the Marxist one(s) which suggest that the educational system does just the opposite. Marxists claim that the system oppresses and harms people, benefitting only the powerful. Interactionism provides a very different approach and concerns itself with what goes on inside schools, arguing that this area of life is socially constructed by the activities of the students and teachers.

The debate which has almost completely dominated the sociological analysis of education concerns the factors which affect the educational attainment of the students in schools. Why do some children do well and others less well? If you believe in natural ability determining success then the answer is that some children are cleverer than others. Sociologists reject this premise and instead seek the social factors which ensure that children who are basically similar in ability attain very different levels of examination success. The majority of the chapter focuses on these sociological explanations. They range from stressing the importance of the economic and political system, or the home, or culture, through to the school itself. We apply these theories to the differences that sociologists have uncovered which exist between social classes, the two sexes, and the various ethnic groups.

Finally, the chapter looks at the recent changes that have been made to the education system in Britain.

9.1 THEORETICAL APPROACHES TO EDUCATION

Whereas most people accept unquestioningly that an education system is necessary, sociologists have asked what purposes it serves. Answers to this vary, from those who see it as necessary to provide relevant knowledge, to those who see it as merely a way of teaching work discipline and skills to a new generation of workers. These views reflect the differing theoretical approaches of functionalism and Marxism. The third major theoretical tradition – interactionism – has been more concerned to study what actually happens within schools. These three overarching approaches have also provided insights into the positions of ethnic minorities and females within the education system.

THE FUNCTIONALIST PERSPECTIVE

Durkheim: the integrating function

Durkheim claims that schools perform two central functions, relating to **social cohesion** and the **division of labour**.

❶ In order to exist, societal members must share common beliefs and values – these are only partially taught by the family. The school continues this process and broadens the forms of behaviour and shared beliefs of the children.

❷ In modern societies the division of labour holds society so that schools train people for the different jobs available.

Parsons: the positive role of the school

This basic position provided the platform for the work of Parsons, who fits the process of formal schooling in to his theory of society. According to him, the school is the bridge between the home and the wider society, that is between childhood and adulthood.

In the family the child is treated as special and the forms of behaviour expected are really quite flexible. Parsons describes this as **particularistic** treatment. In adult life and in the wider society all children are supposed to be treated according to the same rules, ie **universalistic** treatment. The school prepares the students by treating them the same regardless of sex, race or social class. There are school rules, forms of dress and expected patterns of behaviour which are applied to all pupils. The school is a microcosm of society and therefore when the students emerge from school, they are already accustomed to the wider world.

Values and economic skills

The functionalist view is that two important things are learned at school:

❶ The **values** the students learn are those of achievement – the desire to do well and to improve, and the equality of opportunity – that all students are given equal opportunities to make the best of. The result of these values is of benefit to society in general. The schools turn out a highly motivated, achievement-oriented workforce. The differential rewards that adults receive are seen by both the successful and the less successful as justified and fair, because both groups had equal opportunities.

❷ The **economic** function the school performs is to test and grade students into ability groups. The best take the more complex and important positions in society, and receive greater rewards as a result. The less successful accept this situation because of the stress placed by the school on the value of equality of opportunity. This approach relates to the general functionalist position on social mobility and stratification (see p 77).

Criticisms of the functionalist approach to education

Critics argue that:

● there is little equality of opportunity – the education system largely reflects and transmits the inequalities of society;

● different values are taught to different groups within the education system; eg public schools in the UK teach very different values from State schools and even have different curricula;

- the values of the schools and the very purpose of job training may not reflect the needs of society but the interests of the ruling class.

MARXIST PERSPECTIVES

Marxist perspectives place stress upon the role the schools play in preparing children for their future working role in terms of both skills and values. The crucial difference between the Marxist and functionalist approaches is that the education system for Marxists is seen as a means of exploitation of the population by a ruling class.

Bowles and Gintis: a subservient workforce

Bowles and Gintis examine the values which they claim underlie the subjects taught in school. They suggest that the prime purpose is to produce a willing, subservient workforce which will continue to help make profits for the ruling class and not to challenge their dominance of society.

1 **Subservience** After giving personality tests to 237 New York school children, Bowles and Gintis argue that low marks at school are related to creativity, aggressiveness and independence, and that higher grades are related to perseverence, consistency, dependability and punctuality. Therefore rewards go to 'plodders'.

2 **Acceptance of the hierarchy** Schools are based upon the principles of hierarchy and lines of command. This prepares students for employment and taking orders.

3 **Motivation** Learning ought to be something that young people wish to do, and the knowledge gained should be self-evidently useful to them. But capitalist education rewards success by certification – examination certificates. Learning is transformed from creativity to a search for materialistic reward. This prepares students for work where the enjoyment comes from the wage not the job itself.

4 **Fragmentation of knowledge** The development of knowledge in secondary schools in the UK is based upon the fragmentation of knowledge into subjects with little relationship one to the other; for example, the school day is divided into unrelated segments (maths, history, French). The overall process of learning useful knowledge is unclear to the student. This prepares students for the fragmentation of employment, where jobs are broken into component elements in such a way that the actual process of work (car manufacture) becomes pointless and fragmented to the individual worker.

5 **Appropriate knowledge** Most knowledge at school is not needed for employment (as opposed to the underlying values of the school). Pupils are overtaught so that there is always a surplus of knowledgeable people for all posts, and therefore competition for them. This surplus labour keeps wages low.

6 **Inequality and legitimacy** The education system is not open; it reflects the power of the ruling class to ensure that its members retain the senior positions. The belief in equality of opportunity masks the unfairness of the system.

Criticisms of Bowles and Gintis

Hickox ('The Marxist sociology of education: a critique') suggests a number of criticisms of the Marxist approach to education. His points include:

1 The research element of Bowles and Gintis' work is poor, and they made assumptions about the existence of the hidden curriculum rather than proving its existence. Willis' study (*Learning to Labour*) shows that there is a far more complex relationship between students and the school than that suggested by Bowles and Gintis.

2 The formal curriculum of the school does not necessarily reflect an attempt to create a subservient workforce. In fact, the criticism often made of schools is that they are too academic and the subjects taught are not work-related.

3 The majority of the UK population does not accept that there is equality of opportunity; they argue instead (according to a survey by Scase) that social class background determines the success or otherwise of the student. This suggests that the supposed implanting of values favourable to capitalism has not been successful.

Learning to labour: the interrelation between structure and individual choice

One of the most common criticisms of Marxist approaches to education is their mechanical application of the theory – the analysts know that the role of education is to make the working class fail and they search out the elements of schooling that they perceive do this.

An alternative, and more subtle, approach was taken by Willis. He studied a group of 12 working-class boys over their final year and a half at school, and briefly into their first employment. The boys despised school and looked forward to their time at work. Their indifference to school ensured their failure in education. They treated the dead-end jobs they entered like school, and coped in much the same way. Therefore their attitude at school ensured their failure but also gave them the ability to cope with the nature of their jobs.

Willis concludes that the education system does not automatically produce in children the values and gradings of ability, as claimed by Bowles and Gintis, but that there is a wide variety of responses, one of which was that of 'the lads'. Willis remains within a Marxist position but gives back power and choice to pupils, creating a far more dynamic model.

Criticisms of Willis

1 The sample of 12 children is very small – is it possible to generalise from this sample?

2 Willis does not question the boys' view of the world. In particular, he takes their comments about the other pupils as accurate; but there is evidence of a variety of responses to the schools, not just the two extremes of 'lads' and 'ear 'oles'.

3 Willis can be accused of value bias in that he starts from the assumption that the working class are exploited, and that the responses of the boys are responses to capitalist society.

INTERACTIONIST PERSPECTIVES

Interactionist perspectives concentrate on the way that perceptions of pupils by teachers and other pupils can affect their chances of educational success.

The effects of banding

Early studies by Hargreaves (*Social Relations in a Secondary School*) and Lacey (*Hightown Grammar*) concentrate on the effects of streaming on the pupils. These studies show that the self-perceptions of the pupils were strongly influenced by the stream that they were placed in. Teachers were shown to have lower expectations of the lower-band pupils and responded differently to them. The lower-band pupils in turn felt denied status. They responded by being anti-school and expressed this:

1 in Hargreaves' study by rejecting the middle-class values that underlie the activities of the school, and behaving in ways which demonstrate this rejection;

2 in Lacey's study by seeking alternative out-of-school subcultures which were available to them.

Ball's later study (*Beachside Comprehensive*) found similar processes as a result of banding, which led the boys in his study to dissociate themselves from the school. Ball found a more complex set of subcultures in the school compared to Hargreaves and Lacey, arguing that there are more than just pro- and anti-school groups. Ball distinguishes between four types of pupil:

Pro-school

- **Supportive** – pro-school because they believe in it;
- **Manipulators** – pro-school because it suits their interests.

Anti-school

- **Passive** – those who drift into non-conformist behaviour;
- **Rejecting** – those who actively reject the school.

Interactionist studies of girls at school

1. **Role models from outside the school** Griffin studied a group of girls in year 11 of a secondary school (*Typical Girls?*), and later into the job market. She found very great differences between males and females at school. The girls did not go around in gangs but in small groups, and they did not appear to form strong pro- and anti-school attitudes. They were more concerned about their positions in terms of attractiveness to possible partners and about their preferred career patterns.

2. **Awareness of race and gender** In Fuller's study (*Black Girls in a London Comprehensive School*) of black female pupils, the importance of the future career was also emphasised. The role of teachers and other pupils was not regarded as particularly important: the girls had a clear idea of what they wished to achieve and concentrated on this.

3. **Reputation and social control** Lees' study (*Losing Out*), however, suggested that female pupils were very concerned about their reputation, especially concerning sexual behaviour (or perceived sexual activity), and that this had a strong effect upon self-perception and behaviour. Girls were concerned to avoid being labelled into the 'extreme' categories of promiscuous or not sexually active.

The actions of teachers

According to Hargreaves, Hester and Mellor (*Deviance in Classrooms*), teachers engage in a process of differentiation of pupils, by which they type them and then respond to their own typing. However, the typing process moves from a vague category on initially meeting the pupil through to a more refined model as they encounter them more often and get to know them.

There are three stages in the process of typing:

1. **Speculation**: an initial tentative typing based on such things as appearance.

2. **Elaboration**: initial hypotheses are confirmed or rejected and substituted.

3. **Stabilisation**: the teacher believes he/she knows the pupil and the correct way to respond to them.

Of course, pupils also type each other and teachers. The process is not solely one-way.

9.2 SOCIAL CLASS AND EDUCATIONAL SUCCESS

Statistics indicate that social class is directly related to educational success or failure. The higher a person is in the social class structure, the more likely his/her child is to succeed in the education system (see Table 9.1). Explanations which have been put forward include:

- material deprivation,
- family socialisation,
- cultural explanations,
- structural explanations,
- the school as an institution.

Table 9.1 *The highest qualification attained[1] in Britain: by socio-economic group of father, 1990–91*

	Professional	Employers and managers	Intermediate and junior non-manual	Skilled manual and own account non-professional	Semi-skilled manual and personal service	Unskilled manual	TOTAL
Degree	32	17	17	6	4	3	10
Higher education	19	15	18	10	7	5	11
A level	15	13	12	8	6	4	9
O level	19	24	24	21	19	15	21
CSE	4	9	7	12	12	10	10
Foreign	4	4	4	3	2	2	3
No qualifications	7	19	18	40	50	60	35
Sample size (= 100%) (numbers)	961	3,963	2,028	8,618	2,931	1,168	19,669

Percentages and numbers

1 Persons aged 25–59 not in full-time education.

(Source: *Social Trends* 23, p48)

MATERIAL DEPRIVATION

The National Child Development Study found that at age 7 children from overcrowded homes with low incomes are educationally over 9 months behind their peers. 1 in 16 children suffer from **multiple deprivation** such as low income, poor housing, poor diet etc. Bull points out the hidden costs of free education, such as clothing, transport, school uniforms, books etc. Finn suggests that the need of children from low-income families to work in the evenings and weekends in part-time jobs has effects on their concentration on school work. Halsey, Health and Ridge's study of post-war education (*Origins and Destinations*) and its relationship to social mobility found that material circumstances significantly affected the type of secondary school attended and the decision about whether or not to stay on at school into the 6th form.

Criticisms

This approach ignores the causes of the low income in the first place, and has no awareness of issues, such as parental interest and cultural background, that could also affect educational success.

FAMILY SOCIALISATION

Families vary in the degree of support and interest they show in their child's education. This can have a critical effect on the child's success at school.

Douglas' longitudinal study (*The Home and The School*) stresses that the single most important influence on educational success was parental interest. He also claims that middle-class children receive 'better' standards of care. (The obvious criticism of this is how is the standard of care judged?) The Newsons (*Seven Years Old in The Home Environment*) studied child-rearing patterns in Nottingham and claim that middle-class parents provide more stimulating home environments. Sugarman stresses in 'Social class, values and behaviour' how middle-class children are brought up with the concept of **deferred gratification**, that is being prepared to give up short-term benefits for long-term ones. Bernstein ('Social class and linguistic development') emphasises the differences in language use and development between different classes of family. Middle-class families are more likely to use language forms which develop conceptual thought and the ability to express oneself.

Criticisms

Who decides which socialisation patterns are better or worse than others? These approaches exclude discussion of the context of school, family and socialisation – that is the wider structural factors.

CULTURAL EXPLANATIONS

Cultural deprivation

Closely allied to the idea of family socialisation is the argument that certain groups in society may be 'cut off' from the mainstream values of the society. This lack of culture can influence children's ability to benefit from school, as the work there does not reinforce knowledge that is acquired in the home. This can happen, it is claimed, where English is not the first language of the home.

Criticisms

On what grounds is it possible to say that a particular culture is less profound than another, and therefore that a child is deprived?

Cultural capital

This is a very different approach to the concept of culture. Rather than certain groups being deprived of culture (and it being the fault of the parents), children from middle- and upper-class homes are seen as having very significant advantages at school. The values of school are those of the ruling classes of society. The function of schools is to reproduce those values, and ensure that they pass from one generation to another. Those who come from the appropriate backgrounds have a very great advantage in that their home and the educational values mutually support one another. The working-class pupils have much further to go to achieve these values.

Bourdieu (*Cultural Reproduction and Social Reproduction*) calls this advantage of the middle and upper classes **cultural capital**. There is little or no content to the culture, rather the differences lie in manners and style. Bourdieu argues that the major role of the educational system is to exclude working-class children – **the social function of elimination** – and this is partly achieved through the cultural processes. Not only this, but the successful children will be the children of the upper and middle classes – proving that they are superior. Bourdieu's work should be linked with the neo-Marxist school.

Criticisms

Bourdieu is very vague as to what constitutes the *content* of the cultural capital. Specifically, he could then demonstrate how this culture benefits the ruling class. He is unable to show this.

STRUCTURAL EXPLANATIONS

Functionalists

Functionalist writers point out that schools act as sieves grading out higher ability children. The least able therefore fail.

Criticisms

The functionalist explanation is demonstrated to be inaccurate as large numbers of intelligent working-class and black children do not succeed in the education system.

Marxists

These approaches argue that the education system:
- imposes the dominant values of the ruling class on the population;
- grades children according to class background;
- trains people for jobs – in order to produce greater profits;
- makes failure inevitable for the majority of the population, as that is the point of the system – to achieve and legitimise this failure.

A more subtle version of this approach is given by Willis, who argues that working-class boys, aware of their inevitable failure, cope with the boredom and irrelevance of school to their lives by playing up in the classroom. This behaviour guarantees their future failure. However, these very skills, learned to get them through school, also prepare them for their dead-end employment as adults. Griffin and Lees have found a very similar process happening to working-class girls, who prepare themselves for a perceived career as housewife/mother and part-time employee. To them, school is largely irrelevant.

Criticisms

Working-class children do succeed. According to Heath (*Social Mobility*), about 60% of those in social class I come from origins outside that class. There is also very limited evidence that the values of subservience really are taught by the schools.

THE SCHOOL AS AN INSTITUTION

This approach stresses the importance of the school itself, as an *organisation* to influence success or failure. There are four subtypes of this approach:

- organisational study approaches,
- interactionist-based approaches,
- interaction/structure approaches,
- classroom knowledge.

Organisation approaches

Rutter (*Fifteen Thousand Hours*) studied 12 London comprehensive schools and measured four factors:

- attendance,
- achievement,
- behaviour and
- level of delinquency outside the school.

Allowing for social class, Rutter concluded that these four factors were determined by:

- the ethos of the school (a general commitment to good practice shared by all staff members);
- good teaching (teachers are punctual, well organised, patient, encourage pupils, inspire by example);
- an established consistent set of rewards and punishments.

Interactionist-based approaches

These owe much to the early work of Hargreaves and Lacey, and stress the way that the labelling of certain (usually lower-set) groups by teachers and other pupils can produce anti-school behaviour. There is no need, according to these approaches, to look outside the school for further explanation.

Ball shows that teachers' attitudes to lower-band pupils helped to produce an anti-school culture among the middle band by the third year. Interestingly, when banding was abolished and mixed ability groupings brought in, teachers continued to distinguish (informally) between bright and dull pupils and treated them accordingly, with varying consequences.

Interactionist and structural approaches

These combine **structural** factors, such as class, race, gender etc, with the activities and perceptions of teachers – the **interactionist** approach. Teachers respond differently to pupils according to these criteria, it is suggested, and there are consequences for the educational success and failure of the pupils. Sharp and Green (*Education and Social Control*) studied 'Mapledene', a progressive primary school. They argue that pressures from both within the school and the wider society ensure that teachers tend to have higher expectations from middle-class pupils.

Classroom knowledge

This approach links to the work of Bourdieu and to the Marxist approaches. Classroom knowledge, it is argued reflects the teachers' beliefs as to what constitutes appropriate knowledge (and behaviour), and the teacher responds and categorises the pupils accordingly. Keddie studies a humanities department in a large comprehensive ('Classroom knowledge') and found that the children who were regarded as clever by the teachers were those who uncritically accepted the teachers' assumptions of what constituted academic knowledge.

Criticisms

These approaches generally isolate explanations from the wider society. Schools, it could be argued, reflect the values of the wider society and, therefore, explanations should be sought outside the school in the structure of the society.

WHICH APPROACH IS MORE ACCURATE?

Halsey, Heath and Ridge studied 800 males and concluded that family cultural background and attitudes of parents were crucial up to the age of 11; at this point, their influence declined and then the organisation of the school was overwhelmingly important. However, material circumstances were crucial in determining whether boys stayed on into the 6th form and therefore attained better academic results. It should be noted that this was, in effect, an historical study which studied adult males (there were no females in the sample) and then looked back at their schooling. This means that the majority of the study of childhood was conducted in the 1950s.

9.3 GENDER AND EDUCATIONAL ATTAINMENT

ATTAINMENT DIFFERENCES BY GENDER

Girls are more likely to be successful throughout the education system.

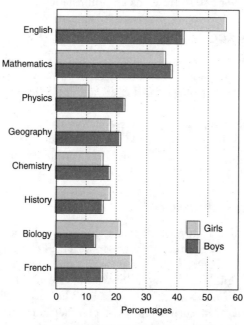

1 Includes GCSE/GCE/SCE levels/grades A–C and CSE grade 1.

(*Source: Social Trends* 23, Table 3.13, p43)

Fig. 9.1 Comparing GCSE[1] results between male and female school-leavers in the UK, 1989–90

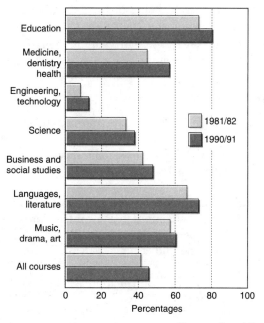

(*Source: Social Trends* 23, Table 3.18, p45)

Fig. 9.2 The percentage of female students to all students on full-time degree courses in the UK, 1981–2 and 1990–91

SUBJECT DIFFERENCES BY GENDER

More noticeable than different levels of achievement, however, are the different subjects which males and females study and achieve success in. Once pupils have the choice of subjects at GCSE/GNVQ and beyond, males choose maths, science, technology and computing, whereas females are more likely to take humanities, caring subjects, human biology and clerical/business studies.

The significance of subject choice is that it strongly influences the choice of higher education and the choice and possibilities of employment.

EXPLANATIONS FOR DIFFERENCES IN EDUCATION

Explanations for the different choices and routes taken in education by males and females include:

● socialisation,

● peer groups,

● differentiation within schools,

● females' expectations,

● the wider society.

Socialisation

Girls are treated differently from boys by parents and relatives. Goldberg and Lewis found that parents expected daughters as young as six months old to be quieter, cleaner and more restrained than boys of the same age. According to Sharpe, young children are given sex-differentiated toys, with construction ones being regarded as more appropriate for boys. Different forms of language are used to describe boys and girls. Van Gelder and Carmichael found that even 'feminist' mothers did not conform to their avowed intentions of breaking with gender norms. The Newsons, in their study of Nottingham child-rearing practices, found that parents exercised much greater control over the activities of girls than boys.

The result of these patterns is that girls may be more cautious and may come to regard domestic activities as more a female role.

The peer group

Griffin's study of Midland schoolgirls examined the appropriateness of Willis' model of boys' behaviour in secondary school to girls (see p 194). She found that there was no clear anti-school culture among the girls although academic success was seen as 'unfeminine'. Primarily, the aim of schoolgirls was to get white-collar jobs of some kind as these were viewed as relatively glamorous.

Fuller's study of girls of Afro-Caribbean origin (*Qualified Criticism; Critical Qualifications*) shows that they had a mutual expectation not to show interest in studying nor deference to the teachers; they were expected instead to show a limited degree of disinterest and insolence. However, they did work hard and did aspire academically to achieve white-collar or management posts.

Kelly (*Science for Girls*) takes a very different approach, however, in her study of science lessons. She claims that the boys in science classes dominate the classes by insisting that they do the experiments, shouting out answers to teachers and generally taking control. Kelly sees this as a microcosm of the wider patriarchal society. This male behaviour, allied to the fact that the majority of books were illustrated by male figures, made science a subject for boys.

Differentiation inside schools

In school, teachers respond differently to boys and girls and expect different patterns of behaviour from them. This re-affirms socialisation in the home and wider society. It also helps to direct girls and boys into different subject choices and hence different future areas of employment.

In primary schools, French found that boys were more active and demanding, so teachers responded more to their wishes and views. When children were gathered for discussion around the teacher, French found that the seating arrangements were such as to make the girls relatively 'invisible'. In secondary schools, Stanworth (*Gender and Schooling*) claims that teachers spent disproportionately large amounts of time dealing with boys to the exclusion of females. Girls also suffered from very low self-esteem, underrating their ability when compared with the views of teachers. The invisibility of females in the classroom was supported by Spender (*Invisible Women*) who recorded her own lessons and, although consciously trying to divide her time equally between males and females, found in reality that, according to her recordings, she gave more time to male pupils.

Teachers are influenced by the values of the wider society and import these values into the classroom. Deem notes in her study how interaction in the classroom is built around these values. For example, boys are asked to help lift things. Textbooks and readers in primary schools are still often gender-biased, with males being the more dominant characters.

Spender suggests that the nature of the knowledge taught in school is sexist and patriarchal. The curriculum consistently ignores the contribution of women to the advance of knowledge, such as in the area of scientific research, where the overwhelming majority of great scientists are men and the role of women has been ignored or covered up. This is true in areas as far apart as the discovery of DNA and the development of computer software.

Criticisms

Both Stanworth and Spender have been criticised by Randall who points out the potential bias in Spender's work, and that Stanworth's research was based upon the girls' *perceptions* of interest shown by teachers (she questioned them on the amount of time they thought the teacher gave them, but did not actually measure it). In her study of classes in a comprehensive secondary school, Randall found no evidence to support Stanworth and Spender.

Girls' own expectations

The result of the socialisation in both the family and the wider society is such that girls actively choose jobs in the caring professions or courses in the humanities. They regard these as appropriate and 'natural' courses of action. Sharpe and Lees, in two separate studies, point out the acceptance by teenage girls of the inevitability of motherhood and marriage. Teachers, too, advise girls on which subjects to choose, based partially on the girls' choice of future career and partially on a realistic awareness of where girls are most likely to be successful. This, according to Thomas and Stuart, is in 'female' areas, such as the health and caring professions.

The wider society

Influences on females' self-perception and aspirations exist everywhere in British culture. Newspapers and magazines portray females in a narrow range of stereotyped images and encourage the continuation of the female role. Female specialist magazines urge women to be both career women and good wives, according to Ferguson (*Forever Feminine*). Marital roles continue to be **asymmetrical**, giving girls their first role models of adults.

9.4 ETHNICITY AND EDUCATIONAL SUCCESS

ACHIEVEMENT AND RACE

The Swann Report (*Education for All*) of 1985 found very significant differences between the educational achievement of people of Afro-Caribbean origin and whites. Only 5% of people of Afro-Caribbean origin obtained an 'A' level, and less than 1% went to university. People of Asian origin had similar success levels to whites, but people of Bangladeshi origins had the worst performance in the education system of all groups. See Fig. 9.3.

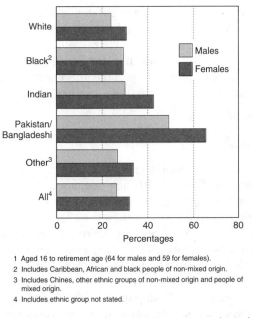

1 Aged 16 to retirement age (64 for males and 59 for females).
2 Includes Caribbean, African and black people of non-mixed origin.
3 Includes Chines, other ethnic groups of non-mixed origin and people of mixed origin.
4 Includes ethnic group not stated.

(*Source: Social Trends*, 1993, Table 3.25, p48)

Fig. 9.3 Percentage of the UK population[1] without a qualification: by ethnic origin and sex, 1992

EXPLANATIONS FOR DIFFERENTIAL EDUCATIONAL ACHIEVEMENT

Explanations for the differences in achievement include:

- innate differences,
- language and cultural differences,
- family and socialisation,
- social class,
- racism, both inside and outside the school.

Innate differences

A number of writers have suggested that there are innate differences in intelligence between blacks and whites. Jenson in the USA and Eysenck in the UK have both argued this on the basis of IQ tests. However, the Swann Committee found that when environmental differences were taken into account, the differences were so slight as to be irrelevant to the debate.

Language and cultural differences

Where the home background is not English or is a variation of the English model, it is claimed that this may hold back the pupil. However, the Swann Report found this was a significant factor in only a small number of cases, primarily for Bangladeshi children.

Family and socialisation

Driver and Ballard ('Contemporary performance in multi-race schools') found that the Asian children in their study did particularly well because of the strong emphasis that the family placed on educational success. They discovered that the Asian families were prepared to make sacrifices to ensure the success of their children in the system. The Swann Report argues that the Asian family structure was more tight-knit than that of either whites or Afro-Caribbeans, and that it 'may be responsible for higher achievement'.

Social class

The differences in performance by pupils from different ethnic backgrounds may be heavily influenced by social class. We know, for example, that the income, employment and housing standards of people of Afro-Caribbean origin are significantly lower than those of the majority of the population. Therefore, much of the poor performance could be related to the same factors that make the white members of the working class perform relatively poorly. The Swann Report suggests that this probably explains about 50% of Afro-Caribbean underachievement.

Race inside school

Schools are organisations, or mini-societies, that reflect in their own specific ways the wider racist culture and practices of society. Although teachers and pupils may not intend to be racist, there are often practices and attitudes which can limit the achievement of some people of Asian and Afro-Caribbean origin.

According to Green's research of boys in junior and middle schools ('Multi-ethnic teaching and the pupil's self-concepts'), some teachers favoured white boys when teaching. Teachers appeared to have lower expectations of Afro-Caribbean pupils and failed to encourage them as much. The result was a lowering of the boys' self-image. Tomlinson points out the way that teachers expect less from pupils of Afro-Caribbean origin. The teachers in the study claimed that they are slower learners, lacking concentration, and are less well behaved.

Brah and Minhas claim that teachers expect Asians to be industrious and courteous, but that Asian girls are often overlooked by teachers as they are regarded as 'passive'. This can often result in their abilities being underestimated. Fuller studied black girls in a London comprehensive; although they were often academically successful and not overtly anti-school, they were not interested in attaining a good reputation with the teachers. Fuller suggests that their identity as female and black was more important to them than being successful and attentive pupils.

Stone's study (*The Education of the Black Child in Britain*) of 264 pupils of Afro-Caribbean origin found that they were often hostile to the teachers and felt that the teachers discriminated against them on the grounds of race. Coard (*How the West Indian Child is Made Educationally Subnormal in the British School System*) argues that children of Afro-Caribbean origin are made to feel inferior by the way that the curriculum ignores black perspectives (on history/music etc) and by the way that blacks appear in subservient roles in, or are totally absent from, books. Coard claims that this leads to Afro-Caribbeans having low opinions of themselves and consequently contributes to their failure. However, the Swann Report did not find any evidence of low esteem among those of Afro-Caribbean origin. Nor did Stone find evidence of low esteem among her sample.

Race outside school

What happens inside school cannot be separated from what happens in the wider society: the institutional racism that it is claimed happens in school reflects racism in society at large. The evidence for the continuation of racist practices lies in low employment levels, restricted careers and lower standards of living for people of ethnic origin. In addition, it could be argued that as the majority of those from ethnic minorities are members of the working class, then the same factors which limit the success levels of the working class also apply to them.

RACE, GENDER AND STEREOTYPING

The problem with any discussion of race and gender issues is that of stereotyping the debate. Although children of Afro-Caribbean origin do relatively less well overall than whites and Asians, it is not a sociological law that all children of Afro-Caribbean origin do worse educationally than whites. Tizzard's work and Driver's research both show the importance of not stereotyping.

Tizzard (*Young Children at School in the Inner City,*) studied 343 primary-school children (171 black, 106 white). The study took place over three years in 30 schools. She concludes that white and black parents of primary-school children were equally likely to support their children and to read to them at home. So the argument of the less supportive Afro-Caribbean family was a myth. She also claims that race was of much less importance than gender in predicting overall success at primary school.

Driver studied pupils in five inner-city comprehensives. His conclusion is that black girls were more successful than either white girls or boys, whereas black male pupils performed worse.

Both these studies show that factors of race and gender are quite distinct in their influence on educational performance.

9.5   EDUCATIONAL CHANGE

THE CHANGE FROM A SELECTIVE TO A COMPREHENSIVE SYSTEM

In pre-World War II Britain, schooling beyond the age of 14 was possible only for those who could pay or who had won a scholarship. The 1944 Education Act extended free secondary education to all up to the minimum age of 15 (extended in 1972 to 16). Three types of school were to be set up, although in reality only two types were found in large numbers. Secondary moderns took the less academically able pupils, and grammars took the cleverer ones. The children were divided by an examination at the age of 11.

This system reflected the class divisions of British society, as the majority of working-class children went to secondary moderns and the majority of middle-class children to grammar schools. The examination was flawed and was biased towards the middle-class child.

Numerous studies showed the enormous waste of working-class talent in this system. It was gradually replaced during the 1960s and 1970s by comprehensive schools. Today approximately 90% of British children attend comprehensives. However, the question remains – do comprehensives eliminate the differences?

However, throughout the 1990s the comprehensives have begun to split into different types as a result of the 1988 Education Act. The Act introduced the Grant Aided School which allowed comprehensives to move out of local authority control and to receive funding directly from the government. These 'grant-aided' comprehensives have been allowed to 'select' a proportion of their intake, although critics suggest that they may informally select a very high proportion of the children they accept, effectively screening out the majority of difficult children.

They have also been given greater financial assistance than those remaining under local education authority (LEA) control. Parents were also encouraged by the Act to start making choices of schools rather than simply accepting the school for their neighbourhood. The basis of choice was to be the National Curriculum and examination results which schools were obliged to publish.

The promotion of grant-aided comprehensives has, in effect, re-introduced the issue of selection which was believed to have been put to rest in the 1970s. The Conservative government also encouraged selection by introducing privately financed state schools known as City Technology Colleges, which have been set up to provide a high level of technological expertise.

THE NATIONAL CURRICULUM

Introduced in 1988, the National Curriculum requires schools to teach students a specific range of subjects, depending upon their age. A wide range of subjects was included, but by 1994 this was limited to English, Maths and Science.

Students are expected to meet certain attainment targets, as designated points in their educational careers. Schools' examination results are published.

The justification for a National Curriculum is that it makes sure all students have access to the same standards of teaching and the same important subjects. It also fits the New Right agenda in that it takes away power from local government, and supposedly from even central government itself, and puts power in the hands of parents. This helps undermine the power of 'experts' and also introduces an element of the market into education. Parents, armed with the right information (i.e. school results), will be able to make an informed choice over which school to send their children to.

The National Curriculum has been criticised by Whitty, amongst others, for a number of reasons:

1. It has destroyed the tradition of school and teacher freedom to choose what curriculum to offer.

2. It has led to further centralisation of power over education in the hands of the government.

3. It has prevented new experiments in curriculums and subjects.

4. Through the publication of results, it has led to schools being compared solely in terms of examination results rather than in terms of what they could achieve for pupils in other ways.

5. Because of the publication of the results, it has encouraged schools to compete for 'brighter' pupils through some form of selection – this is more likely to occur with the gradual extension of grant-aided comprehensives.

6. It is based very much on an Anglo-Saxon view of the world, and excludes the experiences of Asian and Afro-Caribbean groups in society.

7 The schools may also be said to disadvantage religious minorities by being expected by law to have a predominantly Christian act of worship each morning.

8 Johnson has pointed out that the National Curriculum, and the linked reintroduction of streaming has strengthened the ways in which children are ranked at an early age, and that once ranked, this determines their future educational success.

VOCATIONALISM

In schools

The National Curriculum is meant to ensure that students study a range of subjects which will give them knowledge and skills for the workplace. Throughout the history of education there has always been a tension between education for itself and education for employment. The 1990s saw the balance tip in the favour of education for employment or **vocationalism**.

In colleges

Apart from the National Curriculum, a series of new qualifications – the NVQ (National Vocational Qualification) and the GNVQ (General National Vocational Qualification) – have been introduced to provide a skill-based alternative to GCSEs.

For the young unemployed

For those young people who leave school at 16 and who have no employment, there are no state benefits available in normal circumstances. Instead, they are required to take employment training schemes which involve vocational training while undertaking a work placement.

For the unemployed

Similar schemes, based on the US 'workfare' programme have also been introduced for the long-term unemployed. They are required, as a condition of receiving benefit, to have a period of skill training and work placement, usually doing some form of 'voluntary work'.

Arguments for skills-based or vocational training

- In a period of rapidly changing technology, skills can soon become outdated and therefore it is important to keep reskilling.
- Work is available for those with skills – it is only the unskilled and the inappropriately skilled who cannot find employment.
- Those who do not want to work can use their lack of skills as an excuse to claim state benefits.

Criticisms of vocational training

- It lays the blame for unemployment on the lack of skills of workers rather than on structural changes in the economy. Therefore the unemployed are scapegoated as having personal defects.
- Skill training, according to P. Cohen, does not actually teach skills but more a set of attitudes which help create a compliant and deferential workforce.
- Clarke and Willis claim that in a period of unemployment, youth training schemes merely keep young people in 'suspended animation', in that they are not included in the unemployment statistics yet ready for work when it is created.
- Training schemes in general are merely a means to lower the unemployment statistics.
- Finn has argued that youth training schemes were originally introduced as a means of lowering wage levels and weakening the power of trade unions. This was part of the same process that saw the government introduce legislation abolishing minimum wages and undermining the trade unions in the 1980s.

COMPREHENSIVES: A SUCCESS IN ACHIEVING EQUALITY?

The most recent large-scale study by Heath (*Class in the Classroom*) showed that the move towards comprehensive education has hardly changed the inequalities between social classes as they existed in the 1950s. Heath suggests two reasons for this:

1. The reform of the education system into comprehensives was not particularly radical, so that the types of comprehensives very often reflected the social class composition of the neighbourhood.

2. The more affluent parents were able to buy private education for their children when they wanted.

McPherson and Williams disagree with Heath, and point out that in their Scottish study they found that the longer a school is comprehensive the greater is the improvement in the educational attainment of working-class children. They do note, however, that social class differences remain – they are simply saying that the differences are diminishing.

THE NEW VOCATIONALISM

Since the late 1980s the education system has undergone significant change. This came from the belief that it was failing to deliver an adequate vocational education to the majority of British school pupils.

1. The requirement for all schools to become comprehensive was withdrawn.

2. The government introduced State scholarships for the 'most able' to enter private schools – the Assisted Places Scheme.

3. A national curriculum was introduced that all State schools must follow.

4. Standardised testing was introduced at ages 7, 11, 14, 16.

5. Schools were encouraged to withdraw from Local Education Authority control and to become grant maintained – obtaining money directly from the government.

6. Specific vocational courses were introduced for the 16+ age range, such as BTEC national courses. These are now grouped into categories based on a progression within a framework called GNVQ.

7. Those leaving school with no qualifications and no employment are required by the government to enrol on Youth Training Programmes in order to qualify for State benefits.

The aim of these changes is to make education relevant to the world of work and to ensure that Britain has an adequately trained workforce to compete internationally. Critics of the **new vocationalism**, such as Cohens, argue that it is not that the schools turn out low and inappropriately educated young people who are unable to do jobs properly, but that there are actually no jobs for young people to do. Individuals and schools are being blamed for the failure of government to create a high level of employment.

Test yourself questions and answers

Questions

1 According to the functionalists, what is the purpose of schools?

2 What criticisms can you make of this approach?

3 According to Marxists, what is the purpose of schools?

4 Outline the argument proposed by Willis in *Learning to Labour*. Give one criticism.

5 What are the effects of streaming?

6 Outline, very briefly, the competing explanations for educational success by social class.

7 What explanations have been offered for gender differences in education?

8 What explanations have been offered for differences in education between Whites and Asians/Afro-Caribbeans? Is it true to say that people of Asian and Afro-Caribbean origin do worse than Whites at school?

9 What is meant by the term the 'New Vocationalism'?

Suggested answers

1 According to functionalists, school teaches the values and the economic skills necessary for society to survive.

The values include:
- achievement – the desire to do well and to improve;
- equality of opportunity – all students are given equal opportunities to make the best of their abilities.

The schools therefore turn out a highly motivated, achievement-oriented workforce.

The economic function the school performs is to test and grade students into ability groups.

2 Critics argue that:
- there is little equality of opportunity;
- different values are taught to different groups, and social classes within the education system;
- the values of the schools and the job training skills may not reflect the needs of society but the interests of the ruling class.

3 Marxist perspectives stress the role that schools play in preparing children for their future working role, in terms of both skills and values. The crucial difference between the Marxist and functionalist approaches is that the education system is seen by Marxists as a means of exploitation of the population by a ruling class.

Bowles and Gintis suggest that the values include:
- subservience – doing what you are told;
- acceptance of hierarchy – accepting the superiority of some;
- motivation – preparing students for work, in which the enjoyment comes from the wage not the job itself, by transforming learning into the obtaining of a certificate;
- fragmentation of knowledge – preparing students for the fragmentation of employment, where jobs are broken into component elements in such a way that the actual process of work (car manufacture) becomes pointless and fragmented to the individual worker;
- appropriate knowledge – pupils are overtaught so that there is always a surplus of knowledgeable people for all posts, and competition for them. This surplus labour keeps wages low;
- inequality and legitimacy – the belief in equality of opportunity masks the unfairness of the system.

4 Willis studied a group of 12 working-class boys over the final year and a half at school, and briefly into their first employment. The 'lads' showed no interest in their

school activities, and passed their time by 'having a laff' in lessons, and looked forward to their time at work. Having failed at school, they got dead-end jobs, but got by in much the same way. Therefore 'having a laff' at school ensured their failure but also gave them the ability to cope with the nature of their jobs.

There are, however, some criticisms of Willis which include:

- the sample of 12 children is too small;
- Willis can be accused of value bias in that he sympathises with the responses of the boys to capitalist society.

5   Studies by Hargreaves and Lacey and Ball show that the self-perceptions of the pupils were strongly influenced by the stream/band/set in which they were placed. Teachers were shown to have lower expectations of the lower-band pupils and responded differently to them. The lower-stream pupils, in turn, felt denied status and responded by being anti-school.

Hargreaves argues that children rejected the middle-class values that underlay the activities of the school, while Lacey says they sought alternative out-of-school subcultures which were available to them.

Ball found more complex set of subcultures in the school than had been suggested and he distinguished between four types of pupil:

- **Pro-School** (i) supportive – pro-school because they believe in it; (ii) manipulators – pro-school because it suits their interests
- **Anti-School** – (i) passive – those who drift into non-conformist behaviour; (ii) rejecting – those who actively reject the school.

6   Explanations which have been put forward include:

- Material deprivation,
- Family socialisation,
- Cultural explanations,
- Structural explanations,
- The school as an institution.

Material deprivation This sees poverty and deprivation as the most significant problems. The best known study is the National Child Development Study, a longitudinal survey.

Family socialisation Families vary in the degree of support and interest they show in their child's education and this can have a critical effect on the child's success at school. The best known example of work is Douglas' longitudinal study.

Cultural Explanations are either of the cultural deprivation type which stress a lack of 'normal' culture, or the cultural capital approach which argues that those from the appropriate middle class backgrounds have a very great advantage in that their home and the educational values mutually support one another. Bourdieu argues that the major role of the educational system is to exclude working class children – 'the social function of elimination'.

Structural explanations These include those of functionalists, who argue that schools act as sieves grading out higher-ability children; those of Marxists, who claim that the education system imposes the dominant values of the ruling class on the population; grades children according to class background, and trains people for jobs. Failure is inevitable for the majority of the population, as that is the point of the system.

The school as an institution This emphasises the school as an organisation and uses interactionist analyses.

7   Explanations for the different choices and routes for girls in education include:

- Socialisation: girls are treated differently from boys from an early age, for example the work of Goldberg and Lewis.
- Peer groups: Griffin found that there was no clear anti-school culture among the girls although academic success was seen as 'unfeminine'. Primarily, the aim was to get white-collar jobs of some kind as these were viewed as relatively glamorous.
- Fuller's study of Afro-Caribbean origin girls showed that they had a mutual distrust of school, but a desire to achieve.

- Differentiation within schools: In school teachers respond differently to boys and girls and expect different patterns of behaviour from them. French found that in primary schools, boys were more active and demanding, so teachers responded more to their wishes and views. In secondary schools, Stanworth claimed that teachers spent disproportionately large amounts of time dealing with boys to the exclusion of girls.
- Females' expectations: The result of the socialisation both in the family and the wider society is such that girls actively choose jobs in the caring professions or courses in the humanities. They regard these as appropriate and 'natural' courses of action.
- The wider society: Teachers are influenced by the values of the wider society and import these values into the classroom. Deem noted in her study how interaction in the classroom is built around these values.

8 Explanations include:
  - Social class: The differences in performance by pupils from different ethnic backgrounds may be heavily influenced by social class. The Swann Report suggests that this probably explains about 50% of Afro-Caribbean underachievement.
  - Family and socialisation: Driver and Ballard found that the Asian children in their study did particularly well because of the strong emphasis of the family on educational success.
  - Racism both inside and outside the school. For example, according to Green's research in junior and middle schools, some teachers favoured white boys when teaching. Teachers appeared to have lower expectations of Afro-Caribbean pupils and failed to encourage them as much. The result was a lowering of the boys' self-image.

9 This refers to the development of skills training in schools and colleges in the UK and the move in State schools away from traditional humanities and academic work. The government has also introduced a range of training schemes for those in unemployment. It has been criticised on a wide variety of grounds, including hiding the true levels of unemployment and punishing young people without work, so that they cannot claim benefits.

Illustrative question and answer

Question

Item A

The role of the teacher as an agent of social control is extremely important in assessing the role of the hidden curriculum in maintaining gender inequality. Obviously, teachers' attitudes towards the role of education for women and men will influence their relationship with students. Spender found that in mixed classrooms, boys received two-thirds of the teacher time, benefiting from the teacher's attention and distracting from the amount of time spent with the girls...

Just as the attitudes of teachers can play a role in reinforcing gender inequalities through the hidden curriculum so can the attitudes and behaviour of the students. Jones highlights the high level of sexual violence initiated by boys in mixed schools against females, both students and teachers. Jones argues that school is a system for legitimating male violence against women and for making this violence seem part of everyday life.

(Reynolds, K., 'Feminist thinking on education' *Social Studies Review*, Vol. 6, No. 4)

Item B

Schools can make a difference

Although most people remain in the class they were born in, about one in three working-class children move up the social scale and about the same proportion of middle and lower-middle move down. Individual intelligence is one reason that partly explains upward movement and going to a good school is another. But what is a good school?

Michael Rutter's study *Fifteen Thousand Hours* examined this problem. Rutter and his team looked at only twelve Inner London secondary schools so it is important not to over-generalise their findings. Rutter's research is summarised below:

Factors measured	Teachers' qualities linked with success in these four areas
	Teachers who are:
Attendance	Punctual
Academic achievement	Well organised
Behaviour in school	Patient
Rate of delinquency outside school	Encouraging
	Inspiring
	Willing to share extra-curricular activities with pupils
	Consistent

(O'Donnell, M., and Garrod, J., *Sociology in Practice*, Nelson)

Item C

The self-fulfilling prophecy

When pupils come into a school, teachers make judgements on their ability, based on many different things. These labels are, for example, 'bright', 'able', 'thick', 'less able', 'practical', 'academic' etc. However, these labels are not neutral, nor do they describe the real possibilities of students, but are based on commonsense knowledge of what type of student is 'good' and which 'bad'. Thus, it has been shown that teachers have stereotypes linked to class ('from broken homes'), gender ('she's just a girl'), race ('West Indians are noisy') and even physical attractiveness ('snotty-nosed kid'). Teachers then act towards students on the basis of such stereotypes – for example, those students who are labelled 'bright' are given more time to answer questions than those who are seen as unlikely to know the answer anyway.

(Adapted from Lawson, T., *Sociology: A Conceptual Approach*, Checkmate)
AEB

(a) What does Jones suggest is the way in which schools 'legitimate male violence'? (1)

(b) Identify both factors which Item B suggests contribute to upward social mobility? (1)

(c) The concept of self-fulfilling prophecy described in Item C has been criticised by some sociologists. Identify three ways in which the concept might be criticised. (3)

(d) Using information from the Items and elsewhere, evaluate sociological contributions to an understanding of the hidden curriculum as it affects female pupils. (10)

Suggested answer

(a) Making it seem part of everyday life.
(b) Individual intelligence and a good school.

(c) Answers could include:
- lack of consistency or awareness of complexity in applying labels;
- too mechanical a view of the process;
- why do some get labelled and others not?;
- what about the concept of student resistance and subculture?

(d) Your answer should include a discussion of the concept of the hidden curriculum (values, beliefs and expectations which are not explicitly taught, but which are the basis for much of the teaching). You need to show how the hidden curriculum has an effect on the outcome of schooling for females and in their choice of subjects at school. To gain top marks you should refer to studies such as those by Deem, Stanworth and Lees, among others. Finally, do not forget that you need to evaluate and therefore you should criticise the concept. A useful point is made by Oakley who argues that the hidden curriculum is not so much a cause of differences in the education of males and females, but much more a reflection of the wider, patriarchal society.

Question bank

1 (a) Briefly explain how social class might explain one aspect of ethnic inequality in education. (4)

(b) Identify and illustrate two problems with using IQ tests to examine educational differences between ethnic groups. (4)

(c) Outline the view that the family life of ethnic groups influences their educational attainment in the UK. (7)

(d) Examine the significance of racism in the UK educational system in explaining ethnic inequalities in education. (10)

Integrated Boards

Points

(a) Social class defined largely in terms of 'lower levels' of occupation. Members of ethnic minorities more likely to be in these jobs than average.

(b) IQ tests are in English and it is claimed that the sorts of words used reflect 'middle-classes' English. English may not be first language of ethnic minority member, or it may not be used at home. Type of English (colloquialisms) used in the home may be different.

(c) Driver and Ballard argue that 'South Asian' families provide high level of support. (But it is important not to over-generalise as there is a wide variety of "Asian" groups in Britain.) On the other hand, children of Bangladeshi migrants in East London have very significant problems in achieving because of language difficulties at home. Asian families vary too in the expectations of their children, possibly differentiating between males and females. There is considerable dispute about those of Afro-Caribbean origins. There does appear to be a correlation between never-married mothers and children's educational achievement and there is a higher proportion of this category amongst those of Afro-Caribbean origins. *Be very careful not to stereotype in your answers.*

(d) Very limited evidence for overt racism amongst teachers. Although Coard has argued that this occurs. However, studies by Wright and the Swann Report did not find any significant racism. They did find that Afro-Caribbean students perceived teachers as racist however. Studies by Stone and by Taylor suggest that teachers may have lower levels of expectations from children from Afro-Caribbean backgrounds, and that they tended to assume more negative attitudes towards Afro-Caribbean children's behaviour compared to their attitudes to white or Asian pupils. Mac and Ghaill studies of sixth formers showed an awareness of racism in UK society including the school, but also a determination to succeed, and a sense of their own worth.

2 Evaluate the success of sociologists in explaining class-based inequalities in educational attainment.

Integrated Boards

Points

A large amount of research material. Best to divide it into (a) home and material factors, such as parental support, language development, etc; (b) the influence of the school and college, stressing teacher/pupil and pupil/pupil interaction; (c) wider 'structural' factors such as the Marxist critiques of the inevitability of failure of working class children, or the more complex Marxist approach associated with Willis.

CHAPTER 10

POWER AND POLITICS

Units in this chapter

Chapter objectives

We begin this chapter by exploring the nature of power. When people discuss politics they rarely see the subject as simply one aspect of the wider discussion of the nature of power. Power can be applied to virtually every aspect of an individual's life from the family through to debates on the nature of health. Therefore we examine the explanations of power and suggest the relationship of these definitions to major theoretical perspectives in sociology.

The next part of the chapter discusses the traditional class-based voting patterns and gives explanations for voters who do not vote according to their social class. These are often referred to as **deviant voter** explanations. By the mid-1970s it was clear that the traditional class loyalties were fragmenting in possibly the same way that social class appeared to be. Sociologists therefore turned their attention anew to the examination of the voting choices, and a series of new points emerged for discussion.

The following section brings us back more directly to the issue of power and how it is implemented. In particular, we look at the nature of how decisions are arrived at. The differing models which have been suggested include the pluralist, the Marxist and the elitist. All three provide very different ways of understanding the nature of decision-making and the role of the State.

The final section of the chapter looks at the evidence that exists for the concentration of power.

10.1 DEFINITIONS OF POWER

There are four major approaches to defining power:
- power and authority,
- zero-sum model,
- variable-sum model,
- non-decision-making.

POWER AND AUTHORITY

Weber makes a distinction between power and authority. **Power** is the ability to impose one's will on another, using force if necessary. It is the term used to describe any means of gaining compliance. This type of method of imposing one's will on others is relatively rare in contemporary societies, according to Weber. **Authority** is where people accept the right of others to tell them what they should do. He suggests three types of authority:

1. **Charismatic** The person is obeyed for their exceptional qualities. This is very rare and occurs only in a few historical occasions, such as Christ or Mohammed.

2. **Traditional authority** This is the authority which is obeyed on the simple grounds that traditionally the holder of the office has always been obeyed.

3. **Legal-rational** This type is the most prevalent today. It occurs where a subordinate accepts that for a specific end, and in specific matters relevant to the organisation, the senior person has the right to ask them to do something. The authority is vested in the office, not in the individual who holds the office. Therefore all modern, hierarchical organisations have authority holders who 'order' subordinates to perform discrete tasks, and are perceived as having the right to give these orders.

These are all **ideal types**, by which Weber means that they are essentially pure and abstract concepts which are unlikely to occur in reality quite so distinctly from each other.

ZERO-SUM MODEL

This view of power stresses a rather different aspect. Essentially it is a Marxist view of power, and regards power as something that is finite – such that it can only be held by one person or group at one particular time. For Marxists, the class struggle consists of two groups vying for a resource which only one can hold. This resource is then used to the benefit of the group holding it.

The distinction between power and authority, it is claimed in this model, is a false one, for authority is simply a disguised form of power such that the subordinated are persuaded (falsely) to accept the legitimacy of the rights of the power-holders to do what they want.

VARIABLE-SUM MODEL

A slightly more complex view of power is given by Parsons who argues that power can be seen as a resource which is to all intents and purposes infinite. Power is not a resource that one group holds, and another attempts to wrestle off them; instead it is something which can expand or contract depending upon the extent to which people believe in its legitimacy. The easiest way to understand this is to think of the parallel of money. In itself a coin has no value; it is only because we believe that the coin can purchase certain things that we accept and use it. The value of a coin is effectively based on our belief in it. So too with power: the more people who believe in the right of the power-holders, then the more power they have. This is an extension of Weber's concept of authority.

In contradiction to the Marxist view, which sees power as benefitting a small group, the functionalist view sees power as having the potential to benefit the society in general. Parsons points to the example of the democratic process where, if the politician loses the belief and support of the people he/she is no longer able to exercise effective power.

NON-DECISION-MAKING

This approach has been linked with Lukes (*Power: A Radical View*), who argues from a different viewpoint on the nature of power. He suggests that power has three different 'faces', and that the other approaches we have discussed so far tend to concentrate only on one of these:

1. **Decision-making** This is where there is a clear ability to make decisions and implement them. It is the most obvious element of power and is clearly important; however, it does not reflect all the possibilities of exercising power.

❷ **Non-decision-making** The second face of power concerns the ability of certain groups to prevent decisions being made or even being discussed. This is less obvious than decision-making but is just as important.

❸ **Manipulation of wishes** The third aspect of power is the one where the group's wishes are actually shaped: they may desire something and be happy to have it, as a result of the powerful group's ability to manipulate them into believing that these are their true desires. This could be the most powerful, and an **invisible** form of power. However, it could be argued that this invisibility is also a weakness because how can anyone other than the people know whether what they wished for would, in any way, have not been what they wanted?

MANN

A more recent version of power has been developed by Mann (*The Sources of Social Power*). According to Mann there are two **types** or power:

● distributional power – held by individuals and is their ability to get others to do what they want,

● collective power – this is exercised by groups. It is either exercised by one group over another or may consist of the control of inanimate objects (the control of nuclear power).

The exercise of power

● Extensive power – the ability to 'organise large numbers of people over far-flung territories in order to engage in minimally stable cooperation'. One example given by Mann is a large religious organisation such as the Catholic church.

● Intensive power – this is where a group can 'organise tightly and command a high level of mobilisation or commitment from the participants'. An example of this is a religious sect with strict and tightly controlled rules of belief and behaviour.

THE FORMS OF POWER

Mann then distinguishes two forms of power:

● Authoritative power is when those in authority make deliberate plans to exercise their power, organising and allocating tasks, and those who are given the orders consciously accept the authority of those in power.

● Diffused power is where the power relationships are more hidden, though still existing. No commands are issued and nobody consciously gives commands, yet a series of activities occur nevertheless. Mann's example of this is the 'market mechanism' meaning the way that all firms must compete in the market place to stay in business. A company will go out of business if it fails to produce goods of the right price and the right quality. No one issues commands to this effect, but the result is going to be that. This sort of power exists everywhere, and because it is hidden people often argue that it is natural or normal. For example, some economists argue that the market is a 'natural' mechanism for maintaining efficiency and freedom of consumer choice.

The relationship between how power is exercised and the form of power allows Mann to devise the schema shown in Table 10.1.

Table 10.1

	Authoritative	Diffused
Intensive	The armed forces	A general strike by workers in a range of industries
Extensive	British empire in 19th century	The international financial markets

(*Source:* Based upon Mann, M., *The Source of Social Power*, Vol. 1, Cambridge University 1986)

The basis of power

According to Marx, power derives from the control of the economy and Mann says this is partially true, but adds a further three sources of power. For Marx, these additional three derive from economic power, while for Mann these are distinct from economic power.

Mann argues that there are four sources of power:

- economic – derived from control of the economy,
- ideological – derived from control over ideas,
- political – derived from the previous existence of political structures,
- military – derived from the threat of violence.

10.2 VOTING BEHAVIOUR

Sociologists have researched extensively into the reasons why electors vote for a particular party. The study of voting choice is interesting in itself, but sociologists are more concerned to examine the way that voting reflects, and possibly helps to shape, the changing social structure and emerging values of British society.

VOTING AND CLASS LOYALTY

Britain has traditionally been regarded as a country that voted primarily on the basis of social class. From the 1950s to the early 1970s social class was by far the most important factor associated with voting choice.

Working-class people generally voted for the Labour Party, and middle- and upper-class people broadly voted Conservative. The Liberal (now Liberal Democratic) Party drew very limited support from across the social class spectrum. People clearly perceived themselves and their voting behaviour in class terms and, as the class structure was relatively stable, there was comparatively little switching from one party to another during this period.

DEVIANT VOTERS

The most noticeable debate at this time among sociologists concerned the explanations for those people who appeared to be voting against the predominant loyalties of their social class. If it had not been for the one-third of the working-class voters who supported the Conservative Party, they would never have gained power. On the other hand, one-fifth of the middle class voted Labour.

Given the assumptions that the two main parties were social class parties, the sociologists developed a number of explanations for these so-called **deviant voters**. These included:

- subjective social class,
- deferential workers,
- political socialisation,
- subcultural factors.

Subjective social class

This explanation suggests that the person votes for the social class which he/she perceives him/herself belonging to, even if this does not accord with the reality of their employment. Factors affecting this could be cross-class marriages, or where the social class of the family of origin was different from that in which the person currently belongs.

The deferential worker

This idea derives from Mckenzie and Silver (*Angels in Marble*) who claimed that two distinctive types of voter could be distinguished – **deferential** and **secular voters**.

1 **Deferential voters** believed that there were natural-born leaders, usually drawn from the upper class of British society, and that people should vote for them. Typically these natural leaders would be Conservative politicians.

2 **Secular voters** tended to look to see what benefits there were for themselves. They would vote Conservative or Labour depending upon which party appeared more likely to benefit them.

Political socialisation

Butler and Stokes (*Political Change in Britain*) argue that people's voting choices were the outcome of three countervailing pressures:

● social class,

● parental influence,

● significant political events occurring in their youth.

They suggest that people pass through a political lifecycle consisting of four periods. The early stages are of particular significance and the effects of parental views and early political experiences (which may reinforce or contradict each other) have considerable influence on voting in later life, and these in turn may be reinforced (or contradicted) by the social class of the person in adult life. The combined effect of the three pressures determine the voting choice of the individual.

Subcultures

Parkin (*Class Inequality and Political Order*) suggests that the voting choices of the working class could be seen from a different perspective. Rather than viewing a working-class person voting Conservative as being a deviant act and trying to explain this, he suggests that the question be turned on its head. According to Parkin, the whole traditional value system of UK society supported the values normally associated with the Conservative Party. The act of voting Labour was a form of deviance. Therefore any explanation needed would be for the fact that two-thirds of the working-class voted deviantly by voting Labour. Parkin suggested that working-class people are more likely to vote Labour when they are cut off from the **dominant values of society**. The key factors making people cut off were when significant numbers of working-class people worked and lived within established communities, which provided a buffer to the dominant values of society.

Parkin also suggested a fairly similar explanation for middle-class Labour voters. He found that they tended to be in particular occupations, such as teaching and social work, and that these provided outposts of deviance in the middle class, where opposition to dominant values was acceptable.

PARTISAN DE-ALIGNMENT

From the mid 1970s, a significant change emerged in British voting patterns. The clear certainties linking voting and social class began to weaken and social class stopped being the determining factor. During the 1980s and early 1990s this benefited the Conservative Party, as 'working class' voters shifted to the Conservative Party. However, in the 1997 general election, the New Labour Party succeeded in drawing votes from the middle class. This phenomenon of the breaking of class loyalties has been described as **partisan de-alignment**.

Partisan de-alignment can be seen as a reflection of two changes in social class in Britain:

● the decline in traditional social class values,

● the changing social class structure.

Decline in traditional values

The traditional working-class value of solidarity, including automatic support for the Labour Party has weakened considerably. Within the working class there has emerged a more affluent, home-owning and materially acquisitive section, more likely to live in the south of England, more likely to own homes in the suburbs and who are interested in voting for a political party which can maintain and promote their gains.

Marshall et al (*Social Class in Modern Britain*) agree that changes have taken place, but argue that the belief in two clear-cut, distinctive social class groups – working class and middle class – each with their own voting patterns is too simplistic. They argue that there were always divisions within the social classes and that the process of partisan de-alignment was merely an extension of already existing divisions, rather than something new.

Changing class structure

If values have been changing to some degree at least, so has the pattern of employment, which in turn influences the nature of the class structure. There has been an expansion in the service industries, a decline in manufacturing and a growth in the professions. The division between those employed in the public sector (who benefit from state spending and a growth in the state bureaucracy) and those in the private sector who benefit from lower taxes has also developed. These structural divisions impact upon the working and middle classes such that an automatic association with one political party no longer applies.

PERCEPTIONS OF PARTY COMPETENCE

This approach, which Heath et al (*How Britain Votes*) see as having considerable importance, considers the perceptions of the public about the competence of the political parties. According to his study, there is overall agreement about certain economic objectives – in particular that of achieving economic growth. The public's perception of the Labour Party in the 1980s was that it was less able to provide the economic conditions for growth than the Conservative Party. However, in the late 1990s, it was perceived by the electorate as more competent.

RATIONAL CHOICE MODEL

Himmelweit, Humphreys and Jaeger (*How Voters Decide*) studied a group of males aged 21 in 1959 over a period of 16 years. They decided that the belief in social structures determining voting behaviour was flawed, and stressed instead a consumerist model. Their argument is that people decide how to vote by considering what they want and then seeing how far each party meets their requirements. Therefore voting is little different from purchasing clothes or a stereo. They argue that the voter's knowledge of politics may be flawed, but that it is their perceptions that are important. According to Himmelweit et al, their explanations could accurately predict 80% of voters' choices.

Criticism

This approach has been criticised by Marsh (*Pressure Politics*) who points out that it fails to explain the basis of the voters' preferences. These may be class-based, for example.

PARTISAN DE-ALIGNMENT AND POLICY PREFERENCE

Sarlvick and Crewe (*Decade of De-alignment*) combine elements of rational choice with the concept of the changing nature of social class in the UK. They argue that voters increasingly make choices about the party that best represents their interests, but they will do so from a class base which provides an important perception of themselves and where their best interests lie.

This model therefore stresses the importance of the choice of voters, but relates this choice to the perceptions of their interests, which in turn are related to (though not determined by) their place in the class structure.

THE 1997 GENERAL ELECTION: THE FINAL COLLAPSE OF SOCIAL CLASS?

The 1997 election in which Labour gained a majority of 179 is regarded by most commentators as unusual. However, it does lend support to the various theories which stress perceptions, rational choice and policy preferences, which we looked at earlier, rather than any explanation based directly upon social class. Table 10.2 shows that voters stated that they voted for a party on the basis of their policies rather than the fact that they 'usually voted for that party', which is another way of saying voting according to social class.

Table 10.2 *Reasons for voting: the 1992 and 1997 UK general elections compared*

	Percentage	
	1992	1997
Party's policies	41	45
Usually vote for that party	20	20
Dislike another party	18	15
Party leader	7	7
Local candidate	5	4
None of these	6	10

(*Source:* 1992 NOP/BBC exit poll; 1997 Harris/*Independent* in D. Cowling, 'A landslide without illusions', *New Statesman*, Special Edition May 1997)

New Labour

By the middle of the 1990s, with Tony Blair leading the Labour Party, there was a conscious decision to respond to the apparently harmful changes taking place in the electorate. These responses included:

● trying to associate itself with the growing white-collar workforce, and dissociate itself from its traditional working class image,

● weakening its links with the trades unions,

● promoting a less class-based image,

● seeking the votes of women by specifically addressing women's concerns,

● attempting to alter the perception of it by the electorate as less competent on financial matters than the Conservative Party.

All of these appear to have appealed to the electorate, and to have very largely crossed class boundaries.

Table 10.3 shows that the Labour Party managed to retain its very traditional base of trade unionists, council tenants and social classes D and E, but moved far beyond that into the higher social classes – though social class differences do remain, with a decline in Labour voting the higher the social class. It also obtained the majority of younger voters, and women were as likely to vote Labour as men, whereas previously women were likely to be slightly more likely to vote for the Conservatives.

Table 10.3 *Where the votes went in the 1997 general election*

	Percentage		
	Conservative	Labour	Liberal Democrat
Men	29	47	18
Women	29	47	18
AB	40	33	22
C1	25	49	20
C2	24	56	14
DE	19	62	14
First-time voter	18	59	19
Other 23–29	21	58	17
30–44	24	51	18
45–64	31	45	19
65+	41	35	17
Trade unionist	16	59	20
Owns home	39	37	17
Mortgage payer	29	46	19
Council tenant	12	66	16

(*Source:* NOP/BBC exit poll in D. Cowling, 'A landslide without illusions',
New Statesman, Special Edition May 1997)

Regions, nationalism and voting

There remain clear differences between the regions of Britain in their voting preferences. In terms of votes:

● Labour is weakest in East Anglia, the South East and the South West, and strongest in the North, North West and Wales.

● The Liberal Democrats are strongest in the South West.

● The Conservatives are strongest in the South East and East Anglia.

● In Scotland the Scottish Nationalist Party (SNP) gained six seats, which doubled its representation. Labour obtained its highest vote ever. This would appear to support the view that strong support for some form of nationalism has developed here as both these parties are in favour of devolution (or eventual independence in the case of the SNP).

● In Wales, although the independence party, Plaid Cymru, only kept its four seats, the vote for Labour partially reflects the electorate's desire for some form of devolution.

10.3 THE DISTRIBUTION OF POWER

PLURALISM

Pluralism is the term used to describe a society (usually democratic) where power is not concentrated solely in the hands of the State but is dispersed among the population. In sociology, there is a debate between those who believe that Western democracies can best be described in this way and critics – mainly Marxists and elite theorists – who argue that power is in fact concentrated in the hands of a ruling class.

The elements of a pluralistic society are:

1 **Law** In a pluralistic society this reflects the genuine democratic will of the population, as reflected by the activities of pressure groups.

2 **The State** This acts as a form of seesaw constantly balancing the weight of public opinion as shown by the activities of pressure groups with its political convictions. It is neutral.

3 **The political parties** These are broad coalitions of interest groups, and in reality appeal to very wide ranges of opinion. People vote more for an 'image' than for specific policies.

4 **Pressure groups** These are groups formed to campaign over a specific issue. They do not seek election but to *influence* policy, eg LIFE (the anti-abortion lobbyists), Friends of the Earth, League Against Cruel Sports etc. Pressure groups allow people to express their opinions on specific issues, especially between elections; their views often cut across party loyalties.

5 **Individual voters** People choose political parties to support on the basis of 'images' such as 'good for the economy' or 'party of law and order', rarely for the details of their manifesto.

How pressure groups operate

Pressure groups are not represented in parliament, and therefore have to find the most effective ways of persuading the decision-makers that their particular viewpoint is the most appropriate. Depending upon their aims and other factors, such as their financial position and their relationship to the decision-makers, they will use one or more of the following methods of persuasion:

1 **Corruption and bribery** Pressure groups operating through bribery and corruption are supposedly uncommon; such matters rarely enter courts or are uncovered. We cannot mention examples because libel laws disallow it. There has, however, been great concern over the creation by the Conservative government of 'quangos' to replace elected bodies across a wide range of public areas. The members are often drawn from leading local commercial figures who are Conservative Party sympathisers.

2 **Consultancies** Trade organisations often ask MPs (generally, but not always, Conservatives) to 'represent their interests'. Trade unions sponsor certain Labour MPs who are in sympathy with their aims.

3 **Paid lobbyists** Pressure groups are increasingly turning to professional organisations whose job it is to persuade MPs to a particular view.

4 **Public opinion via the media** Pressure groups try to buy or obtain favourable publicity which will generate a 'tide of public opinion' in their favour.

5 **Influencing the experts** Governments turn to 'experts' in technical decisions so pressure groups can influence decisions by gaining the sympathy of the experts. This can take the form of companies funding research, for example.

6 **Public demonstrations** These can attract publicity and are often the most visible form of protest. Pressure groups that hold demonstrations are usually those with the fewest resources and the least influence.

7 **Law breaking** If all else fails then activists may turn to civil disobedience and, at the extreme, terrorism.

Criticisms of pluralism

Critics of pluralism from the Left argue that pluralistic societies do not achieve a measured balance of power for three reasons:

❶ **Resources** Some pressure groups have far more resources and contacts than others – does government policy reflect the public support for one side of the argument, or is this the result of powerful groups putting in overwhelming resources?

❷ **Agenda** Powerful groups are often able to set the agenda within which debates take place. So alternative (often left-wing) policies are derided by the media as 'loony' or dangerous. Ecological issues have traditionally been disregarded as fit only for eccentrics, for example.

❸ **Measurement** Pluralists concentrate their attention too much on the *process* of decision-making. What is more important is the *outcome* of the decision-making process which invariably benefits the powerful.

Critics of pluralism from the Right argue that the issues of **drift** and **buying favour** are flaws in the pluralist perspective.

❶ **Drift** Pressure groups do not lead to rational decision-making. The situation exists where there are **veto groups**, when the majority of pressure groups have enough power to block or veto other groups' initiatives but not enough to initiate action of their own against objections. This leads to weak government and **policy drift**, according to Kornhauser.

❷ **Buying favour** Governments are concerned with staying in power by making excessive promises and giving in to demands by pressure groups in order to maintain popularity and stay in power. This leads to erratic government.

ELITE THEORIES

Elite theories have been propounded by various sociologists. **Mosca** (*The Ruling Class*) introduced elite theory. He claims that a superior group rose to political power and retained this power through being a relatively small, cohesive group that is well enough organised to co-ordinate action and maintain control.

Pareto (*A Treatise on General Sociology*) believed that there are two essential types of personality:

❶ straight-forward, strong people who do not shrink from violence to achieve their aims;

❷ more manipulating types who prefer negotiation to force.

Pareto argues that certain periods of history require one type as a political leader and other periods need the alternative type. This alternating of one elite for the other Pareto calls the **circulation of elites**.

Michels introduced the concept of the **iron law of oligarchy**; this means that, no matter how hard an organisation (or society) tries to be democratic, it will inevitably finish by being controlled by a few people (an oligarchy). He took as an example the German Socialist Party at the turn of the century, which (like the German Green Party of the 1980s) attempted to be democratic; however, the leadership gradually took control through its hold on information (the party newspaper) and money (party funds).

Burnham (*The Managerial Revolution*) writing in the 1940s, argues that capitalism had moved from the stage of owner–controller to the point where share ownership was so widespread that control passed from owners to managers. In the political sphere, Burnham argues that power has passed to top civil servants. Therefore the new elite consists of **technocrats** in industry, commerce and wealth.

Mills (*The Power Elite*) writing in the 1960s, argues that the USA is dominated by a **power elite**, which consists of three separate but interconnected elites:

- the economic,
- the political and
- the military.

Members of the elites move from one elite to the other, for example Eisenhower from the military to the political, Bush from the economic to the political. According to Mills, the elite members are linked by **psychological affirmatives** and personal relationships caused by similar family socialisation and schooling.

Power blocs

Scott (*The Upper Classes: Property and Privilege in Britain*) has suggested that the most accurate description of the control of the State is that provided by the concept of **power blocs**. He argues that dominant groups in society co-exist with each other, forming alliances in order to gain control. Another way in which dominance has been maintained is through absorption by intermarriage. Scott shows how in the 19th century, land owners (the traditional ruling class) intermarried with the industrial *nouveau riche*.

Other power blocs have also entered the scene, such as the financial rich, whose attitudes and interests are taken into account by the State. Some groups, for example the trade unions, have seen their power wax and wane.

RULING CLASS (MARXIST THEORY)

According to Marx, the State is 'but a committee for managing the common affairs of the bourgeoisie'.

Miliband (*The State in Capitalist Society*) writes in the direct tradition of Marxist thinkers. He argues that the top positions in the State and the government are taken by members of the upper class. (The hallmark of upper-class membership is public-school attendance.) He points to the way that most of the senior industrial, financial and government figures are drawn from a closely interconnected upper class.

A separate, opposing Marxist interpretation is given by Poulantzas ('The problem of the capitalist state'). He argues that there is a relationship between the rich and the ruling class that is more complex than the fact that members of the rich fill top positions in the State. Poulantzas suggests that the relationship can best be described by the term **relative autonomy**. He argues that the State need not be staffed by members of the ruling class and that it would run just as effectively in the interests of the rich if it were staffed by people from any social background. Indeed, the assumptions that underlie the actions of civil servants, politicians and managers are ones that ensure that decisions are taken which reflect the interests of the rich. This, however, is not deliberate. Furthermore, the rich are not a cohesive ruling class: they have their differing sectional interests (for example the city versus manufacturing interests) and consequently the State is partially freed from direct control by any one group.

STATE-CENTRED THEORIES

The approach we have looked at so far tends to assume that the state (that is, the organisation which runs society on behalf of the politicians) simply carries out directly or indirectly the wishes of the powerful. Real power is located elsewhere. Marxists see the ruling class who own the means of production as most important. Elite theorists see small groups of people sharing certain characteristics as most powerful. Pluralists see the democratic will of the people as determining what the state does. These approaches are known as society-centred models.

State-centred theories however are different in that they argue that the state in itself is very powerful and that it is only by understanding the wishes and needs of those who comprise the state can we understand political decisions.

Norlinger: the state organisations seek autonomy to make decisions

Nordlinger (*On the Autonomy of the Democratic State*) suggests that the state is autonomous, following its own needs and interests in three situations.

First, when it has different wishes from the majority of the population, but is able to carry out its preferred policies despite the opposition of the majority. IT can do this by:

- being secretive in decision making and excluding outsiders,
- threatening to harm those who oppose its measures, by changing state policies towards them (for example withdrawing subsidies or state protection),
- using state resources to support its policies,
- providing disinformation about its opponents.

The second circumstance in which the state can be autonomous is when it is able to persuade its opponents to change their mind and support its views. It generally does this by manipulating public support.

The third set of circumstances which allows the state to act autonomously is when the state actually does have the consent of the people, or powerful groups in society.

SKOCPOL – THE STATE ORGANISATION SEEKS TO ACHIEVE ITS OWN GOALS

Skocpol (*States and Social Revolutions*) argues that one of the main desires of state bureaucracies is to extend their own power and influence. The extent to which a state can achieve its own goals are as follows:

- It must have a clear territorial base, upon which to act,
- It must have a reliable source of income, and the richer it is, the more powerful it can be. It can do this through tax collection of various kinds. Conversely, the more it needs to borrow, the less powerful it is.
- It must recruit a significant proportion of the academic and social elite.

Criticisms of state-centred theories

Jessop (*State Theory*) has criticised the state-centred theories for drawing an artificial distinction between previous society-centred theories and themselves. He claims that most neo-Marxist theories do give state organisations considerable autonomy in their analyses. Secondly, he points out that state and society overlap so intimately that it is impossible to distinguish a totally separate source of power to the state (or to society). The interplay between state and society is the only possible location of power analyses.

Finally, it has been pointed out that the state is not necessarily to be seen as a unitary organisation but as a fragmented set of groupings competing with the framework of the state for their own specific interests. Baggott in his analysis of the UK government's approach to alcohol, for example, has shown that the policy is driven by the different demands of competing departments in the civil service. The Departments of Trade and Agriculture argue for the liberalisation of alcohol and the Department of Health argues for its tighter control.

RULING CLASS AND ELITE MODELS: CONTRAST AND COMPARISON

Both types of theory share the belief that power is concentrated in the hands of relatively few people. This opposes the pluralist view that power is dispersed among the population. However, there are a number of differences between ruling class and elite models:

1. Ruling class theory derives from Marx and stresses that *political* power derives from *economic* power. Elite theories vary in exactly what brings a group to power and keeps them there – but they would argue that economic factors are only one of a number of possibilities.

❷ Elite theory (except for Mills) tends to be politically right wing. Ruling class theory on the other hand is to the left.

THE EVIDENCE FOR THE CONCENTRATION OF POWER

Table 10.4 *The educational background and gender of senior civil servants*

Department	Total	Oxbridge	% proportion	No. of women
Trade and Industry	54	38	70	5
Defence	143	35	25	1
Treasury	34	24	71	2
Environment	42	19	45	5
Foreign Office	33	18	55	2
Inland Revenue	39	15	39	0
Health	36	14	39	9
Home Office	29	14	48	6
Employment	21	13	62	3
Transport	32	12	38	1
Social Security	15	10	67	6
Education	19	7	37	0

There is plenty of evidence to indicate how power is concentrated in the hands of a few top individuals. Statistics show that the following people attended public school:

- 66% of under-secretaries (a high civil service grade);
- 80% of high court judges;
- 76% of ambassadors;
- 81% of chairmen of major financial institutions.

In addition, the richest 10% of the UK population own at least 54% of the wealth. The Conservative governments between 1979 and the mid-1990s were dominated by ministers who attended public school and came from wealthy families. Senior figures in insurance, finance and government are connected through intermarriage, shared schooling and overlapping directorates.

GLOBALISATION AND POWER

State-centred theories are particularly important in helping us to analyse the development of supra-national organisations which are playing an increasingly important part in our lives. The most important of these is the European Commission, which is above the member states and is not directly democratically controlled by the people of Europe, (though there is a European Parliament with some powers). Society-centred theories are less useful here as they are generally based on the analysis of one nation or society.

However even state-centred theories, according to Held, fail to help us to understand the development of a wide range of supra-national organisations which enmesh societies within regional and global networks. Traditional theories fail to analyse the power of multi-national companies, of world financial markets and international miliary organisations such as NATO. Held points out that for the poorer or weaker countries there is limited autonomy in what choices they can make, as these will be dictated by the international organisations which control the finances or the military power.

The development of trans-national or supra-national organisations also has further implications for inside the nation-state (see pp 111–12). Ethnic and nationalist groups within large 'empires' or nation-states may use the international organisations in order to assert their right to independence. The Basque and Catalan groups within Spain have funded their own delegations to the European Commission to press for recognition as autonomous regions. The countries which were client states of the former Soviet Union have also used applications to join the EU and NATO as ways of asserting their independence.

Test yourself questions and answers

Questions

1 What is the distinction between power and authority, according to Weber?

2 Distinguish between zero-sum and variable-sum models of power.

3 Explain 'partisan de-alignment'.

4 The changes in the class structure have been construed by some as helping Conservatives and by others as having only minimal effect on the Labour vote. Summarise this debate.

5 What are pressure groups? Outline the ways they operate in the UK political system.

6 What are the similarities and differences between elite and ruling class models of society?

Suggested answers

1   Power is the ability to impose one's will on another, using force if necessary. Authority is where people accept the right of others to tell them what they should do. There are three types of authority:
   ● charismatic: the person is obeyed for their exceptional qualities;
   ● traditional authority: the authority which is obeyed on the simple grounds that traditionally the holder of the office has always has been obeyed.
   ● legal-rational: where a subordinate accepts that for a specific end, and in specific matters relevant to the organisation, the senior person has the right to ask them to do something.

2   The zero-sum model is a Marxist view of power which regards power as something that is finite – such that it can only be held by one person or group at one particular time. For Marxists, the class struggle consists of two groups vying for a resource (power) which only one can hold. In the variable-sum model, power is not a resource that one group holds, and another attempts to wrestle off them, instead it is something which can expand or contract depending upon the extent to which people believe in its legitimacy.

3   From the mid-1970s a significant change emerged in British voting patterns, with voting and class links beginning to weaken, to be replaced by the fact that although the majority of people voting for the Labour Party were from the working class, a majority of the working class no longer voted Labour.

4   Crewe has suggested that changes in UK society are likely to continue to go against support for the Labour Party.
   ● Employment: Decline in the numbers of people involved in manual work. These traditionally voted Labour.
   ● Housing: Growth in the numbers of people owning their own homes. Home ownership usually favours the Conservative Party.
   ● Trades unions: Decline in trades union membership. Union membership has traditionally been associated with Labour voting.
   ● Demographic change: Large sections of the population have moved from cities to suburbs and smaller towns, which has weakened traditional working-class communities.

On the other hand it is claimed that the changes will do only limited harm to the Labour Party:
   ● Social mobility: The shift of the working population into middle-class occupations means that those from manual backgrounds might retain their class loyalty and be less likely than the traditional middle class to vote Conservative.
   ● Women and employment: The increase in white-collar employment is taking place among women, and these newly employed women would have been likely to vote Conservative before so there may not be such a significant growth in the Conservative vote.
   ● Home purchase: The argument that the new owners of council properties were switching their votes from Labour to Conservative has been exaggerated, as 35% of council tenants had historically voted Conservative.
   ● The idea of a solidaristic working class has been exaggerated, there has always been a division in the working class vote.

5   They are groups formed to campaign over a specific issue. They do not seek election but to influence policy. Pressure groups allow people to express their opinions on specific issues, and these views often cut across party loyalties.

They operate by using some of the following possible tactics:
   ● Corruption/bribery;
   ● Consultantships;
   ● Paid lobbyists;
   ● Public opinion via the media;
   ● Influencing the experts;
   ● Public demonstrations;
   ● Law breaking.

6   The similarity between ruling class and elite models is that they share the view that power is concentrated in the hands of a few. They differ from each other in that ruling class theory derives from Marx and stresses that political power derives from economic power whereas elite theories tend to emphasise other factors. Elite theories (except for Mills) tend to be politically right-wing.

Illustrative question and answer

Question

Outline and evaluate different sociological accounts of the apparent volatility of voting behaviour over the last twenty years.

AEB

Suggested answer

The essay should begin with a relatively short section on the traditional voting patterns and how they were associated with social class. You should emphasise that sociological theory assumed that this was 'normal' and that the majority of theorising centred on groups who did not vote according to the way that sociologists perceived was appropriate to their social class. You can then quickly comment on a couple of these attempts to explain 'deviant' voting patterns. Butler's work and Parkin's would convey the flavour of these approaches well.

You should then point to the fact that these patterns of voting were gradually breaking down over a relatively long period starting in the early 1960s and that the emergence of the Conservative Party as the major party of government did not suddenly happen but was the outcome of a process. You should make it clear that you are aware that the Conservative Party was in power throughout the 1980s and into the 1990s.

You should then go through the various explanations offered for this. These include the changing nature of the class structure, including such factors, according to Crewe, as employment, housing, trades unions and demographic change. The changing nature of the values of the working class is more of a disputed area, with Robertson arguing that fundamental changes have taken place which lead working class people to sympathise more with the Conservative Party, and others such as Marshall and Heath suggesting that there is no concrete evidence to show a massive shift in values. Other explanations which have been put forward are the 'Perceptions of Party Competence' model, by which the Labour Party has simply been seen as incompetent, and the 'Rational Choice' Model of Himmelweit et al, who argue that people basically vote for the party which they perceive as benefitting them most. The final approach of Sarlvick and Crewe is that people do make a choice on the basis of personal interest, but this has to be linked to the social class from which they come (even though they may be in a different social class now).

You should point out that all commentators agree that the partisan dealignment which has taken place has to some extent been influenced by the changing nature and fluidity of the class structure.

Question bank

1 Critically examine the usefulness of pluralist theories to an understanding of the relationship between power and the state of modern societies.

AEB

Points

Need first of all to define pluralist theories and briefly demonstrate their differences from the centralised power models of ruling class and elites. Need to explore pressure groups and demonstrate how they operate. Use contemporary examples.

Criticise by pointing out the great disparities in power, and look at the arguments from writers such as Lukes about the power of certain groups to 'set the agenda'. Move on to look once again at the elite and ruling class theories showing how they correlate with the huge disparities of wealth – in particular, refer to Scott's work and the 'coalitions of interest'.

2 Examine the extent to which class remains the basis of voting behaviour in UK society.

Integrated Boards

Points

Need to provide an overview of the voting patterns in the last 30 or so years. The statistics will show that class patterns were weakening ever since the early 1960s and were only ever a guide to voting preferences than an exact correlation. Nevertheless, the 1970s saw a significant change in voting patterns with other factors becoming important. Examine the debate on party dealignment. In particular, talk about the argument from

Sarlvick and Crewe regarding rational choice and self interest allied to the changing nature of social class. A reasonable argument was that the majority of people have always voted for the party which would appear to look after their interests. Historically, the working class association with the Labour Party, and as they perceived themselves as changing class, so their allegiance changed to the Conservatives. More recently the Labour Party has moved itself to appeal to the 'newer class structures'.

3 Compare and contrast Marxist and New Right perspectives on the role of the state in society.

AEB

Points

Marxist approaches see the state as being the puppet of the ruling class. You need therefore to discuss general Marxist theory. Need to demonstrate familiarity with the different approaches to the state within Marxist theory, for example, Poulantzas and Miliband.

New Right also is critical of the state, but sees it acting for its own interests, i.e. for politicians, bureaucrats and others with vested interests. Distorts free choice and the market by interfering.

Two approaches in agreement that the state is a bad thing. Both would seek to demolish it. In disagreement as to whom benefits from the state and the purpose of the state.

MEDIA

Units in this chapter

Chapter objectives

The term **the media** refers to all the means by which activities are transmitted and published for the use or enjoyment of the public. Each individual method of distribution – radio, television, books etc is known as **a medium**.

In this chapter we explore the ownership and control of the media in the UK. What we find is that there is a very great concentration of ownership, and that relatively few individuals or groups control the majority of all forms of media output. In a democracy where the role of the media is crucial in informing (as well as simply entertaining) the public, and through which ideas are formed and confirmed, the importance of the media is very great. If biased information is presented then there are political and social consequences, perhaps even affecting our views of ourselves.

The first section examines the ownership of the media and the related debate about whether the owners really do have control over what goes into television transmissions or newspapers.

We then move on to discuss the claimed effects of the media on people. The views vary from those who claim that, as a result of the media, crimes are committed, to those who argue that there are effects but that these are much more subtle and are closely intertwined with the culture of a society.

The next section examines the issues surrounding media exaggeration and distortion, in particular the concept of media amplification, by which an initial (usually deviant) activity is reported in such a way that it actually creates more of that deviant activity.

The final section discusses the way that the media choose events and then shape them into what we regard as news events. The point here is that the news is not 'out there', simply waiting to be found, but is actually manufactured by the media.

11.1 RELATIONSHIP BETWEEN OWNERSHIP AND CONTENT IN THE MEDIA

The concentration of ownership is quite marked in the British (and increasingly the world) media (see Fig. 11.1). However, because the media tend to be dominated by a few companies, does this mean that the content of the media is controlled by the owners? Opinions vary, and there can be said to be four main approaches – although these overlap so much that it is difficult to separate them clearly from each other:

❶ The owners directly control the content of the media – the **instrumentalist approach**.

❷ The owners indirectly control the content of the media – the **structuralist approach**.

Both of these approaches have been associated with neo-Marxism.

❸ The content of the media is determined by a **plurality of values**, but in particular the concept of news values.

❹ The content of the media reflects the wishes of the buying public – the *laissez-faire* **model**.

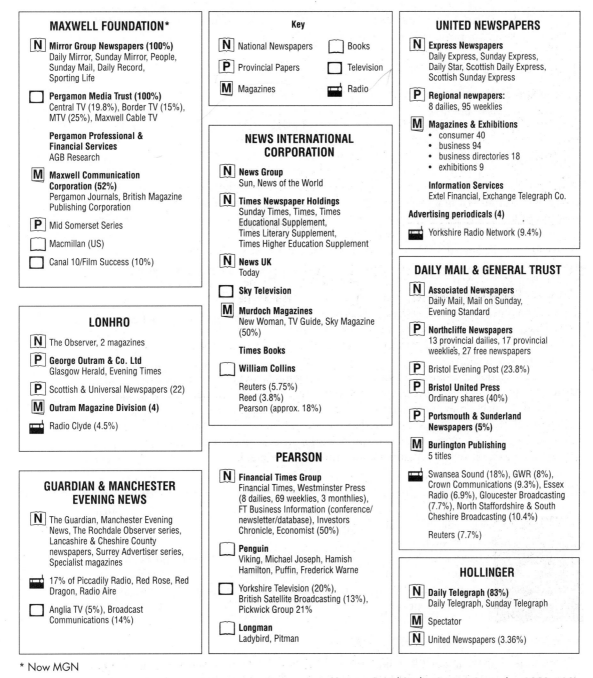

* Now MGN

(*Source: Social Studies Review*, September 1989, p19)

Fig. 11.1 National newspaper ownership of publishing, television and radio in the early 1990s.

THE INSTRUMENTALIST APPROACH (DIRECT CONTROL)

This approach can be described as traditional Marxist. Owners exercise direct control over the content of the media through a number of mechanisms, most importantly:

1 Through telling editors or directors (of films and broadcasts etc) what they feel ought to be included or excluded.

2 By making decisions about whom to employ – so choosing a right-wing editor is likely to ensure the right-wing content of the newspaper or magazine.

3 Through making decisions on investment and publication.

The owners are seen as direct representatives of the ruling class, often coming from the same privileged backgrounds and being linked through interlocking dictatorships of different media companies.

From this perspective, the role of the media is to help control the working class by providing a diet of news and information which distorts the reality of life to the benefit of the ruling class. The media can be seen as the mouthpiece of the ruling class.

News values and commercial pressures

The instrumentalist approach has no interest in the idea that there are other values which guide the contents of newspapers. News values are seen as merely a product of the decisions of owners/managers and senior editors. Commercial pressures do not seem to be analysed.

Criticisms

This approach stresses the personal and conspiratorial nature of the production of news. It ignores the need to sell newspapers as well as the complex issues of why certain activities are regarded as news. It reflects a crude, naive Marxism which seeks to understand the nature of society through the activities of a few conspiring people.

THE STRUCTURALIST APPROACH (INDIRECT CONTROL)

This approach is normally associated with neo-Marxist theory, although all approaches under this heading are not necessarily so.

In essence, this approach argues that no deliberate bias takes place in the media – or at least that this is not the main reason for the content of the media. Rather, the media reflect a set of taken-for-granted attitudes concerning what is normal and sensible. Opposing viewpoints are regarded as 'lunatic fringe' or 'extremist'. Thus the media promotes 'traditional' attitudes on the economy, the role of women (domestic/sexual), and the position of blacks in society (immigrants/trouble).

The media operate within a series of assumptions on reality; these assumptions support the status quo. The control of what goes into the press and television depends upon salaried employees, who dislike 'extremism' of any kind. They therefore seek political balance, reflecting the belief that political debates are like pieces of string – with two ends and a middle. The role of the media is to inform about the views of both ends and to stress that the truth lies somewhere in the middle. Supporters of this structuralist approach argue that the middle simply reflects establishment values.

Marxists relate this view of reality back to Marx's idea that all values and beliefs are determined by the economic structure. The basic values of our society are therefore ones which are sympathetic to capitalism. Thus private property, the freedom of individuals, the value of hard work etc are all praised.

News values and commercial pressures

News values and commercial pressures are accepted as playing a significant part in the process of news and media production; however, they exist within a framework of capitalist values, and this is more important as an area of analysis. Hall et al (*Policing the Crisis*) says: 'The process of "making an event intelligible" is a social process – constituted by a number of specific journalistic practices which embody (often only implicitly) crucial assumptions about what society is and how it works… One such assumption is the consensual nature of society… This consensual viewpoint has important political consequences… It carries the assumption that we all have roughly the same interests in the society and… roughly equal share of power.' This shows how journalistic values are stressed in relation to capitalism not in terms of a professional ideology as in the pluralist model.

THE PLURALIST APPROACH

This takes a much broader view of the way that the contents of the press and television appear. The view is that the contents are determined by a whole range of countervailing forces, which buffet newspapers, magazines and broadcasts rather like a small boat in fierce winds. No one force is regarded as dominant, although the importance of ownership and the wider culture is accepted.

However, other forces are regarded as more important. The forces influencing the content of the newspapers (apart from ownership and wider culture) include:

- commercial pressures,
- journalistic values,
- political and legal pressures,
- press agencies.

Commercial pressures

Newspapers (and television) exist in a commercial environment in which they must make money to survive. In order to do so they must attract viewers and advertising. This results in the provision of material that is regarded as attractive to the particular target audience at which the newspaper or broadcast is aimed. Mass-circulation papers, such as *The Sun*, aim for large numbers of working-class readers, while *The Guardian* targets a smaller, middle-class readership and aims to obtain a significant income from advertising to this affluent group.

Journalistic values

These consist of a series of assumptions concerning what the elements of a 'good' news story are. Only if the event has these elements will it be produced as a piece of news. Newsworthiness includes the following elements:

- **Frequency**: the time period of the event should be short.
- **Threshold of importance**: usually local (national) events are regarded as more important than those far away.
- **Clarity**: the simpler an event the better.
- **Meaning**: events must be culturally meaningful.
- **Unexpectedness**: there must be an element of surprise.
- **Composition**: there has to be a mix of news, eg sport, human interest, politics etc.
- **Personalisation**: there must be a stress on people rather than events.

Political and legal pressures

Here is an awareness that pressures exist outside the field of journalism. For example, the government is able to enforce D notices on newspapers and broadcasting organisations to stop them publishing restricted information. In 1988, the government attempted to stop publication of the book *Spycatcher* by an ex-MI6 employee which detailed information embarrassing to the government.

Press agencies

Most companies and official organisations have press officers whose duty it is to present the activities of their clients in the best possible light. The result is that news is presented to journalists in a packaged form. An extreme version of this is the lobby system in politics, whereby the government gives information to the newspapers but will not allow journalists to attribute it officially to ministers.

THE *LAISSEZ-FAIRE* APPROACH

This is the traditional non-academic approach used by journalists themselves. Here the argument is that the media produce what people want. If the people do not like the products, then they switch off or do not buy the papers. The market rules, according to this approach. What appears is therefore the result of public taste.

News values and commercial pressures

The concept of news values is acknowledged in this approach, but this is regarded as the normal process of news gathering, reflecting the good journalists' ability to spot a 'good story' and to present it in a way that will be exciting to the general public.

Commercial pressures are very strong and are stressed in this approach; however, these are not presented in a negative light but as a reflection of the ability of the media to respond to the demands of the public.

11.2 THE INFLUENCE OF THE MEDIA

There is considerable discussion concerning the portrayal of sex and violence on television and in films. The main complaint is that these incidents stimulate people to commit crimes or to behave in anti-social ways. Feminists have been particularly critical of the way the media portray women, claiming that it influences both women themselves and the way men act towards them.

There appear to be two questions one needs to ask of this debate:

❶ To what extent, if at all, does the media actually influence people?

❷ In what ways does the media influence people?

There are four approaches to understanding the influence of the media on behaviour:

● behaviourist,
● opinion leader,
● audience selection,
● cultural.

THE BEHAVIOURIST APPROACH

This was the first theoretical model advanced for the effects of the media; it derives from **behaviourism** in psychology. Behaviourism is the psychological approach to behaviour based upon the belief that behaviour is learned through rewards and punishment, just like someone training a dog to obey its owner by being rewarded for responding correctly. Most modern psychologists regard this as naive, and sociologists tend to reject behaviourism.

In this model the media were seen to provide a model of behaviour which influenced people by convincing them that they could achieve the same results as those portrayed in a film. If watching a rape scene excited a person sexually (the reward), the argument was that they would copy the rape and act it out in real life, in search of similar excitement.

Much of the appeal of this approach to understanding the effects of the media appeared to be the simple answer it provided to complex problems. The key to violence or crime lies in the effects of the media, rather than in urbanisation, differences in income etc.

Criticisms

This approach holds a naive view of human action, oversimplifying it to an extraordinary extent. People do not simply respond as animals might do (most of the original studies which developed the theory of behaviourism were based on research on rats and birds); they actively make sense of the world, as thinking beings.

Related research

A number of research projects were undertaken within this model. Bandura, in the early 1960s showed groups of children a film which included scenes of violence towards a doll. One group saw a version in which the person committing the violence was punished, another group saw the person being rewarded and the third saw the aggressor being neither rewarded nor punished. The children were allowed to play with the doll themselves. Only the group that had seen the aggressor punished was not violent towards the doll.

In 1972 Liebert and Baron divided 136 children into two groups. Half were shown a violent film, the other half were shown one on sport. Afterwards they were taken individually into a room where there was a box with 'help' and 'hurt' buttons. A child in the room was playing with a model car. The children were told that by pressing the help button they would make turning the wheel of the car easier, and by pressing the hurt button they would make the wheel uncomfortably hot to hold. The children who had watched the violent film were more likely to press the hurt button.

Methodological issues

The studies are usually in the form of small-scale experiments with a very positivistic orientation. The problem is that no-one knows the attitudes of the subjects of the experiment before they were experimented on. As experiments are always artificial, how can they reflect the complexity of the real world?

THE OPINION LEADER APPROACH

The point of this approach is to stress the social context within which the media's messages are received. It developed from the work of Katz and Lazarsfeld. They studied voting patterns and found that the media was far less influential in altering people's voting behaviour over the period of an election. Much more important were **molecular leaders**, more commonly known as **opinion leaders**. Most people had one or a number of individuals whose opinions they respected on one or more issues. They were more likely to be swayed in their opinion by the views of these opinion leaders than by the media.

The influence of the media was then viewed as affecting opinion leaders, who in turn influenced those around them. It is important to note that the opinion leader role is fluid and may vary across groups on particular issues and over time. There is no idea of a particular opinion leader who dominates all discussion around him/her.

Criticisms

The model has been criticised because it is untestable in practice: the opinion leaders change for different areas, and the relationship between their views and those influenced by them is extremely complex.

Furthermore, it stresses the importance of individuals but fails to take into account that advertising, business etc have the power to dominate the agenda of the media so that only a certain set of views is placed before the opinion leaders. In this case, the issues are already decided before they are seen or read, it is argued.

Related research

In *Personal Influence*, Katz and Lazarsfeld conducted a detailed survey of Illinois – 'a middle sized American city'. They interviewed people to find out who the opinion leader was, how he/she influenced people and in what areas. They found that the opinion leaders tended to read, watch and listen to the media more than ordinary people did, but that the opinion leaders emphasised that they made personal decisions as a result and did not just reflect the media's views. They distinguished four main areas in which the opinion leaders were influential:

- the buying of food and household items;
- fashion;
- in going to see a film; and
- judgements about current affairs.

Methodological issues

The methods used were surveys and interviewing, the only practicable research methods. Experiments were inappropriate as the influence of the opinion leader took place within the ordinary context of day-to-day living.

THE AUDIENCE SELECTION APPROACH

This model suggests that the media's audience is active, rather than the passive one portrayed in other approaches. The *audience* chooses which films and programmes to watch, which newspapers to buy.

Furthermore, the audience interprets and uses the same broadcast or item of news in different ways. For example, music can be regarded as background noise to compensate for loneliness or as a central leisure interest.

Blumler and McQuail have been closely associated with this approach and in their study of soap operas they argue that they provide a form of companionship for some people and a sense of community to which they belong. Research in Sweden by Rosengren and Windahl supports this, as people appear to use the media as an alternative to meeting other people.

Criticisms

This model is a significant step forward from the behaviourist and opinion leader approaches, but it has the defect that it almost denies that the media have any influence at all. The argument appears to be that people choose what they are watching and reading, and in so doing, control the media. This is doubtful, as clearly the media do have some influence: otherwise the millions of pounds spent on advertising would be wasted.

More significant is that all the research of behaviourist, opinion leader and audience selection approaches were concerned about short-term changes in behaviour that could be measured in some clear-cut way. Yet no-one had critically examined the ability of the media to set the agenda by continually presenting one version of reality to their audience. It is not that opinions are changed by the media but that a narrow range of opinions is simply formed and strengthened daily through the media. Few, if any, real alternatives are presented.

Related research

Morley (*The 'Nationwide' Audience*) studied the way in which different groups perceived a well-known television programme at the time. He interviewed 29 different groups of people, including apprentice electricians, sociology students and management trainees. He found that middle-class viewers disliked its patronising tone but accepted the factual correctness of its contents. On the other hand, working-class viewers liked its tone but were unhappy about the content. Black students interviewed found the content and the tone irrelevant to them. No specific research was done on the reaction of women.

Methodological issues

The research was conducted through interviews with selected groups, which were assumed to represent the range of opinions; why was there no separate group of women? It would be possible to do large-scale survey work on this issue, using interviews.

THE CULTURAL EFFECTS APPROACH

This approach relates the media to the general culture of society. It is not concerned about the immediate, short-term effects of a particular programme but about the long-term effects of constantly presenting certain groups or their activities in a particular manner. The long-term effect, it is claimed, is to translate these attitudes into reality, which then provides the basis for further media portrayal. Feminists, in particular, subscribe to this approach towards the media, arguing that they are portrayed in a few stereotyped ways, usually in terms of how attractive they are, or what their sexual orientation is, rather than what they have achieved. A second element of cultural effects theory is its awareness of the way different groups respond to the same information; in this it includes an awareness of the audience response model.

For Marxists, the portrayal of situations in particular ways is the direct result of the capitalist system attempting to control the population through biased information and entertainment. For non-Marxists, the source of media content is more likely to be found in the professional activities of journalists and their background assumptions.

Criticisms

The main problem with this approach is that it is not really testable and, although intuitively makes sense, there are problems in providing evidence for it.

Related research

The best known research is the work of the Glasgow University Media Group, which analysed news bulletins in the late 1970s and 1980s. They argued that the language and settings of interviews and the presentation of the information all led to a strong bias against the unions in industrial matters. The unions are presented as the trouble-makers, and the assumption underlying strike reporting was that the unions were the cause of the problem. The Glasgow University Media Group argues that the bias derives from the uncritical acceptance by the journalists of a **hierarchy of credibility** in which the views of the powerful are regarded as the ones which set the framework for the reporting.

Ferguson's work on women's magazines analysed their contents over two periods (1949–74 and 1979–80) and found that certain dominant themes ran through them, which stressed what the ideal woman ought to be doing. The perfect woman today, for example, combines being an excellent mother and wife with a successful business career.

Troyna (*Public Awareness and the Media*: *Reporting of Race*) examined the press in 1976–8 and found that the central theme was of 'outsiders living among us'. The impression given by them was that far more members of the ethnic minorities are in the UK population than actually exist here, and the media stressed the problems they caused.

Methodological issues

This approach generally uses **content analysis** in which the researcher examines copies of magazines/newspapers or film and then collects the information required. This may involve counting references to males and females, and then categorising how they are referred to; it may also involve detailed examination of the language used when referring to different groups etc. From this, 'evidence' is produced to show the patterns which exist in the portrayal of certain groups or themes in the media. The major problem is that the researcher has a large amount of freedom to interpret the material in any way he/she prefers. This can easily lead to bias.

11.3 MEDIA AMPLIFICATION

The interactionist perspective (see pp 233–4) provides an alternative view on the reporting of the media, particularly on issues of deviance. Their analysis focuses primarily on the process of media amplification.

THE ACTIVITY

A group of people are performing an act which is regarded as anti-social by certain more powerful groups in society, but which to the neutral observer is of little importance. This group almost always has to be one with little power, eg youth, blacks, the poor, etc. Examples include football hooligans, drug taking, child abuse, beggars in the street.

DEFINED AS NEWSWORTHY BY THE MEDIA

The media in some way or other finds out about the group's activities (above) and regards these as 'newsworthy'.

Why does the media become interested in a particular group?

There are two very different explanations for the interest that the media takes in the activities of a particular group.

1 **Cohen: Lack of news** The explanation first used by Cohen in *Folk Devils and Moral Panics* is that the activity or group is chosen by the media for interest because there is little alternative news of greater importance. The point here is that if something more 'newsworthy' were happening, these peripheral events may not be reported.

2 **Neo-Marxist: Deliberate news manipulation** Hall et al argue that capitalism needs to control the population. One means of doing this is through the media, that by focusing on certain groups and activities and portraying these in a negative light, control can be enforced. Furthermore, the media can be manipulated to emphasise issues which draw attention away from the real problems of capitalist society and to make scapegoats of powerless groups for the problems caused by capitalism.

Media success of the story

The media produce news stories which are successful in gaining the interest of the public. Papers are sold and viewers gained. At this point the newspapers or broadcasting stations are forced to compete for the most 'interesting' stories.

COMPETITION OF MEDIA

The resulting competition of the media for stories results in three processes, according to Cohen:

- exaggeration and distortion,
- prediction,
- symbolisation.

Exaggeration and distortion

The media exaggerates events, including the numbers taking part and the amount of damage caused or the costs incurred. Distortion takes place through the use of evocative language to heighten the power of the story, so that a series of fights becomes a riot, a group of people becomes a mob.

Prediction

This is the assumption underlying the reporting that the events will inevitably happen again. The result of this is that people are more attuned to the event. This may possibly act as a self-fulfilling prophecy.

Symbolisation

The language used becomes a symbol through which a whole variety of other activities or groups are compared or assimilated. For example, the term 'mugging' changed to refer to a wide variety of street crimes. The term 'punk' or 'lager lout' covered a whole range of young people. This affected how others responded to them.

MORAL PANIC

The audience has become so sensitised to the issue of football hooliganism, 'acid house' parties, mugging by young blacks and so forth that people are almost actively seeking out these problems. Every activity which can vaguely be put into the stereotyped category is placed there. People are distressed and fascinated.

Different groups in the population respond differently to the problem, as they see it. The outcome of the moral panic is the result of the confluence of the response of various groups: for example the State, the police and the public.

The State's response

Marxists see the ruling class as having initiated this whole process and therefore moral panic is used as a means of 'punishing' groups that pose a threat to the stability of the capitalist order. Interactionists see the politicians responding as a result of public pressure. Individual politicians, for example, might want to become involved as a way to gain personal publicity and therefore political advancement. It may be that the State perceives the problem as a threat to law and order and therefore must respond to public fears.

Thus, the introduction of football identity cards can be viewed by Marxists as a means of controlling the population by getting them accustomed to the idea of carrying identity cards; according to the interactionists, it is a response to public fears and a way to gain the prestige of having defeated hooliganism.

The police's response

Again the Marxists and interactionists differ in their interpretation of the police response. Marxists argue that the police justify their actions through manipulation of the media. Through contacts and press releases they are able to have their version of events printed in a way that is sympathetic to them.

Interactionists point out that the police, too, gain much of their information and views from the media and are led into action by the moral panic as much as the politicians or the public are. Their response reflects their view of their own role plus their perspective on the 'problem', as it has been provided by the media.

The public's response

Marxists see the public as being manipulated and controlled by the media, and encouraged in false consciousness. Usually, Marxists regard the public's role as being manipulated into demanding that they be protected from this menace – just what is required of them to do.

Interactionists argue that the outcome of the public response is not automatic and can vary depending upon a wide variety of factors. Generally, the public demand protection and help, but this is a result of the exaggeration and distortion practised by the media in their attempts to sell more papers or to gain viewers.

HOW DOES THE AMPLIFICATION FINISH?

- For Marxists, when the media have successfully done their job.
- For interactionists, when the media lose their interest and turn to a subject with greater novelty.

A Marxist example of amplification

The best known example is of Hall et al. Here Hall argues that the police and the State deliberately manipulated the reporting of mugging by young blacks in south London. They connived to have the extent of this problem exaggerated so that a 'moral panic' ensued. The result was that the public and the newspapers called for the police to do something radical. This was just what the police wanted.

The manipulation by the State had occurred because in one of the periodic **crises of capitalism**, which Marxists claim happen, the inner-city areas were becoming increasingly difficult to police using traditional means. The police wanted to use more repressive methods (such as transit vans full of police officers) to control the potential trouble. The public was not yet ready for this, so by preparing the public through the media and the panic over mugging, the police were able to introduce the new-style 'military policing' with public support.

An interactionist example of amplification

The best known example of this is the work of Cohen (*Folk Devils and Moral Panics*), a study of the original mods and rocker youth groups in the early 1960s. Cohen claims that, as a result of a sparsity of news, the media fastened their attention on the activities of youths in seaside resorts over an Easter Bank Holiday weekend. The media classified the youths into two groups – mods and rockers – a distinction that had not been made clearly by the youths themselves.

Cohen shows how the exaggeration and distortion of the media concerning what happened there meant that youths identified themselves with the images portrayed and *became* mods or rockers. The police were highly sensitized to the possible problems that these youths were likely to cause and so introduced a much higher level of policing. This inevitably brought about higher arrest rates. The unrest that the media had first reported (and largely invented) thus occurred.

11.4 THE SOCIAL PRODUCTION OF NEWS

The news that appears in the papers and on television does not reflect a reality that is waiting to be discovered. Instead, the facts and opinions that are broadcast and printed are the result of a complex weave of social activities. As such, we can make the statement that the news is a social product. The sociologist's task is to find and explain the various components of this process of news creation.

POLITICS

The political circumstances within which the media operate determines the extent of news gathering and presentation. In Britain, for example, the unrest in Northern Ireland led to some degree of media control, notably in the reporting of speeches by Sinn Fein (the political wing of the IRA) and the ban on the broadcasting of Sinn Fein leaders speaking, which has since been lifted. Other media controls available in Britain to the government consist of:

- the D notice system which restricts the publication/broadcasting of information of a 'sensitive' nature;

- the appointment of directors to the BBC and its funding;
- the laws relating to what can be broadcast on television in terms of obscenity.

CULTURE OR HEGEMONY

The media largely reflect the culture of the society around them, in terms of what they choose to focus on and what they see as the main elements of the story. Marxists argue that the dominant values which structure the contents of newspapers reflect the values of the bourgeoisie, either directly or indirectly. The media constantly set the agenda so that oppositional criticisms of capitalism are excluded and debates are thereby kept on safe ground. Pluralist approaches tend to stress that the media stay within the general culture of society. They may help to construct definitions of reality (differences in power are recognised) but there is no 'plot' to benefit the bourgeoisie.

STEREOTYPING

There are stereotyped images of certain groups:

- Blacks and Asians = immigrants,
- women = attractive/unattractive,
- youth = trouble etc.

This clearly links to the previous point concerning culture and hegemony.

AUDIENCE

Newspapers need to sell, and television and films need to be watched. Therefore, the media need to attract an audience. The size and type of the audience are the two important factors:

1 **Size** The media attempt to attract as large a number of people as possible. Therefore the contents must reflect this to a certain degree.

2 **Type** It is not just size that determines the programming and content of the media: the right type of people must be attracted. Newspapers cater for very different social class groupings – for example the tabloids cater for the lower middle/working class and the broadsheets aim at the middle class.

It is important to get the balance right between sheer numbers and types of reader, as advertisers look for particular markets for their goods. The result is that the presentation, style of writing and the content itself varies according to the desired (or actual) readership.

ADVERTISING

Advertisers do have a strong indirect influence on the content and style of newspapers (and television programmes) in that the media must provide a particular targeted audience for the advertisers. Advertisers can also sponsor television programmes, and presumably influence their contents.

NEWS VALUES (OR JOURNALISTIC VALUES)

These are the values which guide journalists in their search for news and which are used to provide a framework for understanding and presenting the information. They are discussed on p 233.

PROFESSIONAL AND CAREER INFLUENCES

The content of the news is also affected by the desire of individuals to be promoted, to gain an exclusive story etc. Decisions which are taken concerning the writing, presentation and publication of stories are partially determined by individual ambition.

Running counter to this in some ways is the desire of journalists to be objective; they do this, according to Tuchman's US study, as a means of reducing the tremendous pressures of the job. She claims that journalists engage in strategic rituals which help to defend them against claims of bias. The problem they face is that they cannot always make sure that their information is correct. Therefore she suggests journalists have **strategic rituals** to help them with this. These involve:

- gathering supporting evidence,
- searching out alternative 'balancing' views,
- using quotation marks judiciously.

MEDIA TECHNOLOGY

The rapid changes in media technology have had their effects on the content of the media and the amount of media output.

The content

The development of lightweight cameras means that news is far more visual and events can be transmitted directly and 'live'. Satellites have allowed intercontinental communication so that even the newspapers are able to bring stories to the attention of the public immediately and dramatically. This ease of communication has also helped to 'shrink' the world, so that events taking place far away are becoming more relevant and meaningful to the home audience.

The amount

New printing technology, satellites, cables etc have all allowed an increase in media output. This does not mean that there is a greater diversity of ownership or opinion, however, as the new media are dominated by the owners of the old.

AGENCIES

News is not spontaneous, in the sense that it is 'discovered' by eagle-eyed journalists. Much of what appears in the newspapers, is the result of:

- news agency reports,
- press releases by companies/government departments (British and other),
- formal or informal tip-offs by people with 'newsworthy' information.

Thus the starting point for information is one in which the news is, in a sense, manufactured.

A good example of this is given in the work of Chibnall (*Law and Order News*) on the reporting of crime. Here Chibnall examined the way in which specialist crime reporters obtain their news. Because of the difficulty of getting good stories out of the Scotland Yard Press Bureau, crime reporters developed close personal contacts with police officers. The benefits of the relationship work in both directions. The police officers receive free meals and drinks (very rarely cash payments), and can give the reporter information which is sympathetic to the police view of a case. The journalists get their 'exclusive stories'. For Chibnall, the result is that the stories in newspapers are social products which depend upon the relationship of police and reporter.

AMPLIFICATION

The idea behind amplification of news is that a story develops which becomes increasingly exaggerated and distorted over time as a result of media reporting. This results in the object of the reporting possibly changing its habits along media lines, and other agencies (the police) at the same time responding to media hype rather than any reality. This can, for example, result in an increase in the original problems considered newsworthy – **copycat riots**.

Test yourself questions and answers

Questions

1 Name the four approaches which seek to explain the content of the media.

2 What do we mean by news values? Give some examples.

3 There are four approaches which give differing accounts of how, if at all, the media contents influence behaviour. What are they?

4 What criticism can be made of the 'behaviourist approach'?

5 What is the audience selection approach?

6 What criticisms can you make of this approach?

7 What is meant by media amplification?

8 Compare and contrast, very briefly, the Marxist and Interactionist approaches to moral panics, in relation to (a) the State and (b) the police.

Suggested answers

1 ● The owners directly control the content of the media – the instrumentalist approach;
   ● the owners indirectly control the content of the media – the structuralist approach;
   ● the content of the media is determined by a plurality of values, but in particular the concept of news values;
   ● the content of the media reflects the wishes of the buying public – the *laissez faire* model.

2 News values are assumptions about the elements of a 'good' news story. Only if the event has these elements will it be produced as a piece of 'news':
   ● frequency: the time period of the event should be short;
   ● threshold of importance: usually local (national) events are regarded as more important than those far away;
   ● clarity: the simpler an event the better;
   ● meaningfulness: events must be culturally meaningful;
   ● unexpectedness: there must be an element of surprise;
   ● composition: there has to be a mix of news: eg sport, human interest, politics etc;
   ● personalisation: a stress on people rather than events.

3 Behaviourist approach, opinion leader approach, audience selection approach, cultural approach.

4 This approach holds a naive view of human action, as people do not simply respond as animals might do, but actively make sense of the world.

5 This model suggests that the media's audience is active rather than passive, as is portrayed in the behaviourist approach. The audience chooses which films and programmes to watch, as well as which newspapers to buy. The same broadcast or film may be used in different ways – so music is either a background noise to compensate for loneliness, or a central leisure interest.

6 This model is a significant step forward from the behaviourist and opinion leader approaches, but it has the defect that it almost denies the media have any influence at all: the argument appears to be that people choose what they are watching and reading, and in doing so, control the media. This is doubtful, as clearly the media

does have some influence or otherwise the millions of pounds spent on advertising would be wasted. More significantly research of behaviourist, opinion leader and audience selection were concerned about short-term changes in behaviour that could be measured in some clear-cut way. Yet no-one had critically examined the ability of the media 'to set the agenda' by continually presenting one version of reality to their audience. It is not that opinions are changed by the media but that a narrow range of opinions is formed and strengthened daily through the media. Little or no real alternatives are presented. Morley's research on the way different groups interpreted the same programme differently supported this approach.

7   Where an event is taken up in an exaggerated and distorted manner by the media in such a way as to actually create more of the deviant behaviour than would have been likely to occur without the reporting.

8   a   Marxists see the ruling class as having initiated the whole process of a moral panic and therefore it is used as a means of 'punishing' groups which pose a threat to the stability of capitalist order. Interactionists see politicians responding to moral panics as a result of public pressure. Individual politicians, for example, might want to 'climb on the bandwagon' to gain personal publicity and therefore political advancement. It may be that the State perceives the problem as a threat to law and order and therefore must respond to public fears.

   b   Marxists argue that the police justify their actions through manipulation of the media. Through contacts and press releases, they are able to have their version of events printed in a way that is sympathetic to them. Interactionists point out that the police, too, gain much of their information and views from the media and are as much led by the moral panic into action as are the politicians or the public.

Illustrative question and answer

Question

'Newspapers may appear to be run by professional managers and journalists but, in reality, it is the owners who wield ultimate power.' Discuss this statement with reference to sociological evidence and arguments.

AEB

Suggested answer

This question needs a discussion of the way in which ownership of the newspapers is becoming increasingly concentrated in the hands of relatively few people. The concentration of ownership has been documented by Golding, among others. Three forms of relationship between ownership and control have been suggested by Cohen and Young:
● the free market model;
● the mass manipulative model;
● news values.

Free market model This rejects the idea that concentration of ownership means that owners wield ultimate power. This approach stresses the fact that owners seek to maximise profits, and that without these profits the newspapers cannot exist. Therefore, the owners will attempt to make the newspapers profitable through high sales, or sales to targeted groups. The readership will want different things and therefore the professionals who write and edit the papers will strive to satisfy these tastes as best they can. Therefore, ultimately, the consumer decides what they want and is in control.

Mass manipulative model This is the Marxist approach and emphasises the way in which newspapers serve the interests of capital by reflecting the values which support the continuation of control by the ruling class. There are a number of writers contributing to this perspective, among them Miliband who argues that ownership is one of the four key elements of control over the mass media in general and these determine the output.

Your essay should spend some time discussing the idea of 'relative autonomy', in that the owners may not directly control, but, as the question states, will have ultimate control.

News values The final approach is based on the idea of there being news values which the newspaper journalists believe constitute a story and which they use to fill the newspapers. You can interpret this through a version of phenomenological theory, or link it to the Marxist approaches, with journalists' values operating directly or indirectly to the interests of capital.

The best examples of this sort of work comes from the Glasgow Media Group studies, and specifically Philo. They have covered strikes and the Falkland Conflict, analysing in detail the ways in which the news was presented. News values comprise a number of factors and you should work through these – they include such things as the frequency and duration of an event, the extent to which it is unusual, and consonance (unusual but not too unusual).

The essay should then summarise the debate between the various positions – and you may wish to go over the strengths and weaknesses of each position and indicate which model appears to you to present a more accurate picture. Do not forget to link these comments to the essay question.

Question bank

1 What does sociological research on audiences tell us about the impact of the mass media?

Integrated Boards

Points

This question is asking you to explore the various ways in which audiences receive and interpret the information given to them by the media. You should start by explaining that a number of approaches in sociology have stressed the construction of the media messages and made an assumption about their impact on the public. This criticism can be made of the Marxist perspective for example, another is the 'hypodermic syringe' or behaviourist approach.

You need to compare the various approaches. The behaviourist or 'hypodermic syringe' model, the opinion leader approach of Katz, the audience selection approach of Blumler and McQuail, as well as Morley.

2 'The selection and presentation of the news depends more on practical issues than on cultural influences.' Critically discuss the arguments for and against this view.

AEB

Points

This question is asking you to look at the differences between the writers who argue that the content of the media is determined by the wider cultural context, with the view that it is actually journalistic values and practical problems which influence what goes into the media as news.

Having explained this, you need to give an overview of writers such as Hall and Philo who basically take a Marxist view as to the content of the media. You should then look in some detail at news values, commercial pressures, the role of press agencies and the political and legal pressures.

You should however point out that all of these journalistic values and pressures take place within an economic and cultural or ideological framework which is not explored in these approaches and this is a serious omission.

HEALTH

Units in this chapter

Chapter objectives

In this chapter we explore the social dimensions of health. Sociologists have argued that we should be aware that health and illness have two issues to them. The first is biological, and it is clearly true that there are states of discomfort, pain and abnormality that we call ill-health. However, the other issue concerns how we define these states, and what objectively is the difference between being well and being ill? The answer for sociologists lies in the cultural definitions, and they start their analysis by examining these definitions.

The next section of the chapter deals with the way that different groups of people in the population have different levels of illness and different expectations of premature death. The fact is that class, gender, ethnicity and region all have varying relationships to expectations of premature death or high levels of illness.

Having uncovered and examined these, we then look through the complete range of theories that sociologists have suggested for the variations in health.

The final section of the chapter covers the importance and influence of the medical professions and how they can be seen either as beneficial to ill people or as actively dangerous.

12.1 THE MEANING OF HEALTH

DEFINING HEALTH

There is a simple model of health and illness to which most people in contemporary British society subscribe. If you do not feel 'normal' then you are unwell. If you are 'sufficiently' unwell then you go to the GP. It is his/her task to find out what is wrong with you and then to make you 'feel better', usually with some form of drugs or, in more serious situations, possibly surgery.

However, you can see by the way we have put some words in quotes that the actual feelings of illness or of being better are all rather vague. At what point are you ill? How do you know that your 'normal' feelings are in fact the same as everyone else's? Why do you simply accept some aches and pains and yet visit a GP for others? Why is the concept of 'health' always defined by the negative concept that being healthy is not being ill? These are the sorts of question that have been raised by sociologists.

THE IMPORTANCE OF HEALTH AND ILLNESS FOR SOCIAL POLICY

When the NHS was begun in 1948, the belief was that there was pool of illness that would be eradicated in a few years, after which everyone would be healthy. In fact, by the early 1950s, it became clear to the government that what was viewed as health was socially defined in much the same way as poverty. Health, it was found, was relative to the society in which it was defined. As people became healthier, they became more aware of being ill.

Furthermore, the whole idea of 'curing' people as the remedy for illness has come under question. If illness is not an individual, random occurrence, as sociologists suggest, and the true causes are in the nature of society and the way people behave, the answer lies in 'curing' society rather than the individual.

THE BIO-MECHANICAL MODEL

This is the model that dominates medicine today. It draws a parallel between a body and a machine. Just as a machine breaks down and needs repairing, so does the human body. Again, like a machine, the body has a fixed period of life, which can be extended slightly by good handling and regular 'servicing'. The role of the doctor (like the mechanic) is to decide exactly what has gone wrong and then to cure it through drugs or surgery.

The distinction between health and illness is quite clear – health is the state of not being ill. This model is relatively recent, with medicine emerging as a science in the latter part of the last century and dominating other forms of healing. The basic model now used was developed from researchers such as Koch, who isolated the bacillus causing tuberculosis. The result was the search for the 'germ' causing the illness and the belief that once this was isolated then a cure could be found.

The current model of bio-mechanical model of illness is based on four elements:

● curing

● individuals (of)

● episodic bouts (of)

● organic disorder.

What this means is that medicine always searches for some **cure** and believes that there always is one. This could be contrasted to the idea that death and illness are an integral part of normal societies and should be understood and accepted as such. The stress on **individuals** being ill suggests that there are no social or economic causes of disease and that the wider circumstances of poverty or pollution are irrelevant.

Episodic bouts refers to the idea that illness is something that arises temporarily and is then cured. Yet the majority of people with ill-health are long-term disabled or ill. Finally, the **organic disorder** refers to the fact that illness is regarded as simply a physical condition and that the cure lies solely in drugs or surgery, rather than looking at the person as a whole.

Criticisms

This model fails to relate illness to the wider factors in people's lives, for example the role of stress, working environments, pollution in the environment etc. It also fails to account for the fact that people cope daily with aches and pains without defining themselves as ill and going to the doctor. For example, a government survey in the late 1980s showed that 56% of men and 70% of women reported a health problem, yet only 9% of men and 12% of women had seen their doctor in the fortnight before. Finally, this approach fails to explain why different societies have different views on what health is. For if illness were solely biological, all societies would show the same patterns of health and illness.

NON-WESTERN MODELS OF HEALTH

In simple societies, most explanations of illness are based on religion. Supernatural power can flow between people, and everyone is in some way connected. Health can be restored only by rearranging the relationships and events that may have brought about the illness, or by 'expelling' the offending spirit. So, contrary to the Western model, illness is not just physical but also reflects the social circumstances of the individual. Illness is caused by either deliberate evil acts or the unintentional acts of others. This model of health is **holistic** in the sense of seeing the illness as related to the whole person and his/her environment.

ILLNESS AS A SOCIAL CREATION

This approach can loosely be related to the interactionist approach. It argues that everyone feels ill at some time, but that only a proportion of those feeling ill actually see a doctor. When they do, they are either defined as ill or their claims to illness are dismissed. If the doctor affirms that the person is ill, then particular consequences occur - time off work, possible hospital treatment etc.

Interactionists, such as Zola, suggest three stages of this model (which can also be applied to mental illness):

● recognition,

● definition and

● action.

Recognition

Zola suggests that many of us feel ill or suffer from various pains, but that we learn to accommodate these pains for a wide variety of reasons (getting older, damp weather etc). We recognise the existence of pain, but that is all. However, at a certain point, not necessarily when the illness is at its worst, the pattern of accommodation breaks down. It may be because the person can no longer do a particular act or fulfil certain obligations. At this point the person recognises that a particular problem exists, but goes beyond this and defines it as illness.

Definition

The role of the doctor is crucial in defining a particular set of symptoms as illness or as something not to worry about. There is considerable evidence to suggest that the perceptions of GPs are significantly different from those of patients. The GP may be concerned about keeping the interaction with the patient as short as possible, aiming to find the cause of the problem and finish quickly with the patient, for example.

Action

Whatever the motives of the GPs, the outcome of the doctor–patient interaction is one of negotiation and, as in all negotiations, the outcome reflects a host of different factors including power. This is seen as one of the reasons why middle-class people are more likely to obtain medical services than the working class.

THE MARXIST APPROACH

This approach, associated with writers such as Navarro, argues that definitions of health and illness are closely related to the needs of capitalism for a healthy workforce. Navarro (*Medicine under Capitalism*) claims that the introduction of health services was partly the result of working-class demands, and therefore a partial victory for the working class, but also closely related to the needs of capitalism.

Health can be more easily defined as the state at which one can continue to work efficiently. People are therefore checked by GPs to see if they are genuinely ill and therefore unable to work. If the GP decides that they are unfit to work he/she then seeks to make them better. In this sense the British Health Service can be seen to be of use to capitalism at least as much as it is to individuals. Supporters of this idea can point to the fact that originally when health insurance was introduced by the Liberal government at the beginning of the century, the only people who were to receive medical treatment free of charge were the (usually male) employed head of household, indicating the importance placed upon keeping the 'breadwinner' working.

THE FUNCTIONALIST APPROACH

The functionalist approach to illness derives from Talcott Parsons.

The effect on society

Talcott Parsons is less concerned about defining what health and illness are than about the importance of illness to the functioning of society and the way, in turn, society copes with illness.

The sick role

For Parsons, illness is actually a form of deviance which is threatening to society. The threat comes from the fact that anyone who is ill is unable to perform their socially expected role. This could have serious consequences for society.

Parsons suggests that illness may not be entirely random, and argues that there is some degree of conscious or subconscious desire to be sick. Someone who is therefore designated sick (by a doctor) is not expected to perform normally; however, if everyone were sick (for whatever reason), then society would no longer function. Therefore Parsons suggests that a **sick role** exists, with two components:

1 it allows individuals not to perform their normal social role requirements, but only if

2 they agree to give themselves over to the care of the doctor and try to get well again.

According to Parsons, therefore, the social aspects of illness are more important than the biological aspects.

12.2 INEQUALITIES OF HEALTH

Standardised mortality ratios (SMRs) show the relative chances between the various social classes of dying at any particular age. The overall average chance of death in society is assumed to be 100. A social class with an average above 100 has a higher chance of death than the average for society; conversely, below 100 means a less than average chance of death.

SOCIAL CLASS

Health is generally regarded as an individual and biological phenomenon – a person is ill because of a virus or germ, or perhaps because he/she has inherited some problem. If this were the case, one would expect illness to be randomly distributed across the population with virtually everyone having a similar chance of being ill. This is not the case: the lower the social class, the greater the chance of morbidity (sickness) and the lower the age of death.

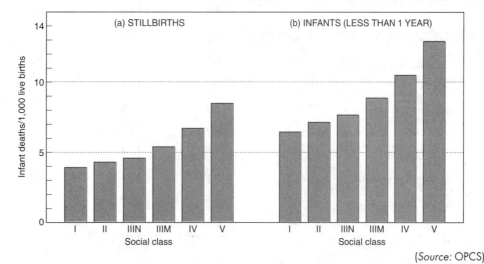

(*Source:* OPCS)

Fig. 12.1 Stillbirths and infant death in England and Wales by social class, 1984

The statistics in Fig. 12.1 show that the chances of a stillbirth (the child born dead) and the death of an infant under one year old are directly related to social class. In both cases, the figure for social class I is approximately half that of the children of unskilled manual workers (social class V).

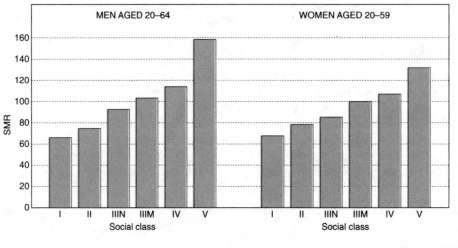

(*Source:* OPCS)

Fig. 12.2 The SMR of men and women in Great Britain, by social class, 1979–83

Fig. 12.2 shows that for men and women aged 20–64 there was a relationship between the chance of dying at any age (and of any cause) between 20–64 and their social class. The class difference for men is significantly higher than that for women. The SMR for social class I men is about 65, while for social class V men it is 160. The relevant figures for women are 65 for social class I, and 135 for class V. Note that from social class II to social class V, women have lower SMRs than men.

Table 12.1 *SMRs for select causes of death in Great Britain among men aged 20–54 and 55–64, 1979–83*

Cause of death	Age	Non-manual	Manual	% of non-manual to manual
All causes	20–54	76	115	0.66
	55–64	82	117	0.70
	20–64	80	116	0.69
Lung cancer	20–54	60	133	0.45
	55–64	67	128	0.52
	20–64	65	129	0.50
Coronary heart disease	20–54	80	113	0.71
	55–64	90	117	0.77
	20–64	87	114	0.76
Cerebro-vascular disease	20–54	73	121	0.60
	55–64	77	119	0.65
	20–64	76	120	0.63

(*Source:* OPCS)

Table 12.1 shows the SMRs for different age groups, divided into manual and non-manual workers for different illnesses. There is a clear class bias in the chances that individuals have of dying from these diseases. Interestingly, there is a different relationship between age and death within each social class. The older a person gets in social class I, the greater is their chance of dying. Yet among the manual workers, this is not necessarily the case. Incidentally, the only disease which was more likely to be found among the higher social classes than the lower is skin cancer – presumably caused by foreign holidays.

UNEMPLOYMENT AND HEALTH

The unemployed tend to have much higher levels of illness, particularly lung cancer, suicide, accidents and heart disease. For example, unemployed men were over 40% more likely to report to a government study (*The General Household Survey*) that they had chronic limited illness than the average for all men. Might this be the very cause of their unemployment? However, another government study (by OPCS), found that unemployed men had SMRs of 136 compared with the average of 100. Even allowing for the fact that ill-health might have been a cause of unemployment and also allowing for the effects of social class (that working-class men are more likely to be ill and working-class men more likely to be unemployed) – there were significant differences in mortality and morbidity rates.

For women whose husbands were unemployed, the SMRs were 120. In areas of high unemployment in Glasgow, children were nine times more likely to be admitted to hospital than the average for all children.

Suicide

People unemployed for more than 12 months have 19 times the chance of committing suicide than the employed.

Mental health

The government *General Health Questionnaire* found that there were significant differences in mental health between the employed and the unemployed. The argument that mental illness causes unemployment cannot be sustained, as the survey found that mental health improved after returning to work and declined with unemployment.

Conclusion

There is no conclusive proof that ill-health is actually caused by unemployment, although there is a relationship between the two. Secondly, there almost certainly is a direct causal relationship between mental health and unemployment.

SEX DIFFERENCES AND HEALTH

Fig. 12.2 has already indicated some important points concerning sex differences in health, and you should refer to this. At birth, females can expect to live six years longer than males. In every age group from birth through to adulthood, males are more likely to die – in adulthood the male to female death ratio is 2:1. Males and females die of different causes too, for example in adulthood, circulatory diseases are prominent causes of death for men, while cancer is the major cause for women. Differences in morbidity and mortality between males and females are so strong that they override social class differences.

Disability

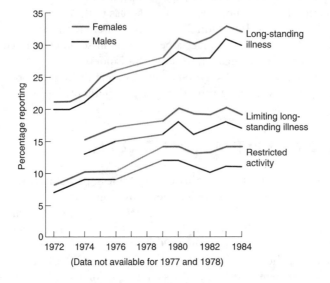

(Source: OPCS)

Fig. 12.3 Percentage of men and women reporting long-standing illnesses and restricted activity in Britain in a single selected period of 14 days

Fig. 12.3 shows that, overall, women are more likely than men to suffer from long-standing illnesses and to have their activities restricted. Overall, women can be said to have more illness during their lifetime, as measured by visits to GPs etc, but to live longer than men. Married women have lower levels of health than single women – although this may be connected with child-bearing.

Mental illness

There are marital and class differences between women's and men's experience of mental illness. Women tend to have higher overall levels of mental illness than men, and in particular they are more likely to suffer from depression. Indeed, depression is the most common mental illness for women. Single women have significantly higher levels of mental health than married women and professional women are three times less likely to suffer from depression than working-class women.

REGION AND HEALTH

Table 12.2 *SMRs for all causes by region and occupational class (men aged 20–64 and women aged 20–59), 1979–80, 1982–83*

	MEN			WOMEN		
Standard region/county	I & II	IV & V as % of IV & V	I & II	I & II	IV & V as % of IV & V	I & II
North	81	152	188	80	136	170
Wales	79	144	182	79	125	158
Scotland	87	157	180	91	141	155
North-west	83	146	176	86	135	157
Yorkshire & Humberside	79	134	170	78	120	154
West Midlands	75	127	169	77	113	147
South-east	67	112	167	71	100	141
East Midlands	74	122	165	73	110	151
South-west	69	108	156	70	96	137
East Anglia	65	93	143	69	81	117
Great Britain	74	129	174	76	116	153

Note: SMR for all men, and for all women, in Great Britain in 1979–80, 1982–83, is 100 Regions ranked by SMR for classes IV and V combined as a proportion of SMR for classes I and II combined. Women classified on own, or husband's, occupation.

(Source: OPCS)

Table 12.2 shows the relationship of health to regions of Britain and social class as well as gender, for people aged between 20 and retirement age. The SMRs show considerable differences by region, for example the highest chances of death are in Scotland and the lowest in East Anglia. Generally, these differences are reflected across the social classes.

When it comes to diseases such as arthritis, rheumatism, bronchitis and heart disease, there is a clear gradient as one moves from south to north. The further north, the higher are the levels of these diseases. However, various small area studies (which take a particular limited geographical area within a region or large city) have shown that within each of the regions in the table there are very significant differences in health patterns. For example, parts of Glasgow have some of the lowest levels of SMR and diseases in Britain, and in parts of Bristol there are high levels of disease and high SMRs, even though it is in the south-west region with some of the lowest SMRs.

It seems that overall, the levels of SMR and diseases are related to deprivation rather than region.

ETHNIC GROUPS AND HEALTH

This is the most difficult area to make generalisations about. The main methodological problems are:

1 the attempt to categorise a wide range of different ethnic/religious groups, such as Muslims, Hindus, Afro-Caribbeans, into one all-embracing category of 'ethnic groups';

2 linked to this is the failure of research to distinguish between British-born blacks and Asians on the one hand and immigrants on the other;

3 the lack of research information available.

We do know that certain diseases are more common among ethnic minorities than the general population:

- rickets in children of Asian origin,
- sickle cell anaemia in people of Afro-Caribbean descent and
- TB among certain Asian groups from the Asian subcontinent and Afro-Caribbeans.

Research so far conducted is summarised in Table 12.3.

Table 12.3 *Summary of main findings of Immigrant Mortality Study England and Wales, 1970–78*

Mortality by cause	Comparison with death rates for England and Wales
Tuberculosis	*High* in immigrants from the Indian sub-continent, Ireland, the Caribbean, Africa and Scotland
Liver cancer	*High* in immigrants from the Indian sub-continent, the Caribbean and Africa
Cancer of stomach, large intestine, breast	*Low* mortality among Indians
Ischaemic heart disease	*High* mortality found in immigrants from the Indian sub-continent
Hypertension and stroke	*Strikingly high* mortality among immigrants from the Caribbean and Africa four to six times higher for hypertension and twice as high for strokes as the level in England and Wales
Diabetes	*High* among immigrants born in the Caribbean and the Indian sub-continent
Obstructive lung disease (including chronic bronchitis)	*Low* in all immigrants in comparison with ratio for England and Wales
Maternal mortality	*High* in immigrants from Africa, the Caribbean, and to a lesser extent the Indian sub-continent
Violence and accidents	*High* in all immigrant groups

(*Source*: OPCS)

12.3 EXPLANATIONS FOR THE VARIATIONS IN HEALTH

EXPLANATIONS FOR VARIATIONS IN HEALTH BY SOCIAL CLASS

The Black Report and Whitehead's review of the research (*The Health Divide*) both found a close relationship between levels of illness, age of death and social class. Four types of explanation were offered by sociologists for these differences in health standards:

- the artefact approach,
- social selection,
- cultural explanations,
- structural explanations.

The artefact approach

This has been suggested by Illsley, who argues that the statistics on health which point to a clear connection between social class and illness are actually misleading. He argues that comparing social class V over time and with other groups is an invalid comparison. The chief reason for this is that the number of people in social class V has declined so greatly over the last 20 years that they form too few a number to be a valid point of comparison with the other social classes (see Fig. 12.4). In effect, he is saying that social class V is now so small as to be insignificant in terms of the general population to provide an accurate guide to changes in the health of the general population. The standard of health of those in social class V is actually declining in comparison with the rest of the population because very large numbers of people have moved out of class V, making the actual numbers in poor health *lower* rather than higher.

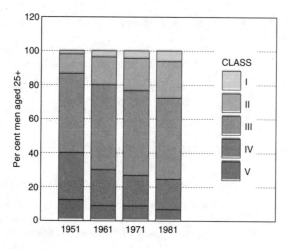

(Source: OPCS)

Fig. 12.4 The shrinking working class

Social policy implications

The artefact approach has several implications for social policy. The first is that campaigns of advertising and health education are carried out as discussed, targeted at the small number of people in the unskilled manual grades. The main implication of this approach, however, is that, overall, health is not as bad as is portrayed in the statistics and therefore tackling health issues need not be a priority.

Social selection

This approach reverses the argument of the artefact approach and claims that social class does not cause ill-health, but that ill-health may be a significant cause of social class. For example, if a person is chronically (long-term) ill or disabled in some way, it is usually difficult for them to obtain a secure, well-paid job. They are therefore in the lower occupational groupings and have lower earnings. Those who are strong and robust are, on the contrary, likely to be successful in life and socially upwardly mobile.

Social policy implications

Health statistics cannot be altered by government action. Ill-health is natural and therefore the social consequences of inability to work flow from this. Those who are genuinely ill should therefore receive State assistance as they are unable to help themselves.

Cultural explanations

This approach has been the one most commonly associated with British government policy in recent years. It claims that people make their own choices in their lifestyles and that these choices influence their health; factors such as exercise, smoking, alcohol consumption and eating habits are the main foci of interest.

The approach stresses that individual lifestyles are best understood as the result of cultural choices made by different social classes, ethnic groups and, to some extent, gender. Working-class people are more likely to eat white bread, less fresh fruit and vegetables and more sugar. So manual workers consume twice as much white bread, 50% more sugar, 60% less fresh fruit, for example, than professionals. Smoking and alcohol consumption, too, are directly related to social class: whereas 21% of professional employees smoke, 55% of male and 41% of female unskilled manual workers do.

Other issues, such as contraception and the use of medical services, such as vaccination, ante-natal care etc, are also raised, as the use of these is directly related to social class and the level of education.

The **culture of poverty** concept has been linked with this approach. According to this thesis, certain of the poorest groups in the population are socialised into a pattern of life that stresses lack of long-term planning, lack of concern over social issues, such as health, crime, the environment, contraception, and, essentially a selfish, live-for-today attitude.

Social policy implications

This approach stresses the need for more education concerning the effects on our health of various foods, drugs and lifestyles. It is the approach taken by the government through the Health Education Authority, which publicises healthy lifestyles and attempts to educate the public through the media and schools.

A second approach has been 'voluntary agreements' that have been made with industries engaged in providing unhealthy products, such as:

● alcohol – agreeing to aim its advertising at the over 25s and to provide low-alcohol beers;

● tobacco – printing a health warning on cigarette packets and restricting cigarette advertising.

Structural explanations

The final approach comes from those who see a direct relationship between differences in health and the nature of Western capitalist societies. Marxists, for example, are drawn to this approach, although it is not reserved exclusively by them.

❶ **Employment** Certain types of work are more dangerous than others, apart from the obvious ones, such as mining. Research on civil servants has shown that routine clerical workers are actually more likely to suffer from stress than more senior managers. We know that stress is a key factor leading to physical illnesses.

② **Unemployment** Brenner, among others, has argued that unemployment leads (after a time lag, he suggests, of about two years) to higher levels of illness in society. The link once again is stress. We also know that unemployment is linked to poverty, which in turn leads to poor diet, inadequate heating and low housing standards.

③ **Types of industry** Industries vary in how dangerous they are to their employees: for example, working in dusty conditions (respiratory diseases), in noisy conditions (deafness), with chemicals and hazardous waste products (forms of cancer). The alternatives, it is argued, are in terms of employees' health *versus* profit levels.

④ **Advertising** People are persuaded to eat and act in ways that are dangerous to health. So advertising campaigns extol the virtues of types of alcohol at one extreme and, at the other, help to create a materialistic society in which people are under pressure to consume ever more. What you possess is what you are.

⑤ **Food products** In order to have a longer shelf life, products are irradiated and treated with additives, with little knowledge of the long-term effects on those who eat them.

The search for profits

Underlying all these points is the nature of capitalist society in which companies need to put profit above any other criterion. It is not that being unhealthy is a choice that people have, it is something that results from the very nature of capitalism.

Criticisms

The obvious retort to those who argue that it is the nature of capitalist society rather than industrial society that causes ill-health, is that pollution and dangerous working conditions were equally bad, if not worse, in State socialist societies.

Social policy implications

The Black Report, although not in any way influenced by Marxism, did come down in favour of the structural explanation of inequalities. It stressed that the main cause of ill-health was poverty. The recommendations of the report included a shift in resources to community care and a rise in child benefit allowances to 5.5% of average gross male earnings. The recommendations of the report were dismissed by the then Social Services Secretary as being 'unrealistic'.

More radical writers in the Marxist perspective, such as Gray, have argued that differences in health by social class are clearly inherent in capitalism and that health issues cannot be tackled until the inequalities of society are eliminated.

EXPLANATIONS FOR SEX DIFFERENCES IN HEALTH

We have noted earlier (pp 251–2) that women live longer than men, but that they are more likely to visit their GPs for treatment and that they have higher levels of mental illness.

Biology

There is some evidence to suggest that women are biologically stronger than men (for instance female foetuses are less likely to die than male foetuses).

Social role

However, women may also live longer because of their social role, which discourages them from violent activities, fast driving, excess alcohol consumption and excess smoking etc.

One group of women who do have significantly high levels of mental and physical illness is housewives. The sheer amount of work, the isolation and the long hours are conducive to ill-health. It is noticeable, for instance, that working women have much lower levels of illness than full-time housewives.

EXPLANATIONS FOR VARIATIONS IN ETHNICITY AND HEALTH

The relationship between health and race is very complex. The different ethnic groups have very different social customs, and these are reflected in their patterns of health.

Asians are less likely to drink alcohol and, therefore, related deaths and illnesses are lower. However, infant mortality and infant abnormality are extremely high to mothers born on the Asian subcontinent. This can be explained partially by poverty, but other factors such as the late age for bearing children and the short timespan between births are more important.

Overall, people of Afro-Caribbean origin are healthier than the general population. Whitehead suggests that this is partly biological – only the fit and healthy would undertake the trauma of migration to Britain, and it is only in the last ten years that the original Afro-Caribbean immigrants are starting to enter old age and with it encounter the problems of ill-health and infirmity. However, people of Afro-Caribbean origin do have above-average rates of certain forms of heart disease and liver cancer; at present there is no explanation for this.

12.4 THE ROLE OF MEDICINE AND THE MEDICAL PROFESSION

Medicine is currently dominated by a bio-mechanical model of health, which stresses the importance of cure rather than prevention. At the top of the hierarchy of medicine are doctors who have been extremely influential in devising this model of health care. The role of doctors in society has been the centre of some controversy among sociologists.

Three clear views on doctors have emerged:

1. **Marxists**: that doctors engage in a form of social control on behalf of capitalism.

2. **Functionalists**: that doctors are dedicated professionals helping people, although there is an element of social control in what they do (the sick role).

3. **Radicals**: those who see the professions as existing to benefit professionals. Writers such as Friedson are in the tradition of Max Weber.

THE MARXIST APPROACH: MEDICINE AS REPRESSION

Doctors as agents of the large corporations

McKinley, an American Marxist, argues (*The Business of Good Doctoring, or Good Doctoring as Business*) that health care exists because it provides massive profits for the medical companies involved in supplying drugs and equipment to hospitals and doctors' practices. In the USA, health care is dominated by private insurance schemes, so that health is a commodity, just like a car or a video. As a result, the practice of medicine can be seen as another form of exploitation, alongside all the others that exist in capitalism. However, McKinley argues that it is not doctors who have control over medicine but the large insurance, private health and drug companies that dominate. Doctors exist merely to deliver the goods in much the same way as shop assistants. The control they feel they have over their work is illusory.

Doctors as agents of social control

Navarro argues that the prime roles of medicine and therefore doctors are:

- to keep the workforce healthy so that they can create greater profits;
- to mystify people as to the real causes of illness in the world.

257

1 **To keep the workforce healthy** Navarro claims that doctors keep the workforce healthy; this ensures that they can go into work and be more productive. By struggling to maintain free health care for all, Navarro points out that workers are actually struggling to allow themselves to make greater profits for the capitalists. Furthermore, as health care is provided by the State not employers, then the State is effectively subsidising the employers.

Criticisms However, it appears that GPs have been increasingly generous in their support of time off work through ill-health. Far from curing people and driving them back to work, it would appear that GPs are increasing the amount of time they give people off work. Furthermore, the Conservative government changed the sickness benefit rules so that a substantial amount of early sickness benefit is now paid by employers. Both these points run counter to Navarro's arguments.

2 **To mystify people** Althusser, in his writings on capitalism, has stressed the role of certain **ideological State apparatuses**, as he calls them, in preventing people becoming aware of the true unpleasant nature of capitalism. These agencies exist to create **false consciousness**, that is to mystify people and create a belief that capitalist society is the 'normal' form of society.

For Navarro, the second function of medicine is just such a process of creating false consciousness. Medicine (and in particular the NHS) creates an illusion of the caring society. It concentrates on the individual end results of disease, drawing attention from the fact that capitalism itself creates the conditions that cause disease. The role of doctors is to help continue this false consciousness, while creating the belief that capitalism has a caring side to it.

Criticisms The first criticism surrounds the concept of false consciousness itself, as this remains an element of Marxist belief and not necessarily a fact. The second criticism is that there is little evidence to show that capitalism as such is responsible for poor health. Certainly the practices of industrial society lead to poor health, but these conditions could be found in communist societies as well.

THE FUNCTIONALIST APPROACH: DOCTORS AS DEDICATED PROFESSIONALS

Functionalist writers, such as Parsons, argue that the reason why doctors have a monopoly over medicine is that there are particularly important reasons why medical treatment should be strictly controlled. Indeed, the stringent professional codes of conduct imposed on doctors guarantee the patient of receiving the highest standards of health care and being treated on ethical lines.

According to Parsons, the sick are vulnerable to exploitation in the following ways:

- Methods of healing are physically invasive, with one's body becoming the object of highly intimate contact.

- Doctors must have the highest levels of competence if serious consequences are not to occur to the patient.

- There is the need for the highest standards of trust, as the doctor is told highly personal information.

A profession, according to the functionalists, has the following five elements and therefore fits the needs of medicine perfectly:

1 **A body of systematic knowledge**.

2 **Professional authority** An unquestioning acceptance of the opinion of the expert by clients, and separately, the right to discipline its own members rather than to receive discipline from outside.

3 **The sanction of the community** This involves the monopoly of the provision of the service and a concern for the interests of the community (rather than self-interest).

4 **A strict code of ethics**.

⑤**A professional culture** This involves a common sense of identity and purpose. Those who offend against this (and/or the code of ethics) can be disciplined.

The functionalist approach therefore sees professions as beneficial to society.

Criticisms

It is highly debatable that the professions actually benefit anyone except the professions themselves, and certainly there is no evidence to prove that a monopoly of medical services has been beneficial to the public. Indeed, most evidence points to the fact that the contribution of doctors to eliminating illness in society is marginal. Far more important have been changes in diet, higher standards of living and housing etc, according to McKeown (*The Role of Medicine: Dream, Mirage or Nemesis?*).

THE RADICAL APPROACH: SELF-INTEREST AND PROFESSIONALS

A completely different approach to doctors, and the professions in general, comes from Friedson (*Profession of Medicine*), who argues that professions exist to benefit the professionals themselves rather than the community. **Professionalisation**, according to Friedson, is one of a number of ways in which groups of workers band together to raise the rewards for their labour. The working-class means of doing this is through trades unions and is generally less successful than professionalisation.

Doctors have been particularly successful in eliminating other groups who claim to treat illnesses, such as homeopaths, faith healers and physiotherapists. By adroit political manoeuvring they obtained a legal monopoly over the practice of 'medicine' and then proceeded to mould our image of illness and healing along lines most beneficial to them.

Parry and Parry (*The Rise of the Medical Profession*) have suggested the following attributes of professionalisation which contrast with the functionalist approach:

① **Restriction of entry** This raises wages and prestige; for example the Family Health Service Authorities limit the number of GPs allowed to practise in an area.

② **Controlling the public image and conduct of doctors** This gives the impression of people who are morally above reproach and who are committed to public service.

③ **The claim that only professional members are qualified to perform the service** This excludes others from performing these services (possibly in a more effective way) and therefore gives the profession a monopoly.

In conclusion, doctors are primarily concerned with their own interests, according to this approach, and professionalisation is simply a smoke screen to hide this.

Iatrogenesis

Illich (*Medical Nemesis*) provides an even more negative view of the medical profession, claiming that much of the professional mystique is to hide the fact that doctors are actually responsible for a large amount of ill-health. Illich calls this situation **iatrogenesis**. He distinguishes three types of iatrogenesis:

① **Clinical iatrogenesis** Poor diagnosis results in illness, particularly through the prescription of inappropriate drugs and harmful surgery.

② **Social iatrogenesis** The control of medicine has also given doctors the control over our bodies. This has helped make our own bodies alien to us. Doctors have taken over the right to decide what should and should not be done to us; for example their control over childbirth.

③ **Cultural iatrogenesis** Pain and death are natural parts of our lives. Medicine has hidden these away and made them taboo subjects. People shy away from the inevitability of death and pain which are part of the natural cycle, and are therefore unable to live their lives fully and naturally.

Test yourself questions and answers

Questions

1 What different models of health exist?

2 What do we mean by SMR?

3 Outline the effects of unemployment on health.

4 Women have higher levels of disability and certain types of mental illness, briefly give the sociological explanations.

5 What are the four types of explanation for the relationship between health and class suggested in The Black Report?

6 What explanations have been offered for the greater life expectancy of women?

7 What is the contribution of Friedson to our understanding of the medical profession?

8 Explain the meaning of the term 'iatrogenesis'?

Suggested answers

1 Bio-mechanical, holistic (or non-Western), interactionist, Marxist and functionalist.

2 SMRs show the relative chances of dying at any particular age between the various social classes. The overall average chance of death in society is assumed to be 100, and a social class with an average above 100 has a higher chance of death than the average for society. Conversely, below 100 means a less than average chance of death.

3 The unemployed tend to have much higher levels of illness, particularly lung cancer, suicide, accidents and heart disease. For example, unemployed men were over 40% more likely to report chronic limited illness than the average for all men. Another government study found that unemployed men had SMRs of 136. For women whose husbands were unemployed, the SMRs were 120. In areas of high unemployment in Glasgow, children were nine times more likely to be admitted to hospital than the average for all children. There is no conclusive proof that ill health is actually caused by unemployment, though there is a relationship between the two.

   People unemployed for more than 12 months have a 19 times higher chance of committing suicide compared to the employed.

4 Disability – women live longer, and the majority of the disabled are elderly. Mental illness – it has been suggested that the high levels of schizophrenia may be caused by the role of women in society.

5 Artefact; social selection; cultural explanations; structural explanations.

6 In *The Health Divide*, Whitehead argues that there is some evidence that women are biologically stronger than men. Women may also live longer because of their social role which discourages them from violent activities, fast driving, excess alcohol consumption and excess smoking etc.

7 Friedson argues that professions exist to benefit the professionals themselves, rather than the community, as suggested by functionalists. Professionalisation, according to Friedson, is one of a number of ways in which groups of workers band together to raise the rewards for their labour. The working-class means of doing this is through trades unions and is generally less successful than professionalisation. Doctors have been particularly successful in eliminating other groups who claim to treat illnesses, such as homeopaths, faith healers and physiotherapists, and have obtained a legal monopoly over the practice of 'medicine'.

8 Illich suggests that doctors are actually responsible for a large amount of ill-health, and he calls this 'iatrogenesis'. There are three types of iatrogenesis:

- clinical iatrogenesis: Poor diagnosis results in illness;
- social iatrogenesis: doctors have taken over the right to decide what should and should not be done to us;
- cultural iatrogenesis: pain and death are natural parts of our lives; medicine has hidden these away and made them taboo subjects.

Illustrative question and answer

Question

Outline and assess different sociological explanations of the continuation of social class inequalities in health and health care.

AEB

Suggested answer

You should start the essay by looking at the facts concerning the distribution of health and illness by social class, using the research in the Whitehead and Black Reports, for example. It is probably worth pointing out early on that you are fully aware that there are other dimensions of inequality besides social class, and you should mention (but no more than this) the issues of gender and race. You could also argue that there are very significant regional differences which may well be related to social class and reflect, to some degree, differences in the social class composition of different parts of the UK.

There have been four main approaches identified:

- artefact,
- individual,
- cultural,
- structural.

The artefact approach consists of the debate over whether the statistics really reflect an accurate picture of the differences in health care. Illsley, in particular, has argued that, although there is a widening gap between the lowest social class and the rest, this reflects changes in the class structure. He points out that there are far fewer individuals in the lowest social class and that therefore the percentage of people with poor health has actually declined. There are also debates about what exactly poor health is, as the majority of the population have higher standards of health and live longer than in the past.

A second approach stresses individual choices and biological backgrounds. This sees health as separate from social class, or puts the relationship a different way around – that those with poor health are less likely to have good jobs and therefore are more likely to be in the lower social classes. You should criticise this heavily by referring to the evidence which clearly shows the impact of poverty on families' health, in particular the work of Townsend in London.

A third approach stresses the cultural choices that people make in the food they eat and the influence of those around them. This sees it as being possible to change attitudes to food and living styles by publicity and medical advice. It is the approach supported by the Health Education Authority.

The final approach comes from Marxist-influenced writers who place the blame for ill-health on the actual structure and demands of capitalist society. In particular, they point to such things as low income, stressful jobs and, increasingly, stress from lack of employment, danger at work, poor housing and lifestyles which are the result of living in an unequal society. Townsend, in particular, has been associated with this form of critique of capitalist society and health. There have been innumerable studies on this and work on the effects of unemployment. You should look at Brenner and Doyal, for example. You should point out that standards of health in socialist societies are probably worse than in capitalist ones.

The final part of the essay is to give an overview of the strengths and weaknesses of each approach and to make it clear that some provide greater insight than others.

Question bank

1 *Critically* assess the view that mental illness is a 'social construct'.

Integrated Boards

Points

This approach is associated with the labelling perspective. You should start with a very brief overview of this approach and the significance of symbols, roles and, most importantly, a 'career', etc. You should then apply this to mental illness.

Work through the writing of Scheff and his argument concerning the career of a mental patient. You should then move on to an examination of Goffman's work on asylums. You might wish to criticise/debate your answer so far with examples about the higher levels of defined mental illness associated with those from Afro-Caribbean backgrounds and secondly the levels of depression amongst women. It could be argued that these groups really do have greater problems to contend with – racism and sexism – and that this does actually cause greater levels of disturbed behaviour. On the other hand, it could be interpreted as a labelling of their actions by more powerful groups of whites and males as mental illness, rather than as reasonable behaviour.

2 'The artefact view of health inequalities asserts that the apparent differences between social groups are simply the result of the inability to measure a complex phenomenon such as health.' Critically examine the sociological arguments for and against this view.

AEB

Points

This question refers to the debate over the causes of inequalities in health care and to elements of the Black Report. This report suggested that the best way to understand the differences in health care by social class was through one of the following artefact explanations; social selection, cultural and structural explanations. You should work through these different explanations, but spend more time on the artefact explanation and then structure your answer in terms of pitting the other three explanations against it. The question does not refer solely to social class so you must include a discussion on race and gender and health.

3 Assess the view that improvements in the health of the population in modern society are the result of better health care.

AEB

Points

This question is suggesting that the medical professions have overplayed their role in raising health standards and lowering the levels of morbidity and mortality. You should really criticise this view and the bulk of your essay should be against it. You should look at the development of the profession of medicine, and how it managed through a process of closure to gain itself a monopoly on the decision-making regarding health care – use Parry and Parry's points about their profession too. You should comment on iatrogenesis and Illich's critique. You can also refer to the statistics on the decline in mortality which show that these occurred with the changes in living standards rather than through medical breakthroughs.

However, do not take too extreme a view. After all, some forms of surgery, most inoculation and vaccination programmes and the introduction of such drugs as penicillin have been particularly effective.

POVERTY AND WELFARE

Units in this chapter

Chapter objectives

The chapter begins with a detailed discussion of the importance of defining poverty and the various competing definitions available. This debate is linked to the implications for policies to combat poverty, and we explore the different political attitudes shown by the government and its critics.

The next section deals with the various groups of people in poverty and their experiences of living in conditions caused by their poverty. The groups we look at cover a wide spectrum of the population and in some cases overlap – they include the low paid, the disabled, single parents, the unemployed, older people (women are overrepresented in most of these groups).

The next section of the chapter turns our attention to the differing explanations offered for the continuation (and, some would argue, extension) of poverty in Britain. These explanations are closely connected to the different definitions of poverty we examine in the first section.

The remaining sections of the chapter consider the Welfare State. Different theories on welfare are described first of all, followed by an examination of the effectiveness of the Welfare State in redistributing wealth through taxation and benefits. Finally, we look at the debates on targeting versus universalism and welfare dependency.

13.1 DEFINITIONS OF POVERTY

There are three broad, and opposing, definitions of poverty; these are:

- absolute,
- relative and
- consensual.

ABSOLUTE POVERTY

In the 1890s, Rowntree set out to prove that there was an immense amount of poverty in Britain, but before he could do this, he had to define a poverty line to distinguish the poor from the majority of the population.

Rowntree argued that there were three essential elements of expenditure that every person or family makes. These are:

1. **food**: he used a basic diet which would keep people healthy;

2. **clothing**: he calculated the minimum necessary clothing for a person to keep warm and dry;

3. **housing**: he took the average rents paid by working-class people at that time.

Rowntree then totalled the amounts and this said that level of income equalled the poverty line.

The continuing relevance of Rowntree's work

The Conservative governments of the 1980s and 1990s supported absolute definitions, arguing that the aim of social security should not be to improve the living conditions of the poor but to make sure that the least well off in the population can afford the basic things in life.

The advantages and disadvantages of absolute definitions of poverty

Table 13.1 *Advantages and disadvantages of the absolute definition*

Advantages	Disadvantages
1 Absolute definitions of poverty are clear and unambiguous.	1 It is extremely difficult to define necessities or 'minimum standards of living'. These clearly change over time/place etc.
2 Relative definitions of poverty (see following sections) lose their usefulness at a certain point in the general standard of living, for in very rich societies, people who have far more than the necessities of life, by any definition, can still be classified as poor.	2 Even those who subscribe to an 'absolute' definition of poverty tend to relate 'necessities' to their own society. For example, even Rowntree accepted that the housing that people found reflected not basic shelter but the reality of life at that time.

RELATIVE POVERTY

Supporters of the relative definition argue that one cannot isolate what is considered poverty from the general expectations of people in society and their everyday living standards. Expectations change over time within societies and vary from one society to another. Relative definitions of poverty stress not so much necessities, but **social exclusion** from normal patterns of life in a society, through lack of income.

The measurement of poverty in relative definitions

There are three main ways to measure poverty in this way:

- 'low income family' statistics,
- income,
- disposable income.

Low income family statistics

The first way to measure poverty is to take the government's own level of income support, plus an allowance for housing etc, as a guide. The amount added up to approximately 140% of income support. The reasoning behind this is that income support reflects the minimum level of income the government itself believes it is reasonably possible to live on. This was used by the British governments in the period 1972–88, and the term used in discussions was LIFs. Fig. 13.1 shows the number of people on the poverty margins, as generated from LIF statistics.

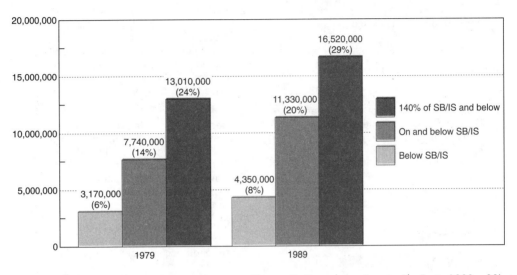

(*Source:* C. Oppenheim, *Poverty: The Facts,* 1993, p33)

Fig. 13.1 Numbers of people living in or on the margin of poverty in 1979 and 1989 (defined as 140% of supplementary benefit and below

Income

A line is drawn at a certain percentage of average income, below which people are said to be poor. The line may be at 50% or 80% of average income. In a society based on inequality of income, poverty will therefore always exist.

There are problems with statistics of poverty based on income because:

❶ They only show a snapshot of poverty at one time and do not show how long people have been living in poverty. Clearly, the longer they have been in poverty the worse is their situation.

❷ All statistics underestimate the extent of poverty. They exclude the homeless and those in residential care. They disregard the additional costs of being poor, such as the fact of buying poor-quality goods which do not last as long as good-quality ones, shopping in small quantities in small shops etc.

❸ They are based on income not expenditure and thus do not reveal much about the reality of living standards.

Spending power or disposable income

This is the measure now used by the European Union. It says that having less than 50% of average spending power is an approximate guide to poverty. This of course means that there is no way that poverty can ever be eliminated.

The advantages and disadvantages of the relative approach to measuring poverty

Table 13.2 *Advantages and disadvantages of the relative definition*

Advantages	Disadvantages
1 It relates the poverty to the expectations of society.	1 Taken to its extreme, this approach means that as long as there is inequality there is poverty.
2 It gives a realistic picture of deprivation within a society.	2 It might be claimed that because a person does not have the 'extras' which most people have come to expect in contemporary Britain, they are poor. As long as they are fed, housed and clothed then they are not truly poor. Poverty is destitution.
3 It broadens the idea of what poverty is, from basic necessities to a range of other needs that people have in a society, and which make life bearable.	3 The relative approach can lead to people ignoring the differences *across* societies, thus the approach seems to say that in a Third World society, as long as a person is not starving they are not poor – because expectations are so much lower in that society.
	4 If income support is used as the measure of poverty, the absurd situation occurs that the higher the level of income support the greater numbers of people there are in 'poverty'.

CONSENSUAL DEFINITIONS OF POVERTY

We have seen that there are a number of problems with the absolute and relative approaches to defining poverty. For absolute poverty, a problem lies in knowing exactly what a 'necessity' is in any particular society. A second problem, associated with the relative approach, is that it is generally based on **levels of income**. Yet a person's standard of living does not always reflect the amount of money coming into a house. For example, one disabled person may be on income support but have a pleasant house, in a decent area of town, with a large garden, supportive relatives and efficient social services, yet another in the same town may have none of these things. In this case, the incomes do not reflect the different **levels of deprivation**.

To overcome these problems, a consensual measure has been suggested. The method was first devised by Townsend in his 1979 study (*Poverty in the UK*), and then refined by Mack and Lansley in 1985 and 1991 (*Poor Britain*). In Mack and Lansley's study, people were asked to rank in order of importance what they considered to be necessities. These were then put together, and as a result a group of necessities was formed which were agreed by a large majority of the people questioned. Using these agreed (hence **consensual**) necessities, they were then able to work out a level of deprivation which the majority of the population felt to be unacceptable.

The measurement of poverty according to the consensual approach

In 1985 and 1991, Mack and Lansley asked over 1,000 people what they thought necessities were, and then from their replies made a list of the most commonly agreed ones (see Table 13.3).

Table 13.3 *An example of a consensual poverty line*

Examples of items included	Examples of items excluded
Basic designs, mass manufactured furniture, textiles and hardware	Antiques, handmade or precious household durables
Prescription charges, dental care, sight test	Spectacles, private health care
Fridge-freezer, washing machine, microwave, food-mixer, sewing machine	Tumble-dryer, shower, electric blankets
Basic clothing, sensible designs	Second-hand, designer and high fashion clothing
TV, video hire, basic music system and camera	Children's TVs, compact discs, camcorders
Second-hand 5-year-old car, second-hand adult bicycle, new children's bikes	A second car, caravan, camping equipment, mountain bikes
Basic jewellery, watch	Precious jewellery
Basic cosmetics, haircuts	Perfume, hair perm
Alcohol – men 14 units, women 10 units (⅔ HEA safety limit)	Smoking
One week annual holiday	Holiday abroad
Walking, swimming, cycling, football, cinema, panto every two years, youth club, scouts/guides	Fishing, water sports, horse-riding, creative or educational adult classes, chidren's ballet/music lessons

(*Source:* C. Oppenheim, *Poverty: The Facts*, 1993, p49)

Items are included in the budget if more than half the population have them or if they are regarded as necessities in public opinion surveys. People who do not have the budget to purchase these items would be considered by most people to be in poverty.

13.2 THE CATEGORIES IN POVERTY

THE EXTENT OF POVERTY

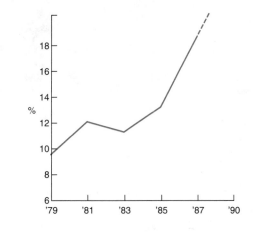

Fig. 13.2 The proportion of individuals with below half average income after housing costs

Fig. 13.2 shows how the proportion of people with below half the average income after housing costs has risen sharply during the 1980s. The numbers of people living in poverty depends upon how poverty is defined. If we take the *absolute* definition then there are very few poor or more accurately *destitute* people in Britain. Taking the measure of 50% of average income, as many as 12 million people can be considered poor. This measure is known officially as Households Below Average Income (HBAI).

Fig. 13.3 shows which family groups compose the poor. For example, 33% of pensioner couples are living in poverty, and 50% of lone parents.

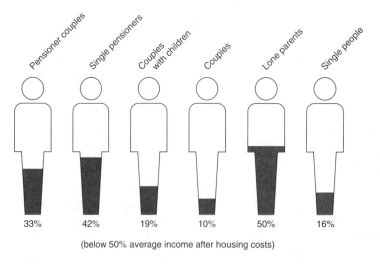

(below 50% average income after housing costs)

(*Source:* C. Oppenheim, *Poverty: The Facts*, 1993, p43)

Fig. 13.3 The proportion of people living in poverty, by family status, 1988–9

Fig. 13.4 shows what proportion of each economic category is living in poverty. For example, 69% of families where the head of the household is unemployed live in poverty, but only 4% of couples where both are in full-time work.

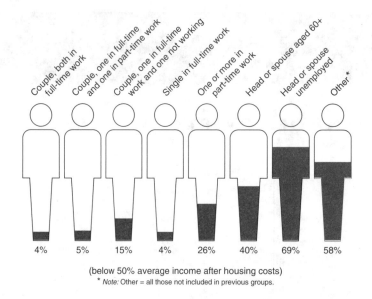

(below 50% average income after housing costs)
* *Note:* Other = all those not included in previous groups.

(*Source:* C. Oppenheim, *Poverty: The Facts*, 1993, p43)

Fig. 13.4 The proportion of people living in poverty, by economic status, 1988–9

The categories of people living in poverty only tell part of the story, however, as certain groups of people are likely to be in all or at least most of these groups; for example, women form the majority of older people, the disabled, single parents, and the low paid. Very often too, as single parents they are unable to work because, although they would like to have employment, their family responsibilities prevent it. In 1990, approximately 5.1 million women were living in poverty compared to 3.4 million men. Similarly, we know that Afro-Caribbeans and certain groups of Asians are more likely than average to be in more than one of these categories, thus they are disproportionately represented among the poor.

Fig. 13.5 shows the changes that have occurred between 1979 and 1988/9 in the way that the poor are categorised.

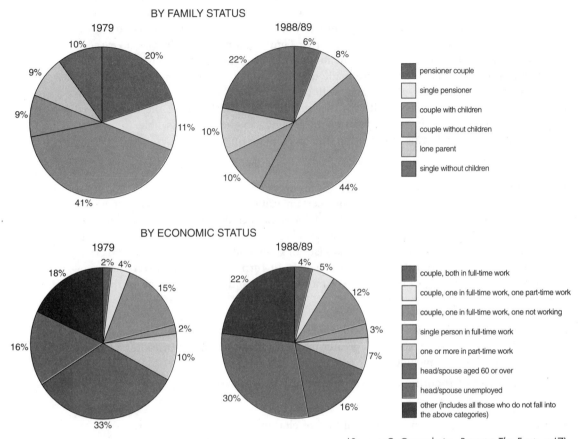

(*Source:* C. Oppenheim, *Poverty: The Facts*, p47)

Fig. 13.5 Changes in the categories of the poor over time

THE UNEMPLOYED

The numbers of people who are out of work change with the economy. However, there have been very significant changes in the British economy over the last 15 years, which seem likely to maintain a permanently high level of unemployment. The main changes include: increasing automation in industry and related increasing productivity so that fewer workers are required, and the general decline of British manufacturing and commerce.

Certain groups in the population, however, are more likely than others to be made unemployed. These include:

1 The least skilled As automated machinery has replaced them. Unemployment levels for unskilled manual workers can be as high as six times that of professional workers.

2 Those living away from the south/south-east of England The south-east of England has a number of advantages for employers, including a skilled workforce, proximity to Europe and a large, affluent population to purchase the goods or products.

3 Ethnic minorities Partly as a result of racism and partly because skill levels are lower overall among Afro-Caribbeans and some of the Asian communities, there are significantly higher levels of unemployment among the ethnic minorities. It is estimated that twice as many blacks and Asians are unemployed as whites.

The effects of unemployment

Official statistics indicate that after three months of unemployment, the average disposable income of a family drops by 59%.

Individuals

If a man becomes unemployed, it is likely that his wife will have to give up work as well, because the benefit system works in such a way that what she earns he loses from income support – by the time travel etc is taken into account the family becomes worse off if the wife continues to work. As a result, the two-earner family becomes a family with no earners.

Unemployment has powerful effects on an individual's mental state too, which can help trap them in poverty. When people are made unemployed, they lose their self-esteem, and of course this affects their ability and will to seek a job. The stress resulting from unemployment affects people's health, so that standards of health among the unemployed are significantly lower than the population in general, so they are less able to take on employment. A cycle begins, preventing the person getting employment and thereby escaping from poverty.

Communities

Unemployment is more likely to occur among certain groups and in certain areas than others. When this occurs, a gradual rundown of an entire area can begin. Without adequate income, people cannot afford to maintain their accommodation, they cannot afford to shop or to purchase good leisure services. The result is a lack of shops and leisure amenities, high crime levels and a general dowdiness of the area, which, in turn, puts off employers and new businesses. So a cycle begins leading to yet more poverty and further decline in the area.

Long-term unemployment

A distinction exists between long- and short-term unemployment, as those who are unemployed for a long time face much greater problems than those out of work for a limited period. These problems include:

1. a **lower level of income**, as a result of the way benefits are worked out;

2. **exhaustion of savings**;

3. a gradual **running down** in the condition of clothing, furniture and general possessions;

4. the **psychological effects** of lack of confidence, stress and depression are more acute for the long-term unemployed.

THE LOW PAID

Low pay is defined as two-thirds of the average male wage. The Low Pay Unit estimates that 45% of British workers are on low pay; this is composed of 78% of part-time workers (4 million people, mainly women) and 29% of full-time, adult workers. 71% of women in all forms of employment are on low pay.

Reasons for the increase in the numbers of the low paid

1. **Legislation** Government legislation since 1981 has weakened workers' employment and union rights, and has even excluded part-time employees from having many effective rights at all. Examples include the fact that a person has to be employed for more than two years to make an appeal against unfair dismissal, and minimum wages for young people have been abolished.

2. **Working conditions and employment pattern** A second important change has been the changing nature of employment in Britain. There has been a growth in part-time workers, so that between 1984 and 1994, the increase in the number of these is estimated to be nearly 20%, while the comparative figure for full-time employees is about 8%. Table 14.4 shows the difference in employer-paid benefits given to male and female full-time employees and how these fall off for female part-time employees.

There has been an increase in temporary employees, so that between the early 1980s and early 1990s the number of temporary employees grew by 12%. Women make up 90% of this temporary workforce.

Table 13.4 *Percentage of jobs where the employer provides benefits, by gender*

	Male full-timers	Female full-timers	Female part-timers
pensions*	73	68	31
sick pay*	66	58	27
paid time off	64	48	30
unpaid time off	54	54	57
company car or van	30	10	5
free/subsidised transport	31	24	17
goods at a discount	47	40	31
free or subsidised meals	39	47	25
finance/loans	21	20	12
accommodation	14	17	5
life assurance	39	19	5
private health	31	22	9
recreation facilities	40	36	24
maternity pay	–	31	16
childcare	1	13	10

* above basic government scheme

(*Source:* C. Oppenheim, *Poverty: The Facts*, 1993, p36)

3 **Unemployment** Levels of unemployment affect the low paid in the sense that employers are able to offer lower wages when unemployment is high.

Low-paid workers in particular are often caught in the **poverty trap**, whereby an increase in earnings means the loss of means-tested benefits. In 1990, over 400,000 people in Britain were caught in this poverty trap.

The low paid with children

Over half of all those living in poverty comprise the low paid and their children. The income earned from employment is inadequate to pay for the extra costs of having children.

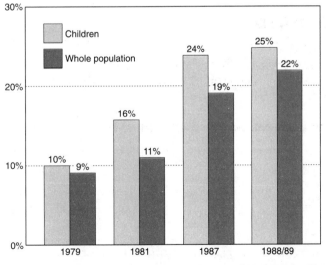

(*Source:* C. Oppenheim, *Poverty: The Facts*, 1993, p44)

Fig. 13.6 Proportion of children and population living in poverty, (living below 50% average income after housing costs), 1979–1988/89

SINGLE-PARENT FAMILIES

One of the more common causes of poverty derives from the high costs of having children and the low income that can be earned because of limited earning opportunities. If we look at the lowest earning quarter of the population, those without children earned significantly higher amounts of money than those with children. An example might make this clear: in 1990, a couple in the lowest earning group without children earned £50 per week more than those with two children.

Single parents with one child earned only half the average income of single people in the lowest quarter of earners. Single parents are likely to be the poorest of the poor; indeed 6 out of 10 single parents are in poverty.

Reasons for the increase in the number of single-parent families

There has been a rapid increase in the number of single-parent families since the 1970s. Today, more than 1 in 7 families in Britain is headed by a single parent. This is caused mainly by the growth in the divorce rate and, to a much lesser extent, the increase in single-parenthood.

SICK AND DISABLED

According to government statistics, there are 6.2 million adults, comprising 14% of all adults, and 360,000 children, comprising 3% of all children, who suffer from one or more serious disability. There have been significant increases in the number of people with disabilities, as a result of:

- people living longer and therefore being more prone to disabilities in old age;
- improvements in medicine leading to higher rates of survival of younger people and infants with disabilities.

Incomes

For people under pensionable age, the average income for an adult with a disability was 72% of that of non-disabled people. Of these people with disabilities, 34% are living in poverty. Those with disabilities are unable to work, or are limited to particular kinds of employment, usually that which is low paid.

Outgoings

A person with a disability not only has problems obtaining employment but has greater outgoings than fully able people. Approximately 8% of disabled people's incomes were going on expenses related to their disability.

OLDER PEOPLE

Approximately 18% of the population are over retirement age, numbering approximately 11 million people. Women form over 65% of older people. With the gradual raising of life expectancy, the numbers of older people in the population are likely to continue increasing until the end of the first decade of the 21st century.

Poverty in old age is not something that happens to all pensioners – rather the poverty reflects the divisions in employment, income and fringe benefits that exist throughout a person's employment. Those who are poor in old age, are most likely to be people who have earned least in their lifetime.

Incomes

Older people are generally dependent upon pensions for their income, and the State pension is pitched so low that living in receipt of this means that older people will be in poverty. The State pension in 1990 was about 16.5% of the average male weekly earnings; this means that elderly people are forced to live off savings or apply for State assistance if they do not have an employment-based pension.

RACE AND POVERTY

Racism and discrimination in society as a whole have often excluded black people from employment opportunities and access to welfare. Afro-Caribbeans and Asians have substantially higher rates of unemployment – almost twice that of whites. This holds true even if the black or Asian person has the same educational qualifications as a white person. They are also more likely to earn lower wages than whites, and to be employed in the lower paying sectors of the economy (although Afro-Caribbean women earn more than white women).

There is evidence of discriminatory practice in the provision of welfare benefits. For example, it is becoming normal practice to request passports from black and Asian claimants. Social Security policy has been directly and indirectly discriminatory, often leaving black people without support from the State.

Family patterns and the age structure of ethnic minority groups means that some groups are more likely to be vulnerable to poverty. For example, there is a higher proportion of single-parent families among people of Afro-Caribbean origin than among whites or Asians.

WOMEN AND POVERTY

The majority of the poor in Britain are women. In fact there are approximately 4.5 million women in poverty today. Each one of the categories of people in poverty discussed in this section of the chapter is dominated by women, except perhaps the unemployed (and there is a fierce debate about that too). For example, 71% of the low paid are women, as are over 90% of single parents.

Why women form the majority of the poor

The following reasons have been suggested:

1. Women are more likely to be in low-paid jobs because they are restricted by family responsibilities (whether married/cohabiting or single) from pursuing a career. It is generally regarded as the woman's role to take primary responsibility for care of the family.

2. Child-bearing disrupts the continuity of employment, which is necessary to gain promotion.

3. The disruption of a woman's working life caused by child-bearing and family responsibility also prevents her from building up enough contributions for non-means-tested benefits. This means that when she needs State assistance she almost always has to turn to income support. In 1990, 96% of single parents on income support were women, and over three times as many women over pensionable age were receiving income support compared to men.

4. Women are expected to care not only for their children but also for older people and for disabled partners/relatives. There are almost 4 million women carers in Britain today, of whom about half spend more than 50 hours a week in unpaid caring.

5. Within the two-parent family, it is usually the woman who goes without if there is any shortage. So although the family may not be poor the woman often is.

13.3 THE CAUSES OF POVERTY

There are two different types of explanation for the causes of poverty:

- the first type stresses the **process of dependency**;
- the second type tends to stress the **process of exclusion**.

DEPENDENCY EXPLANATIONS

Explanations that centre on the concept of dependency basically stress that people who are poor are in that state because of some deficiency that is in themselves or that is passed on in their social group. They have become dependent on the State, and have no desire to work or to cope with the problems of budgeting, which the bulk of people have to do. There are considerable similarities to the views on poverty in the 19th century.

Within this overall approach to explaining the causes of poverty, we can distinguish:

- the individual,
- the underclass and
- the culture of poverty.

The individual

Here the stress is placed on the failure of the individual to achieve through his/her own efforts. People who are poor are lazy and should try harder.

The underclass

This is a development of the individual explanation, but is more sociological in orientation. The argument, which was first developed by an American writer, Charles Murray, is that an **underclass** exists of people who are lazy and make no effort to work or look after themselves. These people prefer to live off the State rather than having to work.

It is important to remember that the underclass refers only to those poor people who make no effort to help themselves. Murray accepts that there are poor people who are in this state through no fault of their own. Nevertheless, the bulk of poverty is caused by those who do not make the effort to earn a living, and/or squander what they do have.

The culture of poverty

This approach stresses that the way people act is the result of how they are brought up by their family. It differs from the underclass explanation because it does not see poverty as a fault of the person, rather that individuals are brought up in such a way that they never have a chance to escape the poverty of their parents.

Cultures develop to give people a guide to how they should behave. In different societies people do not behave in the same way because they learn different cultures. Usually a particular culture develops because it enables people to cope with their surroundings. Cultures are always changing but the main outlines are passed on from one generation to another mainly by parents and those who influence people when they are young.

The **culture of poverty** argument was first developed by Oscar Lewis when he studied very poor people in Central America. The values and behaviour (the culture) of these poor people was significantly different from the majority of the population. Lewis argued that this was because these particular values enabled the very poor to cope with circumstances which would otherwise lead to despair and hopelessness.

The cycle of poverty

A development from the culture of poverty argument is the claim that a **cycle of poverty** or a **cycle of transmitted deprivation** exists. This idea was developed by a former Secretary of State for Health and Social Services, Sir Keith Joseph. His view of transmission, however, ignored the way in which the culture of poverty was supposedly a response to intense poverty and a certainty that the person had no future. Instead, this concentrated on the way in which some poor people failed to help and support their children.

EXCLUSION EXPLANATIONS

The second set of explanations for poverty is based on the idea of **exclusion** – meaning that the poor are in that situation because they are squeezed out of achieving a decent standard of living by the actions of others. Another term for this process is **marginalisation**.

In essence, this approach is stressing differences in power between the various groups in society. Those who lose out – the disabled, older people, women, the ethnic minorities and, of course, children – have significantly higher chances of living in poverty. Within this approach we can distinguish two strands:

● the dyswelfare view and

● the economic system approach.

The dyswelfare view

Dyswelfare refers to the process in which some people lose out in complex industrial societies through no fault of their own. They are the casualties of industrial and social change. The 'victims' of dyswelfare include the physically and mentally disabled, single parents etc. The points to emphasise here are that their poverty is blameless and is the result of the changes in the nature of society. Secondly, society does not deliberately discriminate against any group (compare this view with the following *power* approach), but it is seen as inevitable that some people will lose out in any form of society.

It was this explanation for poverty that largely underlay the foundation of the Welfare State.

The economic system approach

The final, and most radical, explanation for the continuation of poverty comes from those who argue that society is a competition between various groups. Some groups have considerably more power than others and are able to impose their will on the rest of society. Power and wealth generally go together, as do poverty and powerlessness. The groups in poverty are largely formed from the powerless, in particular women, children and the ethnic minorities. Low pay and poor State benefits are the result of the fact that to pay more would be harmful to the interests of those who are more affluent.

This approach contrasts with the dyswelfare explanation, because it says that poverty is the direct and intended outcome of modern Western society.

The poverty trap

The poverty trap occurs wherein a person (or family) receives a number of means-tested benefits from the State when they are unable to obtain work. If the person then finds employment, it is possible that the gains in income from that employment may well be lost, because the Department of Social Security withdraws some or all of the means-tested benefits.

13.4 A SUMMARY OF THEORETICAL APPROACHES TO WELFARE

Table 13.5 *Approaches to social policy*

Issues	Perspective				
	New Right	Social Democratic	Radical Socialist	Feminist	Anti-Racist
ECONOMICS	A free market unfettered by government interference. People should have very low taxes, and decided what to do with their money.	A free market, but with government control to even out the extremes of wealth and poverty. Relatively high levels of taxation.	State to own all business and commerce. Salaries and conditions related to government decisions.	A radical approach to what is considered work, therefore housework is of equal status to employment. Work should be made more flexible to respond to demands on women (such as family).	Employment practices should be radically examined. Positive action programme should be introduced to give Blacks and Asians preference in employment to compensate for past discrimination.
INEQUALITY between people	Good, necessary and a spur to make people work harder. People should be rewarded for their hard work and should not pay high rates of tax.	Acceptable and inevitable, but *extremes* cannot be allowed. So a Welfare State would provide for the less well-off and this will be paid for by heavy taxes on the rich.	Inequality is wrong and needs to be eliminated by State action. There should be, as far as possible, a classless society. No wealth and no poverty.	Inequality is wrong, women have always been discriminated against, and economic/social policies need to be introduced specifically to benefit women.	Inequality is wrong. Blacks and Asians have always been discriminated against and economic/social policies need to be introduced specifically to benefit ethnic groups.
WELFARE STATE	Bad, creates a **dependency culture**, where people rely on the government for help, instead of self-help or family. Welfare is enormously expensive, wasteful bureaucracy.	Good. Welfare State helps pull people together by providing sense of shared citizenship. Compensates those who 'lose out' in a market economy.	Majority and minority views which differ. *Majority* – Welfare State is good and should be improved. The result of working class pressure. *Minority* – bad, introduced to stop the people demanding a radical overhaul of the capitalist system.	Concept is good, but is based on exploitation of women, both as low paid carers/professionals and as unpaid carers in the home. Needs to be restructured taking into account the specific needs of women.	Concept good, but institutional racism exists. Needs to be more aware of, and responsible to, needs of Blacks and Asians.
HEALTH CARE	Should be private, insurance-based for the majority of people. For those with limited incomes there would be assistance with fees or a residual State health care sector.	National Health Service free and fully funded by the government.	National Health Service, but also a belief that much illness is a result of capitalism and therefore eliminating capitalism would reduce ill health.	Provided (cheaply) by women, both formally and informally. Women suffer worse health than men but some areas of women's lives have been 'medicalised', e.g. drugs for depression, childbirth.	Greater awareness of ethnic groups' needs by the NHS. Large numbers of poor paid Black workers in the NHS labour force.
SOCIAL SECURITY	Bad, undermining individual effort, creates dependency on the State. Has a distorting effect on wages, by forcing employers to pay higher rates – can lead to higher unemployment. If it has to be paid, then strict means-testing and targeting.	Important for social stability. Payments should be at a high level and be as widespread as possible. Certain benefits ought to be universal.	Payments are inadequate and, in the short-term, need increasing. In the long term, social security prevents radical social change by 'muting' opposition to capitalism.	Concern over a number of benefits and how they affect the lives of women, e.g. Income Support is inadequate for lone-parent families of which 9 out of 10 are headed by women. Also, pensions system discriminates against women.	Accusations made of racism in social security offices, e.g. Asians asked to show passports, etc.
PERSONAL SOCIAL SECURITY	In majority of cases self-help/family help is preferable. Should be left to agencies or, as in the provision of elderly persons' homes, to the private sector.	Predominantly by the State, but also a mixture of charity and voluntary encouraged. The private sector should be discouraged.	Many problems caused by capitalism – should this be replaced, then many problems would disappear. However, the only agency that should be allowed to provide personal social services is the State.	They rely totally on women as unpaid carers. Ninety per cent of people being cared for are outside the State sector, and 70% of these people are cared for by women. Greater State intervention is needed.	Services do not respond to specific needs of Blacks and Asians, where they differ from Whites, e.g. in elderly persons' homes. Personal social services need to recognise Britain as a multi-racial society.
POVERTY	Inevitable in any society – but the free market can generate enough wealth to minimise this. The Welfare State only increases poverty. Rejects idea of relative poverty.	A consequence of capitalism that can be eliminated through effective tax and social security systems.	Caused by capitalism. The only real way of combating it is through a radical, socialist, alternative structure.	Majority of people in poverty are women. Economic and welfare systems conspire to keep them there. Need to recognise this and alter the system to give women the chance to escape from poverty.	On every indicator of deprivation, Blacks and Asians score highly. This is the outcome of a racist society. Need to tackle racism through positive action policies.
LAW AND ORDER	Heavier sentences, larger police force and the development of protective schemes such as Neighbourhood Watch. Custodial (prison) sentences.	Good policing, but also an awareness of social causes of crime (deprivation, unemployment). Alternatives to prison.	Crime an outcome of greed and inequality of capitalism. Law enforced against ordinary people, not the rich.	Women are treated differently by police and the judiciary. Often they are likely to be treated as mentally disturbed as their behaviour is at odds with the female stereotype.	Racism by police and the judiciary lead to the harassment and imprisoning of young Blacks. At the same time, high levels of deprivation force Blacks towards crime.

(*Source: Social Welfare Alive!*, Stanley Thornes, 1993)

13.5 REDISTRIBUTIVE EFFECTS OF TAXATION AND THE WELFARE STATE

The Welfare State, it is claimed, is meant to redistribute benefits from the affluent to the poorer sections of society. Critics of the Welfare State have disputed this, and Tudor Hart coined the term **the inverse care law**, meaning that the Welfare State actually benefitted the affluent at the expense of the poor. This is because the middle classes make better use of the health and welfare services, it is claimed. However, there does seem to be statistical evidence from the Family Expenditure Surveys that there is some degree of redistribution caused by the effects of taxation and welfare provision as Table 13.6 shows.

Table 13.6 *Redistribution of income through taxes and benefits, 1994–5*

United Kingdom						£ per year
	Quintile groups of households					
	Bottom fifth	Next fifth	Middle fifth	Next fifth	Top fifth	All Households
Total original income	2,040	5,600	13,380	22,250	40,330	16,720
+Benefits in cash						
Contributory	1,930	2,290	1,620	1,050	680	1,510
Non-contributory	2,730	2,180	1,540	900	490	1,570
Gross income	6,700	10,080	16,540	24,200	41,510	19,800
Post-tax income	4,120	6,700	10,520	15,190	26,570	12,620
+Benefits in kind						
Education	1,600	1,250	1,390	1,200	670	1,220
National Health Service	1,790	1,720	1,660	1,460	1,270	1,580
Housing subsidy	80	80	40	20	10	50
Travel subsidies	50	60	60	90	130	80
School meals and welfare milk	80	20	10	10	–	30
Final income	7,720	9,840	13,690	17,970	28,640	15,670

(*Source: Social Trends 27*, Table 5.16 (Office for National Statistics), p 97)

However, after taxes and welfare benefits have been taken into consideration, the top 20% of the population still retains more than twice the income of the average earners and four times that of the poorest 20%.

THE WELFARE STATE AND REDISTRIBUTION

The welfare state seems then to have only marginally redistributed wealth. Explanations for this are:

- The New Right,
- Marxist,
- Social Democrat and
- Feminist and Anti-Racist Approaches

The New Right

The analysis put forward by the New Right is that Britain since 1945 has been faced by a situation of:

- deindustrialisation – a decline in the industrial base,
- disincentives – a lack of rewards for hard work,
- demoralisation – the growth of the dependency culture.

According to writers such as Joseph (*Monetarism is not Enough*) one of the main causes of the situation of decline was the high cost of public services which imposed too heavy a burden on commerce. This led to a lack of resources in the private sector, too few jobs. By cutting back on the welfare state, the economy could be liberated and more people could be lifted out of poverty. However, there would probably fewer, but considerably poorer people. By providing them with means-tested benefits, the deserving could be helped.

Marxist

Marxist critiques of the ineffectiveness of the welfare state, are of two kinds.

1. the welfare state is a type of smoke screen,

2. the welfare state is the unfinished product of the class struggle.

Smoke screen

This approach, associated with Saville, argues that the welfare state was put into place by the ruling class as a means of preventing revolutionary change. The welfare state allows a small degree of redistribution, but generally leaves ownership and wealth in private hands. The result is that capitalism remains intact at the price of the welfare state.

The class struggle

This explanation is that the welfare state has emerged as a price paid by the ruling class for social harmony. It is a genuine gain by the working class, although it is only part of the way along the road which will lead to a socialist society, where a welfare state will not be necessary.

Social Democrats

These approaches share the view that the welfare state has moved towards redistribution, but that the wider society is best seen as a form of non-violent 'battleground' over resources – this view is largely derived from Weber.

In many ways this approach seems similar to the class struggle model, except that there is no belief that the 'struggle' will lead to (or is intended to lead to) a socialist society.

The nature of the power struggle in advanced democracies is between the economic and the political spheres. For example, Korpi argues that the welfare state reflects the triumph of political power (of working class groups) over economic power.

In essence the more successful the activities of the organised working class, the more entrenched the welfare state, and the more marginalised the 'principle of allocation through the market'.

However, it is claimed by social democrats that the middle classes are powerful enough in the political sphere to ensure that they force the system to give them significant benefits – even if they are at the expense of poorer sections of society. An example of this is housing, with social housing owned by local government or housing associations being forced to put rents at such a level that there is no subsidy, while those who purchase their own homes can receive a subsidy of up to 20% in tax relief.

Le Grand's work in the 1970s has suggested that the middle class also benefit more from services such as education and health services.

Feminist and Anti-Racist Approaches

These approaches state that significant groups in the population are systematically excluded from full citizenship by being denied access to benefits, health and education. The welfare state has not benefited them, and was not designed to do so. Supporters of this approach, such as Williams, point to the high rates of poverty amongst members of the ethnic minorities and amongst women, and to the way that some state benefits work to their disadvantage.

13.6 TARGETING VERSUS UNIVERSALISM

TARGETING AND MEANS TESTING

In recent years there has been considerable debate between those who argue that state benefits should be *targeted* against those who argue for *universal* provision.

Targeting describes a system of welfare provision that delivers state benefits to those identified as most in need. An example of targeting in practice is the *exclusion* of people under 18 from receipt of income support. Underlying this, is the belief that the parents should support them, and they ought to be on a work experience programme.

Targeting is closely linked to *means testing*, whereby individuals are not eligible for certain benefits because they fall into a certain *category*. Means testing is a system of awarding benefits on the basis of comparing the actual income that a person (or family) has against what the state thinks they need in order to have an adequate standard of living. The person then has to prove their income is lower than the official level. This system is the way in which most social security benefits are provided.

Advantages of means testing and targeting

- It targets help to the most needy.
- It does not give money or services to those who could afford to pay and who are currently being subsidised by the rest of the population. Some of these people may actually be worse off than the those they are subsidising.
- Targeting groups should cost less to the State as fewer people should receive benefits.
- The savings could go to providing better services for the recipients, or could be used by the government to lower taxes.

Disadvantages of means testing and targeting

- Means testing is complex and creates a large bureaucracy to administer it, so 'savings' would not return to the government but would be used up in higher administration charges.
- Targeting is complex, which means that quite often mistakes are made.
- People are often confused as to what they are entitled to claim, as the system is often complex.
- People often fail to take up the benefits because they feel embarrassed to ask, (they feel 'stigmatised').
- As income rises, so state benefits decline, this can lead to *the poverty trap*, (mentioned earlier) where people may actually lose more in state benefit than they gain from the increase in income they receive when they get a job.

UNIVERSALISM

The alternative to targeting is to give benefits to everybody who falls into a particular category. For example, every family having a child receives child benefit, even though many may not need it.

When everyone in a particular category receives benefits, then it is known as universalism. Supporters of universalism claim they are defending the welfare state, though few benefits available since the beginning of the welfare state have been truly universal – child benefits and health services are two examples. The of majority of state benefits are actually means tested.

Advantages of universalism

- It eradicates the poverty trap – (because there is no decrease in benefits as income rises through employment).

- It ensures that everyone who is in need obtains the benefits, and no one is omitted through their ignorance of benefits available or through fear of stigma.

- It is cheap to administer because there is no expensive bureaucracy working out entitlement through means testing.

Disadvantages of universalism

Critics point out that it is highly expensive because so many people unnecessarily receive benefits. Money is wasted, which could go to other more needy groups. They also argue that giving people benefits which are not really needed, encourages them to rely upon the state rather than on their own resources – this is known as *welfare dependency*.

13.7 WELFARE DEPENDENCY DEBATE

Associated with the New Right (see Table 13.5). The argument is that over the last fifty years the ease with which people could obtain benefits from the state has taken away:

- the will to look after themselves,
- the sense of obligation of a family to look after its members,
- the decline of the sense of community.

Furthermore, the fact that most state services are free means that people make use of them when they are not really in need. For example, people with trivial complaints call out GPs, thereby wasting the money of the NHS.

The argument can be seen as an update and revision of the *culture of poverty* argument (see p 274). It is also linked with a revised (and New Right) version of the underclass thesis (see p 274). The argument put forward by C. Murray (*Underclass*) is that there are two types of poor:

- those who are on low incomes,
- those with a 'dependency' mentality.

It is the second group which constitute the underclass. Murray characterises them in the following way: people who have 'unkempt' homes; men unable to keep employment; drunkenness (or drug use) is common; the children grow up 'ill schooled and ill-behaved'; high levels of delinquency. According to Murray the indicators of the growth of the underclass include:

- the increase in illegitimacy,

- the growth of violent crime and
- large numbers of low income males choosing not to take jobs – which leads to a collapse in the community and to the high levels of crime.

Critics of the underclass thesis

Dahrendorf argues that it is true an underclass exists, but is the result of being *excluded* rather than any deliberate movement of people out of the social structure. Field develops this criticism further and argues that the 1980s in the UK saw the tradition of shared citizenship destroyed, with a deliberate creation of the gap between the affluent and the rest of the population, while at the same time cutting back on welfare.

MacNicol has argued that the underclass thesis is simply another manifestation of a theme that re-emerges periodically about those who scrounge from the rest of us. The effect is to support those who wish to limit the activities of the welfare state.

Test yourself questions and answers

Questions

1 What three definitions of poverty are there?

2 How do you measure a consensual definition of poverty?

3 Why has there been a growth in poverty among low-paid workers?

4 Is poverty inevitable in old age?

5 There are two groups of explanation for poverty. What are they? Give an example of each of them.

6 Why do women form the majority of the poor?

Suggested answers

1 Absolute, relative and consensual.

2 Mack and Lansley asked people to rank a list of items according to how much they considered them to be necessities. As a result, a group of 'necessities' was found which was agreed by a large majority of the people questioned. Using these, Mack and Lansley were then able to work out a level of deprivation which the majority of the population felt was unacceptable.

3 Government legislation since 1981 has weakened workers' employment and union rights, and has even excluded part-time employees from having many effective rights at all. A second factor has been the changing nature of employment in Britain: a growth in part-time workers and an increase in temporary employees. Unemployment affects the low paid in the sense that employers are able to offer lower wages when unemployment is high.

4 It is only inevitable because pensions are so low in the UK. It is also true that inflation eliminates savings.

5   Dependency theories include: individual explanations, the concept of the underclass, and the culture of poverty. The second group of theories are exclusion explanations which include the concepts of dyswelfare and the nature of the economic system.

6   Women take primary responsibility for care of the family and are therefore less likely to be able to work full-time. The disruption of a woman's working life caused by child-bearing and family responsibility also prevents her from building up enough contributions for non-means-tested benefits. Women also care for older people and for disabled partners/relatives. There are almost 4 million women 'carers' in Britain today. Within the two-parent family, it is usually the woman who goes without if there is any shortage. So, although the family may not be poor, the woman often is.

Illustrative question and answer

Question

The claim that 'the poor have themselves to blame for their poverty' is a feature of some explanations of poverty. Critically examine the sociological arguments for and against this statement.

AEB

Suggested answer

This essay wants you first of all to look at explanations which are based on individual failure – what defects do people have that lead them to be poor? – and secondly to discuss the culture of poverty and the linked concept of the cycle of poverty; and thirdly to discuss the nature of the emerging underclass.

You should work your way through the three elements of the essay, making sure that you criticise as you progress. The words 'critically examine' are crucial here. Blaming individuals as such is not sociological and fails to explain why so many people should be poor in society.

The culture of poverty approach needs to have a considerable amount of attention and you should point out that it developed not in the UK but in marginalised groups in Mexico, and that the originator, Lewis, specifically excluded societies like the UK from having the concept applied. You should point out that no study has found a clearly articulated culture of poverty in the UK.

You should discuss how the cycle of poverty does not explain the cause of poverty, but is a response to it, and how the concept of the underclass which was put forward by Murray seeks to place the blame on the people who have been made the scapegoats for the dismantling of welfare.

You should then move on to compare these approaches with ones pointing out how certain groups are more likely to enter poverty through low pay, temporary employment, part-time work etc, and relate this to the wider economy. It is a good idea to conclude by saying that poverty is related to power differences. Do not forget to point out the high proportion of the elderly and of women in poverty.

Question bank

1   Assess the argument that different definitions and explanations of poverty reflect different ideologies.

AEB

Points

The question requires you to discuss definitions of poverty. Definitions of the poverty line have been provided on three grounds: absolute, relative and consensual. You need to work your way through these noting the strengths and weaknesses of all three. Note that the relative ones based on income and spending power are actually used by states. In sociological research too these have been most useful. You should also point out the use made by Townsend and later Mack and Lansley of the consensual approach – how it is most useful, but also very difficult to employ in cross-country or cross-ethnic groups' analysis because of the cultural component.

It is true that it is not possible to provide a poverty line supported by all, because of political differences between people. Those from the right prefer a type of absolute definition, and those from the left prefer a form of relative or consensual definition. They do so because relative definitions suggest that the true basis of poverty is inequality and until this is eliminated or at least limited, then poverty will continue. The right argue that this is absurd and confuses two very different issues – according to them you can have significant inequality but very limited poverty. They point to the fact that virtually everybody in the UK has higher standards of living than in the early 1950s and then relatively few are 'destitute' or malnourished. For them this is the basic issue.

2 Explain the causes and consequences of the adoption of community care policies in the last ten years.

Integrated Boards

Points

Causes: *Ideological* – the right wish to push back responsibility for care on to the family, e.g. Normal Dennis. They also wanted to undermine the local authorities' provision of care and give it to private agencies. At the other extreme large numbers of radical commentators critical of the nature of institutions and how they treat people ('inmates') badly. *Financial* – spiralling costs of the institutions, particularly residential homes for older people, which were paid for by the DSS at the time of the introduction of the Community Care Act Demographic. The ageing of the population meant that the future perceived 'burden of dependency' would be too great. There had to be an alternative to building more institutions.

Consequences: *Positive ones* included: greater freedom of choice, a raising of standards in residential homes and nursing homes, more support for those who chose to stay at home. Closing down of the majority of Victorian mental institutions. *Negative ones* included: very significant lack of funds, elderly people stuck in hospitals because no funds to move to residential and nursing institutions, mentally ill people released into 'the community', lack of support and medication. Did not recreate family support.

3 Evaluate the view that social policy has tended to promote a culture of dependency rather than a culture of enterprise.

Integrated Boards

Points

Explain the meaning of the culture of dependency and the culture of enterprise (people looking after themselves). Go on to explore the right-wing argument that the policy of having a welfare state undermines the family and community and individual responsibility by providing everything that people need. Link this to the functionalist debate on the loss of functions of the family. You should demonstrate an awareness of writers such as Dennis and Murray who argue that the welfare state has contributed to the growth of an underclass which is dependent on the welfare system as they are not 'forced' to work . The support for single parents, in particular, never-married women with children is a particularly significant factor in the development of the culture of dependency. They also point to the undermining of charity and the idea of voluntarily helping people, and also that the welfare state imposes a high burden of taxation on the wealth creators.

4 'Some have argued that the major reasons for the continuation of poverty are the behaviour and attitudes of the poor.' Critically discuss the sociological arguments and evidence in support of this view.

AEB

Points

You need to cover discussions on the causes of poverty including a full exploration of both the culture of poverty and the debate on the underclass.

In effect the two extremes of explanations are ones which locate the causes of poverty within the poor, i.e. they have some defects which the rest of the population do not have, or at the other extreme the poor are in that state because of the structure of society.

Provide a very brief outline of the extent of poverty. Continue by looking at the culture of poverty first developed by Lewis and then move on to examine Murray's argument for the existence of the underclass. Criticise this by pointing out that Taylor-Gooby's research found no evidence of the people regarded as the underclass having any different values from the rest of society. Move on to discuss wider structural factors which might cause poverty.

CHAPTER 14

DEVELOPMENT, URBANISATION AND COMMUNITY

Units in this chapter

Chapter objectives

We explore the nature of the relationship between the advanced industrialised nations and the poorer ones of the Third World. We begin with a discussion of exactly how one makes a distinction between a poorer and a richer nation.

Then we consider the explanations which have been put forward to explain the state of the differing advanced and Third World countries today. The issues centre on the routes to development that the richer nations took, and the appropriateness of these routes for the poorer nations. There are numerous theories, but one great division. This is between those writers who see the developing nations as not developed because they lack something (either economic or cultural) and those who believe that the poorer nations of the world are actually made poorer by the activities of the richer nations. The structure provided by this debate allows us to examine and compare the strengths and weaknesses of the widely differing theoretical discussions.

The next area we look at concerns life in the Third World. We understand this by examining the changing population trends in the poorer countries and the related move to living in cities, with the consequences that these bring for the economies and cultures of the poorer nations.

Then we look at how the process of urbanisation in the UK has reversed in the latter part of this century, with people moving away from the cities and back to the countryside. This is followed by a discussion on different types of community.

Finally, we look at the relationship between health and underdevelopment.

14.1 DEFINITIONS

Various attempts have been made to categorise different societies by their economic levels of development. Three types of terminology have been used:

- economic development,
- economic and political,
- economic and geographical.

1 **Economic development**: the developed and underdeveloped world; or the developed and developing worlds.

2 **Economic and political**: First World – the wealthy capitalist democracies; Second World – the less affluent ex-communist nations and totalitarian states; Third World – the underdeveloped nations, generally not democracies.

    The use of different terminology is important, as the different words suggest different relationships between the various 'worlds'. The term **developing** implies a positive movement forward by poorer States, while the term **underdeveloped** suggests that they are static. The terms the First and Third Worlds imply, to some, a relationship of superiority and inferiority. It was for this reason that the Brandt Report used the terms North and South, which gave a more neutral geographical slant to the definition.

3 **Economic and geographical**: the North – consisting of the relatively wealthy countries of the world, which are generally in the Northern Hemisphere. The South – consisting of the relatively poor countries of the world (China, India, Brazil, etc) and the very poor countries, such as Bangladesh. This division is an economic one, based on the extent to which societies have industrialised or have retained a traditional agrarian economy.

14.2 UNDERSTANDING DEVELOPMENT

Sociologists are particularly interested in understanding the 'routes' that different societies have taken in their development, and what paths are open to the poorer nations in the future. There are a number of conflicting explanations:

- modernisation,
- convergence,
- structural underdevelopment theory,
- Marxist structural theory.

These are explored in detail in the following pages. They offer radically different explanations for the past of both rich and poor nations, and for the future of the poorer nations.

MODERNISATION THEORIES

Modernisation theories are based on the following assumptions:

1 the technologically advanced Western democracies represent the most advanced forms of society in technological, social and political terms;

2 there is a **pathway**, or series of stages, through which countries pass on their route to development into advanced societies;

③ the development path to advanced technological and democratic societies represents a 'natural' form of development, and the underdeveloped nations have some kind of blockage which prevents them from moving along the path;

④ underdeveloped nations can advance without any significant changes taking place in world trading patterns.

Modernisation theories are generally regarded as politically conservative because they see the underdeveloped nations as such because they lack some quality. This compares with more radical analyses which argue that the underdevelopment of Third World nations is linked to their economic exploitation by the advanced nations.

Types of modernisation theory

Modernisation theorists disagree on the nature of the 'blockage'; basically there are two schools of thought:

① **Economic explanations** These stress the economic problems that an 'underdeveloped' country has to face. The idea here is that underdeveloped nations have failed to move forward towards full industrialisation because they lack the favourable economic conditions which will allow them to develop.

② **Value-based explanations** These emphasise the ways in which the traditional values and attitudes of the local population prevent development.

These two schools of thought are fully addressed in the following two sections.

Economic explanations

The best known approach is that of Rostow (*The Stages of Economic Growth*), writing in the 1960s, who argues that all societies develop through five economic stages. It is best to imagine them rather like a plane taking off from the runway.

The stages of development

① **Traditional societies** Agricultural societies with low levels of science (**pre-Newtonian**), ascriptive social structure based on kinship networks. Poor communications.

② **Pre-conditions for take-off** Trading patterns improve and a considerable surplus develops, often based on extractive industries and the beginnings of services. Communications improve. An elite group emerges with enough wealth (and the desire) to invest. Rational ideas and science develop. Rostow points out that Britain was the first nation to reach this stage in the late 17th century.

③ **Take-off** Investment rises to 10% of national income, which usually ensures that per capita income growth outstrips population growth (therefore people become wealthier). Specific manufacturing industries develop and dominate the economy. Political structures develop which allow growth (this seems to imply a move towards democracy). This period lasts 20 years, eg 1783–1803 for Britain, 1843–60 for the USA.

④ **Drive to maturity** At this stage societies have already developed. This stage includes further advances in science and technology, and the widening of the economic bases (not just one or two areas of manufacturing or services, such as tourism). Political reform continues. A meritocratic attitude dominates. Investment is 10–20% of national income. International trading becomes extremely important. This period lasts about 40 years.

⑤ **Age of high mass consumption** This is the period of most affluence, where individuals live in a consumer society and where the surplus produces enough wealth to allow choices to be made as to how to use this wealth.

Rostow suggests three models, then existing:

- Western Europe, where wealth is used for a Welfare State;
- the USA, where wealth is used for individual consumption;
- the USSR, where power was used to build up 'global power and influence'. Since then, of course, the USSR has collapsed and been partially replaced by Russia and its satellite States.

Criticisms of Rostow

Rostow ignores the fact that developing countries are not starting on a fresh path as the original industrialising nations such as Britain did: there are already existing developed nations. The implication of this is that any attempt by developing nations towards industrial production would pose a threat to the developed nations, as they would be in competition with them. Developed countries will therefore not be enthusiastic to help them move away from their traditional position as suppliers of raw materials.

A second major problem, pointed out by Frank (*Capitalism and Under-development in Latin America*), is the way in which values, cultures, beliefs etc are all swept aside, regarded as being of no importance and merely a reflection of economic changes. This form of economic determinism ignores the fact that people, not societies, make decisions. The history of Britain, the values of the people and the circumstances in which industrialisation took place were very different from African societies today, for example.

Policy implications of Rostow's approach

This approach was heavily favoured in the 1960s until the Brandt Report (an extremely influential report written by a number of senior Western statesmen) showed it to be heavily flawed. However, its influence lingers on, in that organisations such as the International Monetary Fund and the World Bank still lend money to national governments in order for them to instigate manufacturing or structural (eg roads or hydro-electricity) schemes. The aim is to create the conditions for 'take-off'. Furthermore, multi-national companies are encouraged to invest in underdeveloped nations in order to create a manufacturing sector, in the expectation that the spin-offs – in terms of wealth created by employment and the import of technological methods and knowledge – will encourage the further development of industry.

The key to industrialisation, then, is investment from outside to stimulate the conditions for take-off.

Liberal economists and the new right

Old ideas of *laissez-faire* and free market economics have reasserted themselves in the debate on development just as they have in welfare policies. The basic argument is that if the world economic order is left alone without interference from States or from trading blocs, then every nation can concentrate on doing what it does best or most cheaply. If there is high unemployment in a particular country, for example, then multi-national companies will be drawn there to lower its labour costs, as happened in Spain during the 1960s, for example. Aid, international economic planning and any form of trading blocs (such as the European Union) distort this balancing of supply and demand and therefore prevent the development of the poorer (and therefore cheaper) economies.

This approach has been associated with a number of writers, in particular Friedman and Hayek.

The 'North-South' approach

In 1980, the Brandt Report was published with the official title of *North-South: A Programme for Survival*; this was followed in 1983 by *Common Crisis*. Both these reports reflect a social democratic view of the world. The reports argue that it is in the interests of both the North (the developed nations) and the South (the underdeveloped ones) to work together.

In essence, the reports follow Keynsian principles in arguing that the wealthier the South becomes, the greater the number of goods the North can sell them. In order to create the trading conditions that are necessary for harmony between North and South, there should be easier credit for the creation of new industries and an expansion of aid – which is not for the relief of poverty but for the Third World countries to start their own development and to rescue their agricultural resources.

Other recommendations included a switch from the production of armaments to that of peaceful goods and services.

Value-based approaches

These approaches lay emphasis on the ways in which the beliefs of a population can initiate change and innovation. Economic factors are not dismissed but are seen as the result of ideas.

Morimisha (*Why has Japan 'succeeded'?*), for example, compares the present positions of Japan and communist China. He argues that at the beginning of the 20th century Japan industrialised and China did not because of the different value systems that existed. This was the result of the differing interpretations of the Confucianist religion. In China, this religion was interpreted as the need to obey one's own conscience and the family, while in Japan it was obedience to one's superiors that matters. The Japanese version of Confucianism had been deliberately created by the ruling class in order to make the population obey them. Morimisha argues that the obedience led to a pliable workforce and hence industrialisation.

The values approach seems to owe a lot to the ideas of Max Weber. His study of social change *The Protestant Ethic and the Spirit of Capitalism* is an example of economic change initiated by changing beliefs.

A social psychological approach

McLelland argues that underdeveloped societies are in such a state because the individuals do not have the desire to achieve. McLelland calls this **nAch** (need to achieve). He has developed various tests which he claims shows the level of 'nAch' of any society. This desire to achieve can be seen as the basis of British Victorian enterprise. 'NAch' is achieved at an early age through the socialisation process so that by eight years of age a child should be expected by its parents to have gained **'self-reliant mastery'** – this includes the qualities of competition and independence.

Pattern variables

This approach is closely related to the functionalist viewpoint in sociology, and in particular the work of Parsons. He argues that societies are characterised by particular choices from a set of **pattern variables** (for full details of this see p 26). However, it was Hoselitz (*Sociological Aspects of Economic Growth*) who applied Parsons' analysis to the Third World.

The pattern variables are:

1 **Affectivity** *versus* **affective neutrality**: relationships between members are based on emotion (eg small village) *versus* impersonality (the city).

2 **Collective orientation** *versus* **self-orientation**: the person regards him/herself as part of a group to whom he/she owes loyalty *versus* self-interested action.

3 **Particularism** *versus* **universalism**: rules are related to who the person is *versus* the person is dealt with as one of a group to whom the law applies equally.

4 **Diffuseness** *versus* **specificity**: people have a number of roles which they play at the same time (mother, shopkeeper, employer etc) *versus* the individual has one role which predominates.

5 **Quality** *versus* **performance**: the person's main characteristic is who he/she is and is therefore treated according to this (royalty) *versus* the main characteristic is what they have achieved.

For Hoselitz, societies need to shift towards the second example in each of the pattern variables (ie affective neutrality, self-orientation, universalism, specificity, performance) in order to evolve into modern societies as these contain the values necessary for the generation of the correct economic and social conditions.

Hoselitz links these pattern variables to the development of certain **evolutionary universals** which have to be attained before progress can be made. These include:

● written language,

● money,

● a bureaucratic State,

● an academic elite.

Policy implications of the value-based approaches

These approaches stress that there should be a policy of educating and training members of underdeveloped societies. Although economic help is useful, the existence of the correct values will enable the underdeveloped nations to help themselves. Through hard work and a wholesale adoption of Western values, they will become 'modernised'.

This type of approach to development, in which the values of the West are passed on to the rest of the world, has become known as **diffusionism**.

Criticisms of value-based modernisation theories

These forms of modernisation theory suffer from many of the defects of economic-based modernisation theory, although clearly they do recognise the key role that is played by values and beliefs. However, they still accept that Western societies present a model which underdeveloped countries can copy, and that underdeveloped nations can/should become just like the Western democracies. These approaches continue to ignore the fact that the circumstances that the Third World nations face now are different from those that were faced by Western societies when *they* were developing, in that today there are already developed societies.

Finally, these approaches are flawed in that they look at underdeveloped societies and compare them with the developed ones. The *differences* are the causes of development. Yet there is no proof that these differences are the causes; they could equally just be differences. Some societies, particularly Iran, are attempting to follow a path towards modernisation that does not involve Western values.

CONVERGENCE THEORY

The **convergence thesis** was particularly popular in the early 1960s, as a result of the writing of Kerr et al (*Industrialism and Industrial Man*). It was closely related to concepts like Bell's **end of ideology** thesis, in which Bell argued that the economic and political realities of the post-industrial age meant that ideology and rhetoric were out-moded. Bell 'discovered' that the American values were the ones that the rest of the world was coming to see as the 'reality'.

The convergence thesis referred to the process whereby advanced industrial societies were becoming increasingly similar in three areas:

● culture,

● politics,

● social structure.

This convergence was the result of the **logic of industrialism**, by which is meant the demands made upon the social structure by advanced industrialisation.

Culture

Industry requires:

1 people to be competitive, in order to be successful;

2 the extended family to decline in importance as it blocks social mobility and prevents the individual being successful;

3 that people become highly literate and numerate in order to cope with the complex tasks of advanced technology;

4 that societies become urbanised as people come together to work in service industries and commerce, as well as manufacturing;

⑤ that scientific and rational thinking dominate, with the consequent growth of medicine, science etc;

⑥ that socially, there is a consensus that values such as education, the media and urban society all pull people together;

⑦ finally, that **achievement criteria** (treating people on the basis of what they do), replaces **ascription** (treating people on the basis of what they are).

Politics

Industry requires:

① A political consensus based on democracy: without this there would be too much disruption for commerce to take place. Democracy ensures that the political structure reflects the will of the people. Ideological differences will dissipate as the wealth that advanced industrial production produces fulfils most people's requirements.

② Industrial/commercial consensus: large-scale production techniques require workforces who are content. Constant disruption would prevent industry being competitive. Consensus is in employers' interests as well as employees' interests, as high-quality products will ensure satisfactory profits.

③ A movement towards co-ordinated government action, both nationally and internationally: governments are needed to co-ordinate the amazing complexity of advanced industrial societies, especially in economic and social matters. International links develop between similar types of government: governments are increasingly likely to be aware that they are operating within a world situation as in a national one, and adjust their policies accordingly.

④ Welfare States: in order to ensure there is political stability, the governments will ensure that as citizens, people will have access to welfare and health services, and that extremes of poverty will be eliminated (as will extremes of wealth).

Social structure

Industry requires:

① A 'bulb'-shaped stratification structure: there will be large numbers of skilled workers (both manual and non-manual), and a decline in unskilled employment. This will eliminate the bottom of the class structure.

② High levels of social mobility: the most talented must be encouraged to take the highest positions and be rewarded accordingly. This will ensure large amounts of movement.

③ The elimination of extremes of poverty and wealth: in order to ensure that there is political and social consensus and to fund the Welfare State, the government must eliminate the extremes of inequality in society.

The result of this is that societies which do not fit this model will be forced by economic pressures into adopting it. Therefore the extreme market economies (such as the USA), totalitarian societies and communist societies will converge.

Criticisms of convergence theory

The most common criticism is one that reflects a debate which has run through the history of sociology – **economic determinism**. Does the economic structure of any society determine the social structure?

Japan: an example against convergence

Japanese society is strikingly different from the West, although Japan is closely linked to the West economically; indeed it has been described as a **paternalistic** or even **neo-feudal** form of society. It is rigidly hierarchical (although this is based on merit, among other things).

Employees have jobs for life once employed by a large company, irrespective of their ability. Rewards from the company are linked partly to non-economic criteria, such as family size. The company provides a complete range of services for its employees – a mini-Welfare State.

The history of industrialisation in Japan also supports the view that social factors can take precedence over economic ones. Much of the success of Japanese industry lies in the loyalty of the workforce and their extraordinary commitment to their companies. Much of this can be traced back to a version of the Shinto religion which was deliberately introduced in the 1880s to create loyalty to the State authorities – hence the title State Shinto. The point is that the introduction of these values was not the result of industrial 'demands' but of a deliberate decision by the elite.

THE CONCEPT OF UNDERDEVELOPMENT

Frank's work develops from Marxism yet is not a Marxist account of development. In essence, Frank is arguing that there is a close relationship between the conditions of the Third World nations and those of the West. In itself this is not new, but Frank develops a specific explanation of the way in which the international pattern of capitalist trading ensures by its very nature the continuing poverty of the Third World.

Development and underdevelopment

Frank argues that the West is actually 'underdeveloping' certain nations (and/or areas within nations) and actually making them poorer. Frank distinguishes between **undeveloped** societies which have no manufacturing sector but no outside interference causing this situation (for example Britain before industrialisation), and **underdeveloped** societies that are poor and have little manufacturing as the outcome of external interference (such as Mexico today). Underdevelopment is the process by which the economy of Third World nations is systematically 'distorted', by large companies based in the industrialised nations, so that profits and wealth created in the Third World nations flow to the richer Western nations.

When countries are no longer of use to the exploiting Western nations – the **metropolis(es)** – they are discarded and will fall into even greater poverty. Frank gives the example of the north-east of Brazil, once an extremely rich area (at least for the plantation owners), which is now one of the poorest areas of South America because sugar is no longer needed.

The metropolis–satellite relationship

The essence of Frank's analysis is the concept of the **metropolis–satellite relationship**. International capitalism is based in a few world centres, such as New York and to a lesser extent Brussels, which are **international metropolises**. These use their investments and their trading dominance to cover the world markets. However, they do not trade directly with individual peasants or Third World companies; instead, they pass through local offices or local agents operating usually from the capitals of the particular Third World nations. In Frank's analysis, these are the **satellites**.

These satellites are, however, in turn **national metropolises** and they further exploit through local or regional satellites, and the process may happen all over again until finally the peasant is actually exploited by a local landlord who acts on behalf of the local satellite. International capitalism is a chain that drags up the profits from one link to another until finally they arrive in the hands of the international metropolis.

Countries can only develop independently when the major powers are engaged in some crisis, such as a war etc, or if they remain totally isolated from the outside.

The role of multi-national companies

The role of multi-nationals, in Frank's analysis, is to find the cheapest place for labour and production and then to export the product and the majority of the profits back to the metropolis(es). There is very little diffusion of wealth in a Third World country.

Local political elites support the exploitative actions of the multi-nationals because they benefit financially and politically (for example with US military support).

Policy implications

There is no way to develop while locked into the metropolis–satellite relationship, so developing countries must break out of this. According to Frank, isolation may be the best solution, where the country withdraws from international trading as much as possible.

Criticisms of Frank

Frank's analysis is very appealing and certainly describes much of the interlocking nature of the world economy. However, his remedy for underdevelopment – isolation – does not seem to produce any better results; this can be seen in the fact that China, Burma and Romania have all tried isolation with little obvious success.

Secondly, modernisation theorists point to the success of countries such as South Korea and Taiwan in industrialising and becoming affluent within the capitalist world economy. Critics of the Left are discussed in the neo-Marxist approaches below.

MARXISM AND NEO-MARXISM

Marx, as a 19th-century European writer, virtually ignored the rest of the world (apart from the USA) in his writings. However, he appears to have regarded all societies as passing through the various epochs of history on their way to capitalism and eventually communism. It was simply that these Third World societies were at earlier stages in the move forward through the various epochs. However, he did note that the exploitation of the Third World was making the British working class better off, and that this weakened the British working class's sense of class solidarity and therefore willingness to rebel.

Lenin, writing in the 20th century, was more aware of the international aspects of trade. He suggested that the relationship between the more advanced nations and the poorer ones could be characterised as **finance capitalism**. Banks invested money in enterprises outside the advanced countries and because of low wage costs etc were able to achieve greater returns on their investment. Lenin foresaw the world being divided up by **international capitalist monopolies**, which would be supported by capitalist governments (he used the term **state monopoly capital** to describe this).

Warren (*Imperialism: Pioneer of Capitalism*) continues the Marxist analysis. He argues that, in fact, the traditional Marxist analysis is correct and that since 1945 there has been a significant advance through the epochs, just as Marx's theory predicts. Colonialism has actually been a 'powerful engine of progressive social change', by destroying traditional social structures and implanting capitalist ones.

In Marx's analysis, capitalism is the last full epoch before communism, and therefore the faster the shift towards capitalism, the faster the conditions develop for communism.

Complexity of class structures and economies

Laclau (*Feudalism and Capitalism in Latin America*) argues that there is no simple overall pattern which can be used to explain the process of development in the Third World. Laclau argues that the complexity of the Third World countries means that there will be some parts which are agriculture-based and others that are based on industrialisation. The outcome is that there are really mixed economies within each Third World nation and so the idea of clear-cut epochs in the traditional Marxist sense is mistaken.

This form of argument is also taken up by Taylor (*From Modernization to Modes of Production*), who claims that the impact of capitalism on non-capitalist (unindustrialised) societies is to create a very fragmentary class structure within them; this leads to forms of society which have not yet appeared in those countries, such as Britain or the USA, that industrialised without outside interference.

Baran and Sweezy

Baran and Sweezy have attempted to amend the work of Marx to show how the predictions that Marx made about the move through the various historical epochs has simply not occurred. In *Monopoly Capitalism*, Baran and Sweezy describe the process by which

European countries systematically distorted the economies and social structures of their colonies in such a way as to favour the industrial growth of their home economies and do long-term harm to the colonies. Baran and Sweezy argue that, had it not been for the effects of colonialism, there would be no Third World problem today.

For example, India was exploited by the British through heavy taxes levied on exported Indian goods, which made them uncompetitive; restrictions on trading and manufacturing initiatives in India; and straight-forward looting of the nation's wealth. Indeed there was more industry (primarily textile) in India *before* Britain made it a colony than when India won independence in 1948.

In many ways this analysis is similar to Frank's.

Criticisms of the Marxist approaches

Marxist approaches have tended to concentrate on patching up the original 19th-century thinking of Karl Marx and his evolutionary perspective, which sees history as a series of stages or epochs. Most modern thinkers would disagree about this view of history. Marxists have underplayed the expansionist and exploitative actions of communist countries, such as the USSR, which do not have a record significantly better than the West's. Marxists have failed to explain why some countries, such as Japan, have successfully industrialised and others failed, when both have been operating in the same world economic order.

14.3 URBANISATION IN THE THIRD WORLD

By the end of the 20th century, 3 billion people will live in urban settlements (towns and cities), two-thirds of whom will live in the Third World. Mexico City is expected to have over 25 million people by 2000.

CAUSES OF URBAN GROWTH

There are two basic reasons for the growth in Third World cities:

- immigration,
- high birth rates.

Immigration

By this we mean **internal migration** within the country from the rural areas. Country-dwellers are drawn to the towns and cities through:

1 the 'push' of intense rural poverty, lack of medical facilities and, in large parts of Asia and Latin America, violence in the countryside;

2 the pull of possible employment, health care and success.

Intensifying factors

The flight from rural areas has been intensified by the reorganisation of agriculture into cash crops grown in large estates, as opposed to subsistence agriculture on small 'peasant' land holdings. This has caused a surplus of unemployed, landless agricultural labourers. A second intensifying factor has been the development of a small amount of manufacturing industry in or near the major urban areas. There is rarely any industrial development in the countryside.

High birth rates

The urban areas are in the stage of having very high birth rates and a decline in death rates.

This could be due to a number of factors, such as:

① the urban population is very young and therefore likely to have high birth rates;

② they may culturally continue the high birth rates of the countryside (from which many came originally);

③ they may need large families in order to survive.

Fig. 14.1 shows how changes in the birth and death rates as well as war and migration influence population size. Table 14.1 details how the demographic characteristics of a society alter as it moves from an agricultural to an urbanised basis.

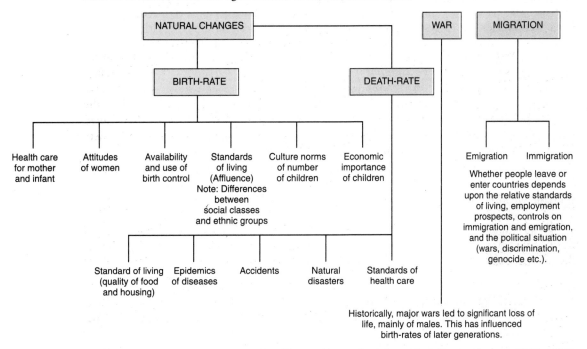

(Source: Moore, Sociology Alive!, Stanley Thornes, 1987, p137)

Fig. 14.1 Factors influencing population size

Table 14.1

	Level of social and economic development	Major demographic characteristics	Examples
Stage One	Societies with low national income per capita. High percentage of labour force in agriculture. Low levels of urbanisation.	**High** birth-rates. **High** death-rates. **High** infant mortality-rates. **Low** expectation of life at birth. **Low** rate of natural increase. **High** percentage of children.	All societies before 1700. Contemporary modernising societies (eg. India, Egypt, tropical Africa, most of Latin America and Asia before 1950).
Stage Two	Societies undergoing the early stages of industrialisation. National income per capita increasing. Percentage of labour force in agriculture declining. Rising levels of urbanisation.	**High** birth-rates at first, gradual decline in later stages. **Declining** death-rates. **Declining** infant mortality-rates. **Rising** expectation of life at birth. **Very high** rate of natural increase at first, gradual decline as birth-rates fall in later stages. **Very high** percentage of children at first, declining later.	Britain, 1780–1880 USA, 1870–1910 W. Europe, 1830–1900 USSR, 1910–40 Japan, 1920–50
Stage Three	Societies with high national income per capita. Low percentage of labour force in agriculture. High levels of urbanisation.	**Low** birth-rates. **Low** death-rates. **Low** infant mortality-rates. **High** expectation of life at birth. **Low** rate of natural increase. **Low** percentage of children. **High** percentage of old people. **High** percentage of persons 15–64.	Contemporary Britain, W. Europe, USA, Japan, Australia, New Zealand, Canada.

ECONOMIC PATTERNS

The economies of Third World cities are usually based on two very different sectors:

- the formal,
- the informal.

The formal

This is the employment sector based on State and commercial bureaucracies, on legal manufacture and on financial services such as banking. These are closely tied into the international economy – for example the manufacturing company is very often owned by foreign companies who invest because of the low costs. Industrialisation in the cities has taken the form of **import substitution**, that is manufacturing locally for the home market goods which are internationally available.

This is the sector that Third World States encourage.

The informal

Estimates vary concerning the proportion of people engaged in this sector in Third World cities. It is probable that the majority of adults (and possibly even children) are engaged in this sector, and estimates have reached 67%. This sector consists of all forms of economic activity outside the legally controlled ones: people may wash cars, hustle in the streets, search the rubbish dumps, sell articles without vendor's licences and perform numerous other activities, all of which overlap the illegal.

In the cities of the richer nations an informal sector exists but it is marginal to the formal one. In the Third World the informal sector is the usual way for a substantial section of the population to make a living.

HOUSING PATTERNS

The growth in the population is so great that there is inadequate accommodation – at least for the price that the majority of workers can afford to pay. This has led to the development of shanty towns, or favelas. The shanty towns develop on waste ground that is not suitable for housing, such as on rubbish dumps or where there is danger of landslips. The occupants are usually the rural migrants who are on the bottom rung of the urban ladder. Usually these shanty towns are illegal, have no sanitation or fresh water and are periodically destroyed by the authorities. However, in some countries, for example Peru, there has been some attempt by the authorities to provide water supplies and sanitation of a sort.

The shanty towns are generally regarded as places of despair and social disorganisation, but a variety of writers, such as Moorhouse and, separately, Turner, have argued that they are sensible responses to the problems of the poor, and that the poor are often organised and socially well integrated. This does not mean to say that there is not terrible poverty nor that the shanty town dwellers would not prefer to live in decent (or even slum) homes.

The most extreme form of 'housing', which can be found in Calcutta for example, is that of street dwelling. Poverty here is so acute that entire families live on the pavements. Here, even the shanty town is a step up.

There is nothing natural or inevitable about shanty towns and street dwelling. They usually result from:

1. intense poverty in the countryside forcing people into the cities;

2. lack of work or low wages in the cities so that the people cannot afford to rent or buy homes;

3. the construction of homes in Third World States for the private sector, rather than State provision;

4. the above, in turn are caused by the inequality in the distribution of wealth in many Third World countries and by the international trading patterns which keep these countries poor.

SOCIAL RELATIONSHIPS

Urban immigration does not mean that the social patterns of the Third World countries are necessarily changed. Most migrants are young people who come from the country to stay with relatives in the city. In turn, they are joined by other family members as they come to settle in the city. It is true that immigrants from ethnic groups or certain regions tend to gather together to form networks in the cities for mutual help. On the other hand, urban relations do slowly undermine certain of the rural traditions: for example the caste system in India is basically a rural phenomenon and in the cities, people are unable to tell from what caste a person comes.

A PARALLEL BETWEEN THIRD AND FIRST WORLD CITIES?

It has been argued that the development of the Third World cities is basically like that of the richer nations: that eventually housing will improve and population growth will decline. However, the evidence does not seem to support this:

1. The population in the urban areas of the Third World is double that of 19th-century Europe. Initially European cities were characterised by high fertility and high infant mortality (and so natural growth was low), and the growth in the population was mainly by immigration. In the Third World however, urbanisation is characterised by:

   - a decline in mortality,

   - a continuing high level of fertility,

   - high levels of immigration.

   Immigration is unlikely to decline and the fertility rate in rural areas is even higher than in the cities – providing a constant pool of aspiring immigrants.

2. European economies developed in terms of the formal sector. In the underdeveloped countries, the development is in the informal sector.

3. Poverty was largely overcome in Europe: there is no reason, given international trading patterns, that this will happen in the developing nations.

INTERNATIONAL TRADE AND URBANISATION IN THE THIRD WORLD

The Third World cities were generally created as a result of colonisation, unlike the richer nations whose cities developed for some local economic reason. Third World cities were therefore centres for colonial administration; power was usually centralised, and alternative centres of power were not allowed to develop. This resulted in one or two enormous cities which have continued to grow. It is therefore typical of the Third World cities that there are fewer of them in each country and that they tend to be larger than cities in the First World.

Trans-national companies, whether left from colonial days or new ones looking for cheap production costs, have centred their production within the few major cities. This has meant that all wealth and employment possibilities are concentrated in the urban areas.

Agricultural patterns influenced by the needs of the richer nations have had an influence on the urban development, too. The move towards cash crops for export, which are grown on massive estates, has meant poverty and unemployment in the rural areas. This is because the small peasant farmers have been dispossessed of their land and are no longer able to practise subsistence agriculture. They are therefore drawn to the cities in search of work.

14.4 URBANISATION IN THE UK

In 1801 about 17% of the population lived in towns, yet by 1851 it had increased to 50%, by 1951 it was 81%. Since then there has been a gradual decline so that about 72% of the population now live in large towns and cities.

Two processes have therefore occurred:

1 urbanisation and

2 de-urbanisation.

These are closely linked with the processes of industrialisation and de-industrialisation.

URBANISATION

The causes of this included

- Changes in agriculture, particularly the enclosures when common land was fenced off.
- The introduction of agricultural machinery which meant that fewer workers were need on the land.
- Industrialisation
  (i) switching manufacture from isolated communities to towns.
  (ii) introducing labour intensive machinery so that large numbers of workers were needed in the factories.
- This led to demand for housing.
- The population growth led to the creation of shops and traders.
- As towns developed so distinctions grew between the various social classes.

DE-URBANISATION

This has occurred at a significant rate since the 1970s, but began in the 1950s. Causes include:

- The development of modern means of commuting allows people to live away from the cities.
- Industry has moved out of cities because
  (i)   it is cheaper,
  (ii) better access is available to motor ways,
  (iii) developments in IT allow communication with commercial and financial centres without having to have a physical presence.
- The inner cities began to decline as a consequence of de-industrialisation and there was a middle class 'flight from the cities'.

14.5 COMMUNITY

Sociologists have been interested in the social effects of the process whereby people move from predominantly rural-based societies into urban based ones. As the process first happened in Europe in the 1st century, the early writers who constructed the framework for the debate were Europeans. However, their arguments have also been used in Third World contexts.

Tonnies distinguished between two types of society:

❶ Gemeinschaft or community,

❷ Gesellschaft or association.

Durkheim agreed with these divisions but called them **mechanical** and **organic**.

These divisions into two types of community relationships are 'ideal types', which serve as examples which draw all the characteristics together of each type. In reality, the characteristics would not all be found.

Characteristics of Gemeinschaft or Mechanical Society

- Relationships are very close between people and are based on personal acquaintance.
- People living in rural areas believe they have interests in common and are united in similar types of views.
- The social network is closely knit.
- People play a multiplicity of roles.
- There is the potential for role conflict.
- The economy is usually simple – agriculture, or at least singular (one company dominates).
- There is relatively little division of labour.
- The society is based upon ascribed status.

Characteristics of Gesellschaft or Organic Society

- Relationships are generally impersonal, shallow and transient.
- There is little sense of sharing a common set of interests.
- The social network is large and dispersed.
- Fewer multiple roles are played.
- Therefore there is little opportunity for role conflict.
- The economy is likely to be complex based upon commerce and industry.
- There is a complex division of labour.

According to Durkheim, people are held together by their mutual need expressed through the division of labour. People are valued for what they achieve rather than for inherited or family characteristics.

Reasons for the change in types of community relations

Wirth has suggested that there are three main reasons for the differences between gemeinschaft and gesellschaft:

size: towns and cities cover larger areas and therefore need roads, public transport etc. Furthermore, the sheer size allows social class and ethnic divisions to emerge in terms of housing areas.

density of population: the density of population leads to housing shortages, traffic, pollution, shopping centres and therefore creates a more complex situation.

social heterogeneity: people from a much wider range of backgrounds mix together.

THE CONTINUING EXISTENCE OF COMMUNITY

The idea that there is a clear difference between rural and urban life has been heavily criticised. Studies of city and village life have not substantiated the existence of clear-cut differences.

Pahl (*Patterns of Urban Life*) studied Swansea and found that it was divided into quite distinct neighbourhoods. These formed separate communities each having an individual identity, where people seemed to exhibit behaviour very similar to that of Gemeinschaft.

Pahl explains this by pointing out that Swansea developed as a tinplating town with successive waves of immigrants arriving and settling into specific areas depending upon their origins. Successive generations retained the sense of community.

Young and Willmott found that working class East London in the 1950s (*Family and Kinship in East London*), and middle class North London in the 1960s (*Family and Class in a London Suburb*) had both retained clear senses of community. In Willmott's work in a different area of North London in the 1980s a sense of belonging and kinship still emerged, even if it was more fluid and less restraining.

In Pahl's study of Hertfordshire commuter villages (*Urbes in Rure*) he found that the Gemeinschaft style of life was missing. There were deep divisions between the villagers.

We can therefore conclude that it is not the place that is important in determining relationships, but factors such as social class, ethnicity etc.

14.6 THE THIRD WORLD AND HEALTH

MORTALITY AND MORBIDITY IN THE THIRD WORLD

There are considerable differences between life expectancy in the First and Third Worlds: for example in the First World life expectancy at birth is 70–75 years, in South America 61, East Asia 52, South Asia 49, Africa 46. Infant mortality in the Third World is six times higher than in the First; indeed the chances of death in the poorest countries are so high that babies are more likely to die than to live. Half of those dying each day in the Third World are children, compared to about 3% in the industrialised nations.

Children in the Third World are 400 times more likely to die of a disease than in the richer, industrialised nations. Illnesses that are relatively minor in the industrialised nations, for example measles, are killers in Africa. There are also a number of major Third World killer diseases that are not common in the industrialised nations:

● vector-transmitted diseases,

● air-borne diseases,

● contact diseases.

Vector-transmitted diseases

1 Via faeces: include cholera, diarrhoea.

2 Via insects and parasites: include polio and infections, such as filiariasis, which affects over 300 million people (often known as elephantitis as it causes enormous swelling), and Bilharzia, which affects 250 million people. Mosquitoes carry malaria, which affects 200 million people, killing a million people per year in Africa; it is even so on the increase.

Air-borne diseases

These include TB (eliminated in Britain), influenza (which kills in the Third World), diphtheria etc. Only smallpox has been eradicated, as a result of the World Health Organisation.

Contact diseases

These include leprosy, which affects up to 15 million people. Trachoma, which is the major source of blindness in the world, affects 500 million people.

REASONS FOR HIGH LEVELS OF MORTALITY AND MORBIDITY

Undernourishment

The image of millions of people dying of starvation each year, as has recently occurred in the Sudan, is a distortion of reality. Lack of food is rarely the direct killer. Much more important are the long-term effects of undernourishment and malnutrition. The result of undernourishment is to weaken resistance to diseases which people in the richer countries can shrug off. For example, each year in India 150,000 children become blind as a direct result of lack of vitamin A. In Europe, TB was eliminated not by the activities of the medical profession but by increases in living standards, including decent diets and housing conditions. These do not exist for the vast majority of people living in the Third World.

Undernourishment also means that unhealthy mothers give birth to weak babies, and so the cycle of infant mortality continues.

Environmental factors

It has been suggested that 80% of disease is related to water. Impure water supplies and inadequate sanitation are responsible for many of the vector diseases mentioned earlier. If the sanitation systems found in the Third World resembled those of the industrialised nations, these diseases would be eliminated. Other diseases are partially caused, or at least transmitted, by poor housing, so that overcrowding and dirt lead to disease passed by humans or by insects who thrive in the poor-quality housing conditions.

COLONIALISM AND HEALTH

Importing disease

The first effect of colonialism was the importing of diseases from the European nations against which the local populations had no defences (such as influenza and VD). This was generally done unwittingly, but the British deliberately spread smallpox among the Canadian Indians (through the gift of infected blankets) to take their land.

Slavery, too, although not a disease, killed millions of people through the conditions of work.

POVERTY

A second result of colonisation was the theft of the wealth of the colonised nations, such as India, and the destruction of industry that was competitive with the European colonisers. The result of this was poverty which indirectly leads to ill-health and death.

Cash crops

One of the most common activities of colonisers was to prevent the normal agricultural patterns and to force the farming of 'cash crops' (rubber, coffee, tea etc). The result was inadequate production of foodstuffs for the indigenous population, resulting in starvation at worst and undernourishment at best. This resulted in weak people, prone to illness.

The development of medicine

Medicine developed in Third World nations in response to the demands of the colonial elite. These demands were influenced by:

1. their expectations of what constituted medicine – ie scientific, curing and technological;

2. the fact that their illnesses were typical Western ones, as their wealth protected them from the diseases of poverty around them. The result was a copy of Western-style medical organisation and practices.

There is considerable doubt about the usefulness of this model to the industrialised nations, but undoubtedly this was irrelevant to the needs of the Third World, where illness is caused primarily by poverty in its various forms.

POST-COLONIAL SITUATION

The problems caused by the colonisation did not disappear with its removal. National elites developed in most Third World nations and perpetuated the unequal economic order of colonialism in another form. Poverty in the Third World is caused largely by the trading practices of the richer countries, but there would be considerably fewer health problems if the distribution of resources were more equal within the Third World countries.

The continuation of cash crops has meant that Third World nations are often importers of food; this means that food is expensive and that large numbers in the population remain undernourished and therefore susceptible to illness.

Inequality has been exacerbated by urbanisation, so that most of the resources of the underdeveloped societies are consumed by those living in cities and there is little left for the rural poor. In the cities, the poor who gain their living through the informal economy (see p 296), often live in appalling conditions in the shanty towns, often situated on rubbish dumps, with the attendant health hazards.

Western medical patterns persist. The original bio-mechanical model (see p 247) of health has been left by the colonial elite and taken over wholesale by the new national elite. It is irrelevant for the majority of the population, but not for the rich elite who suffer from Western conditions of overconsumption.

THE ROLE OF TRANS-NATIONAL COMPANIES

Trans-national companies crucially influence health patterns in the Third World through:

- employment,
- dumping.

Employment

First, they do so through their trading and employment patterns which continue to keep these nations poor. They seek (and enforce with the help of local elites) low wages which cause poverty directly and ill-health indirectly. They also employ people in terrible working conditions, even having special permission to operate in special trading zones in which the laws regulating labour of the country involved can be ignored. Finally, profits are shifted out of the poorer countries back to the 'metropolises', so that there is little increased wealth in those countries.

Dumping

Secondly, the trans-national drug companies use the Third World as an area to dump drugs that are rejected by the richer nations and to test drugs for the more strictly controlled developed nations. Perhaps the most famous example of **dumping** is Nestlé's campaign to sell baby milk to the poorer nations by means of advertising campaigns. The poor were being persuaded to spend their scarce resources on a product inferior to the one women can make naturally.

HEALTH CARE IN THE THIRD WORLD

Health care provision in Third World countries mirrors that of the developed nations. The new ruling elites have retained the old colonial-style provision of health, which was based on the needs of urban, wealthy people. This kind of health care is hospital- and curative-based rather than preventative. There remains a strict hierarchy of doctors/surgeons and nurses; these jobs are usually available to the children of the elites.

The education systems of most Third World countries are based on the old colonial patterns and so medical schools train doctors as if they were to practise in the developed nations. This leads to them being of little use to the bulk of the population in the Third World nations. Many of the doctors then leave their country to work in the developed nations where rewards are higher.

Drug companies have enormous influence and have used the Third World as an area to try new drugs or to dump ones that are not successful in the developed countries.

An alternative approach would be for nurses or trained auxiliaries to tour the rural areas of the Third World countries teaching methods of hygiene; for intergovernmental initiatives to tackle the poverty that really causes the diseases; and for mass immunisation schemes such as that used against smallpox to be carried out.

Test yourself questions and answers

Questions

1 What four approaches to development are distinguished in the main text?

2 What are the stages that Rostow claimed existed for development?

3 Explain the concept of 'underdevelopment'.

4 Why are there high levels of morbidity in the poorer nations of the South?

Suggested answers

1 Modernisation, convergence, Marxist, underdevelopment.

2 Rostow suggests the following stages:
- Traditional societies: agricultural society, low levels of science ('pre-Newtonian'), ascriptive social structure based on kinship networks, poor communications.
- Pre-conditions for take-off: trading patterns improve and a considerable surplus develops, often based on extractive industries and the beginnings of services. Communications improve. An elite groups emerges with enough wealth (and the desire) to invest. Rational ideas and science develops.
- Take off: income growth outstrips population growth (therefore people become wealthier). Specific manufacturing industries develop and dominate the economy. Political structures develop which allow growth (this seems to imply a move towards democracy).
- Drive to maturity: further advances in science and technology, and the widening of the economic bases. Political reform continues. A meritocratic attitude dominates. Investment is 10–20% of national income. International trading becomes extremely important.
- Age of high mass consumption: period of most affluence where individuals live in a consumer society and where the surplus produces enough wealth to allow choices to be made as to how to use this wealth.

3 Frank argues that the West is actually 'underdeveloping' certain nations (and/or areas within nations) and actually making them poorer. Underdevelopment is the process by which the economies of Third World nations are systematically 'distorted' by large companies based in the industrialised nations, so that profits and wealth which are created in the Third World nations flow to the richer Western nations. International capitalism is a chain that drags up the profits from one link to another until finally it arrives in the hands of the international metropolis.

4   The reasons for the high levels of morbidity include:
- Undernourishment: which weakens resistance to diseases which people in the richer countries can shrug off. Undernourishment means unhealthy mothers giving birth to weak babies and so the cycle of infant mortality continues.
- Environmental factors: impure water supplies and inadequate sanitation are responsible for many 'vector' diseases, such as cholera, typhoid and trachoma.

Illustrative question and answer

Question

Evaluate the usefulness of the concepts of development and underdevelopment in the analysis of the relationships between First and Third World countries.

AEB

Suggested answer

The essay must begin with clear definitions of development and underdevelopment, and make the point that these terms are generally linked with modernisation theories which assume that there is a path which the South could follow in order to become industrialised and affluent like the countries of the North.

You should introduce at this point a discussion of the alternative notion by Franks of dependency and suggest that this provides a far more radical approach. Marxist theories straddle the divide as different versions fall into the different camps.

Then begin to work your way through the different modernisation theories, showing that there is a major division between approaches which stress economic factors as being most important (economic determinism) and those which stress the importance of values (voluntaristic approaches). The clearest and simplest of the economic determinist models comes from Rostow, and you should work your way through the various stages which are discussed in the main text. Do not forget to be very critical of this approach and point out how values are almost completely ignored. A useful example to counterbalance this approach is to discuss Weber's *Protestant Ethic* study. More up-to-date examples of the power of values could come from Malaysia or Iran. A further criticism you should make is that there are different routes to development rather than the single 'path', and this does not square with Rostow's model.

You should then move on to look at the approaches which develop from Weber and which stress the issue of values; for example Hoselitz and Parsons, who both emphasise the need to understand that development takes place because individuals within societies take on certain values that lead to the development of a capitalist, industrial form of society. These values overwhelm the traditional values which are perceived to inhibit development. The easiest framework to use in an essay are Parson's pattern variables which are discussed in the main text in Chapter 1: Theory. You should criticise these approaches for their assumption of a single path towards the presumed 'advanced form of capitalist industrial' society, as well as because there are only a limited number of values, as designated by Parsons.

You could then move on to varieties of Marxism, describing first the traditional approaches of Marx and pointing out that there is a very clear form of historical determinism here with a clear path emerging which all societies will follow. You could certainly criticise this for being historically inaccurate, and point out the different routes that have emerged and the apparent failure of so-called communist societies. There have been a number of debates within Marxism with more enlightened commentators, such as Warren, offering a more complex model.

However, it is best at this point to move to a full and detailed discussion of the contribution of Franks and to point out that this developed from a form of Marxist critique.

Frank's main point is that the poorer countries are not in the process of developing but, to the contrary, are being actively underdeveloped and being made into dependency economies. You need to make a clear exposition of this process of dependency and of the relationship between metropolis and satellites.

Frank's analysis could be criticised for being too negative – countries such as South Korea, Malaysia and Taiwan appear to be successfully industrialising and emerging from their client relationships with larger economies and some element of independence. Perhaps Frank's analysis is most appropriate to agricultural economies.

At this point you should conclude by reviewing the main theories and their strengths and weaknesses and suggesting which ones are of more value in understanding the concepts of development and underdevelopment.

Question bank

1 (a) Briefly explain what sociologists mean by a 'community study'. (4)

(b) Identify, with examples, two methodological problems that sociologists face in studying 'communities'. (4)

(c) Assess the contribution of any one community study you are familiar with to our understanding of either rural or urban life. (7)

(d) Evaluate the view that studies of communities tend to 'romanticise' their ways of life. (10)

Integrated Boards

Points

(a) This may be a suburb, inner city area or even a small town.

(b) Problems include:
   (i) bias – may get drawn into the local community and see things through their eyes,
   (ii) may not get a true cross-section of the local community and see things only through the viewpoint of an unrepresentative group,
   (iii) being able to define exactly what a community is in a particular area and who forms part of that community,
   (iv) researchers may bring their own biases into the study,
   (v) gaining access to certain groups in order to study them.
   Howard Newby's *A Green and Pleasant Land* is a famous study of a rural area of East Anglia which illustrates the problem of definition, and of who is representative. Newby also had considerable problems tracking down a representative sample of farmers and persuading them to talk to him.

   A second famous study (or series of studies) was the Bethnal Green studies of Young and Wilmott. The researchers conducted a pleasant picture of urban life which neglected a whole range of social problems such as violence against women and children. This could have been because of seeing through their own biased male viewpoint. There were no senior female researchers.

(c) Lots of examples. Two of the most famous are given above. Newby's study of rural England (*Green and Pleasant Land*) was conducted in the 1970s. This tried to understand the changing nature of rural Britain and the relationships between the various groups in rural society.
   Newby pointed to:
   - the rate of change in the countryside,
   - the differences in power between various groups,
   - the continuing power of social class,
   - the loss of sense of community and the impact of the commuters with their levels of affluence,

- the decline of the small farms and the growth of the agricultural industries or 'agribusinesses',
- the loss of distinctive nature of rural life and its inclusion in the homogenous British society.

What contribution did the study make? It helped break myth of rural community and distinctiveness of rural style of life. Demonstrated the continuation of social class and the impact of commuters. Related wider changes in UK economy and society to a specific area, thereby bridging the gap that many community studies fail to make between the wider economy and the locality under study.

(d) This is raised in the issue of bias above. Newby's work does not romanticise, but many do. One example of a modern and rather unusual form of community study is Dick Hobb's study of East London, and in particular his study of policing and the informal economy. In this Hobb can be criticsed for constructing a view of working-class life which is fast-moving, exciting and non-harmful to others. There is no mention of women, of violence, of the possible harm that the criminals which he writes about may be doing to others. This reflects the patriarchal views of Young and Wilmott in which women are only minor players in their description and analysis of life in the locality studied.

A classic example of the differences that sociologiests with different research agendas can find in studying even the same area occurs in the comparison of Redfield's study in the 1930s of Tepoztlan in Mexico with Lewis's work 30 years later on the same village. Whereas Redfield, a functionalist, found harmony and integration and stability; Lewis found discord, suspicion and fear and envy.

Studies of suburbs and rural life have tended to emphasise positive aspects of life there, with little awareness of crime or poverty. In the US Kaplan's *The Dream Deferred* and in Britain, groups like ACRE have demonstrated that crime and poverty are commonplace in these communities, just hidden.

2 Assess sociological explanations of both social problems and social conflict in cities. Critically examine the view that de-urbanisation has blurred the differences between rural and urban life.

AEB

Points

This question appears to have two distinctive parts.

The first part of the question asks for a discussion of theories explaining what happens in cities to create social conflict. There are a number of approaches to these issues:

(a) Ecological or Chicago school. This emphasises different constructions of reality based on different cultures and different patterns of immigration. Conflict is caused primarily by different sets of values.

(b) Weberian. The best known approaches are those of Rex and Moore with their work on conflict caused by housing shortage. However, you can widen this to include the fight over any scarce resources including education, employment or whatever is valued. Essentially all social groups in cities (and in society generally) are aiming to maximise their use or control over scarce resources.

(c) Marxist analyses. The best known one is by Castells who argues that cities are locations of consumption, and that differences break out over access to consumption between different groups. He refers to these groups as 'urban social movements'. Interestingly for a Marxist, these groups may cross class lines. Harvey, however, in his work on the city, takes a more traditionally Marxist view and argues that the wider divisions in society are brought more sharply into focus in the city, but ultimately the differences in the city can be traced back to the wider issues.

(d) More specific analyses of urban disorder have hinged upon issues of race – particularly writings of Solomos and Sivanandan who point to the inequalities faced by young people of Afro-Caribbean descent in Britain and argue that they are demonstrating resistance to police and white oppression.

(e) The work of the left realists is also useful here, in that their work on subculture and relative deprivation is extremely useful.

The second part of the question needs to examine the distinction between rural and urban life as described by Tonnies and later by Parsons. Writers such as these made a clear distinction between the two structures of community and association. You need to run through these differences in a good degree of detail.

A second approach which can be found in the work of Gans, Pahl and Newby is that there never was a clear distinction between rural and urban life, at least not the sort of 'community' and 'association' distinctions which had previously been made. The argument here is that community can be found in the city just as much as in rural areas, and also many of the social problems which are associated with cities are to be found in suburban and rural areas.

Other writers, such as Cooke have argued that there has been a blurring of this distinction as the significance of both national and global processes of cultural and economic change have begun to impose a uniformity on all localities. In the UK, there has been a decline in industry, a growth in the service sectors, a process of suburbanisation followed by a move to smaller towns and into rural areas.

3 'The key reasons why the Third World remains underdeveloped is not because of its own inadequacies, but because the West has deliberately underdeveloped it.' Assess this view.

NEAB

Points

This question is asking you to work through the modernisation-based theories and compare them with those which stress the role of the industrialised and post-industrialised societies in maintaining the poverty of the poorer countries. Point out there are two types of modernisation theories: economic-based ones and value-based ones.

Economic-based: You should explore Rostow's explanation of five key stages, and point out that it does not fit the history of many countries, particularly the Pacific Rim ones (Japan, Korea, etc). Secondly, it underestimates the importance of value systems. It tends to be based on the USA and Europe. You should also mention the liberal economic school of Friedman and Hayek.

Value-based: Derives from functionalist theory. Sees certain values as being as crucial as economic factors. Possibly most famous example is the work of McLelland. Also comment on Hoselitz.

Finally, examine convergence theories, associated with Kerr et al, and point out that they have been criticised for not fitting the facts. Although more recently the concept of globalisation and the increasing dominance of worldwide media systems and consumption patterns may make countries more similar in culture. Against these approaches you need to explore in considerable detail the underdevelopment theories of Frank and his arguments concerning metropolis and satellites. Explore the role of international companies – perhaps using the example of how fashion brand names, such as Nike and Reebok, buy from producers in the underdeveloped countries who use child labour and impose very poor working conditions, and then sell in the developed nations at high profits. You need to point out that there are variations on this essentially Marxist theme by looking also at the work of Laclau, and at Baran and Sweezy.

CRIME AND DEVIANCE

Units in this chapter

Chapter objectives

In this chapter we explore the explanations that sociologists have offered for crime and its related concept of deviance. The chapter begins with a discussion of the nature of crime statistics, as an example of how sociology helps us to understand that objective facts, when analysed in more detail, stop being objective and possibly stop being 'facts'. We explore the socially constructed nature of official crime statistics and what factors occur for an act to be classified as a crime.

The nature of many theories of crime is influenced by the perception of the statistics, and so we move on to explore the relationship between different approaches to criminal statistics and sociological theories which claim to explain the nature of crime and criminality.

In the next, and largest, section of the chapter we undertake a detailed analysis of all the contemporary theories of crime. These range from functionalist, through a variety of subcultural theories, to Marxist and interactionist approaches. Each approach provides fundamentally different, and therefore often contradictory, explanations of the nature of crime and criminality. Furthermore, within the various traditions, such as Marxism, there are a number of competing approaches. These are all clarified and explained. Apart from the theories we look at issues of corporate crime and moral panics.

The following two sections look at the relationship between gender and criminality, and finally there is a discussion of the area of crime and race. The final section considers the models of policing.

15.1   CRIME STATISTICS

METHODS USED TO UNCOVER THE ACCURACY OF OFFICIAL STATISTICS

Two different methods have been used to try to uncover the true extent of crime:

- self-report studies,
- victimisation surveys.

Self-report studies

These consist of confidential questionnaires in which the respondents are asked to record whether they have committed any of the criminal acts which are listed. An example of a self-report study is that done by Campbell (*Girl Delinquents*), in which she tried to find the extent of deviant acts committed by adolescent girls.

Results of self-report studies indicate that common criminal acts are spread across much of the population, and that the clear differences which appear in the official statistics between the social classes, the sexes and ethnic groups are far smaller in reality, if these self-report studies are to be believed. Differences between the social classes, for example of 6 to 1 (working to middle class) decrease to 2 to 1. The same change in ratios is apparent for the sexes.

Criticisms of self-report studies are based on their lack of validity, relevance and representativeness:

1 **Validity** How do we know that the respondents are telling the truth?

2 **Relevance** The results obtained vary with the categories of crime which the researcher has put on his/her list. Most lists have included large numbers of very minor criminal or deviant acts. As most people commit some minor infringement of the law (under-age drinking in pubs, speeding etc), the results obtained are not significant for an understanding of 'true' criminality.

3 **Representativeness** The majority of surveys have been conducted on young people, and so there is little or no information on adult crime.

Victimisation surveys

This approach asks people to list and name the criminal acts that have been perpetrated against them, even if they have not reported the crimes to the police. An example of this has been the British Crime Surveys (BCS) which are regular surveys of the population of England and Wales, carried out by The Home Office, in which one person over 16 in 11,000 households is questioned. The latest survey was in 1994 (see Fig. 15.1 for results of the 1992 survey).

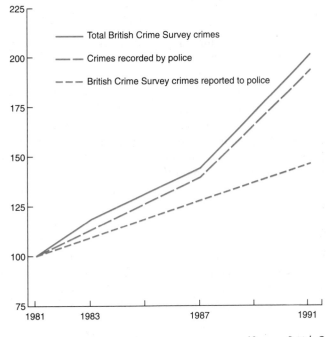

(*Source: British Crime Survey, 1992*)

Fig 15.1. Indexed trends in crime 1981–91 (1981 = 100).

Results indicate that the number of crimes actually reported is massively fewer than the number of crimes people believe to have been committed against them. For example, only 18% of robberies or thefts from the person, and about 23% of burglaries are reported. Criticisms include:

❶ **Exclusion** The BCS exclude many types of crime, such as drug dealing, prostitution, white-collar crime.

❷ **Reliance of individual memory** People may forget, regard the matter as unimportant or be reluctant to mention it because of embarrassment.

❸ **Classification of crimes** People need to define and classify acts as criminal. They may be inaccurate in so doing.

FACTORS AFFECTING THE REPORTING AND RECORDING OF CRIME

Whatever may be the defects of the sociological studies of the extent of crime, there is no doubt that there are considerably more crimes committed than are recorded in the official statistics. Explanations for this centre on the reporting of criminal acts to the police, and the recording and classifying of these reports by the official criminal justice agencies.

Factors affecting the public's reporting of crime

❶ People do not report crimes they regard as too trivial for the police to deal with.

❷ Some crimes are regarded as private matters between individuals.

❸ The victim may not wish the 'criminal' to be harmed, for example if the criminal is the son of the victim.

❹ The victim may be too embarrassed to report the crime, for example sexual assault.

❺ The victim may not be in a position to report the crime, for example if he/she has died.

❻ People are more likely to report crime if there is some benefit in it for them, for example car theft or house burglary where there is an insurance claim to be made.

The Merseyside Crime Survey studied the extent of crime in the Liverpool region. It showed that in inner-city areas the local community was less likely to report crime to the police because of a mixture of lack of faith in the police and a fear of reprisals.

Invisible crime

Often individuals are unaware that they are the victims of crime, for example in the cases of false accounting, computer fraud, overcharging by garages and commercial organisations. Also, many jobs include an element of 'fiddling' as part of the accepted way of earning extra money above the basic wage. Mars, in *Cheats at Work*, describes a number of jobs where these fiddles take place, including waiters who routinely steal food and overcharge customers, and garages where the minimum of work was done but extensive repairs were claimed to have been performed.

Corporate crime

This consists of illegal acts performed by large companies to inflate their profit. Pearce, in *Crimes of the Powerful*, studied corporate crime in the USA and claimed that even the detected levels of corporate crime were twice as great as the total value of all robberies in the USA. Corporate crime is rarely, if ever, uncovered and when it is, it is rarely treated as crime.

Factors affecting the recording of crime by the police

Fig. 15.2 shows the construction of criminal statistics, indicating the relationship between police activities and the official clear-up rate.

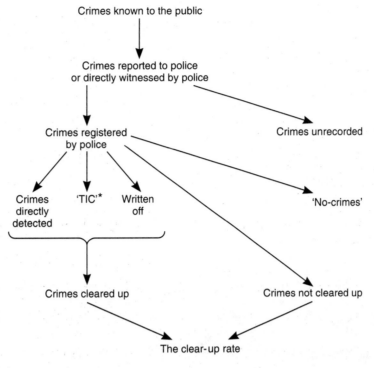

* Crimes 'taken into consideration' at the request of an offender

(*Source:* Kinsy et al, *Losing the Fight Against Crime*, 1986; reprinted in Moore, *Investigating Deviance*, 1988, p138)

Fig. 15.2 How the crime statistics are created

There are a number of factors affecting how the police record crime:

1 **Categorisation** How an act is categorised by the police in official criminal terms determines the statistics on crime. When an act is reported to the police they must classify it for the records. But why are crimes put into particular categories, for example assault with intent to rob or just assault?

2 **Dispersal** The more police officers the greater the likelihood of acts being seen by the police and possibly defined as illegal. More police are used to patrol working-class areas.

3 **Differential enforcement** Police forces in Britain have considerable autonomy and may take very different approaches to similar crimes. Enforcement may be strict in one city and less so in another, for example enforcement of drink-driving laws or street prostitution.

4 **Police culture** It is argued that the police operate with stereotyped views on who criminals are and are therefore more likely to concentrate on young males, particularly Afro-Caribbeans. This increases the likelihood of arrests among these groups.

5 **Moral panics** At any one time there tends to be national concern over a particular criminal issue. When this occurs the police (and public) are sensitised to this issue and are likely to seek out examples of this form of behaviour. Moral panics have concerned youth violence, football hooliganism, 'black' crime, child abuse.

THEORETICAL APPROACHES TO CRIME, AND CRIMINAL STATISTICS

Criminal statistics are not neutral summaries of a real situation. They reflect a complex world of different experiences, definitions and power.

Interactionist theories

These stress the negotiated nature of criminal statistics in much the same way as Atkinson and Douglas have pointed out the way in which suicide statistics are constructed (see p 67).

Marxist theories

These point out the way in which street crime and burglaries are overrepresented, and how there is a lack of concern over corporate crime. They also point out that the very definition of crime and policing practices represent the power of the ruling class.

Realist approaches

These point out that the official statistics distort the true picture but do indicate the real problems that people face in inner cities etc. Victimisation studies are the most useful and accurate of these.

15.2 USING THEORETICAL APPROACHES TO EXPLAIN DEVIANCE

The following theoretical approaches have been taken to explain deviance:
- functionalist,
- subcultural,
- labelling,
- Marxist,
- new Left realism,
- control and situational theories.

FUNCTIONALIST

This approach derives from general functionalist theory in interpreting activities in terms of their uses to the continuation of society.

Durkheim suggested that deviance and crime were beneficial to society in two ways:

1 Crime can bring about social change by providing a public forum (the courts) where public acceptance of the law is constantly being tested.

2 If there is a general outcry that the law is inadequate or out of date, then the law is changed. This helps to legitimise social change.

On the other hand, crime can strengthen social solidarity in that it draws people together in mutual horror at particularly abhorrent crimes.

Merton: anomie

A more detailed version of functionalist theory that sought to explain actual *behaviour* derived from Merton. He suggests that all societies set clear goals for people to attain (in modern Western societies these are primarily financial success). Societies also give socially approved means of obtaining these goals (hard work and success in business). Merton argues that as long as there is seen to be a reasonable chance of achieving success through approved goals, the society will function well. If, however, there is perceived to be little chance of success through these goals, then a situation of **anomie** results.

In this situation, people respond to the fact that they have very little chance of achieving socially approved goals by adapting to their situation, in one of five ways:

1. **Conformist**: they may simply continue to attempt to achieve success through the socially approved channels.

2. **Innovation**: they may accept the goals but reject the socially approved means of obtaining these goals, eg organised crime.

3. **Ritualism**: they follow the approved means without necessarily expecting to achieve the goals.

4. **Retreatism**: they lose sight of both the goals and means, eg drug addiction.

5. **Rebellion**: they develop an alternative set of goals and means to achieve these goals, eg a new religion.

For Merton, crime and deviance are the results of the response to the situation of anomie.

Illegitimate opportunity structure

Merton's work was developed by Cloward and Ohlin, who argue that there is not only a set of socially approved means to obtain the society's goals but also an illegitimate subculturally approved set of means. They suggest that there are also different responses to success and failure in this **parallel illegitimate opportunity structure**.

Criticisms of Merton

The majority of criticisms have been that there is an assumption that society has only one commonly held goal – financial success. It has been pointed out that there are a variety of goals held by individuals and different sectors of society. Secondly, the goals have been taken as neutral, or as given by society in some impersonal way. Critics argue that Merton ignored real issues of power: who sets the goals and the means?; who benefits from the nature of success and failure? Thirdly, Merton was criticised because he failed to explain clearly why a person would follow one adaptation rather than another.

Crime and power

Erikson also followed the tradition of Durkheim, but whereas Merton tried to explain the causes of crime, Erikson wanted to examine the element of *power* missing from Durkheim's work. Erikson examined the way in which the leadership of the puritan settlers in America in the 18th century used their power to define as officially evil certain religious beliefs which might have challenged their leadership, and in doing so were able to establish the unchallenged right to make decisions on behalf of the settlers.

SUBCULTURAL APPROACHES

A wide range of competing and contrasting theories are generally placed together under the rubric of subculture. The one thing linking them together is that they all stress the fact that groups of people create values which both reflect their circumstances and influence their patterns of behaviour.

US subcultural studies

1. **Ecological approach** In 1920s Chicago, researchers at the University observed that there were clear differences in the amount and type of crime which occurred in different parts of the city. The research of Shaw and McKay suggests that there were five concentric zones in the city, and one of these, the second zone out from the centre, had much higher levels of crime than the other four. They suggest that this was because the zone was one in which waves of immigrants to Chicago arrived and settled for a while before the more successful moved out to better housing in the suburbs. Eventually, this zone became the area where the less successful of each wave of immigrants lived. Because of the complexity and transience of the variety of

cultures in the zone, there was a lack of clarity of the correct ways to behave and thus children socialised in this transient area were more likely to develop criminal attitudes as they grew up.

Later versions of this approach, such as that by Sutherland, stress that the individuals learned a more or less coherent set of alternative values to the mainstream ones of US society.

② **Inverted values** The next development of subcultural theory came from Cohen (*Delinquent Boys: The Culture of the Gang*); in this work Cohen suggests that everybody needs to see themselves as having high status, and that adolescent males who fail at school seek alternative ways of gaining status. According to him, they deliberately adopt values which are almost the opposite of those which gain status in mainstream society.

③ **Distorted values** If Cohen's explanation was based upon a subculture which inverted normal values, then Miller's work was just the opposite. He stresses the fact that delinquent youths just carried traditional working-class values to an extreme, and this led them into their criminality. Miller summarises these values as trouble/ toughness/smartness/fate/autonomy.

UK studies

Studies of British society began to be conducted in the 1950s and have covered a very wide range of interpretations of subcultural theory. The best known are:

① **Morris** (*The Criminal Area*) This is a study of Croydon, based on an ecological approach. Delinquency was found to be concentrated in certain areas, but this was the result of the local council's policy of putting problem families in certain council estates.

② **Downes** (*The Delinquent Solution*) He studied male adolescents in east London and found that delinquency was associated with young people trying to amuse themselves and that the intention was rarely evil. He describes their attitudes as **dissociation** – meaning that they were not attached to work or a career and were simply interested in having a good time. This led them into conflict with the law on occasion.

③ **Baldwin and Bottoms** (*The Urban Criminal*) This is a detailed and complex study of Sheffield which tried to find out if there was evidence for any of the major subcultural and ecological theories. The conclusions were ambivalent. Like Morris 20 years earlier, they found very significant variations in crime rates in different areas of the city. They found no evidence for the idea of social disorganisation or that the council directly created criminal areas as suggested by Morris.

④ **Subculture and interactionism** Gill used an interactionist perspective in his subcultural study of a street in Liverpool renowned for its criminality. In *Luke Street*, Gill argues that the residents of the street were aware of their reputation, were rather proud of it and, as a result, tried to live up to it; therefore, a self-fulfilling prophecy was created and maintained.

⑤ **Structural subculture** In *A View from the Boys*, a study of Liverpool youths who steal car radios, Parker suggests that their specific situation and attitudes must be understood in the wider context of British society. Using a Marxist analysis, Parker shows that the activities and attitudes of the boys are a relatively sensible and rational response to their situation as 'bottom of the heap' in British society. Their deviant actions allow them to cope with their situation, but at the same time trap them in their inner-city, low-wage, petty-crime existence. Further development of this sort of approach came in the form of new Left realism discussed on pp 319–20.

Criticisms of subcultural and ecological theories

Because of the wide variety of approaches, it is difficult to give a few general criticisms. Some that have been made are:

❶ There is little evidence to show that there is either any one dominant set of values or any clear-cut alternative sets of subcultural values. In reality, the nature of values is such that they are confusing, overlapping and constantly changing. This is taken up in the work of Matza (see p 321).

❷ There is generally no discussion of crime other than delinquency or, at the very best, working-class crime. There are no discussions of white-collar or corporate crime, for example.

❸ Linked to the above point is the fact that there is rarely discussion of the nature of power and its relationship to crime.

❹ Subcultural theory is essentially **positivist** in that it seeks to show the differences in culture or values between criminals and non-criminals; yet interactionists argue that there are no differences.

❺ There are no discussions on the extent (or lack) of deviancy in women and its causes.

❻ The concept of social disorganisation, and many of the assumptions about crime and the inner city, are racist in that they associate social disorganisation with immigration, ethnic minorities etc.

❼ They rarely explore wider contexts in which crime and immigration occur.

INTERACTIONIST OR LABELLING THEORIES

These derive from the work of the symbolic interactionist approach developed in late 19th-century Chicago. As you will know from Chapter 1: Theory, the central point of the symbolic interactionist school is that the world is not fixed and given, but instead depends very much on how people define things around them. Furthermore, people do not live in a social world which is simply fixed, but they negotiate with each other, make choices and define (often incorrectly) the nature of their situations.

The significance of this for deviance was not fully developed until the 1950s (although it was an important influence on the Chicago subcultural studies). When it was first used by Lemert and Becker they tended to use the term **labelling** to describe this approach.

The key questions asked are:

● why some people rather than others come to be labelled as deviant;
● what the effect of that labelling is on them (the deviant career);
● why and how certain acts come to be labelled as deviant or criminal.

Labelling of individuals

It is not what a person does that is important but how the actions of that person come to be labelled. If someone commits an act in one situation it may be acceptable, in another it may not.

It has been suggested that the determination of an act as deviant varies with:

● who performs the act (eg adult or child);
● when the act is committed (during a party or at work);
● where the act is committed (on the beach or in a factory);
● in which group or society the act is committed (Victorian or contemporary Britain).

The implication of this for the study of deviance is that if there is little difference between those who commit deviant acts and those who don't then there is no point looking for the *causes* of an individual's deviancy.

Exactly why one individual is labelled and another not is never clearly explained in interactionism. It is clear that the issue of power is important (ie those who are powerful label the less powerful), but no clear theory of power has ever been developed by interactionists.

The effects of labelling

Lemert distinguished between primary and secondary deviance. If a person commits an act but is not labelled as deviant then no further consequences follow; however, if for the same act a person *is* labelled as deviant then **secondary deviance** takes place. By secondary deviance, Lemert meant the further responses of the labelled individual as a consequence of her/his initial labelling.

❶ **Variability** As mentioned earlier, there is no automatic relationship between committing an act and being labelled as deviant. There are few agreed definitions of exactly what deviance is, and so in practice the labelling of acts is very variable.

❷ **Negotiable** Labels are not fixed and permanent; they are the outcome of negotiations by people in which the person's label may be altered as a result of new information or the re-evaluation of earlier views. Here power is important, as some people are more able than others to reject negative labels. Becker coined the term **master status** to describe how, once a label is applied to someone, then all the activities of that person are seen in the light of that label.

❸ **How people perceive themselves** Becker points out that it is not just that other people see an individual differently once he/she is labelled, but that the person him/herself may alter their self-perception. Once labelled as a thief, I may gradually come to see myself as such, and to act in a way which reflects this.

Labelling acts as deviant

Just as people can be labelled as deviant and can respond in different ways, so acts come to be labelled as deviant and the performing of them may have symbolic value for people.

The process of rule creation

Laws are created according to this approach and reflect the activities of moral entrepreneurs, that is of individuals who try to get laws passed and enforced either because they directly benefit them or because they believe that the enforcement of these laws will benefit society. In a sense, the actual motivations are unimportant; the point the interactionists wish to make is that laws do not reflect any central values of society as functionalists would have us believe, nor do they necessarily reflect the interests of the ruling class, as the Marxists would claim. The process of law creation is complex and is, above all else, the result of a successful campaign by a group to introduce a particular definition of the situation.

Two examples of law creation follow:

❶ **Becker (*The Other Side*)** In 1937 the use and growing of marijuana was made illegal, except under certain special conditions. Becker's historical study explains this as a result of the campaign launched by the US Bureau of Narcotics who were motivated partly by moral feelings against marijuana and partly by the perceived benefits of a ban to their own organisation. The Bureau placed lurid articles in newspapers and magazines and lobbied members of the US Congress.

❷ **Platt (*The Rise of the Child-Saving Movement*)** In this study Platt showed how a group of well-connected women in the USA in the late 19th century changed the way in which crime committed by young people was actually defined and responded to. Historically, it was the act of criminality that was punished and it was irrelevant who actually committed the act. In the UK, for example, children were punished in exactly the same way as adults (including executions) until the 19th century. The US reformers campaigned for young people to be treated differently by the law and to be subject to different forms of punishment. Platt argues that the campaign was brought about and won because the women were the wives of successful businessmen; they were unable to use their talents in business themselves because of the attitude towards women at that time and therefore turned their talents to charitable work and to doing good. The redefinition of youth crime into juvenile delinquency and the introduction of special juvenile courts were part of this process.

These are two examples of the activities of moral entrepreneurs leading moral crusades and the interactionist contribution to the issue of law-making.

Deviancy amplification and moral panics

One of the insights of interactionism has been into the way that initial deviance can be significantly increased by the actions of those who apply the labels. Thus the media, in describing and hyperbolising an event, can create greater deviance than had existed beforehand.

The classic book on the effect of the media is by Cohen (*Folk Devils and Moral Panics*). It studies how:

1 the media created a sensation concerning the activities of groups of youths called mods;

2 the public outcry at their activities led to the police overresponding to what was perceived as a great threat to public order;

3 the media's attempt to outsell or outdo the competition vied to create the most sensational stories;

4 the young people themselves began to model themselves upon the exaggerated behaviour shown in the newspapers and thus brought exaggeration into reality;

5 the effect of the media was thus to amplify the deviance that they claimed merely to be reporting.

Evidence to support this comes from Armstrong and Wilson's *City Politics and Deviancy Amplification*. This is a study of the reporting of crime by local newspapers in Glasgow. There was found to be little relationship between the extent of crime and the reporting of it. According to the authors, support for one local political party led to a distortion of the true situation.

Fishman, in *Crime Waves as Ideologies*, points out that the reporting of crime is affected by the following:

1 The amount of other news material available.

2 The search by editors for themes. Crime provides a good linking theme, so that the theme of crime on the streets allows editors to include material on individuals, crime, politicians, good deeds by passers-by etc.

3 Crime waves come together because the media feed off themselves. Each part of the media will repeat, though slightly altered, the themes of its rivals in order to be sure of following the main events of the day.

See Fig. 15.3.

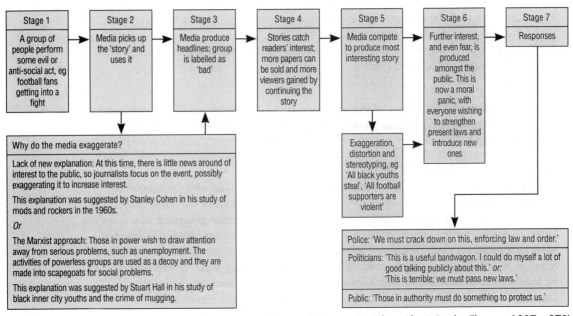

(*Source:* S. Moore, *Sociology Alive!*, Stanley Thornes, 1987, p270)

Fig. 15.3 Deviancy amplification and the role of the media

Criticisms of interactionist perspectives on deviance

1 There is no explanation as to why some people are labelled and some are not.

2 There is no explanation of the reasons why some people respond to their labelling one way and others in different ways.

3 Following from the first two points, symbolic interactionism has a major weakness in its claim to be a coherent theory in that it fails to predict any particular form of behaviour but merely explains after the event what has happened.

4 Its explanation for the introduction of laws reflects no coherent theoretical framework but implies that law-making is simply the result of successful crusades. There is no attempt to place the crusades into a wider structure.

5 Labelling does not explain why people commit crime; it concentrates on the causes and effects of labelling. But all the same, some people do commit crime and others do not – no explanation is given.

MARXIST AND CONFLICT APPROACHES

Marxist theories of crime and criminality are, of course, located in the general Marxist analysis of society, which suggests that capitalist societies exist for the benefit of the owners of capital.

There are four elements to the Marxist analysis of crime:

- the manipulation of values,
- the process of law creation,
- the enforcement of law,
- individual motivation.

1 Manipulation of values

What is defined as crime is a result of the values which the ruling classes have imposed upon society. The laws reflect and uphold these values. Laws enforcing workers' rights or controlling corporate crime are seen as less important than those controlling the activities of youth in inner-city areas.

2 Law enforcement

Therefore policing and public concerns are centred on particular types of crime. People assume that the real criminals are those in council estates or in inner-city areas (see the work of the UK subcultural theorists, pp 312–15). They therefore look for the causes of crime in the differences between the normal (middle class, middle aged) and deviant individuals (young, male etc).

3 Law creation

The law is seen as a reflection of the interests of the powerful in society, and does not exist, as most functionalists claim, to reflect the will and needs of the majority of the population.

4 Individual motivation for crime

In capitalist society, success is measured in terms of ownership and possession of status symbols. For Marxists, greed is therefore the very basis of capitalist society. For those with access to means of success (stock market, senior positions in commerce through public-school connections etc), success is virtually guaranteed and greed is seen as a positive 'wealth-creating' activity. For those with little, crime is one of the ways in which they too can succeed. This is similar in many ways to Merton's theory of anomie – but whereas Merton sees this situation as evidence of an abnormal capitalist society, Marxists see it as the very nature of normal capitalist society.

Policing the crisis: an example of the traditional Marxist approach

In *Policing the Crisis*, Hall and his colleagues studied the apparently rapid growth in street crime in the 1970s and the police response to it. At that time there was great concern over the increase in street robberies (muggings); the response of the public and politicians was outraged and demanded that the police do something about it. The authorities began a series of high-profile policing in inner-city areas, ostensibly as a deterrent to the would-be muggers.

Hall et al argue that this reading of the situation distorted the true picture. In the book, the authors claim that in the 1970s Britain was undergoing great social and political upheaval, and that there was a gradual build-up of trouble in the inner cities (this later climaxed with the inner-city riots of the 1980s). In order to forestall the perceived threat from inner-city youth, the authorities whipped up the concern over mugging in order to justify the implementation of much higher and tougher levels of policing than had ever before been introduced into inner-city areas in Britain.

Corporate crime

Box's *Crime, Power and Mystification* argues that crime committed by corporations is excluded from the **process of criminalisation**, by which he means that the City of London, where large amounts of fraud and illegal trading activities take place, is hardly policed at all. The city institutions are left to police themselves through various bodies. The record of the Serious Fraud Squad, which is given the task of investigating serious crime in the City, is very poor indeed and has rarely brought about successful prosecutions.

Criticisms of traditional Marxist approaches

1 The stress on context and structure limits the analysis of individuals' explanations and motives.

2 The constant explanation that all crime is the result of the interests of the ruling class leads Marxist writers into circular or tautological explanations. All crime is the result of the ruling class looking after its own interests, therefore when Marxists study crime they start from this assumption and look for the possible benefits from any law or police activity that accrue to the ruling classes. They ignore other potential explanations and therefore are bound to find the benefits they are looking for.

3 Marxist explanations of crime are only valid if one accepts the general Marxist analysis of society. The weaknesses of the general theory are also weaknesses of the explanations for crime.

4 These criticisms led to an evaluation of the Marxist position and a new contemporary Left analysis emerged known as new Left realism, which is discussed next.

NEW LEFT REALISM

New Left realism (NLR) is the name given to the form of left-wing analysis of crime that was developed by Lea and Young, among others. Their central argument is that victimisation surveys show that street crime really is a problem for people in the inner cities (as shown by victimisation surveys, see pp 309–10) and that the traditional Marxist analysis which ignored this, or saw it only as a plot against the working class, was wrong. The new Left realists argue that crime is a reality and that criminological studies should do something about it.

They developed a subcultural model or framework which they believe can help explain why groups of young people are more likely to commit crime. The main elements of the framework include:

1 **Subculture as a response to problems** Those who commit crime had developed a subculture which helps them to cope with problems not necessarily of their own making.

2 The macro/micro dimension The problems that people face are not randomly distributed; those with less power and economic resources are most likely to have problems and develop subcultures.

3 The objective/subjective balance Marxists have traditionally ignored the meanings individuals have of their own situation and instead introduced a reading based upon the political situation from a Marxist perspective.

4 The subculture is not completely separated from the values of the wider society Subcultures do not differ very greatly from the general values of British society but are versions of these general values.

5 The historical dimension Subcultures are not passed on but each generation recreates them according to their specific situation.

6 Relative deprivation One of the problems facing Marxists in their explanations of crime is that the poorest and most oppressed may not be those who have the highest levels of crime. The new Left realists argue that the answer lies in the concept of relative deprivation. By this they mean that people are more likely to feel deprived and want to do something about it, not necessarily because they are poor but because they are less well off than they ought to be. According to Young, contemporary youth feel frustrated and bitter because of the disparity between what they are led to expect and the reality of what they can obtain.

Criticisms of NLR

1 There has been no successful implementation in an actual piece of research of the framework described above.

2 NLR, in rejecting classical Marxist approaches, has been accused of ignoring the 'crimes of the powerful'.

3 The issue of the relationship between race and crime has become a major debating point for critics and defenders of NLR. Critics point out that the NLR approach does tend to accept that young blacks are more likely to commit crime than other groups and that this is racist. Defenders point out that, given the marginal position of young blacks in UK society, it would be difficult for them not to be over-represented in certain types of street crime.

CONTROL AND SITUATIONAL THEORIES

Control and situational theories are quite distinct from one another but do share a lack of concern to explain the reasons why people break the law, instead accepting this as quite normal. For control theorists the main question is why people break the law at all. By contrast, for situational theorists the main issue is that, given that people are going to break the law, what limitations can be placed on them to make breaking the law more difficult?

Control theories

Control theories are based upon the rather simple but nevertheless accurate point that instead of asking why people break the rules of society, the question asked is why they follow any rules in the first place.

Hirschi: bonds to society

In *The Causes of Delinquency*, Hirschi argues that individuals are linked to society by four bonds. These are:

1 attachment: the extent to which people care about others' wishes and opinions;

2 commitment: the amount of personal investment that people put into their life in terms of education, hard work, career moves, etc;

3 involvement: this concerns activities – thus a busy person with a wide range of interests and activities may be too busy to engage in deviant activities;

4 **belief**: this concerns the intensity or degree of belief that someone has in the rules of society.

The extent to which a person conforms to these four elements represents the extent to which that person is likely to engage in criminal activities.

Box: the strength of the bonds

Box, in *Deviance, Reality and Society*, asks what factors strengthen or weaken an individual's bonds to society. He suggests the following key factors:

1 **secrecy**: to what extent people are able to conceal deviance;

2 **skills**: having the knowledge to commit deviance;

3 **supply**: of the sorts of equipment needed to be deviant (how to obtain drugs?);

4 **social support**: will peers give their approval?;

5 **symbolic support**: the extent to which the wider community in which the person lives gives support and approval.

Matza: subterranean and drift values

One of the criticisms made against sociological theories that are not interactionist is that they all ignore the possible thoughts, feelings and motivations of individual deviants and concentrate on wider social factors such as housing, working-class culture, social disorganisation or even capitalism. Matza (*Delinquency and Drift*) concentrates much more on the motivations of delinquents or criminals and successfully links these to the broader values of society. In doing so, he provided a death blow to conventional subcultural theories (by showing that distinctive subcultures do not necessarily exist) and also influenced the thinking of the new Left realists (who appreciated the fact that Matza showed that delinquents *share* traditional values, they do not *oppose* them).

There are two key elements according to Matza:

● subterranean values,

● drift.

1 **Subterranean values** Traditional subcultural theories emphasise the differences between delinquents and 'normal' people. Matza suggests that delinquents are no different from the rest of society, they simply *exaggerate* normally accepted subterranean values that we all use. By subterranean values, Matza means a complex set of attitudes that are held by all of us alongside the morally upright values we all claim to hold. The subterranean values are to do with sex, thrills and enjoyment: the sorts of value and action which emerge when people are drunk or drugged.

What we all do when we engage in actions which are considered morally wrong is to justify them; Matza calls these **techniques of neutralization**. These techniques are:

● **denial of responsibility**: it wasn't my fault, I was drunk;

● **denial of victim**: she deserved it, the way she dresses;

● **denial of injury**: he could afford it anyway;

● **condemnation of condemners**: everybody does it;

● **appeal to higher loyalties**: I had to do it, all my friends did.

Delinquents use exactly the same techniques as all of us, but in situations we may not find appropriate.

2 **Drift** But the question remains: why are young males likely to use subterranean values in situations which many of us would find inappropriate? Matza suggests **drift**. By this he means that young males find themselves in a situation in which the bonds of family life and employment are weakened, and where they are therefore more likely to engage in deviant values. This fits closely with the ideas of Hirschi and Box on what holds people into the values of society.

Situational theory

This reflects the belief held by most current activists in the area of crime prevention that actually all the theories which have been produced have failed to halt the increase in the levels of crime, particularly among the young.

The approach is associated with the Home Office Research and Planning Unit and in particular with Clark and Mayhew (*Designing out Crime*). They reject any explanations for criminal behaviour which look for special factors to distinguish deviants from non-deviants (they called these sorts of theories **dispositional theories**). Instead they argue that crime is simply a normal form of risk-taking behaviour which people engage in all the time. The higher the rewards the greater the risks people are prepared to take, and conversely the greater the risk the less likely people are to commit crime.

They therefore shifted explanations of criminality away from motive and assumed, like control theorists, that people were predisposed to crime unless other factors intervened. Whereas control theorists place great stress upon ways of drawing people into society, the situational theory says quite simply that the important factor in limiting crime is to make it harder to commit crime.

Two elements are stressed:

1 **Target hardening** This makes it more difficult for criminals to perform their task – locked cars, alarms, restyled telephone kiosks etc.

2 **Surveillance** This stresses the physical design of cities which allow or prevent crime occurring. Thus street lighting, closed circuit cameras in city high streets etc all make crime more visible and more controllable by the police or passers-by.

15.3 WOMEN AND CRIME

The most interesting thing about female crime is its very low levels: for example, of the 50,000 people in prison in Britain, only 1,500 are women. The relationship of women to crime is more one of victims than of perpetrators.

Debates concerning gender and crime focus on:

- the reasons for the lack of interest in female crime by (male) sociologists;
- the accuracy of official figures on female crime;
- the reasons for the low level of female criminality;
- the situation of women as the victims of crime.

Reasons for traditional lack of interest in female crime

Heidensohn, in *Women and Crime*, has suggested the following reasons:

1 **Vicarious identification** Most studies of crime have traditionally been conducted by male sociologists and have been, in particular, studies of street gangs and similar groups. Heidensohn suggests that these sorts of study provided a form of vicarious identification by middle-class sociologists with the lifestyle and activities of these groups.

2 **Precluded** Most female sociologists have been precluded from doing studies of male street gangs, and most male sociologists have been precluded from studying working-class female crime.

3 **Male domination of sociology** Most sociologists have traditionally been male and most studies have been of males, by males, reflecting male interests, as indicated above.

4 **Low recorded levels of female crime** The very low levels of recorded female crime mean that this area has not been seen as significant or worthy of study.

⑤ **Malestream theories** The theories of crime and deviance developed by sociologists have been male-based, starting from assumptions about the world from a male perspective. The questions and explanations have been framed in such a way that women have been excluded from the central areas of study and relegated to marginal roles.

⑥ **Social class** Theories of deviance have been primarily based upon social class; other variables, such as gender and race, have not, until recently, been studied in detail.

The accuracy of the official figures on crime

Criminality is higher than official figures suggest. Pollack, writing in the 1950s, claimed that there are high levels of female crime but that they are masked. Prostitution and shop-lifting are commonly reported to the police. Pollack suggests that women are therefore as criminal in their behaviour as men.

Campbell and Box, in two different reviews of self-report studies of female crime, found that there were higher levels of crime committed by females than indicated in the official figures. However, for serious crimes the official figures are accurate (see the section on methodological issues of self-report studies, p 309).

Explanations for the possible differences are:

① **Differential treatment by the courts** There is a considerable debate over the treatment of females in courts. Writers, such as Kalven and Zaesel, argue that there is a chivalry factor which encourages juries and judges to be lenient to women. On the other hand, Casburn (*Girls will be Girls*) argues that courts are harsher with females.

② **Actions of the police** The evidence is that the police are more likely to caution females rather than prosecute them in comparison with males. 45% of young males and 70% of young females receive cautions after being stopped for criminal offences.

③ **Female role** The pressure group NACRO suggests that women are treated differently from men by police and courts. They suggest that the circumstances of females, such as pregnancy and care of dependants, are taken into account.

Explanations for the low rate of female crime

The explanations centre on:

- differential socialisation,
- social control,
- lack of opportunity.

① **Differential socialisation** Females are generally socialised into a pattern of values and actions that stresses that women are less aggressive and violent than men. These roles are taught through parents, schools, the media etc. Instead, socialisation is into roles such as parent or carer, which rely upon responsibility and awareness of the needs of others.

② **Social control** Women are not only socialised differently, they are more strictly controlled in their attitudes and activities. Women are expected to base themselves and their lives in the home. There are two spheres of life – that dominated by men (streets after dark, pubs, the workplace) and that by women (homes, shops during the day). Women are restricted from the male sphere in which crime takes place.

- **Male monopoly of violence**: women are strongly discouraged from violence, whereas the potential for its use remains an element of masculinity.

- **Reputation**: women have to be careful of their public displays of behaviour for fear of being labelled as promiscuous etc. Lees' study of schoolgirls (*Losing Out*), shows how girls label other girls and how this constrains behaviour.

3 **Opportunity to commit crime** Throughout their lives, females are shielded from opportunities to commit crime. Socialisation does not equip them with the aggressive male attitudes to violence. Social control keeps them under the surveillance of parents, their peer group and male partners. Women have fewer career opportunities and are rarely in a position to commit fraud or other forms of white-collar crime.

Women as the victims of crime

The British Crime Survey shows that 35% of women aged 30–60 feel unsafe going out in the dark, compared to only 4% of males. Yet women in this age group seem to have very slightly lower levels of attacks on them than males: 1.4% for women and 1.6% for males.

Writers such as Clemente and Kleinman (*Fear of Crime in the USA*) were the first to point out that the fears of women were exaggerated and that women stood very little chance of any form of attack in the street. However, they argue that the effect of fearing crime was to prevent women going out in the streets at night, so that those who did were actually at greater risk. They argue, 'fear of crime...has become a problem as serious as crime itself'.

The Islington Crime Survey indicates that female victims are concentrated in certain age groups and areas of cities. So women's fears are justified in these places and the averaging out of the statistics by the British Crime Survey distorts the situation. Secondly, we know that sexual assaults have the lowest levels of reporting to the police (and possibly to social science surveys) because the victims feel embarrassment. The figures for assault are therefore much higher.

Sexual assaults

Most sexual attacks involve people who are known to each other, including family members. About one-third of rapes take place in the home of the victim, approximately the same proportion as take place in the street or in an isolated spot.

Sociologists largely reject the biological argument that sexual assaults are motivated by uncontrollable sexual desire on the part of men. The following explanations have been suggested:

1 **Rape as control** Brownmiller suggests that rape is a means of controlling women that has been used historically by men to keep women in an inferior position.

2 **Rape as an extension of 'normal' male behaviour** Smart suggests that rape is merely an extension of normal sexual bargaining which occurs in British society. The socialisation of women includes their learning to be sexually attractive to men. On the other hand, men are expected to initiate sexual encounters and women to at least make a show of 'resistance'. Therefore rape can be seen not as being in opposition to the values of our society but as an extension of them.

Marital violence

Underreporting takes place here, as in rape, as wives are reluctant to report crime committed by their husbands. The police will arrest only where the case seems sufficiently serious; this is left to the discretion of the police.

Explanations for marital violence fall under three headings:

1 **Individual explanations** These stress precipitating factors such as violence in the childhood experiences of the male, high levels of alcohol intake, or mental illness.

2 **Subculture of violence** This stresses that among certain groups in society, violence is acceptable. Wolfgang and Ferracuti, for example, argue that this is why violence is more common among working-class couples. However, a criticism of this is that no-one can be sure that violence really is more common among the working class.

3 **Structural (or feminist) explanations** Dobash and Dobash (*Violence against Wives*) argue that violence against female partners is embedded in our culture. Historically, the use of a limited degree of violence by husbands has been culturally (and legally) acceptable. Our culture stresses that the values of family life are of a dominant male and a submissive wife who performs her duties to a very high level; women who fail to do so can reasonably be coerced.

Dobash and Dobash do not dispute that specific factors such as alcohol or jealousy may spark-off violence, but this can only occur where there is a cultural 'context' which allows this.

15.4 ETHNIC ISSUES AND CRIME

This is an area of great dispute among sociologists as some regard the area of discussion itself as being racist; that is, to discuss crime and ethnicity together means that they become associated.

STATISTICS

Evidence to the Scarman Enquiry by the Metropolitan Police suggested that Afro-Caribbean youth had higher levels of street crime than average.

Criticisms

Criticisms of the police statistics are that:

1. They would be higher because of the higher percentage than average for the general population of young Afro-Caribbean males. Young males commit the highest levels of crime.

2. The areas where Afro-Caribbeans live tend to be more heavily policed.

3. Accusations of police racism are commonly made: that the police are more likely to stop and arrest young blacks.

Overview

Stevens and Willis conducted research for the Home Office (*Race, Crime and Arrests*). They concluded that there was a higher level of crime committed by Afro-Caribbean youths than by white or Asian youths. However, the point would be that, given the extent of deprivation, unemployment and exclusion from society experienced by young blacks, the crime level is not racial but reflects the situation of a marginal group in society.

CRIMINALITY AND 'RESISTANCE'

In *The Empire Strikes Back*, Gilroy and Bridges argue that crime among blacks is a continuation of a 'colonial' struggle. Black criminality is a form of political struggle therefore, rather than simply crime.

Marxist subcultural explanation

Subcultural explanations stress the fact that black youth is in a marginalised position in capitalist society and has developed responses which include crime.

Anomie

This approach is similar to the Marxist position in that it stresses the way in which black and some Asian youth are obstructed from obtaining success through legitimate means (the situation of anomie, see pp 312–13), and therefore construct alternative routes for themselves.

New Left realist approach

This approach (discussed on pp 319–20) suggests three key elements in understanding the situation of black youth:

1. **Marginality** They are less successful in education, have higher levels of unemployment etc.

2. **Relative deprivation** Rather than being in opposition to the wider society (as argued by Gilroy et al), young blacks share the same aspirations; and precisely because they cannot obtain the desired standard of life legally, a small number are tempted to obtain it in other ways.

3. **Subculture** They argue that young blacks respond in a wide variety of ways, and a number of different subcultures emerge.

15.5 MODELS OF POLICING

CONSENSUAL MODEL OF POLICING

This is the traditional view of the police. It relies upon large-scale support of the police by the public, who provide relevant information to patrol officers, usually on the beat. Police officers see themselves as part of the community, and the social characteristics of police officers (particularly racial) largely reflect those of the community. Information from, and support of the community allows officers to target specific, individualised offenders. This model is, of course, an idealised one, but one that British police forces claim as the model to aspire to.

CONFLICT MODEL OF POLICING

The model of the police has been criticised by Scraton, who claims the police are an *occupying force*, imposed upon the working class initially, and later the ethnic minorities. According to Scraton the modern police movement was gradually formed and imposed upon the working class over the last two hundred years.

The military style model of policing is one whereby the police are seen as distinctive and separate from the public. Because of the gap between the two groups voluntary information from the public required to make arrests is not forthcoming. So, modern information technology is used, such as surveillance cameras or computerised files on suspects or suspected groups.

Instead of foot-patrols or 'beats' by lone officers, the police use vehicles and will have specialist groups trained in specialist functions. Suspects move away from being individuals (burglars) to entire groups (for example, young, black men) who are harassed, controlled and segregated from the innocent public.

POLICE DISCRETION

Within the models of policing there is always a large element of discretion accorded to police officers, as the law cannot provide a clear, unambiguous guide for police officers in every situation they are called to deal with. Police officers therefore have to use their discretion.

Reiner has suggested that there are three ways of understanding police discretion:

- individualisation,
- cultural and
- structural.

Individualistic explanations

This approach suggests that a particular 'authoritarian personality type' is drawn to policing and that the type of decisions regarding discretion are explained by this. Colman and Gorman studied police officers after the public disorders in Brixton in the early 1980s. They concluded that certain *individual* police officers were racist, and that their policing methods against black people were strongly affected by this racism – but these were in the minority. It was therefore possible to root out racism by tackling the relatively few individuals with racist opinions.

Cultural explanations

This approach places greater emphasis on *police culture*. Skolnick, for example, argues that the *common problems* faced by police officers and the *nature of the job* create a distinctive subculture with three core characteristics of this 'canteen culture'. These are:

1 suspiciousness,

2 internal solidarity and social isolation and

3 conservatism.

Suspiciousness

This is taught to police officers as part of their training, but extends eventually into their daily lives. Because of the need to evaluate individuals in the course of their duties, they have developed shortcuts consisting of a number of stereotyped categories of typical offenders. One of these is young, male and black.

Internal solidarity and social isolation

Policing is potentially a dangerous job and officers need to rely upon their colleagues. The result of this is a strong sense of solidarity, particularly amongst the lower ranks of the police. This solidarity also protects them against complaints against them from disgruntled members of the public.

Police officers also have some difficulty interacting with the public, in that they are authority figures and most keep a social distance from them. This merely reinforces the sense of solidarity and difference.

Conservatism

According to Reiner, politically police officers have tended to be more supportive of the Conservative party than a typical cross-section of the public. It has been suggested that although the police are drawn from the working class, the effect of the police culture is to 'deradicalise them', by pulling them away from their working-class backgrounds and sympathies (this also fits with the concepts of solidarity and social isolation).

It is important though not to become as stereotyped about police behaviour and values as we are suggesting occurs in the police culture. First, there are significant divisions within the police in terms of politics, moral values, career aspirations and openness to change. Secondly, there are regulations and laws which police officers must abide by, and which the majority follow. It is not true to say that because a police officer has racist sympathies he or she will therefore ignore the rule of law in order to provide an outlet for his or her racist beliefs.

One example of the divisions within the police has been suggested by Reiner who claims that there are four variations on the police subculture:

- The peace keepers – officers who seek to maintain order, but not to seek to maximise arrests.
- The law enforcers – officers who perceive their job in terms of combatting crime. This is defined as 'real' police work, as opposed to maintaining order or performing more routine tasks.

- The alienated cynics – officers who are either personally disillusioned with the job or who have failed to obtain promotion. They are merely carrying out the tasks required but have no wider purpose of controlling crime or maintaining peace.

- The managerially inclined professionals – officers who want promotion and are prepared to be excluded from the lower ranks' police culture in order to obtain the desired promoted post.

Structural explanations

These refer to the wider pressures placed upon police officers to do their jobs. The first one is the formal requirements of the law which provide the framework within which discretion operates. For example, in 1984, a major review of the powers and procedures of the police was introduced with the Police and Criminal Evidence Act (PACE). This extended the powers of the police whilst at the same time clarifying the rights of suspects. Perhaps the best-known result of the Act is the recording of police interviews with suspects, to prevent fabrication of evidence. Whether police officers liked the changes or not, they were required to alter their practices to conform to them. Similarly, the Public Order and Criminal Justice Act considerably increased police powers to intervene in a range of activities which they had previously been allowed to ignore, for example the disruption of blood sports.

Taking one step back from this, Marxist writers would suggest that it is necessary to explore the wider implications of the differences in power. Thus the changes in the law are likely to be a reflection of the will of the more powerful in society, so changes in policing largely benefit the more powerful, and that the 'neutral' policing activities which uphold the law are in fact heavily biased towards the powerful and against the poorer sections of society, by the very nature of the law reflecting the interests of the powerful.

Summary

Stop and search

We have seen that there is a police culture, but what we need to find out is just how the culture and the structural factors actually affect the way the police operate. One of the first steps on the path into the criminal justice system is that of 'stop and search' by the police.

A study by Smith and Gray found that police officers had considerable difficulty explaining why they stopped certain people and not others. However, according to the researchers, they tended to choose the stereotypical groups who looked unconventional in one way or another, perceived homosexuals and very significant numbers of young black males. In Willis's study, the police usually gave the grounds for stopping someone as 'suspicious movements', yet the arrest rates following these stops were very low – typically about 10%. To underline the point, 90% of all those stopped were found to have committed no offence. An example of the disproportionate stop rate for black youth, was that despite comprising 5% of the population of the Metropolitan Police District, a Home Office study in the late 1980s found that stop and searches of black males comprised 16% of all stops.

Arrest

McConville (*The Case for the Prosecution*) suggested that there are six working rules which police officers use to guide them over their decisions to stop or to arrest someone. These are:

- **Previous** If an individual is known to the police, then they are more likely to be stopped and more likely to be arrested.

- **Police Authority** If an individual challenges the authority of the police officer then he or she is more likely to be arrested.

- **Type of victim** Some victims are more likely to be responded to than others. In general the higher the social standing, the more serious the offence, or the more 'deserving' the victim, the greater the chance of the suspect being arrested.

- **Workload** The busier the police officer or the police station, the less likely that minor infringements will be acted upon.

● **Degree of suspicion** This is a catch–all category based usually upon some instinct or a belief that the person is out of place. One study by Jefferson and Walker (*Ethnic Minorities in the Criminal Justice System*) found that were likely to be stopped and searched if they were not in 'their own' areas.

Test yourself questions and answers

Questions

1 What two ways are there to find out the true levels of crime?

2 What theoretical approaches are there to explain crime?

3 What do we mean by 'anomie' when used to help explain crime?

4 What is the meaning of 'subculture' – give one example of how it can explain crime?

5 How do sociologists explain the creation of laws?

6 What does new Left realism mean?

7 What do we mean by a 'moral panic'?

8 What criticisms can you offer of the interactionist position on crime?

9 Why do females have lower levels of crime than males?

Suggested answers

1 Self-report and victimisation studies show the true levels of crime.
2 The major theoretical approaches to crime are:
   ● functionalism,
   ● subculture,
   ● labelling,
   ● Marxism,
   ● new Left realism,
   ● control and situational theories.
3 The term 'anomie' was first used by Merton, who suggested that if society provides inadequate legal routes to success then, in certain circumstances, people may turn to crime.
4 A subculture is used to describe a group of people who develop values which are different from the mainstream values and which can lead to them coming into conflict with the dominant values of society. The approach was first developed by Chicago University in the 1920s and was later widely used in British and other US studies. Usually the researchers attempt to discover the values and perceptions of the world by 'deviant' or stigmatised groups, and they do this through observational studies.
5 There are three main approaches to understanding law creation: the Marxist, the functionalist and the interactionist positions:
   ● Marxists see the law as reflecting the interests of the powerful in society.

- Functionalists see the laws as reflecting the changing values of society, and protecting the collective conscience or core values by setting the boundaries of permissible action. The approach is associated with Durkheim.
- Interactionists have developed a detailed position on law creation. Moral panics occur (exactly why is a matter of dispute), and the response is to create or to enforce laws against the perceived culprits.

6 Left realism refers to a modern neo-Marxist approach associated with Young amongst others. The approach has critically developed Marxist ideas and tried to make them operational by police and other control agencies, to combat working class crimes in cities.

7 A moral panic is the situation where an activity or group of people come to be perceived as a threat to the stability of the social order. The activities of the media and police/other control agencies exaggerate and distort the extent of the problem and may actually help create a bigger 'problem' than existed in the first place.

8 Criticisms of the interactionist, or labelling theory, position on crime include:
- inadequate explanation as to why some people are labelled and others not;
- no explanation of the reasons why some people respond one way and others in different ways to their label;
- a major weakness in its claim to be a coherent theory in that it fails to predict any particular form of behaviour, just explains after the event what has happened: for example, law-making is simply the result of successful moral crusades;
- no attempt to place the crusades into a wider structure.
- no explanation why people commit crime, only of the effects of labelling.

9 The explanations centre on:
- differential socialisation,
- social control,
- lack of opportunity.

Differential socialisation Females are generally socialised into a pattern of values and actions which stress that women are less aggressive and violent. They are strongly discouraged from violence.

Social control Women are more strictly controlled in their attitudes and activities. They have to be careful of their public displays of behaviour for fear of being labelled as promiscuous. Women are expected to base themselves and their lives in the home. They are therefore restricted from the male sphere in which crime takes place.

Opportunity to commit crime This is limited for women as their socialisation does not equip them with the aggressive male attitudes to violence, while social control limits their freedom to commit crime, and finally their career opportunities are more limited so they are rarely in the position to commit white-collar crime, for example.

Illustrative question and answer

Question

Evaluate the usefulness of official statistics to a sociological understanding of crime.

AEB

Suggested answer

The point of this essay is not just to show how inadequate the basis of official statistics are in coming to an understanding of the nature of crime, but also to show that the actual study of the process of constructing official statistics is in itself an interesting and useful sociological activity which helps us to understand better the categorisation and response to crime in the UK.

The essay should start with a discussion of what official statistics of crime show, and should move on to look at alternative ways of understanding the extent of crime. The different methods, such as the British Crime Survey or Self-Report studies, should be clearly discussed. What emerges from this is that crime statistics are inaccurate and ought not to be relied upon. You should then engage in a discussion on how positivistic theories of crime have based their theories upon the belief that numbers of crime rates, and criminal offenders are the same as those measured in official statistics. So the first point you should make very clearly is that all the traditional positivistic explanations are thrown into doubt.

You should then look at the way in which official statistics are constructed and what factors influence the crimes reported to the police. Make the point that these are not simply relevant to the construction of official statistics but are useful, too, for the extension of sociological understanding of crime.

Then move on to discuss the way that the police use discretion in their handling of individuals. Here you should bring in the significance of this for blacks and for women. It is claimed by a number of writers that the police show racial bias in choosing who to stop and who should be proceeded against (although you need to say that this is hotly contested by police themselves).

You should then move on to white-collar and corporate crime and point out that these are significantly understated in official crime reports because of low levels of complaints by employers and because they have relatively low levels of enforcement. You could emphasise the importance of this by pointing to Pearce's assertion that in the USA company crime is more costly to society than all other crime put together.

It is useful at this point to bring in explicit discussion of theory and you should point out that this last discussion on white-collar crime provides significant support for Marxist theory. The earlier work on the construction of crime statistics lends support to interactionist approaches to crime.

Question bank

1 'The usefulness of crime statistics in sociological research depends on the theoretical approach adopted by the sociologist.' Critically explain this view.

AEB

Points

This is linking a debate on the nature of crime statistics with the different explanations sociologists offer for crime. Essentially, it contrasts the positivistic-based approaches such as the later UK subcultural models with interactionist or labelling approaches. Start by looking at approaches explaining crime on the basis of the differences between criminals and non-criminals – you have a wide choice, but the best would be those based upon comparing the family life and background of criminals with those who do not commit crime; the Cambridge Criminology studies are useful examples. You could also look at approaches linking crime and unemployment and finally, the work of writers such as Dennis linking the collapse of the family with crime increases. Explore briefly the official statistics and gender differences in rates of crime committal.

Then run through the criticisms of statistics pointing out that they might be dubious and, in particular, look at the way that official statistics are socially constructed. Explore labelling theories and Marxist theories

Finally, you should point out that the use of local surveys and victimisation studies has provided useful information particularly for left realist and gender-based approaches which use the statistics in a different way to show how pervasive crime is for certain groups.

2 Critically examine the relationship between deviance and power.

AEB

Points

Discuss Marxist approaches emphasising the relationship they demonstrate between power and the crime in that street crime or working class crime is heavily stigmatised, as is social security fraud, and compare these with tax evasion and corporate crime. Look also at the way that power issues emerge in terms of gender, in that the extent of women as victims was ignored. Look at the way that those of Afro-Caribbean origin have much higher chances of entering the criminal justice system, and of being routinely stopped by the police.

Do not forget to look at power as it is applied in labelling theory, for example in mental illness. You could also use the example of sexuality.

You could also explore the work of those where power is completely missing as a concept (Durkheim) and then show how introducing the concept can radically change the analysis (Erikson).

3 'There is no such thing as a deviant act. An act only becomes deviant when it is perceived as such by others.' Explain, illustrate and assess the validity of the quotation.

NEAB

Points

This is asking you to explore interactionism/labelling. You should explain its origins and basis. What factors are linked to deviance and its creation? Point out how different it is from other approaches. You should look at the issues of secondary deviance and the role of the media. Note that people can reject the label applied to them, and comment on why this might be. Do not forget to include issues of law creation.

Criticise it for its relativism, i.e. the way that it fails to grasp that some crime really does exist and do harm. This is taken up by left realism. Also criticise it for failing to explain the motivation of people who knowingly commit deviant acts.

TEST RUN

In this section:

Mock exam

Mock exam suggested answer plans

This section should be tackled towards the end of your revision programme, when you have covered all your syllabus topics, and attempted the test yourself questions and the exam questions at the end of the relevant chapters.

The mock exam is set out like a real exam paper. It contains a selection of question styles and topics, drawn from various examination boards. You should attempt this paper under examination conditions. Read the instructions on the front sheet carefully. Attempt the paper in the time allowed, and without reference to the text.

When you have completed the paper compare your answers to our mock exam suggested answer plans.

LETTS SCHOOL EXAMINATIONS BOARD
General Certificate of Education Examination

ADVANCED LEVEL
SOCIOLOGY

Time allowed: 3 hours

Answer all the questions

Question 1

STRATIFICATION AND GENDER

Item A

It is obvious that there are some serious problems in Marx's account. Revolution has occurred in nations on the verge of entry into capitalism, not in societies which are mature and 'ripe' for change. The working class in capitalist society has enjoyed in the long term a rise in the standard of living and labour movements have won enough welfare concessions to ease the lot of many of the poor.

(Bilton, T. et al, *Introductory Sociology*, Macmillan. 1988, p 46)

Item B

Max Weber defines class as a group of people who share a similar position in the market economy, they receive similar economic rewards and they therefore have similar life chances in common.

Weber was not content, however, to classify society solely by class. He also classified social life by status... Status reflects manners, education, family origin, race, how you made your money (from 'trade' or inheritance).

(Joseph, M., *Sociology for Everyone*, Polity, 1986, pp 66–7)

(a) Identify, according to Weber, what status reflects. (1)

(b) Outline the criticisms made by feminist writers of traditional means of classifying social class by occupation. (7)

(c) What views do sociologists hold on the argument that manual workers and non-manual workers are still clearly differentiated from each other? (8)

(d) How true is it to say that Britain is a meritocracy? (9)

Question 2

EDUCATION, RACE AND EMPLOYMENT

Item A

To reproduce the social relations of production, the educational system must try to teach people to be properly subordinate and render them sufficiently fragmented in consciousness to preclude their getting together to shape their own material existence...

The structure of work relations in education not only inures the student to the discipline of the workplace, but develops the types of personal demeanour, modes of self-presentation, self-image and social class adequacy which are the crucial ingredients of job adequacy.

(Bowles, S. and Gintis, H., *Schooling in Capitalist America*, Routledge, 1976, pp 130–131; reproduced from O'Donnell, M., *New Introductory Reader in Sociology*, Nelson, 1993)

Item B

The middle-class parents take more interest in their children's progress at school than the manual working-class parents do, and they become relatively more interested as their children grow older... the most striking difference is that many middle-class fathers visit the schools to discuss their children's progress whereas working-class fathers seldom do.

(Douglas, J.W.B., *The Home and the School*, Panther, 1967, reproduced in Pritchard, D., *Skills in Sociology*, Causeway, 1989)

Item C

The problems females meet in education are much the same as they may meet in the family or in society generally. When studying the family, you will have noticed how females are expected and socialised to do certain things rather than others, and this can also occur in schools.

(O'Donnell, M., and Garrod, J., *Sociology in Practice*, Nelson, 1990 p 41)

(a)   According to Item B, what is the difference between middle-class and working-class parents? (2)

(b)   What criticisms have been made of labelling theory as it applies to education? (5)

(c)   Examine the significance of the hidden curriculum for females in school. (8)

(d)   What have sociologists suggested as the relationship between work and school? (10)

Question 3

THE FAMILY AND MARRIAGE

Item A

Behind this lies the persistence of very widespread notions as to what is appropriate work for women and men. The way in which these differences are formulated is often in terms of responsibilities. Husbands may help perhaps to a considerable extent – in domestic tasks or with child care – but in most cases the responsibility for these tasks rests with the wives and mothers. Such responsibilities it should be noted are not simply in terms of housework or child care but also in terms of wider caring obligations, particularly in relation to elderly relatives.

(Morgan, D., 'Sociology, society and the family', in Lawson, E. et al, *Sociology Reviewed*, Collins Educational, 1993, p 19)

Item B

But there is no evidence at all for the simple association between single parenthood and social class, intelligence or deviance. Nor is there any evidence that children from single-parent families do any worse at school than comparable children from similar social backgrounds... Certainly single parents are likely to be poor and it is their relative poverty that places them at a disadvantage.

(Calvert, S. and Calvert, P., *Sociology Today*, Harvester Wheatsheaf, 1992, p 185)

Item C

Divorce makes an increasing impact upon the lives of children. It has been suggested that nearly 40% of children born in the UK in 1970 would at some stage before adulthood be members of a one-parent family. Since 75% of women and 83% of men who are divorced remarry within three years, they will none the less grow up in a family environment. Only just over 2% of children under fourteen in the UK today are not living with either parent.

(Giddens, A., *Sociology*, Polity Press, 1989 pp397–8)

(a)   According to Item A, what percentage of children under 14 do not live with either parent? (1)

(b)   Identify and explain the factors which have led to an increase in divorce (6)

(c)   Assess the contribution of feminism to an understanding of the family and marriage. (9)

(d)   What similarities and differences are there between functionalist and Marxist accounts of the family? (9)

Question 4

RESEARCH

Critically assess the view that a value-free sociology is impossible.

SUGGESTED ANSWERS

Question 1

(a) Manners, education, family origin, race and how you made your money.

(b) Many contemporary sociologists have characterised these approaches as malestream. By this they mean that these classifications are inappropriate for classifying women:

- Orthodox approaches are designed to distinguish between male occupations

- The important male distinction between manual/non manual is far less important for women given the dominance of non-manual work for women.

- Within occupational groups, women are typically employed at lower levels than men.

- The same job can be very different in terms of its implications, eg clerical work for a man could be a route into management, for a woman a job in itself.

- Where are housewives in traditional occupational-based occupations?

- In most of the classifications, women who work are still based upon their husband's social class, as head of household.

- 14% of households are now headed by women in single-parent families.

(c) In answering this question, you need to look at the changing nature of the occupational structure, noting that the numbers of manual jobs as a proportion of the workforce has declined. You should:

- comment on the huge growth of female labour – much of it in low paid white-collar employment;

- point out that there were always divisions within the manual non-manual workforce, such that the clear-cut division was always suspect;

- cover the studies by Lockwood and Roberts on the fragmentary nature of the non-manual routine workers, and note that many of these overlapped in wage levels and lack of autonomy with manual workers;

- refer to the original affluent worker studies to show that differences existed and that in the new study by Marshall et al class differences still exist and are important in people's lives.

The conclusion is that manual and non-manual workers have always overlapped and they do now, but probably to a much greater extent.

(d) You need to clearly define meritocracy. You need to work your way through the statistics on who moves up and who moves down, linking this with the importance to stratification theory and the proof or otherwise that social mobility gives to functionalism, Marxism and Weberian-based theories. You should then discuss the top positions in society and refer to the work on ruling class and elites, and in particular John Scott's material on power blocs. Then you need to look at some of the factors influencing social mobility and see if they reflect a meritocracy or merely changes in the occupational structure.

Question 2

(a) Middle-class parents are more likely than working-class parents to take an interest in the school progress of their children and to visit the school.

(b)   The main criticisms have been that:

- the labelling is seen as too mechanical with limited allowance for choice and decision-making by the students;

- the wider factors which influence the activities of children are ignored and instead only the actions of teachers and pupils are studied;

- labelling fails to explain why some people are labelled at all and others are ignored;

- a number of studies, such as Fuller's of Afro-Caribbean-origin girls, would indicate that the labels applied to them at school are unimportant.

(c)   The hidden curriculum consists of all those values which teachers and the girls themselves import from the wider society and which constrain and direct their behaviour within schools.

Therefore you need to discuss the expectations of teachers regarding appropriate activities. You need to examine the fact that females are likely to choose arts and languages subjects. You should point to the way that boys dominate ordinary lessons, but in particular science lessons. Then move on to look at the way girls, according to Lees, judge other girls. After this, look at the way the girls view the wider society, and their career and life expectations. The work of Sharpe and Lees is relevant here. Do not forget to include discussions of race and gender: the hidden curriculum does not just apply to all girls in one way.

(d)   This requires you to take a number of different approaches. First you should discuss the way that the school's development and curricula have been very much influenced by the demands of the economy. You should then go on to discuss the introduction of all the measures relating to the New Vocationalism. Next a discussion of theory is required, and you must introduce a discussion of both the functionalist and Marxist approaches to education, as both, though in very different ways, see education as being closely linked to work skills and attitudes.

Question 3

(a)   Just over 2%.

(b)   The factors include:

- the fact it is easier to get a divorce;

- the high expectations of partners and the high value placed upon marriage;

- the changing attitudes of women who refuse to accept oppression within the family;

- the decline in the sanctions placed by the community on couples to remain married.

(c)   Feminist writers have exposed that the study of the family has been from a primarily male viewpoint and they have introduced a wide range of new ideas. The first is that the family is a site of oppression for women and children. This is shown by the way that women do the bulk of the work and caring. Furthermore they are heavily involved in reproducing the next generation of children – with similar sexist attitudes. Feminist research has also led to work on violence and sexual abuse in the family, and further than that into the very nature of sexuality.

A good reply would include discussions on the differing feminist approaches and would not simply give the impression that there is one feminist approach.

(d)   This essay allows you to explore the way in which functionalist accounts have basically seen the family as an institution which benefits both society and the members in it, while the Marxist account has stressed the way in which the family helps serve the continuing oppression of workers. You could also argue that the feminist school of thought which derived from Marxism has shown the way that women in particular are oppressed. But whereas the Marxist account has very limited views on the reasons for the changing structure of the family, functionalists have engaged in a long debate about the loss of functions etc. This needs to be covered.

Question 4

This question requires you to put both sides of the argument regarding value freedom and sociology.

Those who argue for objectivity, see sociology as a science like any other. There are objective social facts such as divorce statistics, crime statistics, and the biases of the researcher are irrelevant, as long as they do not deliberately distort or alter the findings. If the researchers are biased and they publish the methods used in their research then other sociologists can check their research process.

Having made the introduction, you should then put together all the arguments concerning the impossibility of having a value-free sociology. Many critics within sociology reject that a value free sociology is neither possible nor desirable. You should mention the historical background to the debate when Max Weber argued that personal values should be kept separate from the research and teaching of sociology, and mention also Gouldner's critique of this.

Feminists point to the way that sociology has focused on male concerns and interests, whereas Neo-Marxists point to the way that sociology has accepted the values and social structures of capitalism and has sought answers within the framework of capitalism.

You should mention finance – those who pay for research often control the direction of that research. Furthermore, personal values and interests of sociologists may influence the choice, methods, direction and interpretation of research.

Phenomenology and Reality sociologists who subscribe to phenomenological approaches to sociology argue that the process of scientific method, the concept of science and the very basic underlying concepts of sociology are themselves products of society, and reflect only the social activities of people attempting to construct a reality.

Foucault argues that what is considered knowledge reflects no more than the process of certain powerful groups attempting to construct a reality. Yet this reality is not substantial, composed as it is by a mixture of contradictory and essentially meaningless beliefs and values. Foucault rejects any sense of order or meaning in society. Value freedom is impossible.

You could then comment on whether social policy *should* be Value Free, and comment on the Becker versus Gouldner debate.

BIBLIOGRAPHY

Allen, G., *Family Life, Domestic Roles and Social Organisation*, Blackwell, 1985.

Anderson, M., *Approaches to the History of the Western Family*, Macmillan, 1980.

Anderson, *Education, Economy and Society*, 1961.

Archer, 'Morphogenesis versus structure and action', *British Journal of Sociology*, Vol. 3, No. 4, 1982

Atkinson, J., 'Societal reactions to suicide', in Cohen, S., *Discovering Suicide*, Macmillan, 1978.

Baldwin, J. and Bottoms, A.E., *The Urban Criminal: A Study in Sheffield*, Tavistock, 1976.

Ball, S.J., *Beachside Comprehensive*, Cambridge University Press, 1981.

Ballard, R., 'South Asian families' in Rapoport et al, *Families in Transition*, Routledge, 1982.

Barrett, M., *Women's Oppression Today*, Verso, 1980.

Barrett, M., and McIntosh, M., *The Anti-Social Family*, Verso, 1982.

Barron, R.D., and Norris, G.M., 'Sexual divisions and the dual labour market' in Barker and Allen (eds), *Dependence and Exploitation in Work and Marriage*, Longman, 1976.

Barrow, J., 'West Indian families: An insider's perspective' in Rapoport et al, *Families in Transition*, Routledge, 1982.

Becker, H., *The Other Side*, The Free Press, 1963.

Becker, H., *Whose Side are We On?*, Social Problems, Vol. 14.

Bell, N.W., and Vogel, E.F., *A Modern Introduction to the Family*, Penguin, 1966.

Benston, M., 'The political economy of women's liberation', in Glazer, Malbin, and Waehrer, *Women in a Man-Made World*, Rand McNally, 1972.

Berle, A., and Means, G., *The Modern Corporation and Private Property*, Harcourt, Brace and World, reprinted ed. 1967.

Bernstein, B., 'Social class and linguistic development', in Halsey, Floud and Anderson, *Education, Economy and Society*, The Free Press, 1961.

Beynon, H., *Working for Ford*, Allen Lane, 1973.

Blauner, R., *Alienation and Freedom*, University of Chicago Press, 1964.

Boulton, M.G., *On Being a Mother*, Tavistock, 1983.

Bourdieu, P. and Passeron, J., *Reproduction in Education, Society and Culture*, Sage, 1977.

Bowles, S. and Gintis, H., *Schooling in Capitalist America* Routledge, 1976.

Box, S., *Crime, Power and Mystification*, Tavistock, 1983.

Box, S., *Deviance, Reality and Society*, Holt, Rinehart and Winston, 1981.

Brake, M., *The Sociology of Youth Culture and Youth Subcultures*, Routledge, 1980.

Braverman, H., *Labor and Monopoly Capitalism*, Monthly Review Press, 1974.

Breugal, 'Women as a Reserve Army of Labour', *Feminist Review*, No. 3, 1979.

Burnham, J., *The Managerial Revolution*, Putman and Co, 1943.

Butler, D., and Stokes, R., *Political Change in Britain*, Penguin, 1971.

Campbell, A., *Girl Delinquents*, Blackwell, 1981.

Cashmore, E.E., *Having to: The World of One-Parent Families*, Counterpoint, 1985.

Castles, S., and Kosack, G.C., *Immigrant Workers and Class Structure in Western Europe*, Oxford University Press, 1973.

Centre for Contemporary Cultural Studies, *The Empire Strikes Back*, Hutchinson, 1983.

Chester, R., 'The rise of the neo-conventional family', *New Society*, 9 May, 1985.

Clarke, J., and Critcher, C., *The Devil Makes Work: Leisure in Capitalist Britain*, Macmillan, 1985.

Clemente, F., and Kleinman, M., *Fear of Crime in the USA*, Social Forces, 1977.

Cloward, R.E., and Ohlin, L.E., *Delinquency and Opportunity*, The Free Press, 1961.

Clutterbuck, D., *New Patterns of Work*, Gower, 1985.

Coard, B., *How the West Indian Child is Made Educationally Subnormal in the British School System*, New Beacon Books, 1971.

Cohen, A.K., *Delinquent Boys: The Culture of the Gang*, Free Press, 1955.

Cohen, P., 'Subcultural conflict and working class community' in *Working Papers in Cultural Studies*, 2, 1972, University of Birmingham.

Cohen, S., *Folk Devils and Moral Panics*, McGibbon and Kee, 1972.

Cooper, D., *The Death of the Family*, Penguin, 1972.

Crewe, I., *The Grim Challenge of the Ballot Box*, The Guardian, 1 October, 1988.

Dahrendorf, R., *Class and Class Conflict in an Industrial Society*, Routledge, 1959.

Davis, K., and Moore, W.E., 'Some principles of stratification' in Bendix, R., and Lipset, S.M., (eds) *Class, Status and Power* (2nd ed), Routledge, 1967.

Delphy, C., *Close to Home*, Hutchinson, 1984.

Ditton, J., *Part-Time Crime*, Macmillan, 1977.

Dobash and Dobash, *Violence against Wives*, Open Books, 1979.

Douglas, J.D., *The Social Meanings of Suicide*, Princeton University Press, 1967.

Douglas, J.W.B., *The Home and the School*, Panther, 1967.

Downes, D., *The Delinquent Solution*, Routledge, 1966.

Driver, G., and Ballard, R., 'Contemporary performance in multi-race schools' in James, and Jeffcoate, *The School in Multi-Cultural Society*, Harper Row, 1981.

Edgell, S., *Middle Class Couples*, Allen and Unwin, 1980.

Elson, D., and Pearson, R., 'The subordination of women and the internationalisation of factory production' in Young *Of Marriage and the Market: Women's Subordination in an International Perspective*, CSE Books, 1981.

Erikson, K.T., *The Wayward Puritans*, Wiley, 1966.

Ferguson, M., *Forever Feminine: Womens' Magazines and the Cult of Femininity*, Heinemann, 1983.

Firestone, S., *The Dialectic of Sex*, Paladin, 1972.

Foucault, M., *Madness and Civilization: A History of Insanity in the Age of Reason*, Tavistock, 1971.

Foucault, M., *The History of Sexuality*, Penguin, 1984.

Friedson, E., *Profession of Medicine*, Dodd, Mead and Co, 1975.

Fuller, M., 'Black girls in a London comprehensive school', in Hammersley and Woods (eds) *Life in School: The Sociology of Pupil Culture*, Open University Press, 1984.

Gallie, G., *In Search of the New Working Class*, Cambridge University Press, 1978.

Gershuny, J., *Social Innovation and the Division of Labour*, Oxford University Press, 1983.

Gibbs, J. and Martin, W., *Status Integration and Suicide*, University of Oregon Press, 1964.

Giddens, A., *Social Theory and Modern Sociology*, Polity Press, 1991.

Gill, O., *Luke Street*, Macmillan, 1977.

Glasgow University Media Group, *Bad News*, Routledge, 1976. *More Bad News*, Routledge, 1980. *Really Bad News*, Writers and Readers, 1982.

Goldthorpe, J.H., Lockwood, D., Bechhofer, and Platt, J., *The Affluent Worker in the Class Structure*, Cambridge University Press, 1969.

Goldthorpe, J.H., *Social Mobility and Class Structure in Modern Britain*, Clarendon, 1980.

Goode, W.J., 'A sociological perspective on marital dissolution' in Anderson, *Sociology of the Family*, Penguin, 1971.

Goode, W.J., *World Revolution and Family Patterns*, The Free Press, 1963.

Gouldner, A.W., *Anti-Minotaur: The Myth of a Value-Free Sociology*, reprinted in *For Sociology*, Penguin, 1975.

Green, 'Multi-ethnic teaching and the pupils' self concepts', in *The Swann Report*, HMSO, 1985.

Griffin, C., *Typical Girls?*, Routledge, 1985.

Halbwachs, M., *The Causes of Suicide*, Alcan, 1930.

Hall, S., et al, *Policing the Crisis*, Macmillan, 1979.

Halsey, A.H., Heath, A., and Ridge, J.M., *Origins and Destinations*, Clarendon, 1980.

Hammer, J., and Saunders, S., *Well Founded Fear*, Hutchinson, 1984.

Hargreaves, D., Hester, S., and Mellor, F., *Deviance in Classrooms*, Routledge, 1975.

Hargreaves, D.H., *Social Relations in a Secondary School*, Routledge, 1977.

Hart, N., *When Marriage Ends*, Tavistock, 1976.

Harvey, D., *The Conditions of Post-Modernity*, Blackwell, 1990.

Heath, A., et al, *Understanding Political Change*, Pergamon, 1991.

Heidensohn, F., *Women and Crime*, Macmillan, 1985.

Hickox, M., 'The Marxist sociology of education: a critique', *British Journal of Sociology*, December, 1982.

Himmelweit, H. T., Humphreys and Jaeger, *How Voters Decide*, Open University Press, 1985.

Hirschi, *The Causes of Delinquency*, University of California Press, 1969.

Hyman, R., *Strikes* (3rd ed), Fontana, 1984.

Illich, I., *Medical Nemesis*, Bantam Books, 1977.

Jefferson, and Walker, 'Ethnic Minorities in the Criminal Justice System', *Criminal Law Review*, Pennsylvannia State University, 1992.

Jessop, *State Theory*

Jones, B., 'Work and Flexible Automation in Britain' in *Work, Employment and Society*, Vol. 2, No. 4, pp451–86

Joseph, 'Monetarism is not enough', Centre for Policy Studies, 1977.

Keddie, N., 'Classroom knowledge', in Young, *Tinker Taylor … The Myth of Cultural Deprivation*, Pengin, 1973.

Kerr, C., and Siegel, A., 'The inter-industry propensity to strike' in Kornhauser, Dubin and Ross (eds), *Industrial Conflict*, McGraw Hill, 1954.

Kumar, *From Post-Industrial to Post-Modern Society*, Penguin, 1978.

Lacey, C., *Hightown Grammar*, Manchester University Press, 1970

Laing, R., *The Politics of the Family*, Penguin, 1976.

Lane, T., and Roberts, K., *Strike at Pilkingtons*, Fontana, 1971.

Lane, C., 'Industrial Change in Europe', *Work, Employment and Society*, Vol. 2, No. 2, pp141–68

Laslett, P., *The World We Have Lost*, Methuen, 1971.

Lea, J., and Young, J., *What is to be done about Law and Order*, Penguin 1984,

Lees, S., *Losing Out*, Hutchinson, 1986.

Le Grand, J., *The Strategy of Equality*, Allen and Unwin, 1982.

Lloyd Warner, *Social Class in America: The Evolution of Status*, Harper and Row, 1960.

Lukes, S., *Power: A Radical View*, Macmillan, 1974.

Mann, M., *The Sources of Social Power*, Cambridge Univery Press, 1986.

Marcuse, H., *One Dimensional Man*, Abacus, 1972.

Mars, G., *Cheats at Work*, Allen and Unwin, 1982.

Marsh, D. (ed), *Pressure Politics*, Junction Books, 1983.

Marshall, G., Newby, H., Rose, D., and Vogler, C., *Social Class in Modern Britain*, Hutchinson, 1988.

Matza, D., *Delinquency and Drift*, Wiley, 1964.

Mckenzie, R.T., and Silver, A., *Angels in Marble*, Heinemann, 1988.

McKeown, T., *The Role of Medicine: Dream, Mirage or Nemesis?* The Nuffield Provincial Hospitals Trust, 1976.

Miliband, R., *The State in Capitalist Society*, Weidenfeld and Nicholson, 1969.

Miller, W.B., 'Lower class culture as a generating milieu of gang delinquency' in Wolfgang, M., Savitz, L., and Johnston, N., *The Sociology of Crime and Delinquency*, Wiley, 1962.

Mills, C.W., *The Power Elite*, Oxford University Press, 1956.

More Bad News, Routledge, 1980.

Morley, D., *The 'Nationwide' Audience*, British Film Institute, 1980.

Murray, C., 'Underclass', *Sunday Times Magazine*, 26th November, 1989.

Navarro, V., *Medicine under Capitalism*, Croom Helm, 1976.

Navarro, V., *Medicine under Capitalism*, Prodist, 1976.

Nichols, T., and Beynon, H., *Living with Capitalism*, Routledge, 1977.

Nordlinger, E. A., *On the Autonomy of the Democratic State*, Harvard University Press, 1981.

Oakley, A., *The Sociology of Housework*, Martin Robertson, 1974.

Pahl, J., *Divisions of Labour*, Blackwell, 1984.

Pahl, J., *Money and Marriage*, Macmillan, 1989.

Parker, H., *A View from the Boys*, David and Charles, 1976.

Parker, S., *The Sociology of Work and Leisure*, George Allen and Unwin, 1976.

Parkin, F., *Class Inequality and Political Order*, MacGibbon and Kee, 1971.

Parry, N., and Parry, J., *The Rise of the Medical Profession*, Croom Helm, 1976.

Parsons, T., *The Social System*, Routledge, 1951.

Pearce, F., *Crimes of the Powerful*, Pluto Press, 1976.

Platt, J., *The Rise of the Child-Saving Movement*, Annals of the American Academy, 1969.

Poulantzas, N., 'The Problem of the Capitalist State', in Urry and Wakeford, *Power in Britain*, Heinemann, 1973.

Rapoport, R., and Rapoport, R.N., *Leisure and the Family Life Cycle*, Routledge, 1975.

Really Bad News, Writers and Readers, 1982.

Rex, J., and Moore, R., *Race Community and Conflict*, Oxford University Press, 1967.

Rex, J., and Tomlinson, S., *Colonial Immigrants in a British City*, Routledge, 1979.

Roberts, K., *Contemporary Society and the Growth of Leisure*, Longman, 1978.

Sarlvick and Crewe, *Decade of De-alignment*, Cambridge University Press, 1983.

Scott, J., *Corporations, Classes and Control*, Hutchinson, 1979.

Scott, J., *The Upper Classes. Property and Privilege in Britain*, Macmillan, 1982.

Seidler, *Rediscovering Masculinity*, Routledge, 1989.

Sharp, R., and Green, A., *Education and Social Control*, Routledge, 1975

Shaw, C.R., and McKay, H.D., *Juvenile Delinquency and Urban Areas*, University of Chicago Press, 1942.

Shorter, E., *The Making of the Modern Family*, Fontana, 1977.

Skeggs, B., 'Confessions of a feminist researcher', *Sociology Review*, September 1992.

Skocpol, *States and Social Revolutions*, Cambridge University Press, 1979.

Smart, C., *Women, Crime and Criminology: A Feminist Critique*, Routledge, 1978.

Spender, D., *Invisible Women*, Writers and Readers, 1983.

Stacey, M., 'The division of labour revisited', in Abrams, P., Deem R, Finch J and Rock P (eds), *Practice and Progress*, Allen and Unwin, 1981.

Stanworth, M., *Gender and Schooling*, Hutchinson, 1983.

Stevens, P., and Willis, C., *Race, Crime and Arrests*, HMSO, 1979.

Stone, M., *The Education of the Black Child in Britain*, Fontana, 1981.

Sugarman, B., 'Social class, values and behaviour' in Craft, *Family, Class and Education*, Longman, 1970.

Taylor, L., and Walton, P., 'Industrial Sabotage: Motives and Meanings' in Cohen, *Images of Deviance*, Penguin, 1971.

Tizzard, B., et al, *Young Children at School in the Inner City*, Lawrence Erlbaum, 1988.

Townsend, P., *Poverty in the UK*, Penguin, 1979.

Troyna, B., *Public Awareness and the Media: Reporting of Race*, CRE, 1981.

Tuchman, G., *Objectivity as Strategic Ritual: An Examination of Newsmens's Notions of Objectivity*, American Journal of Sociology, Vol 77, 1972.

Wallis, R., *The Elementary Forms of the New Religious Life*, Routledge, 1984.

Westergaard, J., and Resler, H., *Class in Capitalist Society*, Penguin, 1976.

Wilensky, H.L., 'Work, careers and social integration' in Smith, Parker and Smith, *Leisure and Society in Britain*, Allen Lane, 1973.

Williams, F., *Social Policy A Critical Introduction*, Polity, 1992.

Willis, P., *Learning to Labour*, Saxon House, 1977.

Willmott, P., 'Kinship in urban communities, past and present', *Social Studies Review*, 1988.

Wilson, B.R., *Religion in a Secular Society* CA Watts, 1966.

Wilson, B.R., *Religion in Sociological Perspective*, Oxford University Press, 1982.

Wood, S., *The Transformation of Work? Skill, Flexibility and the Labour Process*, Unwin Hyman, 1989.

Wright, E.O., *Class, Crisis and the State*, New Left Books, 1978.

Young, M., and Willmott, P., *The Symmetrical Family*, Penguin, 1975.

INDEX